Ao Haru Ride

The scent of air after rain...
In the light around us, I felt your heartbeat.

7

IO SAKISAKA

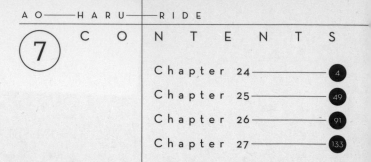

AO——HARU——RIDE

C O N T E N T S

S T O R Y
T H U S
F A R

Futaba Yoshioka was quiet and awkward
around boys in junior high, but she's
taken on a tomboy persona in high
school. It's there that she once again
meets her first love, Tanaka (now Kou
Mabuchi), and she soon finds out she's
not the only one who's changed.

Kou becomes closer to his classmates,
but the friendlier, happier Kou doesn't
remain for long. Yui, his old classmate
from Kyushu, shows up to attend the
school cultural festival. There, Futaba
and Kou share an accidental kiss and
follow it up with a real one. When
Futaba wants to know Kou's intentions,
their conversation shifts to Yui, and
suddenly distance grows between
them again. Kou has decided to act
as Yui's support after learning of her
estrangement from her family.

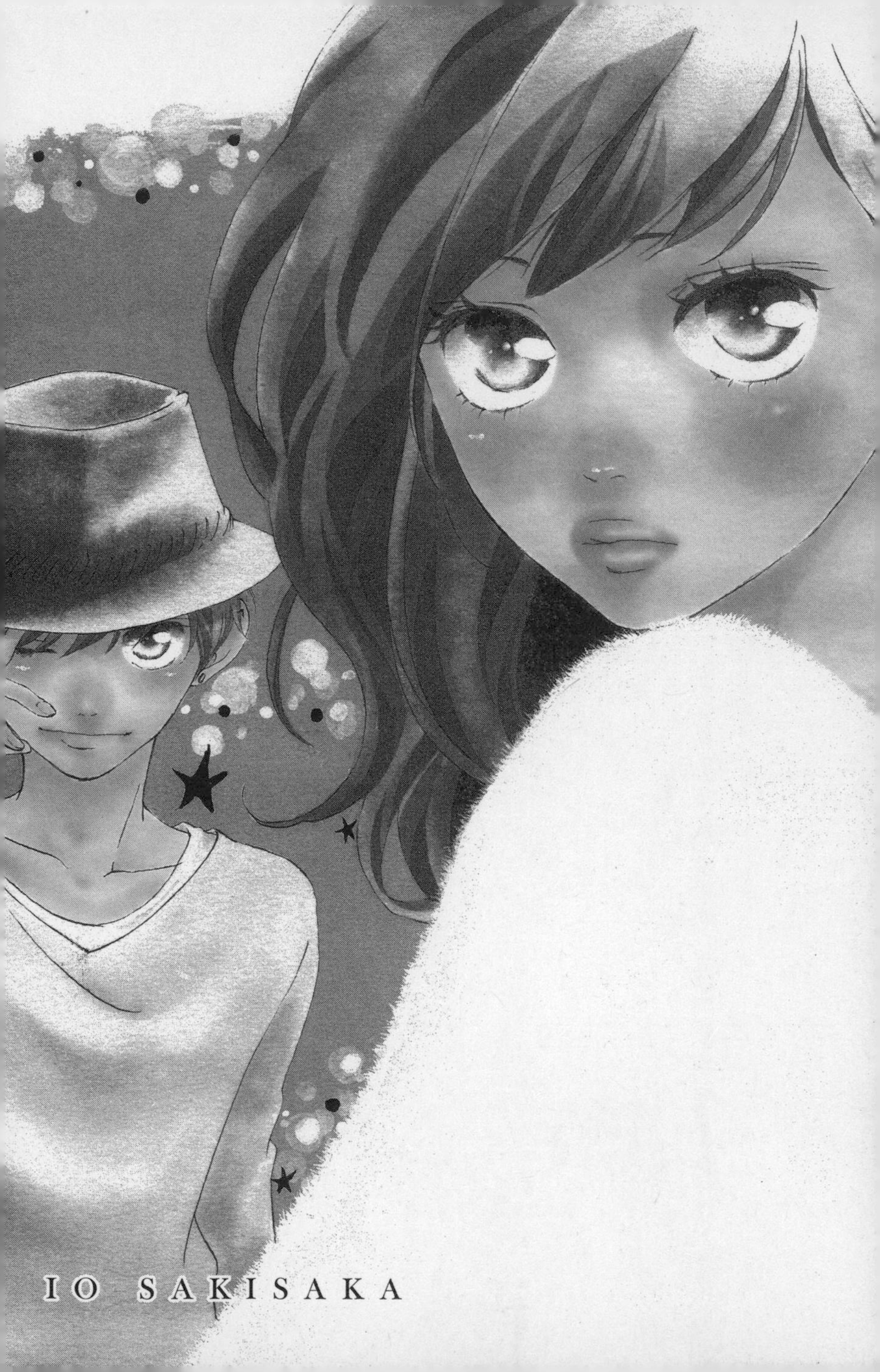
IO SAKISAKA

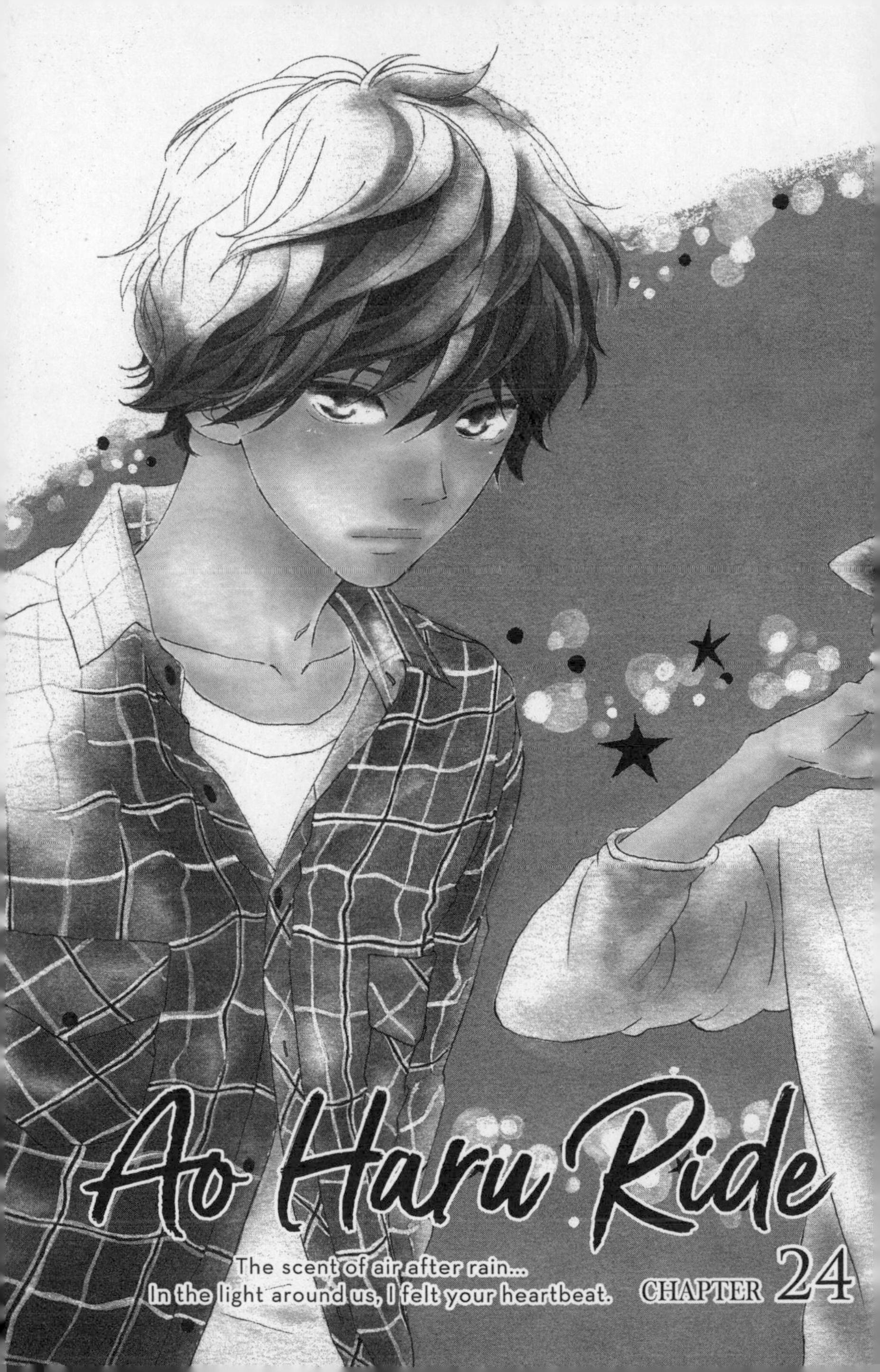
Ao Haru Ride
The scent of air after rain...
In the light around us, I felt your heartbeat.
CHAPTER 24

GREETINGS

Hi! I'm Io Sakisaka. Thank you for picking up a copy of *Ao Haru Ride* volume 7!

Spring is here! It's my favorite season. When the cold starts to fade and you wander outside, wondering if winter is coming to an end, suddenly the scent of the daphne flower hits your nose! It's that moment of excitement and anticipation that I love. I especially enjoy hearing the warbler sing "ho—hokekyo." (The young birds that are not very good yet sing "ho—hokyohokyo.") It's the cutest. Sometimes I think about how wonderful it would be to experience this calm throughout the whole year, but that would mean I'd no longer experience becoming calm. So I shall accept things as they are and continue to bear the cold of winter and the violent rays of summer. For only then can I truly appreciate the joy I feel when springtime comes around. It's such bliss.

And with that, here's *Ao Haru Ride* volume 7. The story is currently in the middle of fall—and is completely unrelated to what I'm feeling right now—but pay no attention to such details and please do read through to the end!

 Io Sakisaka

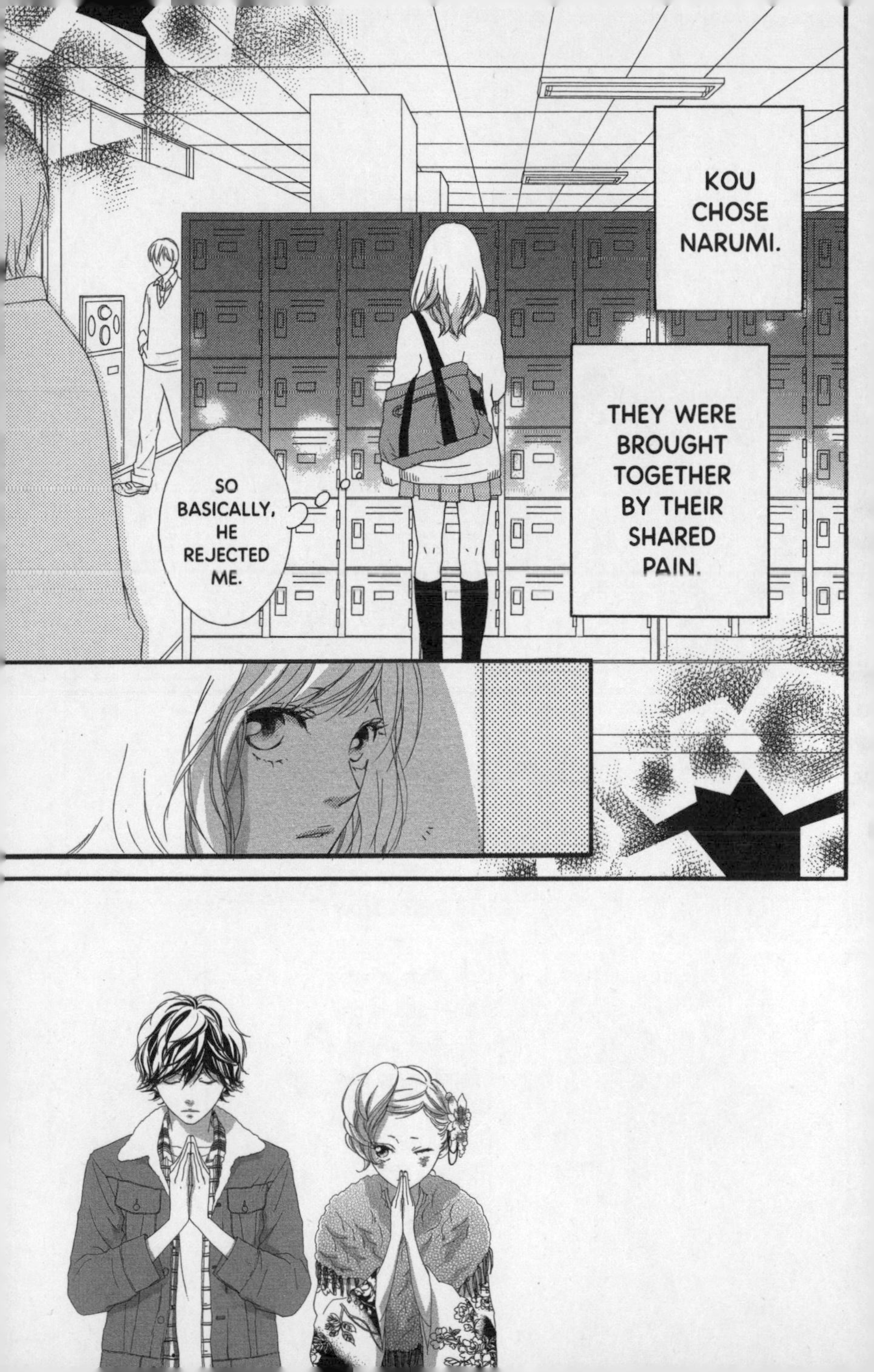
KOU CHOSE NARUMI.
THEY WERE BROUGHT TOGETHER BY THEIR SHARED PAIN.
SO BASICALLY, HE REJECTED ME.

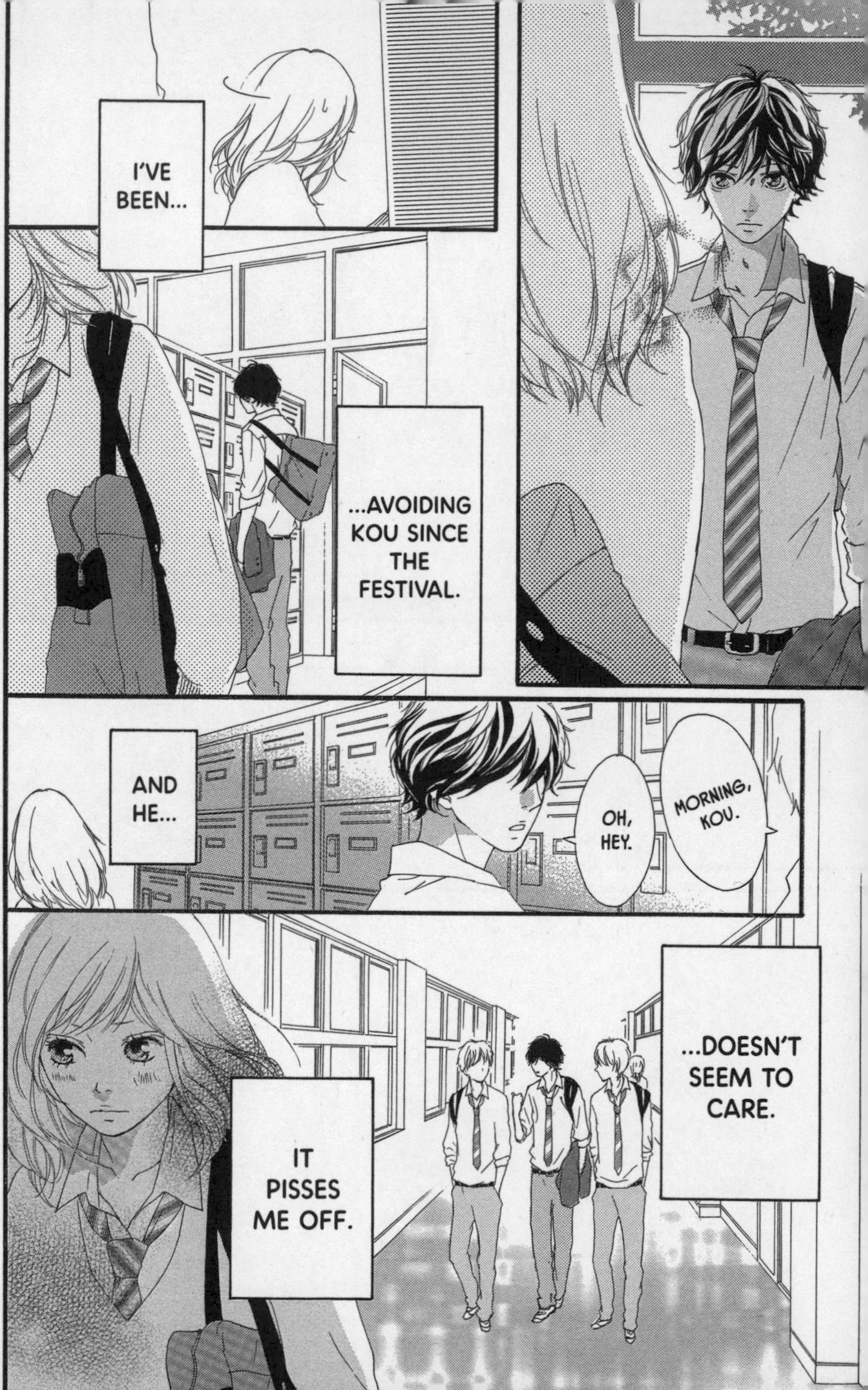
I'VE BEEN...
...AVOIDING KOU SINCE THE FESTIVAL.
MORNING, KOU.
OH, HEY.
AND HE...
...DOESN'T SEEM TO CARE.
IT PISSES ME OFF.

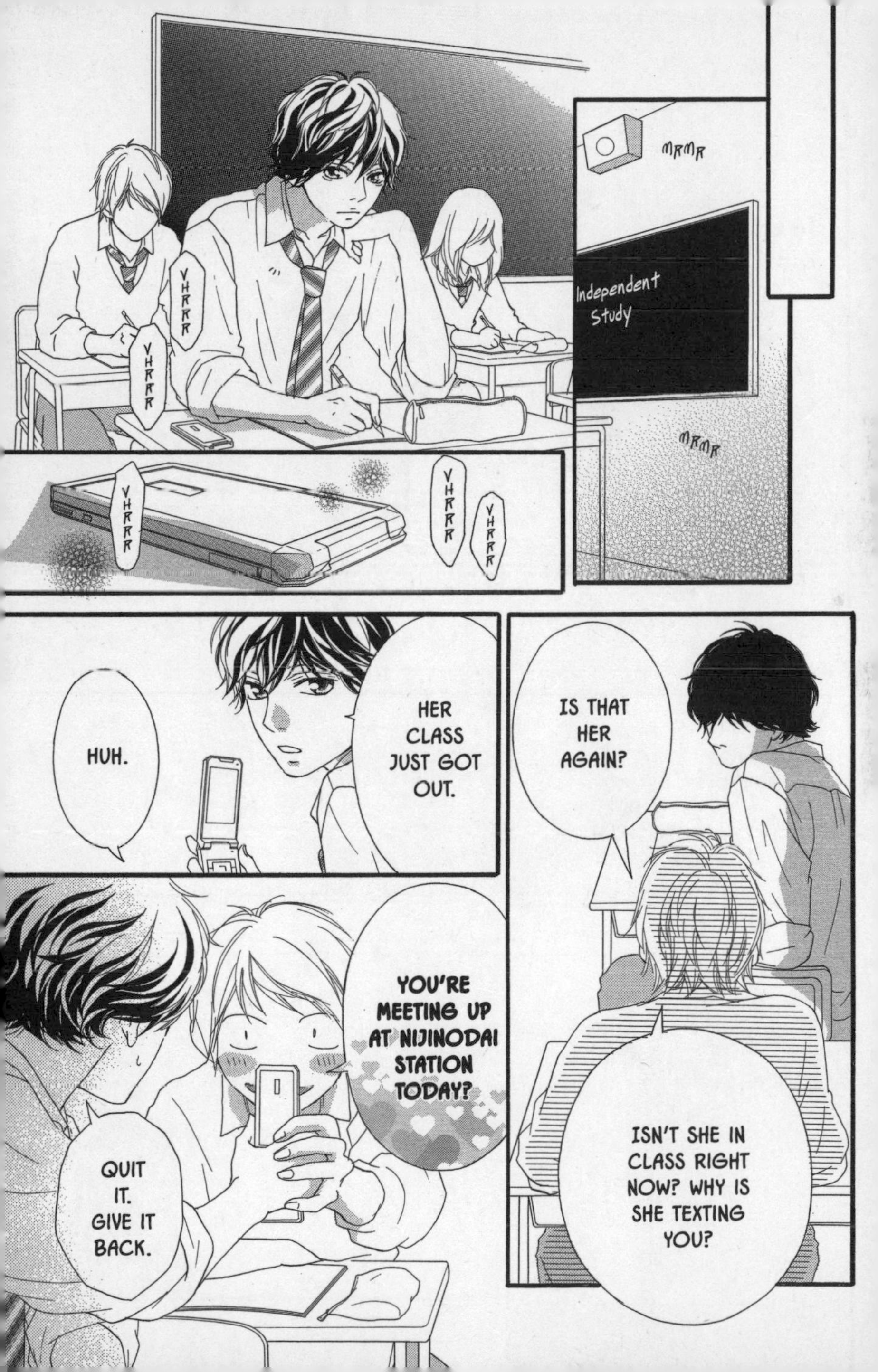
MRMR
Independent Study
MRMR
VHRRR
VHRRR
VHRRR
VHRRR
VHRRR
IS THAT HER AGAIN?
ISN'T SHE IN CLASS RIGHT NOW? WHY IS SHE TEXTING YOU?
HER CLASS JUST GOT OUT.
HUH.
YOU'RE MEETING UP AT NIJINODAI STATION TODAY?
QUIT IT. GIVE IT BACK.

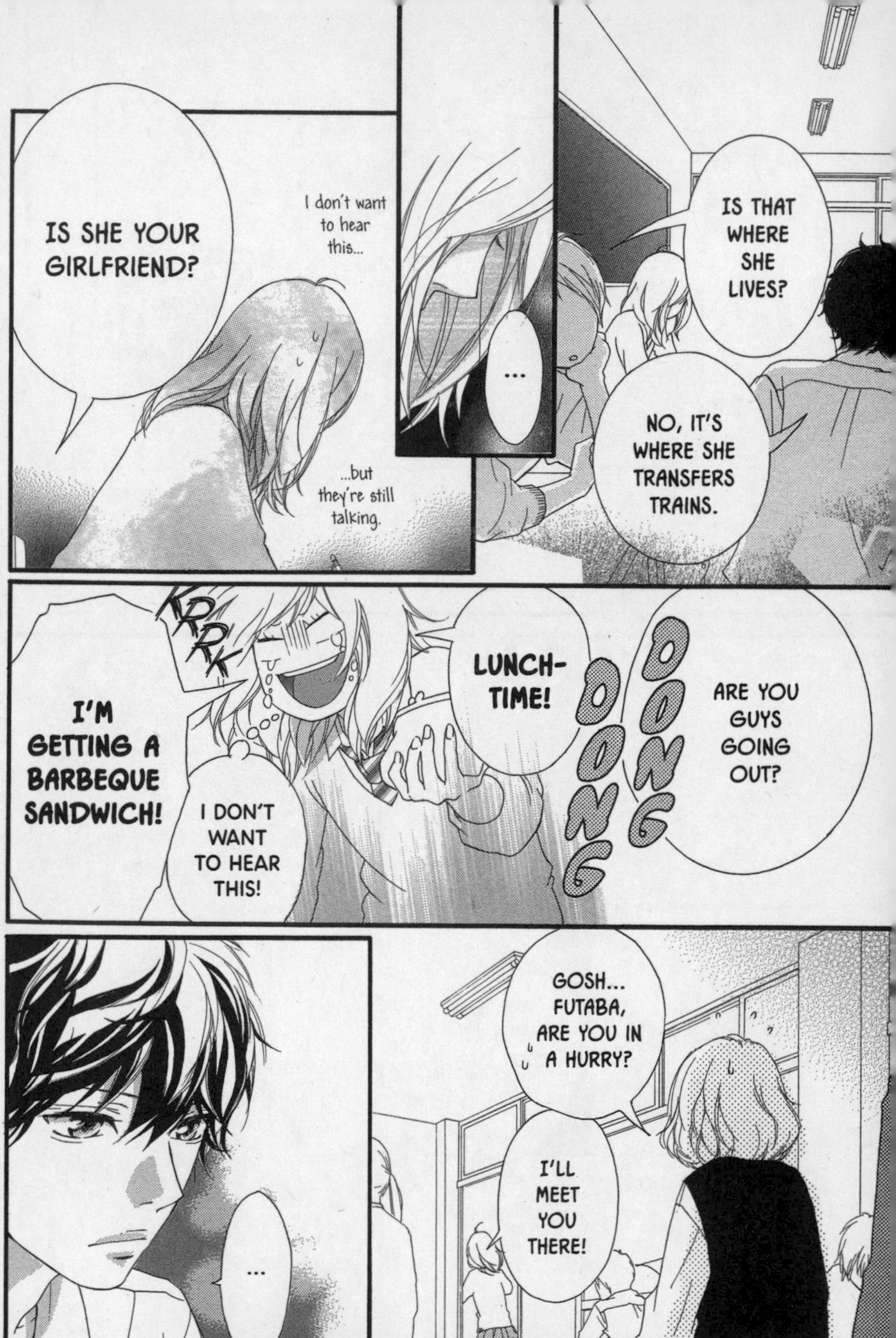
IS THAT WHERE SHE LIVES?
NO, IT'S WHERE SHE TRANSFERS TRAINS.
...
IS SHE YOUR GIRLFRIEND?
I don't want to hear this...
...but they're still talking.
ARE YOU GUYS GOING OUT?
DOONG
DOONG
LUNCH-TIME!
KRRRK
I DON'T WANT TO HEAR THIS!
I'M GETTING A BARBEQUE SANDWICH!
GOSH... FUTABA, ARE YOU IN A HURRY?
I'LL MEET YOU THERE!
...

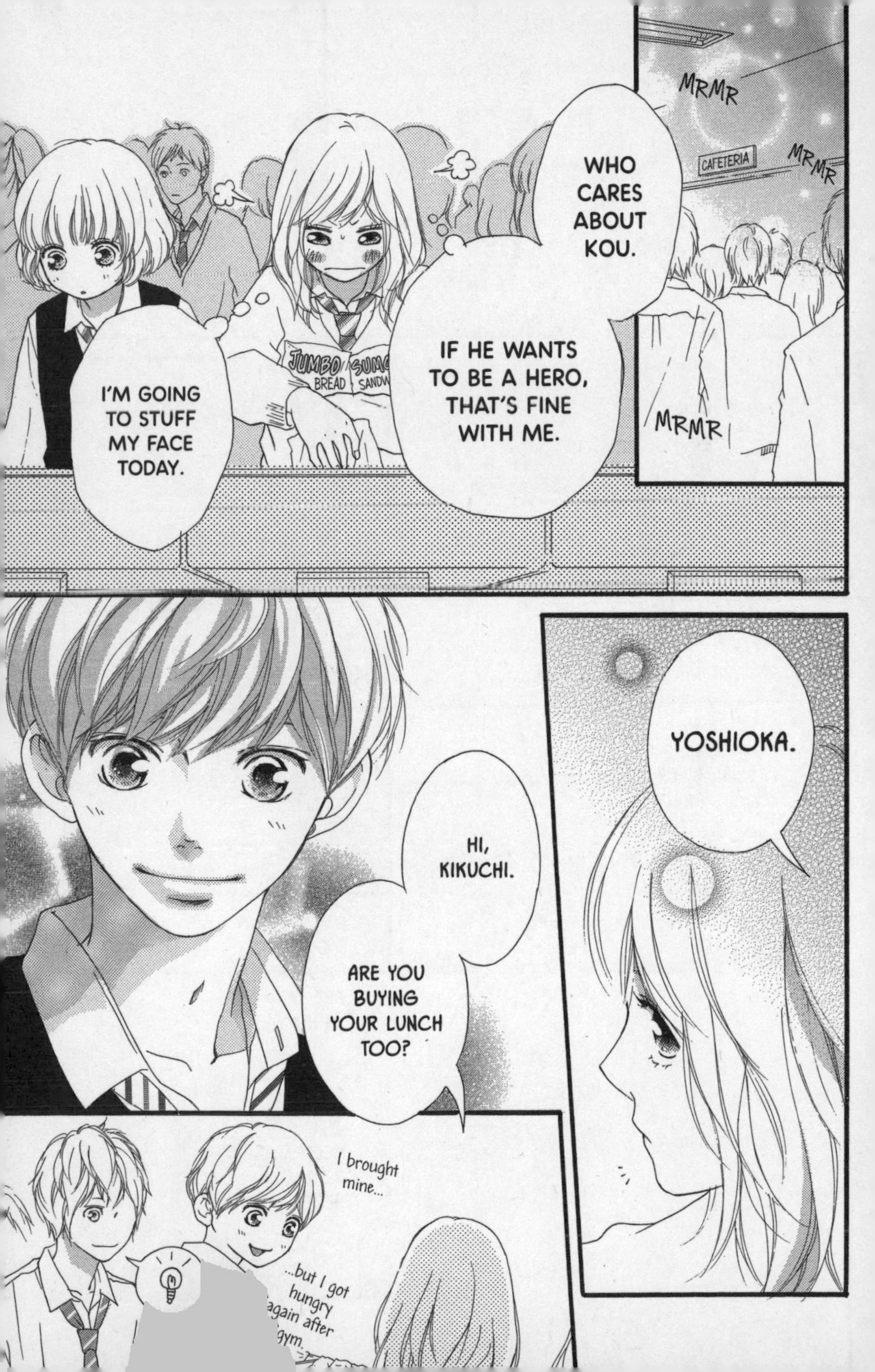
MRMR
CAFETERIA
MRMR
MRMR
WHO CARES ABOUT KOU.
IF HE WANTS TO BE A HERO, THAT'S FINE WITH ME.
JUMBO BREAD
SUMO SANDW
I'M GOING TO STUFF MY FACE TODAY.
YOSHIOKA.
HI, KIKUCHI.
ARE YOU BUYING YOUR LUNCH TOO?
I brought mine...
...but I got hungry again after gym.

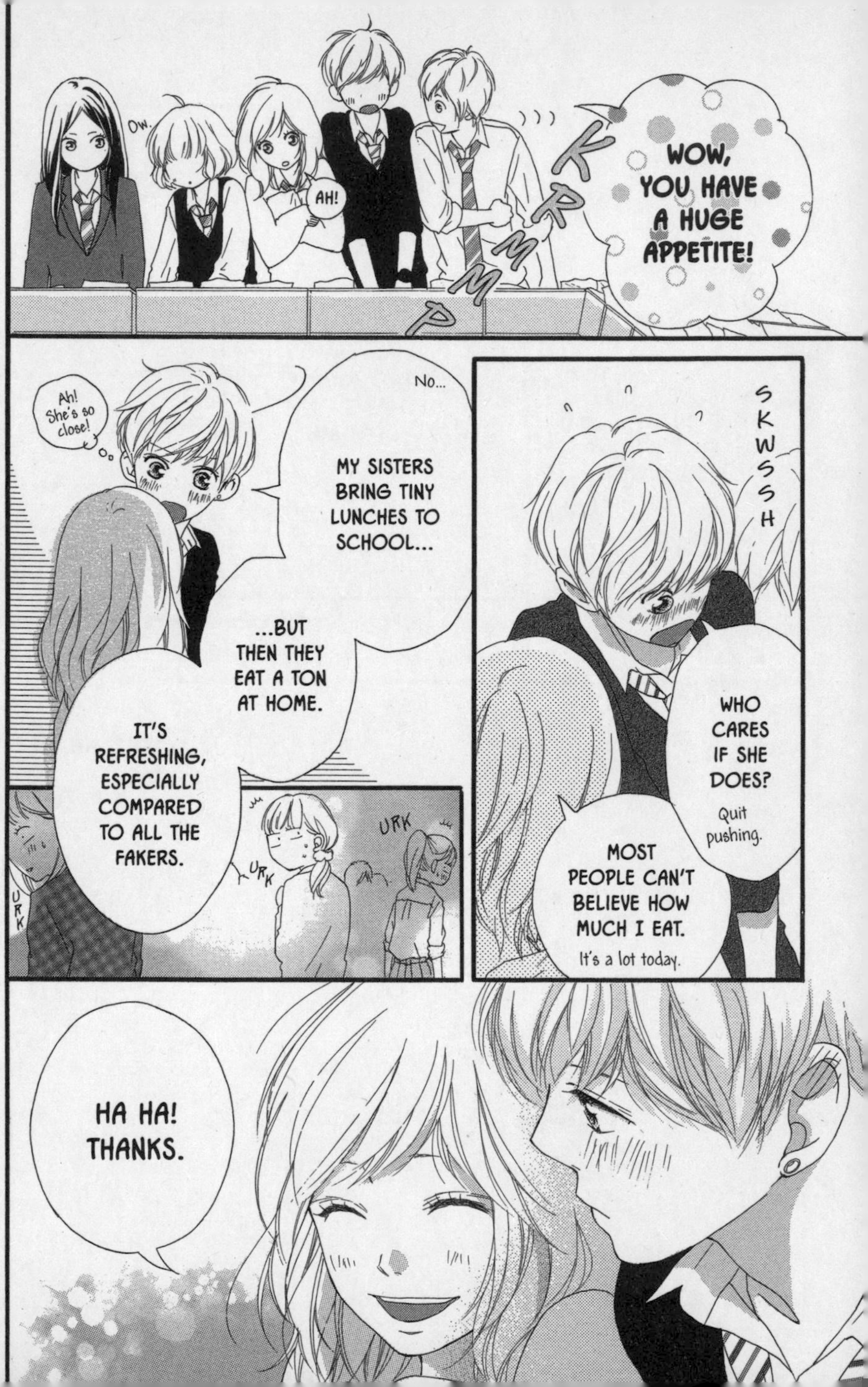
WOW, YOU HAVE A HUGE APPETITE!
KRMMP
AH!
Ow.
SKWSSH
WHO CARES IF SHE DOES?
Quit pushing.
MOST PEOPLE CAN'T BELIEVE HOW MUCH I EAT.
It's a lot today.
No...
MY SISTERS BRING TINY LUNCHES TO SCHOOL...
...BUT THEN THEY EAT A TON AT HOME.
Ah! She's so close!
IT'S REFRESHING, ESPECIALLY COMPARED TO ALL THE FAKERS.
URK
URK
URK
HA HA! THANKS.

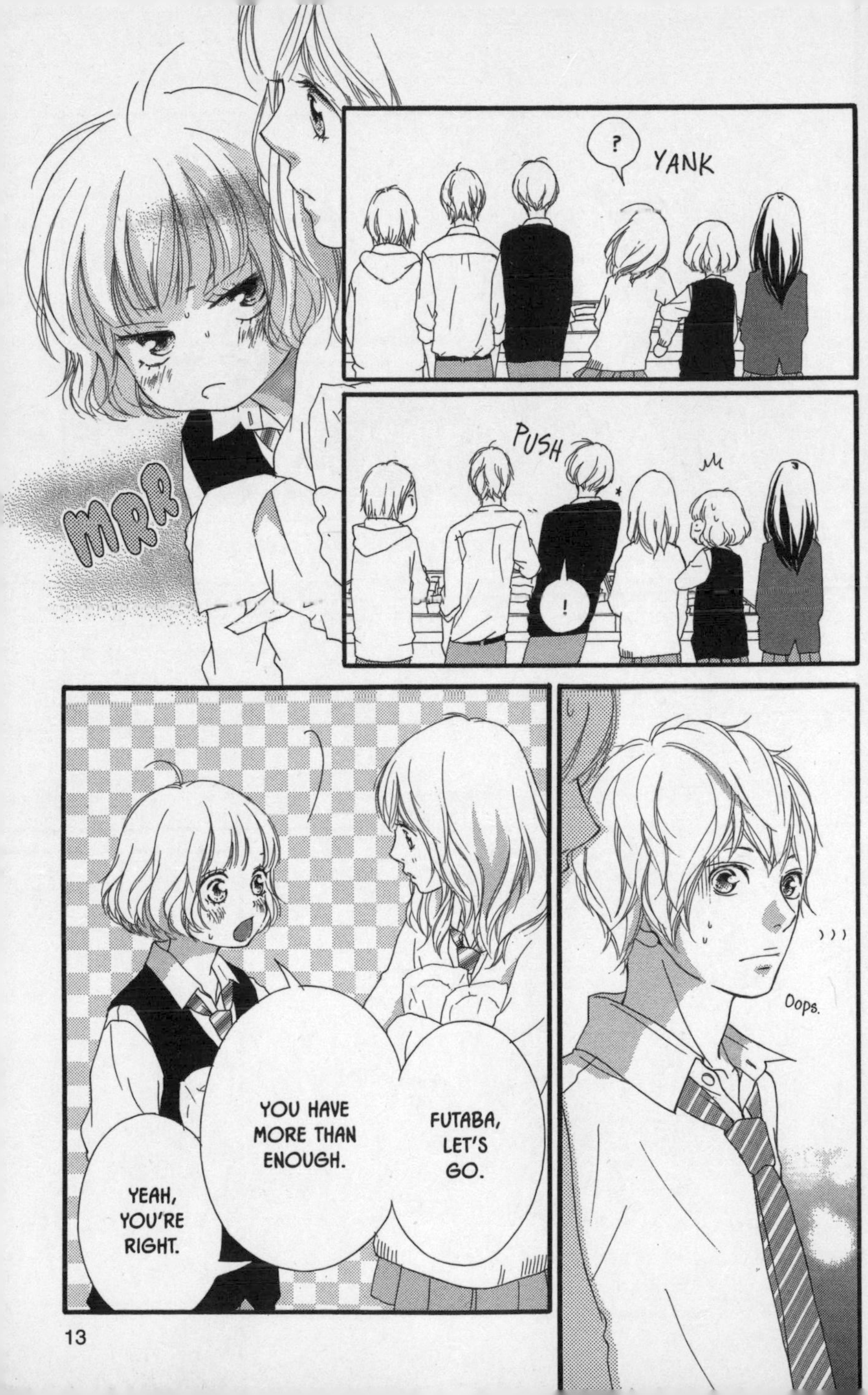
?
YANK
PUSH
!
MRR
Oops.
FUTABA, LET'S GO.
YOU HAVE MORE THAN ENOUGH.
YEAH, YOU'RE RIGHT.

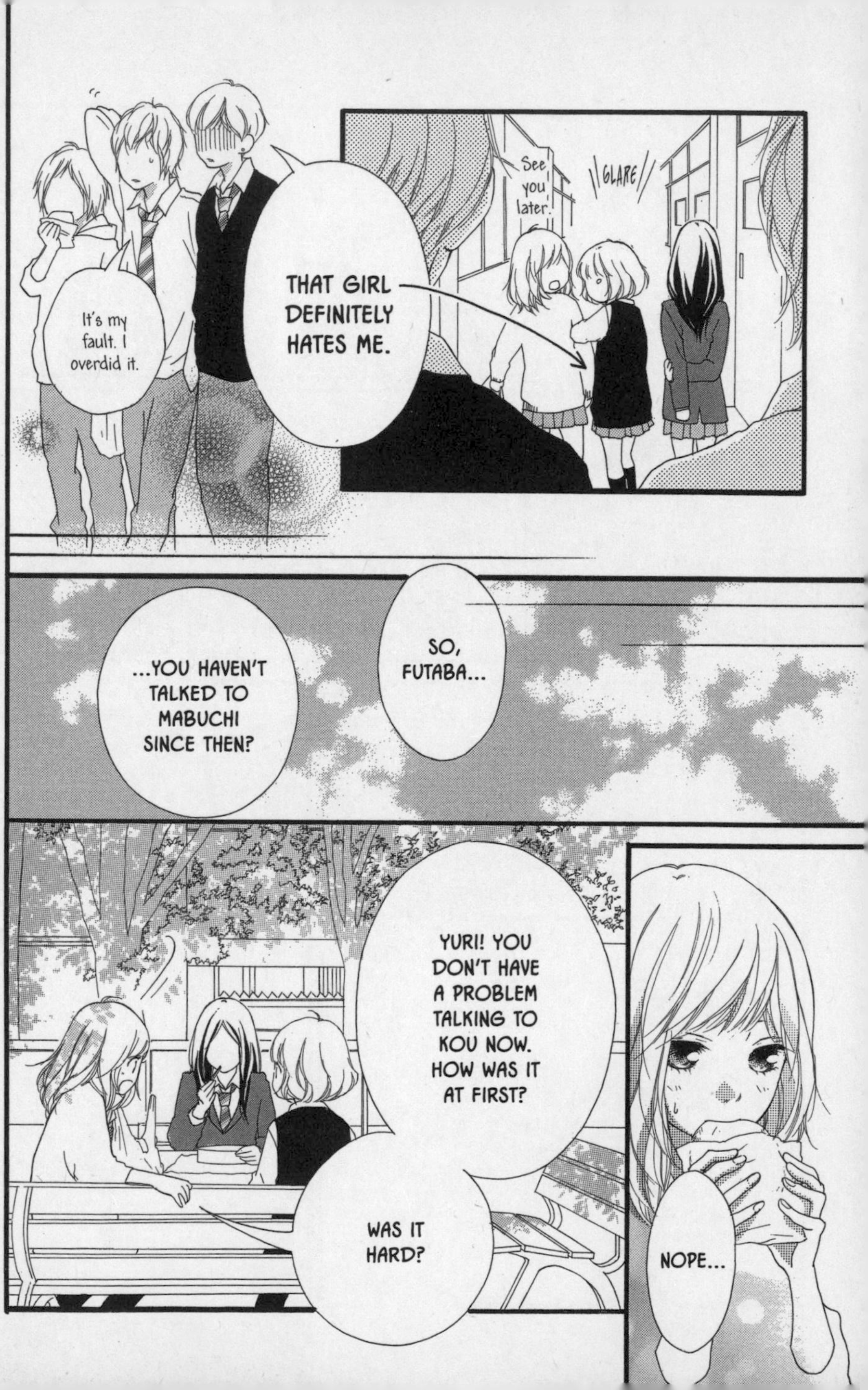
See you later.
GLARE
THAT GIRL DEFINITELY HATES ME.
It's my fault. I overdid it.
SO, FUTABA...
...YOU HAVEN'T TALKED TO MABUCHI SINCE THEN?
YURI! YOU DON'T HAVE A PROBLEM TALKING TO KOU NOW. HOW WAS IT AT FIRST?
WAS IT HARD?
NOPE...

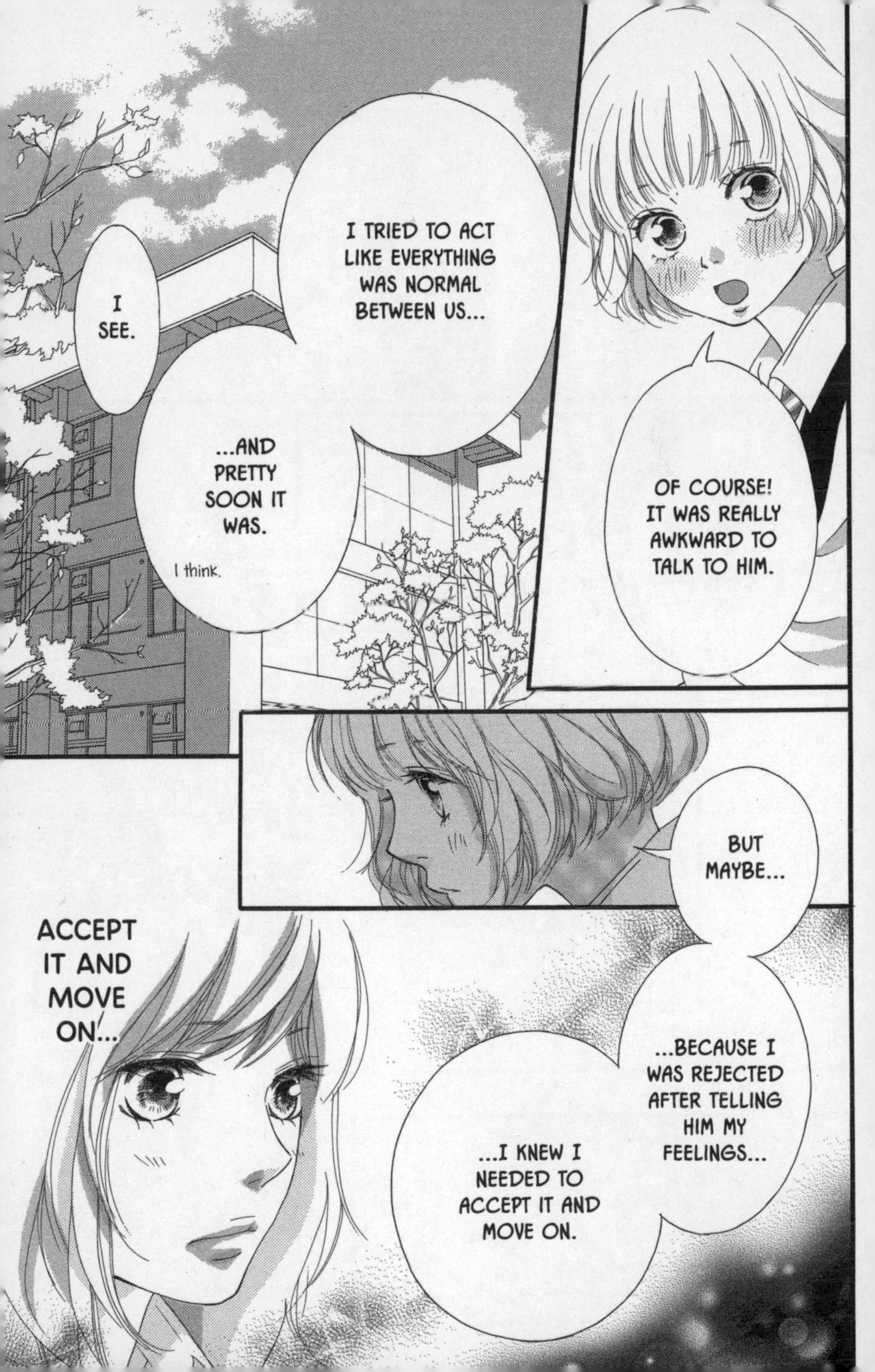
OF COURSE! IT WAS REALLY AWKWARD TO TALK TO HIM.
I TRIED TO ACT LIKE EVERYTHING WAS NORMAL BETWEEN US...
...AND PRETTY SOON IT WAS.
I think.
I SEE.
BUT MAYBE...
...BECAUSE I WAS REJECTED AFTER TELLING HIM MY FEELINGS...
...I KNEW I NEEDED TO ACCEPT IT AND MOVE ON.
ACCEPT IT AND MOVE ON...

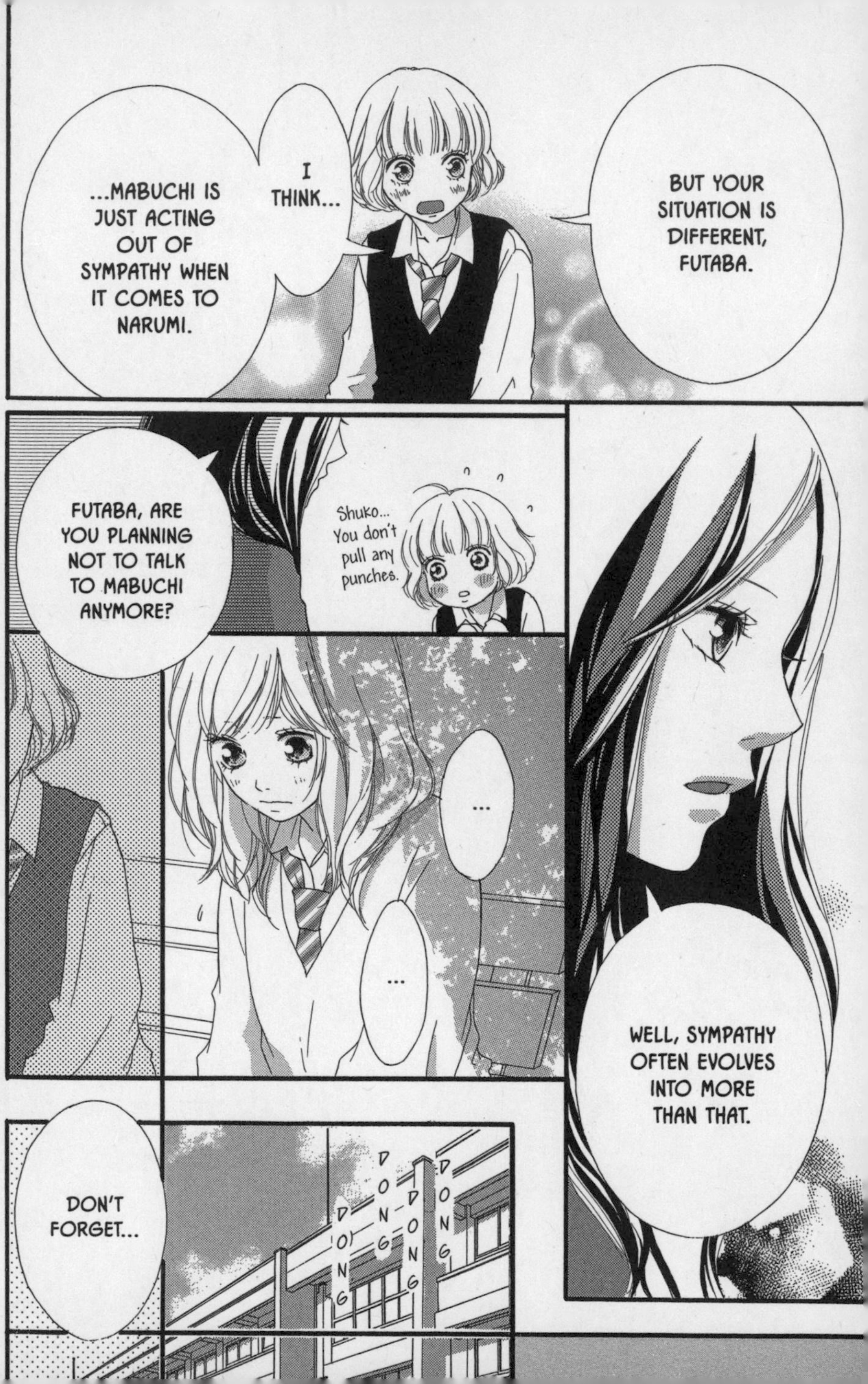
BUT YOUR SITUATION IS DIFFERENT, FUTABA.
I THINK...
...MABUCHI IS JUST ACTING OUT OF SYMPATHY WHEN IT COMES TO NARUMI.
WELL, SYMPATHY OFTEN EVOLVES INTO MORE THAN THAT.
FUTABA, ARE YOU PLANNING NOT TO TALK TO MABUCHI ANYMORE?
Shuko... You don't pull any punches.
...
...
DONG DONG DONG DONG
DON'T FORGET...

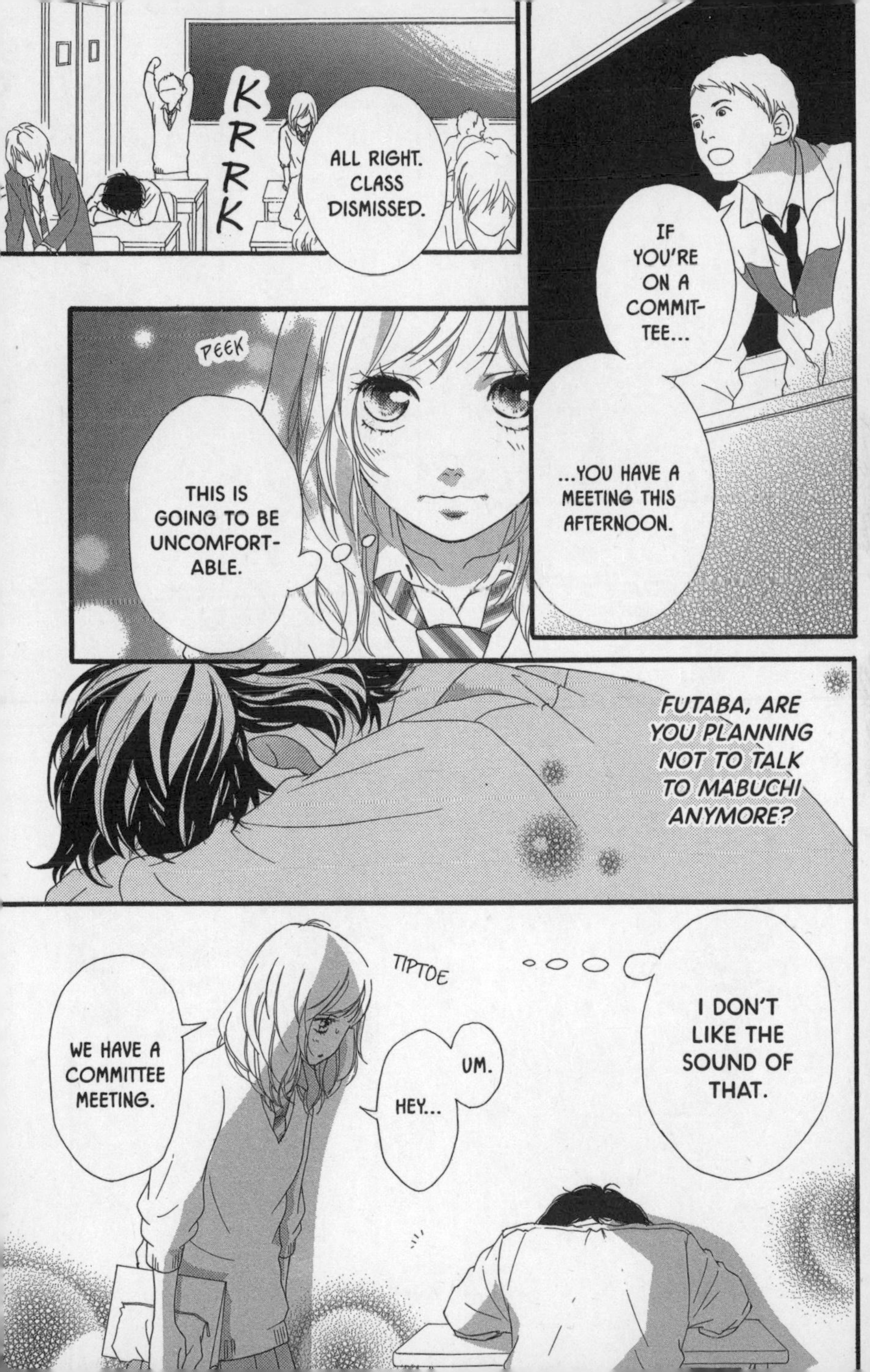
IF YOU'RE ON A COMMIT-TEE...
...YOU HAVE A MEETING THIS AFTERNOON.
KRRK
ALL RIGHT. CLASS DISMISSED.
PEEK
THIS IS GOING TO BE UNCOMFORT-ABLE.
FUTABA, ARE YOU PLANNING NOT TO TALK TO MABUCHI ANYMORE?
I DON'T LIKE THE SOUND OF THAT.
TIPTOE
UM.
HEY...
WE HAVE A COMMITTEE MEETING.

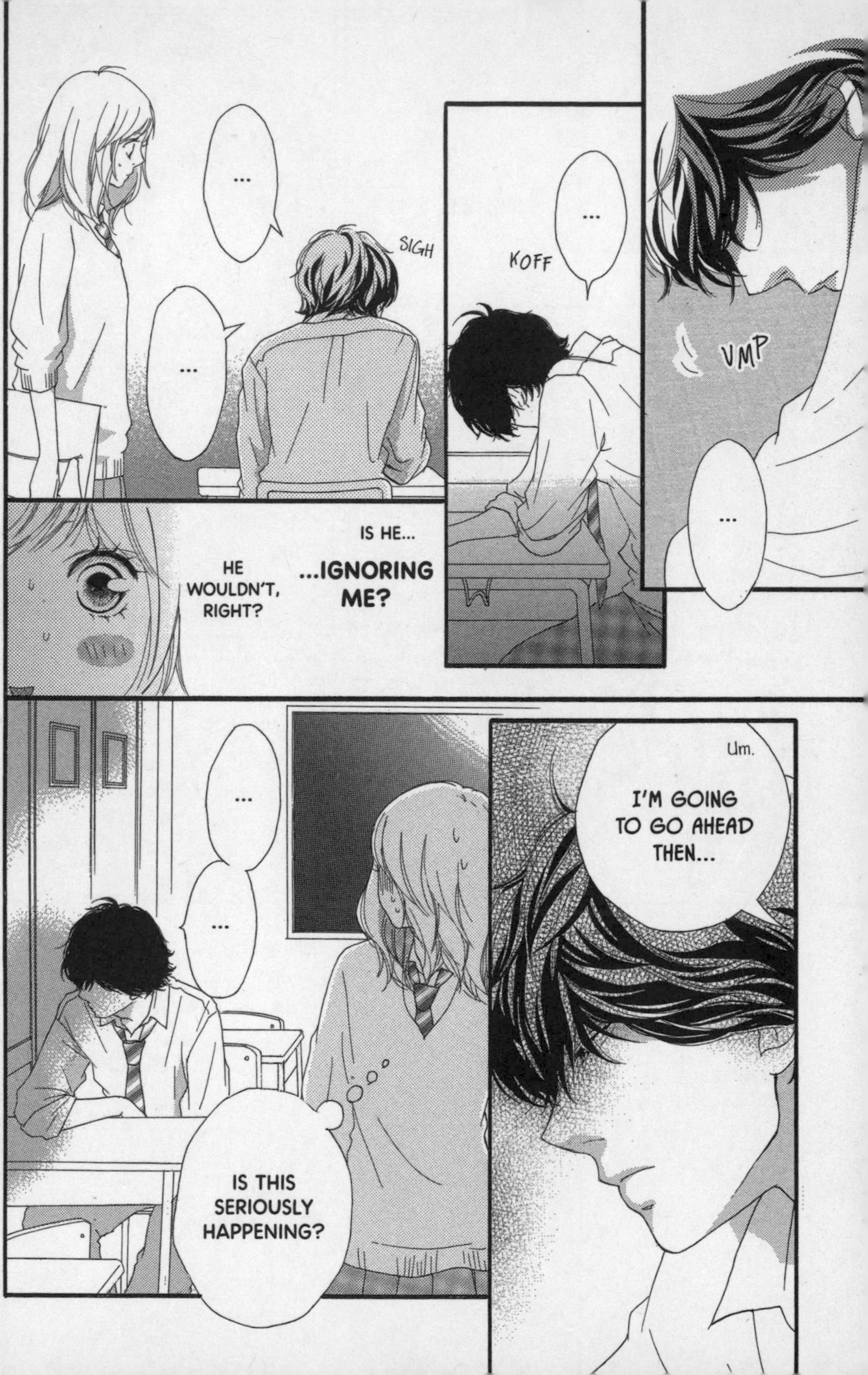
VMP
...
...
KOFF
SIGH
...
...
IS HE...
...IGNORING ME?
HE WOULDN'T, RIGHT?
Um.
I'M GOING TO GO AHEAD THEN...
...
...
IS THIS SERIOUSLY HAPPENING?

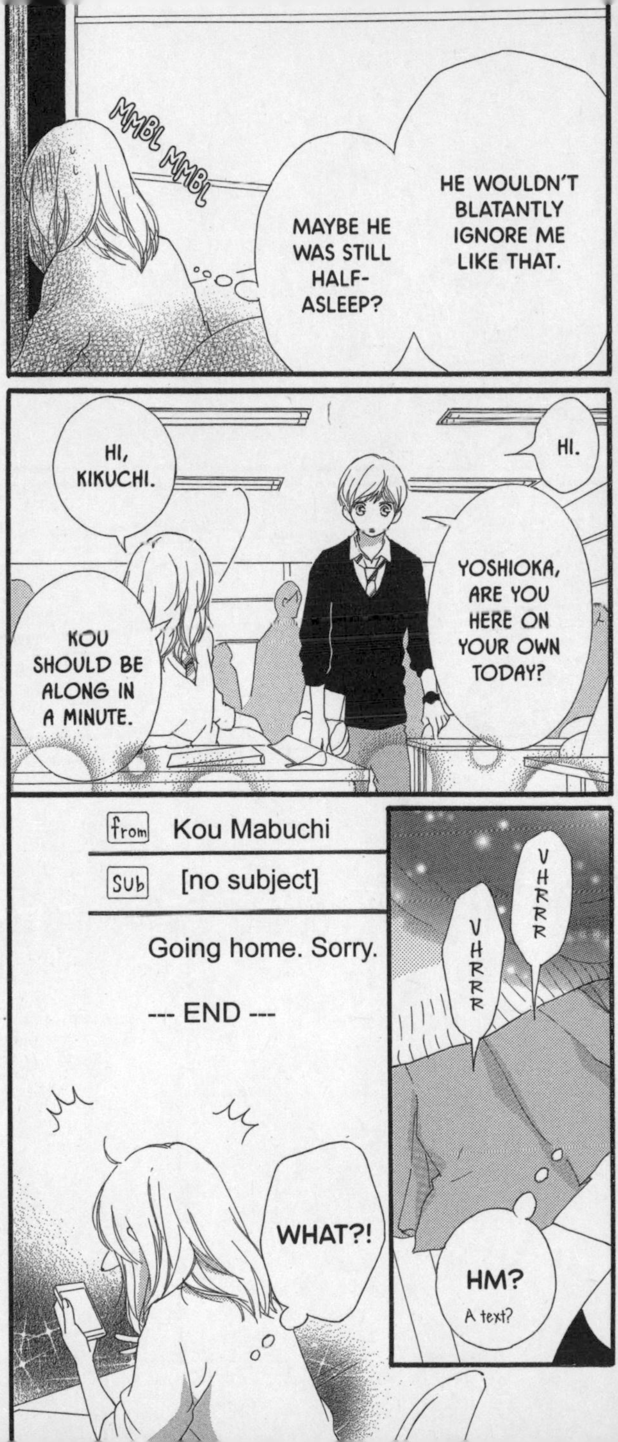
HE WOULDN'T BLATANTLY IGNORE ME LIKE THAT.
MAYBE HE WAS STILL HALF-ASLEEP?
MMBL MMBL
HI.
HI, KIKUCHI.
YOSHIOKA, ARE YOU HERE ON YOUR OWN TODAY?
KOU SHOULD BE ALONG IN A MINUTE.
VHRRR
VHRRR
HM?
A text?
from Kou Mabuchi
Sub [no subject]
Going home. Sorry.
--- END ---
WHAT?!

I listened to Capsule's "Sugarless Girl" nonstop while coloring the cover art for volume 7. The song doesn't have anything to do with the cover—I just happen to like it. For some reason, I made up a rule in which I had to listen to the song on repeat until I finished coloring, so of course I messed up and had to redo everything three times. I doubt there are many people who've listened to "Sugarless Girl" on repeat as many times as I have. Ha ha! So you could say I owe a lot to this song. Now, if I'm being honest, I'll tell you that I broke my own rule and listened to "The Music" a few times too. Both songs are by Capsule, so I let myself bend the rules a bit. Heh heh.

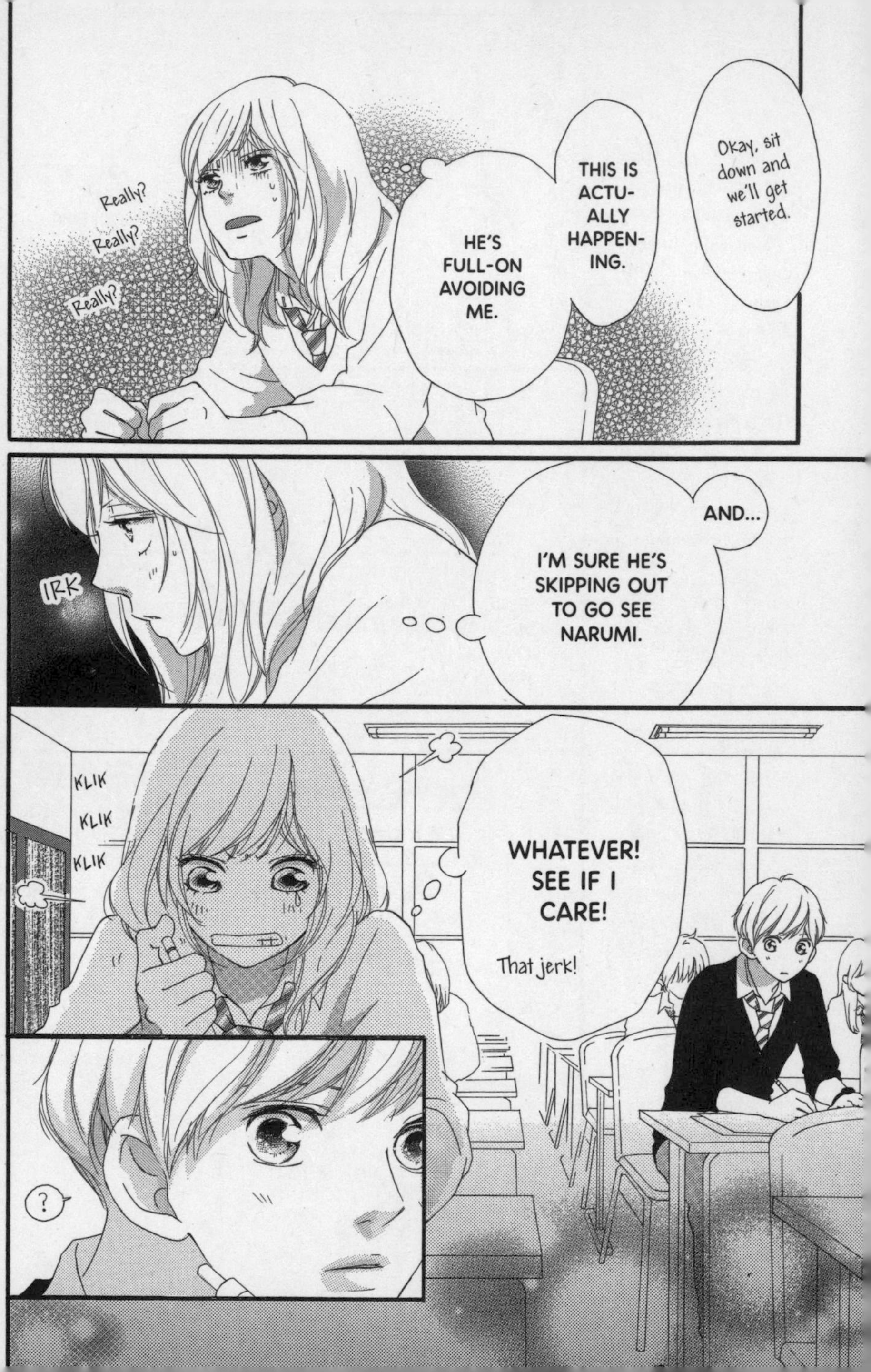

Okay, sit down and we'll get started.
THIS IS ACTU-ALLY HAPPEN-ING.
HE'S FULL-ON AVOIDING ME.
Really?
Really?
Really?
AND...
I'M SURE HE'S SKIPPING OUT TO GO SEE NARUMI.
IRK
WHATEVER! SEE IF I CARE!
That jerk!
KLIK
KLIK
KLIK
?

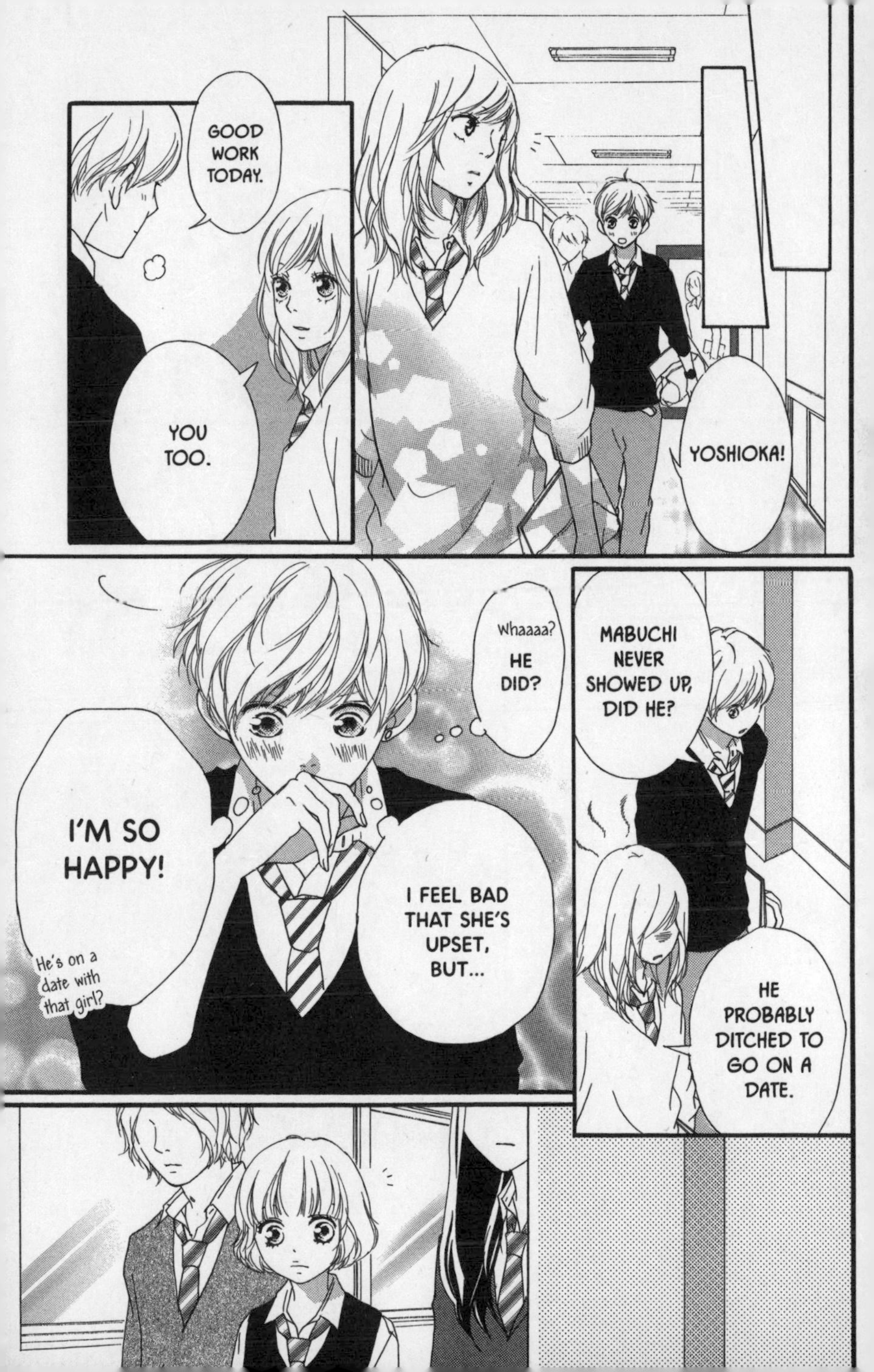
YOSHIOKA!
GOOD WORK TODAY.
YOU TOO.
MABUCHI NEVER SHOWED UP, DID HE?
HE PROBABLY DITCHED TO GO ON A DATE.
Whaaaa?
HE DID?
I FEEL BAD THAT SHE'S UPSET, BUT...
I'M SO HAPPY!
He's on a date with that girl?

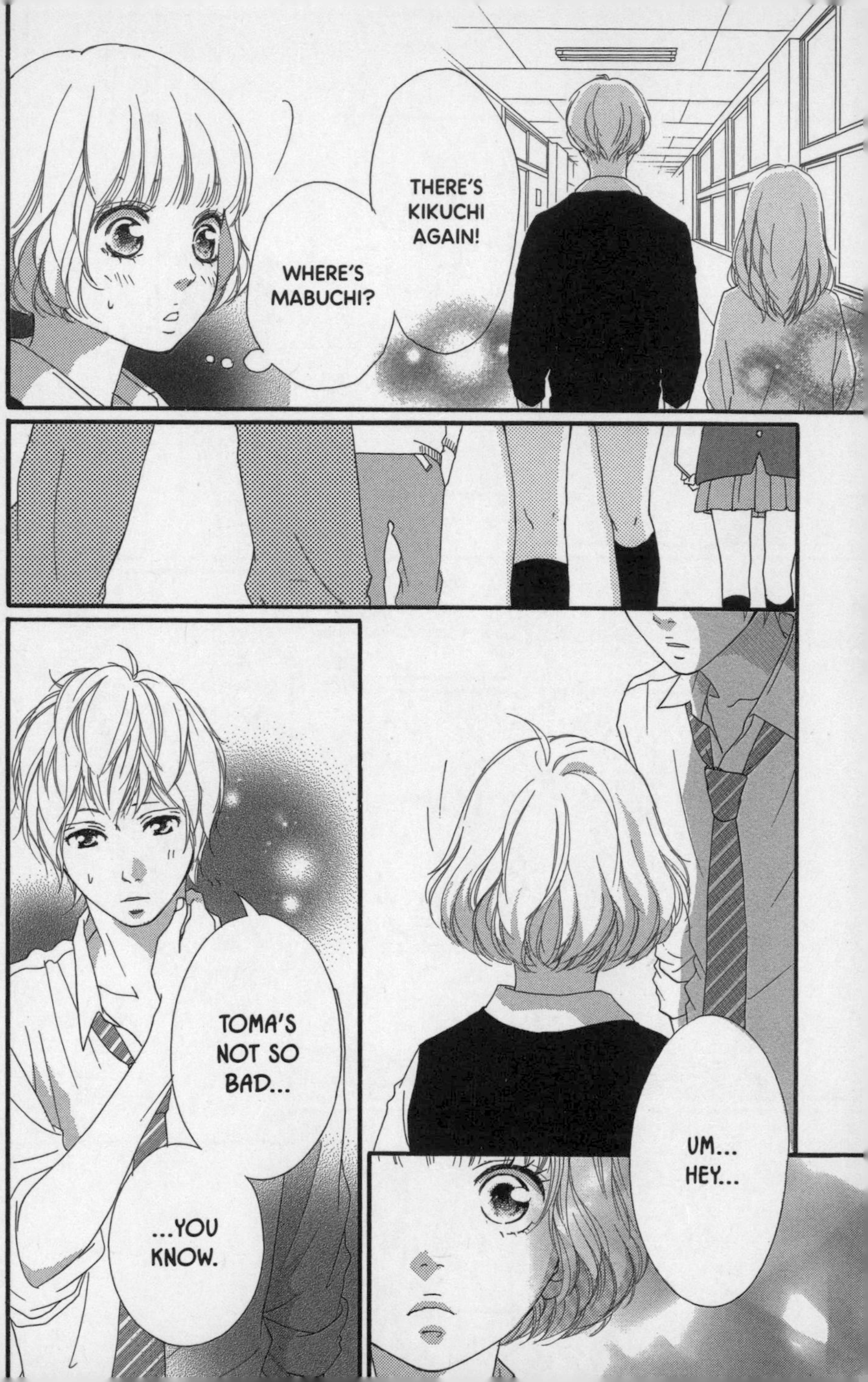
THERE'S KIKUCHI AGAIN!
WHERE'S MABUCHI?
UM... HEY...
TOMA'S NOT SO BAD...
...YOU KNOW.

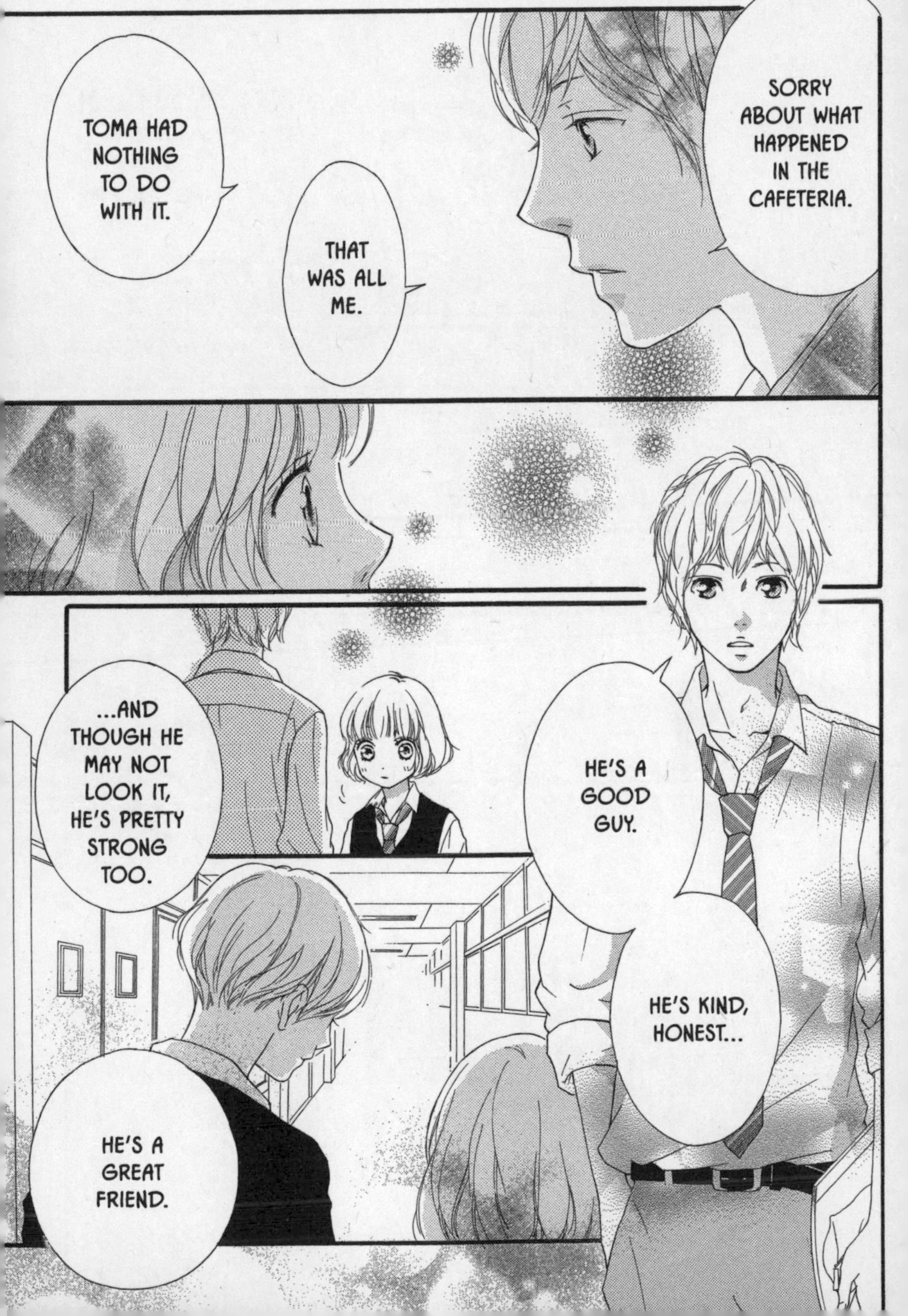
SORRY ABOUT WHAT HAPPENED IN THE CAFETERIA.
THAT WAS ALL ME.
TOMA HAD NOTHING TO DO WITH IT.
HE'S A GOOD GUY.
HE'S KIND, HONEST...
...AND THOUGH HE MAY NOT LOOK IT, HE'S PRETTY STRONG TOO.
HE'S A GREAT FRIEND.

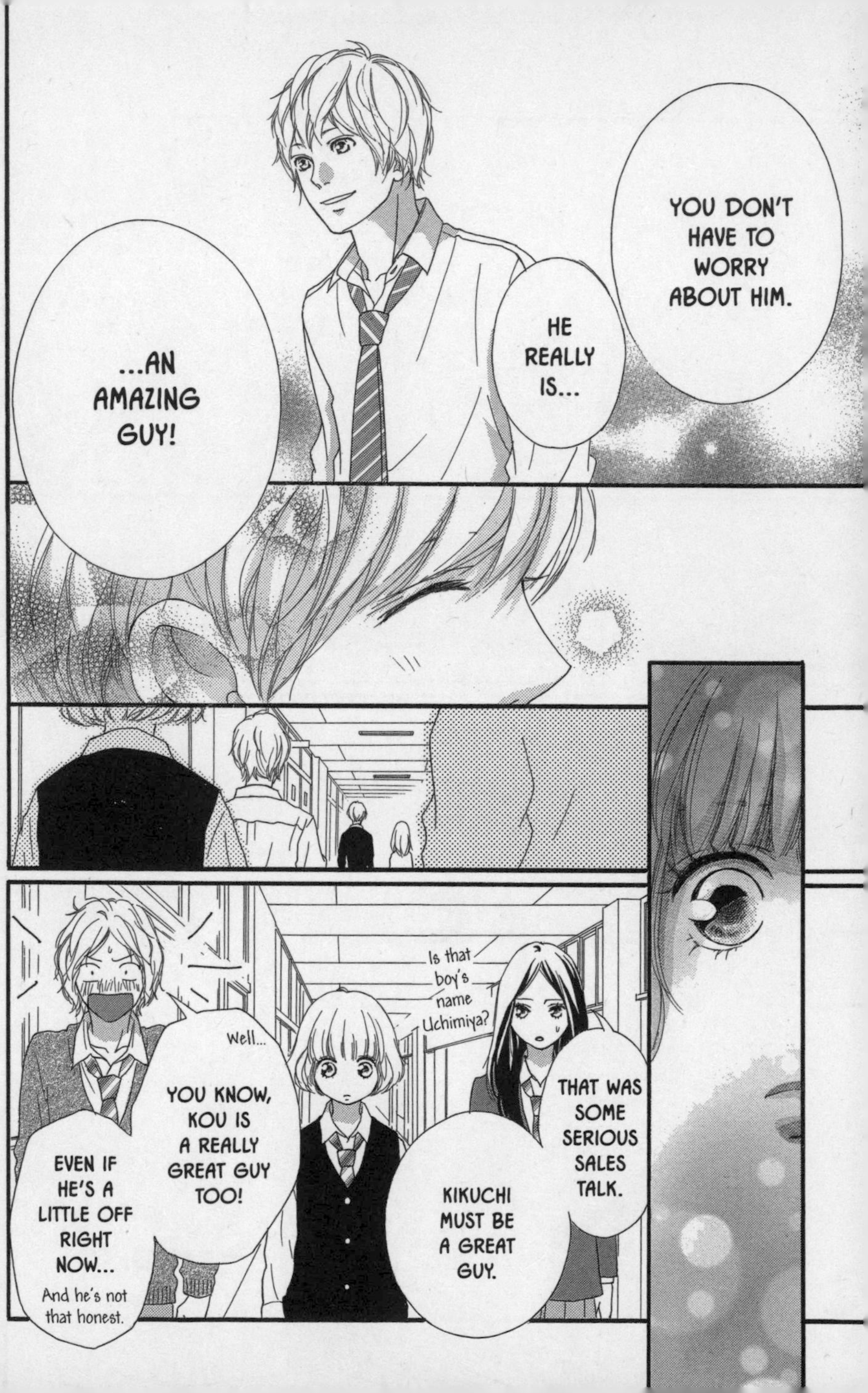
YOU DON'T HAVE TO WORRY ABOUT HIM.
HE REALLY IS...
...AN AMAZING GUY!
THAT WAS SOME SERIOUS SALES TALK.
KIKUCHI MUST BE A GREAT GUY.
Is that boy's name Uchimiya?
Well...
YOU KNOW, KOU IS A REALLY GREAT GUY TOO!
EVEN IF HE'S A LITTLE OFF RIGHT NOW...
And he's not that honest.

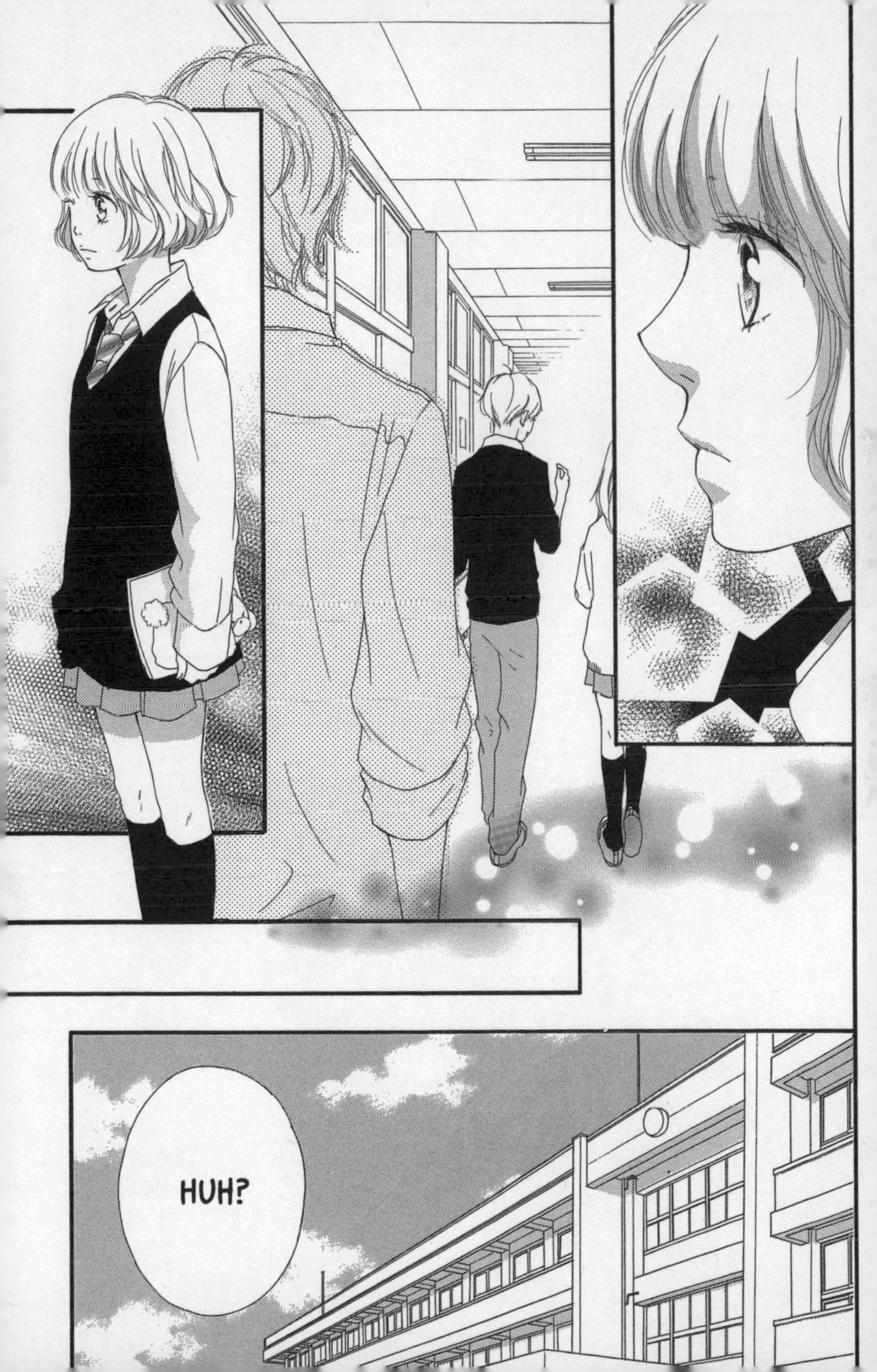
HUH?

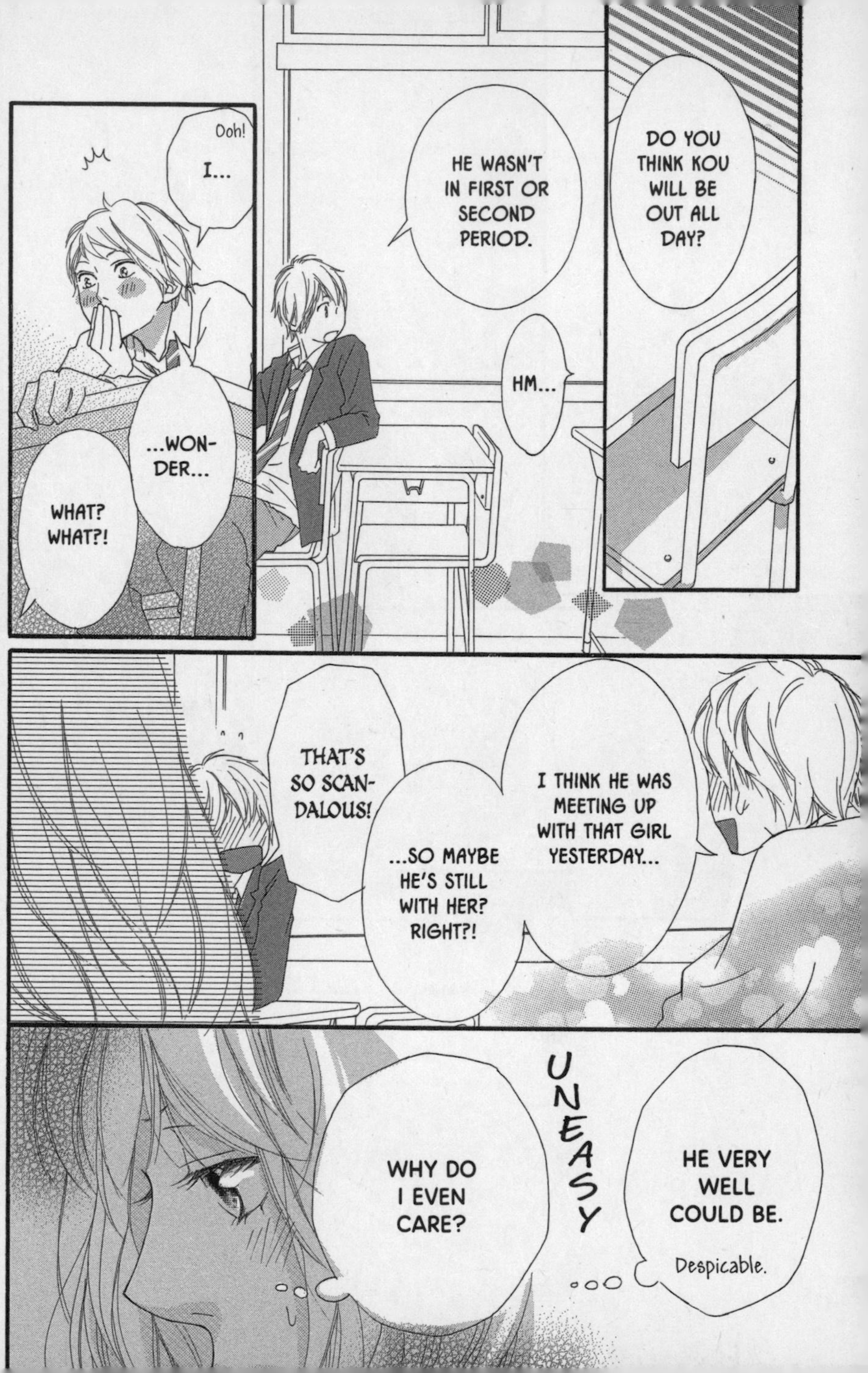
DO YOU THINK KOU WILL BE OUT ALL DAY?
HE WASN'T IN FIRST OR SECOND PERIOD.
HM...
Ooh!
I...
...WON-DER...
WHAT? WHAT?!
I THINK HE WAS MEETING UP WITH THAT GIRL YESTERDAY...
...SO MAYBE HE'S STILL WITH HER? RIGHT?!
THAT'S SO SCAN-DALOUS!
HE VERY WELL COULD BE.
Despicable.
UNEASY
WHY DO I EVEN CARE?

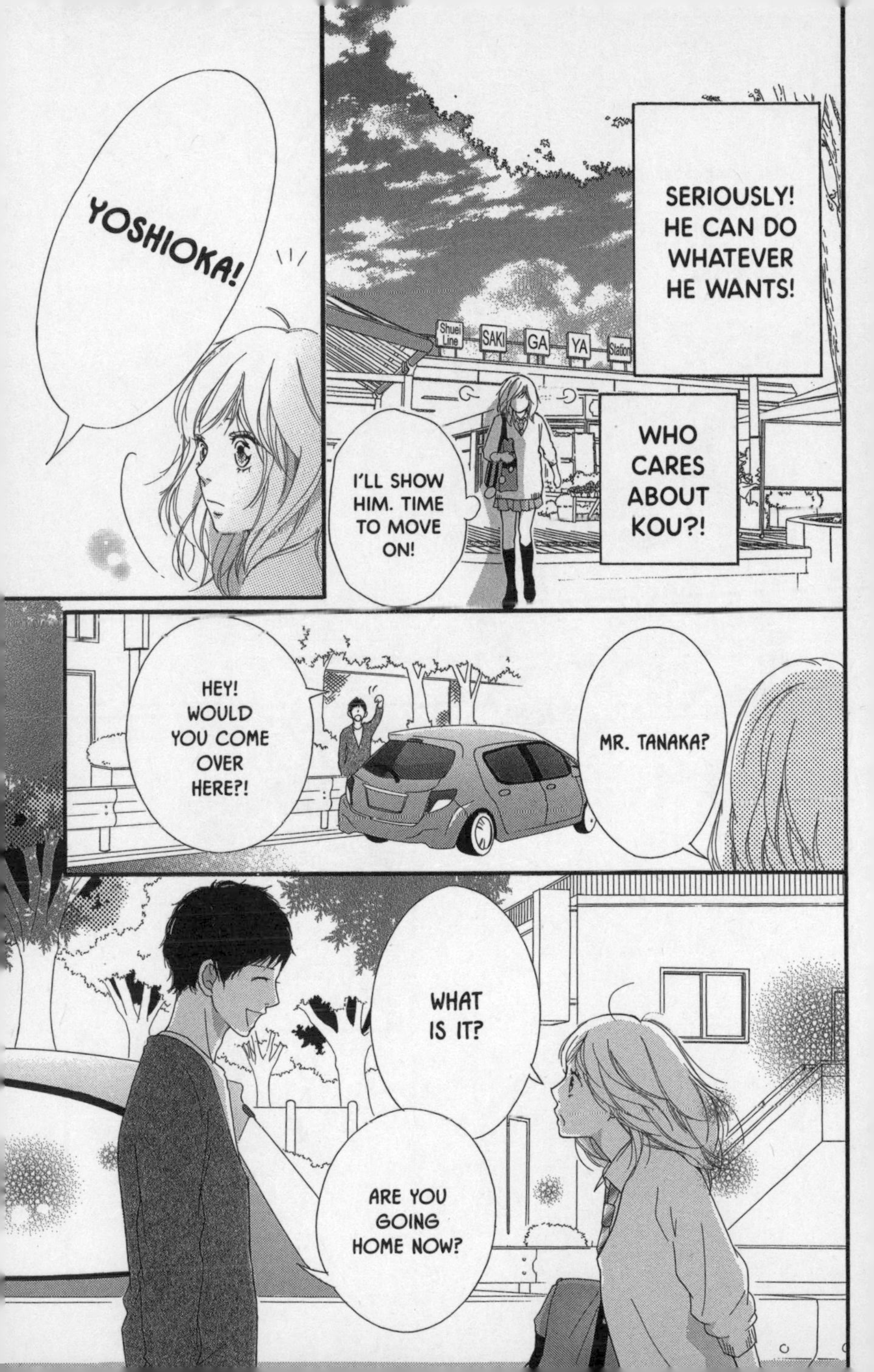
SERIOUSLY! HE CAN DO WHATEVER HE WANTS!
WHO CARES ABOUT KOU?!
Shuei Line SAKI GA YA Station
I'LL SHOW HIM. TIME TO MOVE ON!
YOSHIOKA!
MR. TANAKA?
HEY! WOULD YOU COME OVER HERE?!
WHAT IS IT?
ARE YOU GOING HOME NOW?

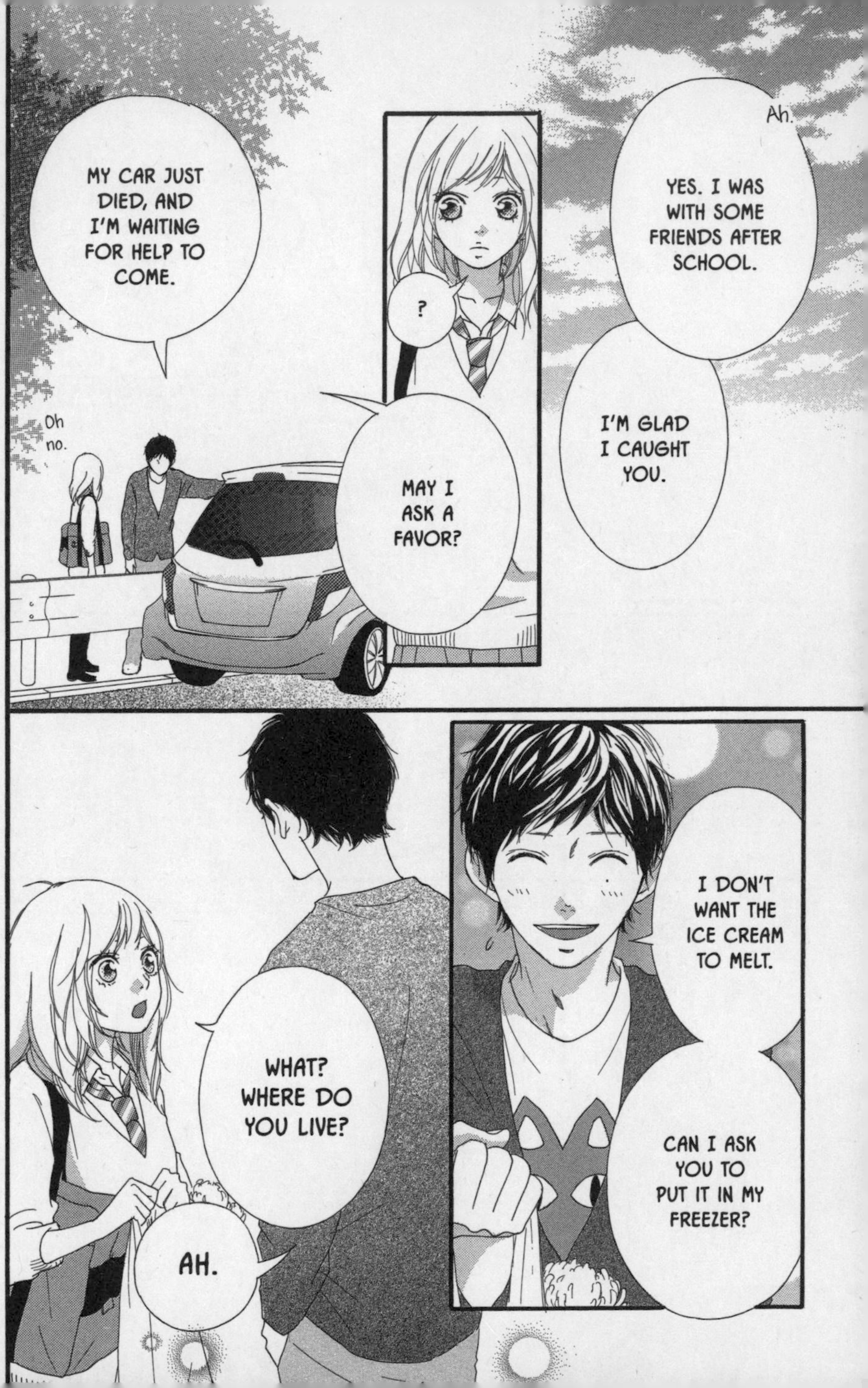
Ah.
YES. I WAS WITH SOME FRIENDS AFTER SCHOOL.
I'M GLAD I CAUGHT YOU.
?
MAY I ASK A FAVOR?
MY CAR JUST DIED, AND I'M WAITING FOR HELP TO COME.
Oh no.
I DON'T WANT THE ICE CREAM TO MELT.
CAN I ASK YOU TO PUT IT IN MY FREEZER?
WHAT? WHERE DO YOU LIVE?
AH.

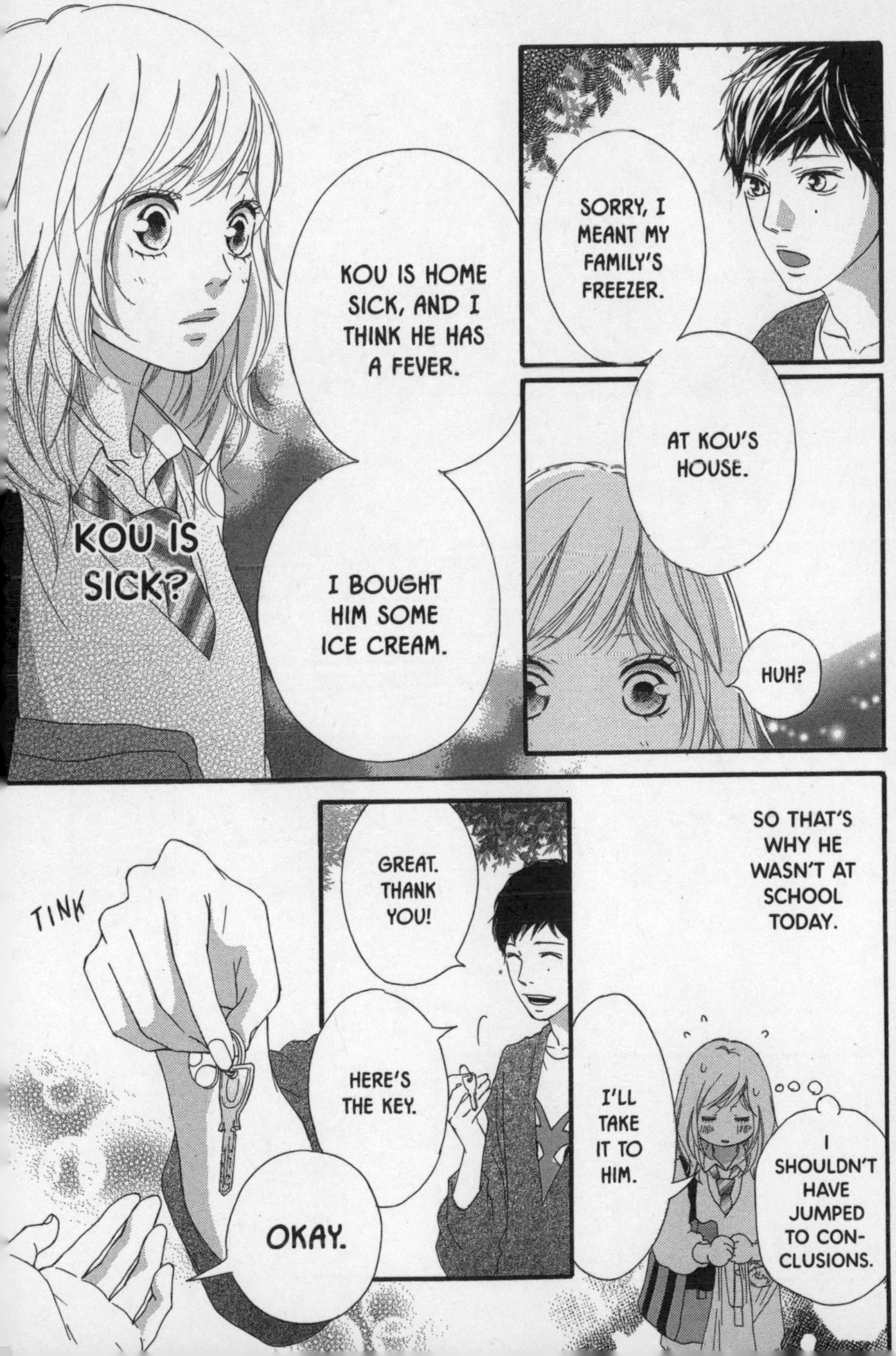
SORRY, I MEANT MY FAMILY'S FREEZER.
AT KOU'S HOUSE.
HUH?
KOU IS HOME SICK, AND I THINK HE HAS A FEVER.
I BOUGHT HIM SOME ICE CREAM.
KOU IS SICK?
SO THAT'S WHY HE WASN'T AT SCHOOL TODAY.
I SHOULDN'T HAVE JUMPED TO CON-CLUSIONS.
I'LL TAKE IT TO HIM.
GREAT. THANK YOU!
HERE'S THE KEY.
TINK
OKAY.

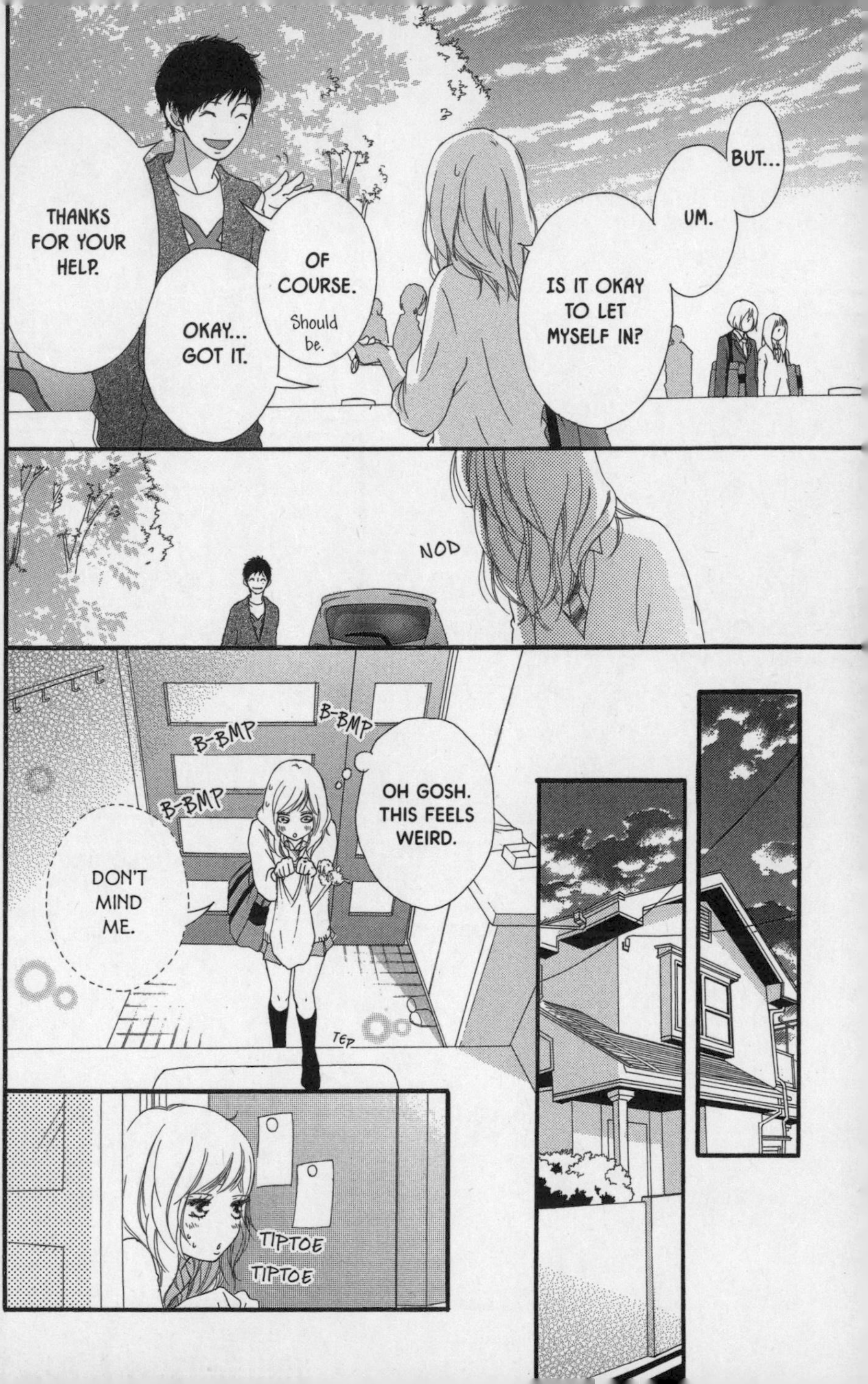
BUT...
UM.
IS IT OKAY TO LET MYSELF IN?
OF COURSE.
Should be.
THANKS FOR YOUR HELP.
OKAY... GOT IT.
NOD
B-BMP
OH GOSH. THIS FEELS WEIRD.
B-BMP
B-BMP
DON'T MIND ME.
TEP
TIPTOE
TIPTOE

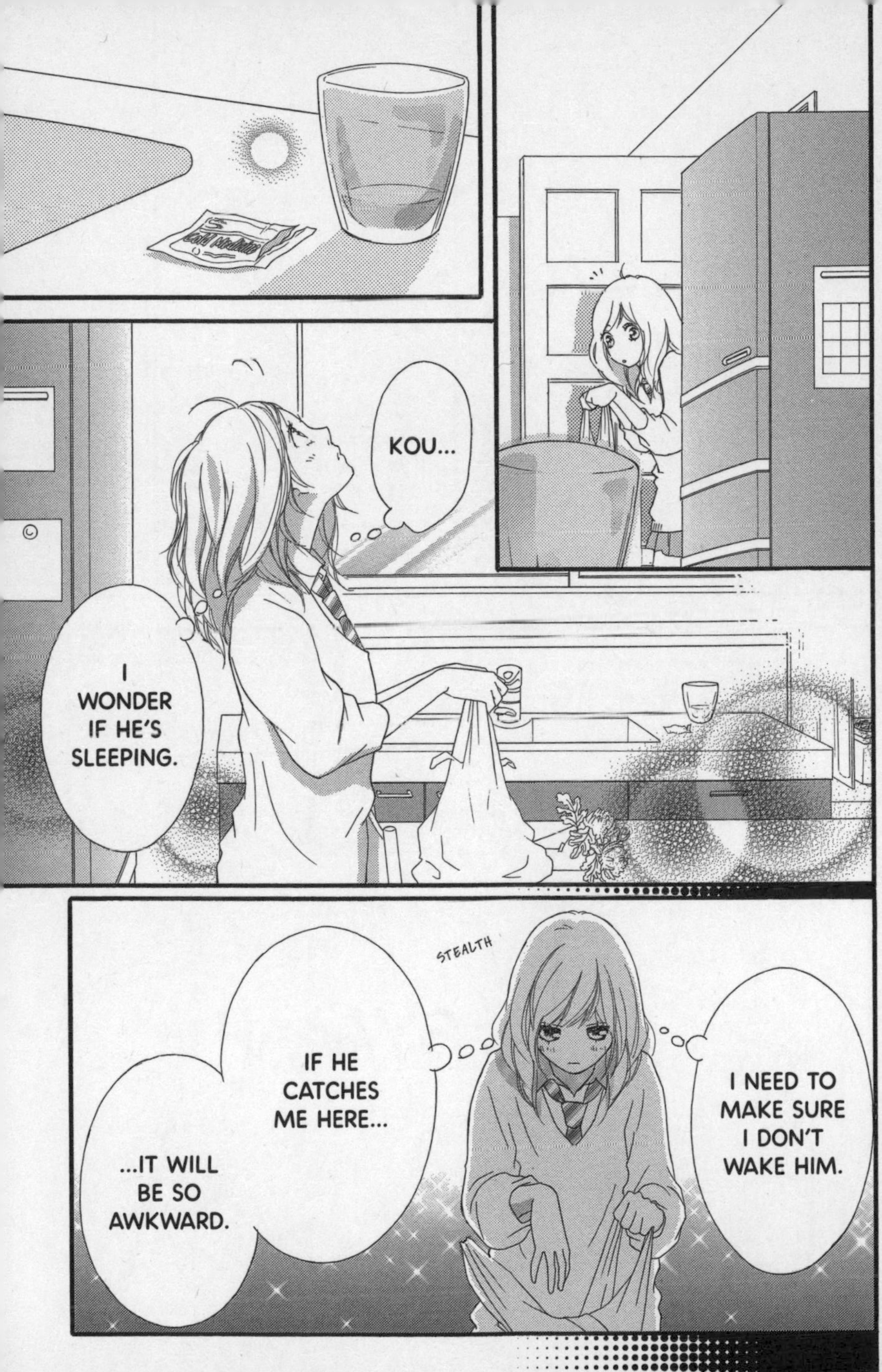
KOU...
I WONDER IF HE'S SLEEPING.
I NEED TO MAKE SURE I DON'T WAKE HIM.
STEALTH
IF HE CATCHES ME HERE...
...IT WILL BE SO AWKWARD.

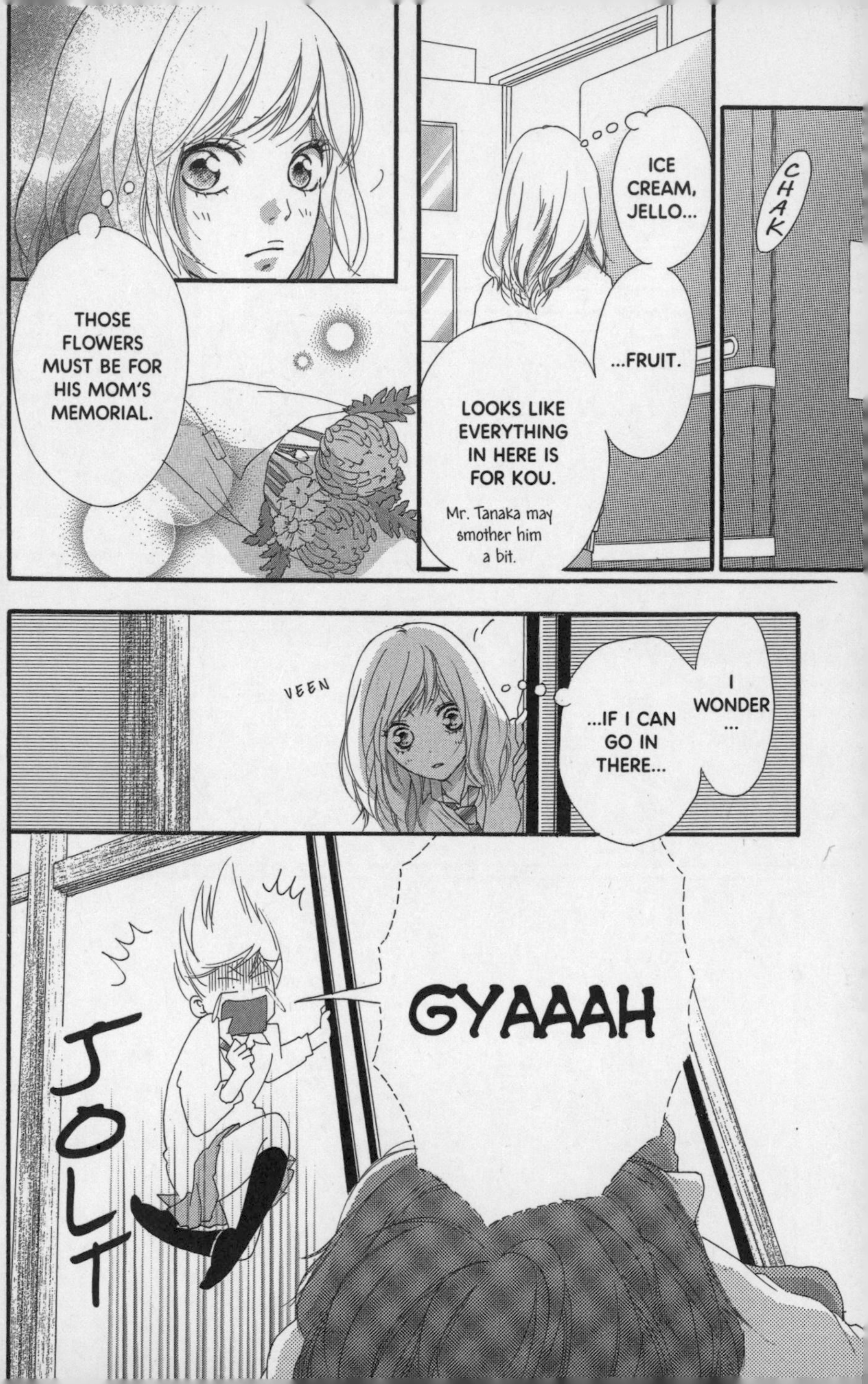
CHAK
ICE CREAM, JELLO...
...FRUIT.
LOOKS LIKE EVERYTHING IN HERE IS FOR KOU.
Mr. Tanaka may smother him a bit.
THOSE FLOWERS MUST BE FOR HIS MOM'S MEMORIAL.
I WONDER ...
...IF I CAN GO IN THERE...
VEEN
GYAAAH
JOLT

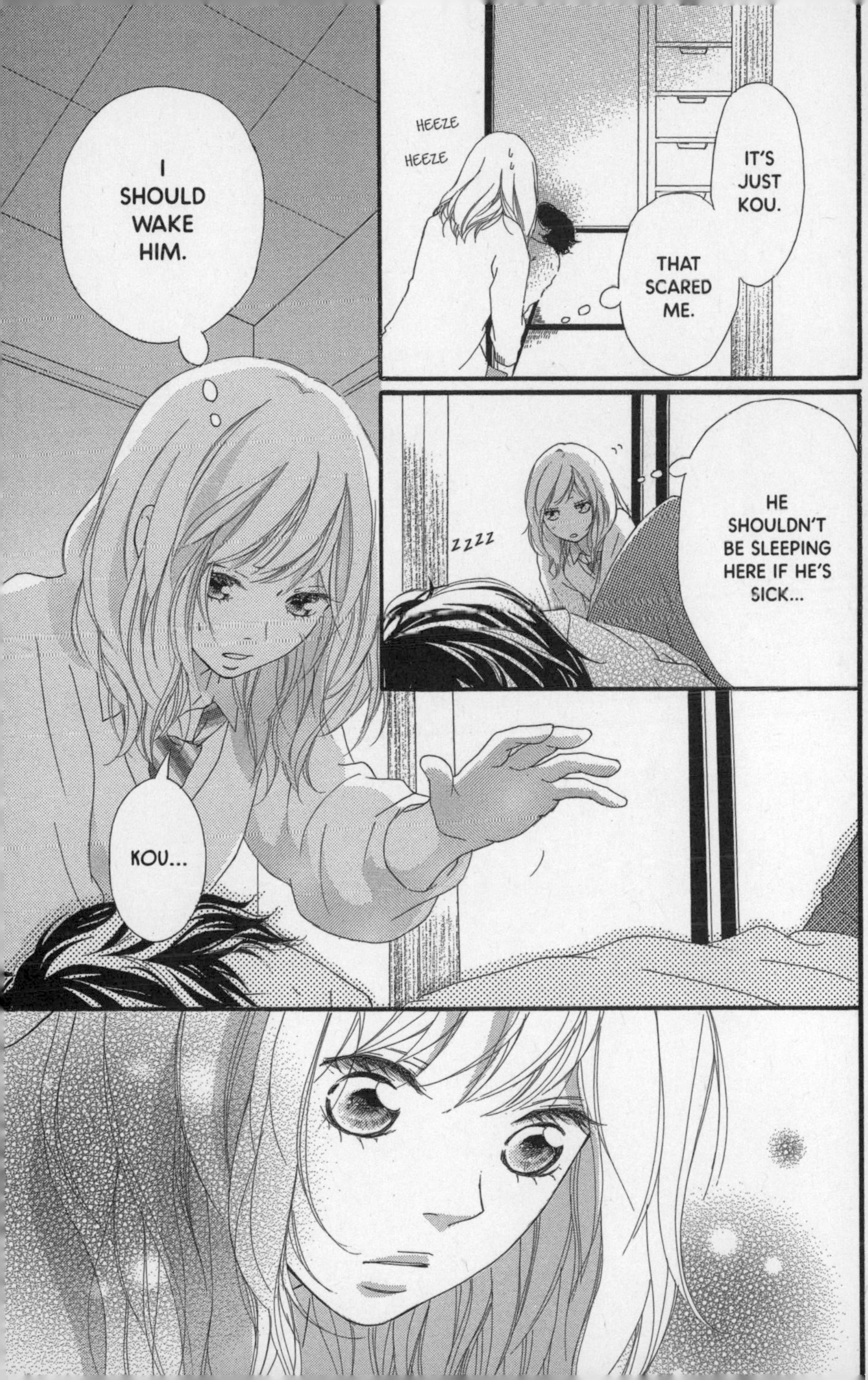
IT'S JUST KOU.
THAT SCARED ME.
HEEZE
HEEZE
HE SHOULDN'T BE SLEEPING HERE IF HE'S SICK...
ZZZZ
I SHOULD WAKE HIM.
KOU...

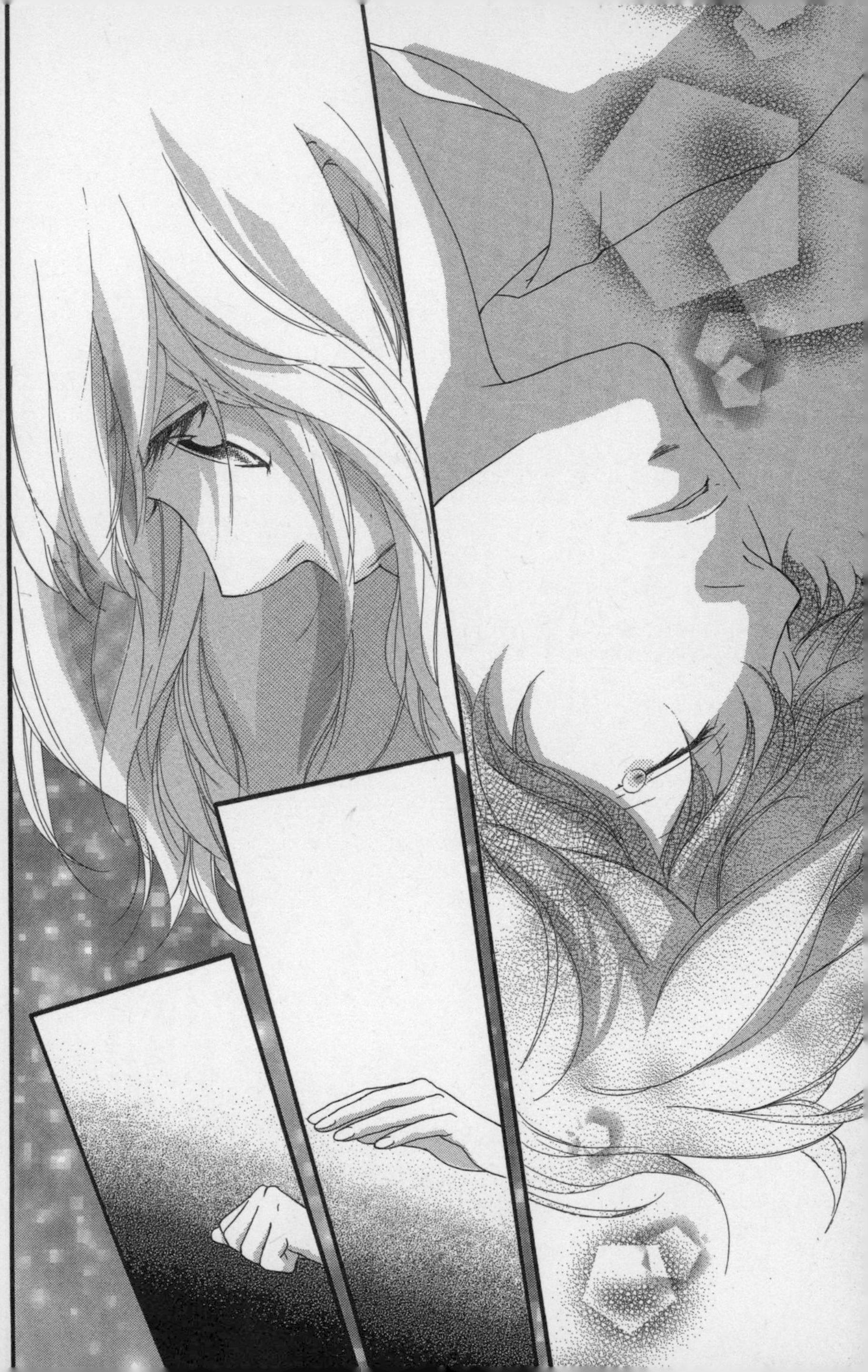

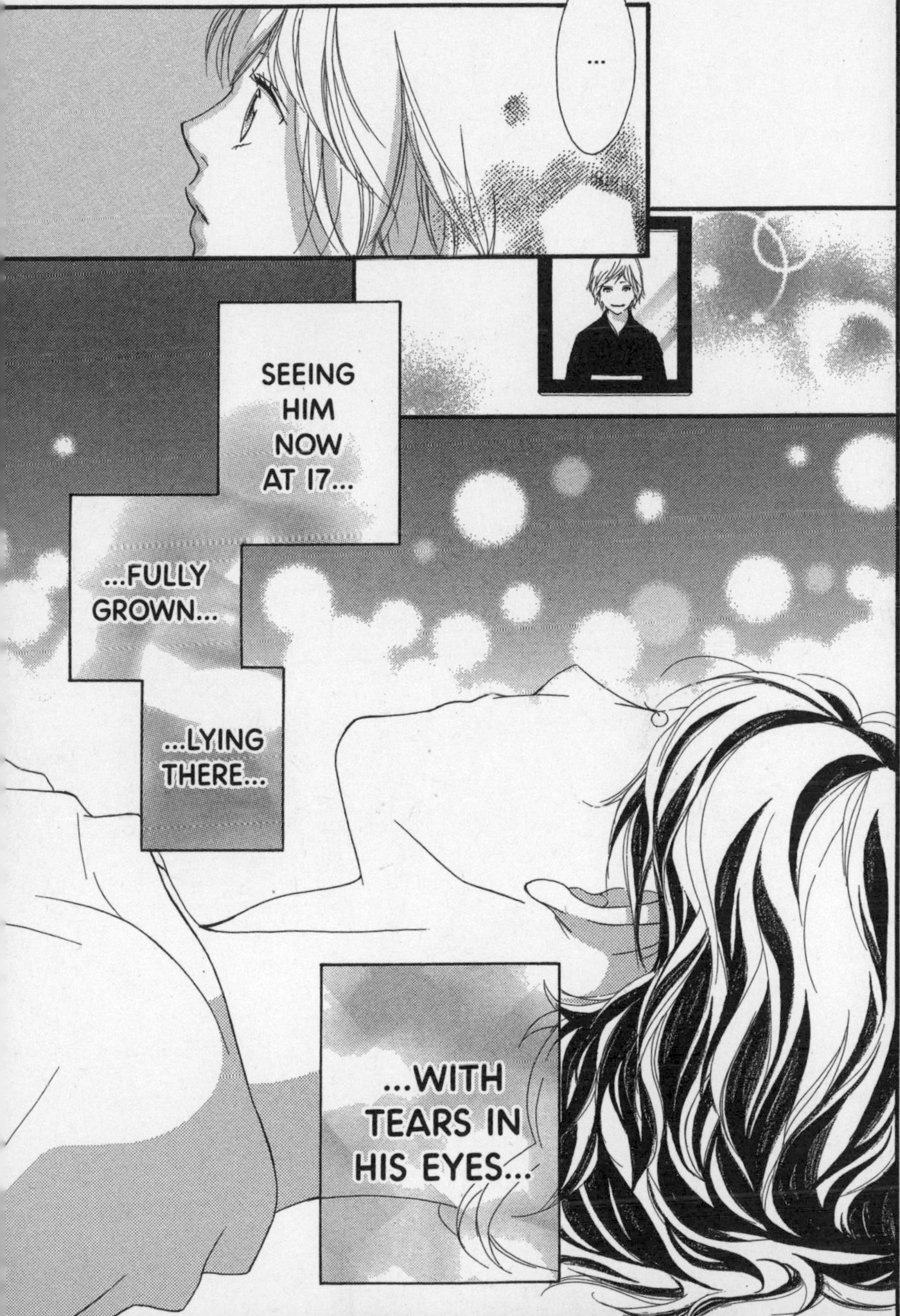
...
SEEING HIM NOW AT 17...
...FULLY GROWN...
...LYING THERE...
...WITH TEARS IN HIS EYES...

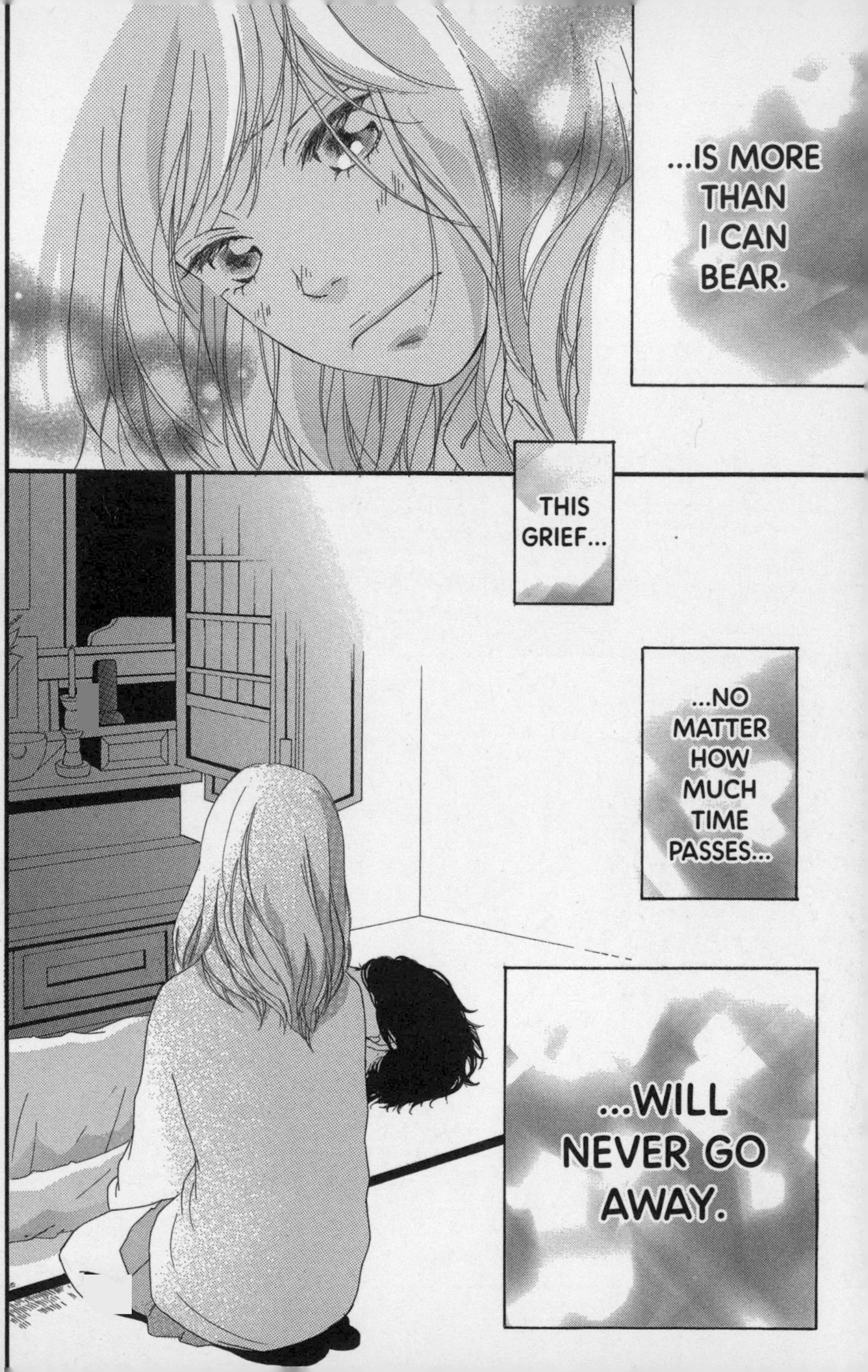
...IS MORE THAN I CAN BEAR.
THIS GRIEF...
...NO MATTER HOW MUCH TIME PASSES...
...WILL NEVER GO AWAY.

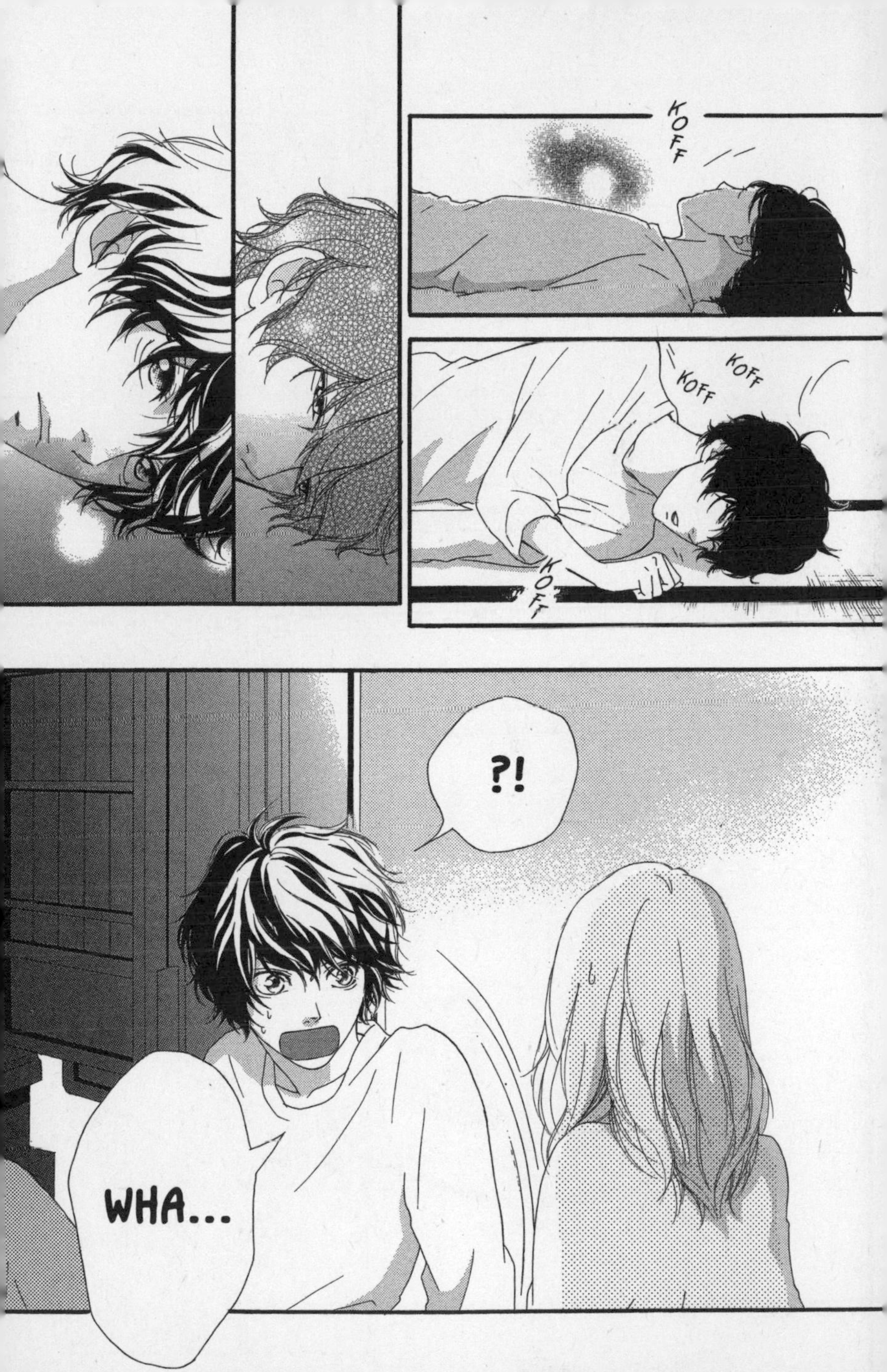
KOFF
KOFF
KOFF
KOFF
?!
WHA...

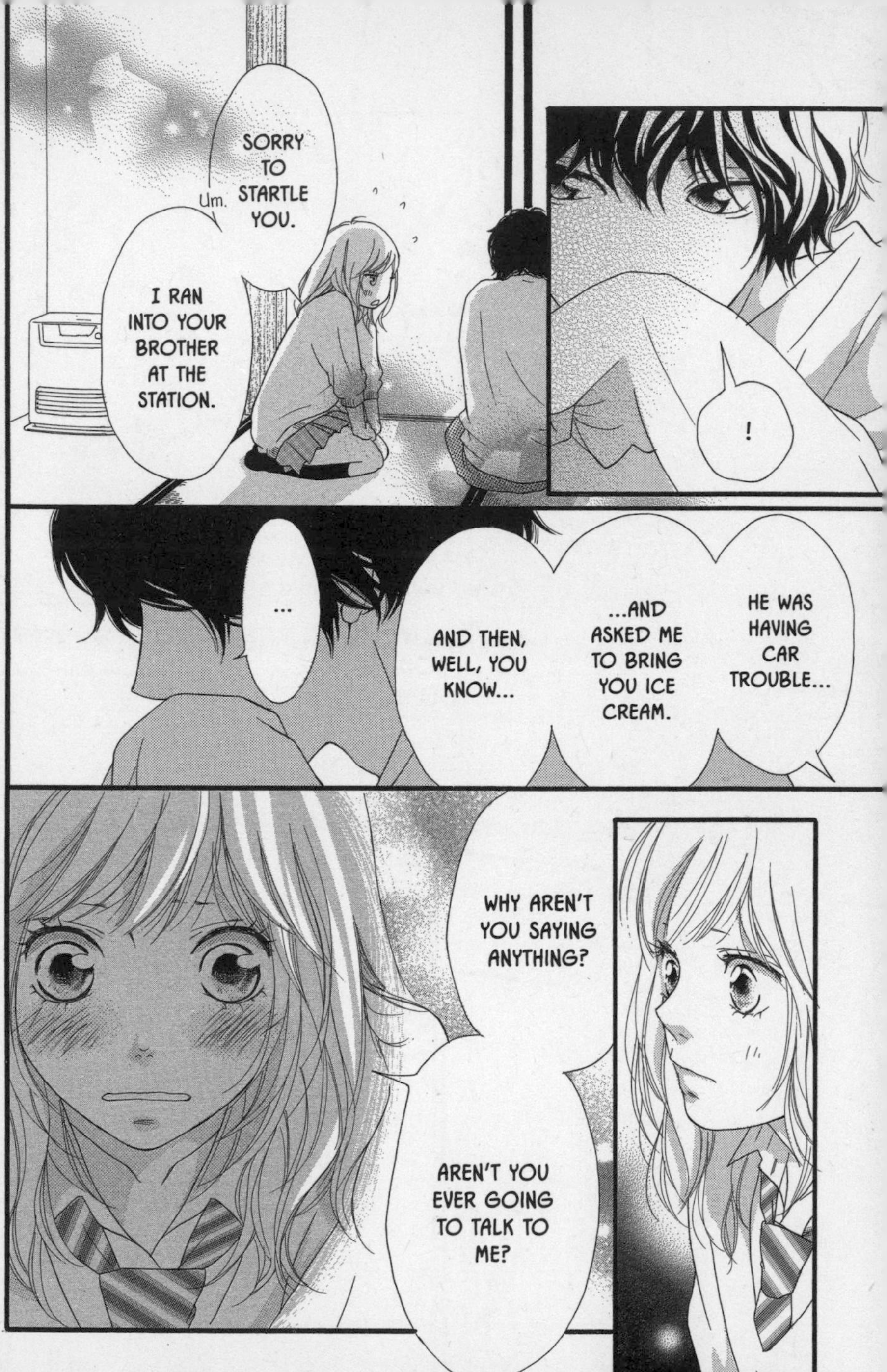
!
SORRY TO STARTLE YOU.
Um.
I RAN INTO YOUR BROTHER AT THE STATION.
HE WAS HAVING CAR TROUBLE...
...AND ASKED ME TO BRING YOU ICE CREAM.
AND THEN, WELL, YOU KNOW...
...
WHY AREN'T YOU SAYING ANYTHING?
AREN'T YOU EVER GOING TO TALK TO ME?

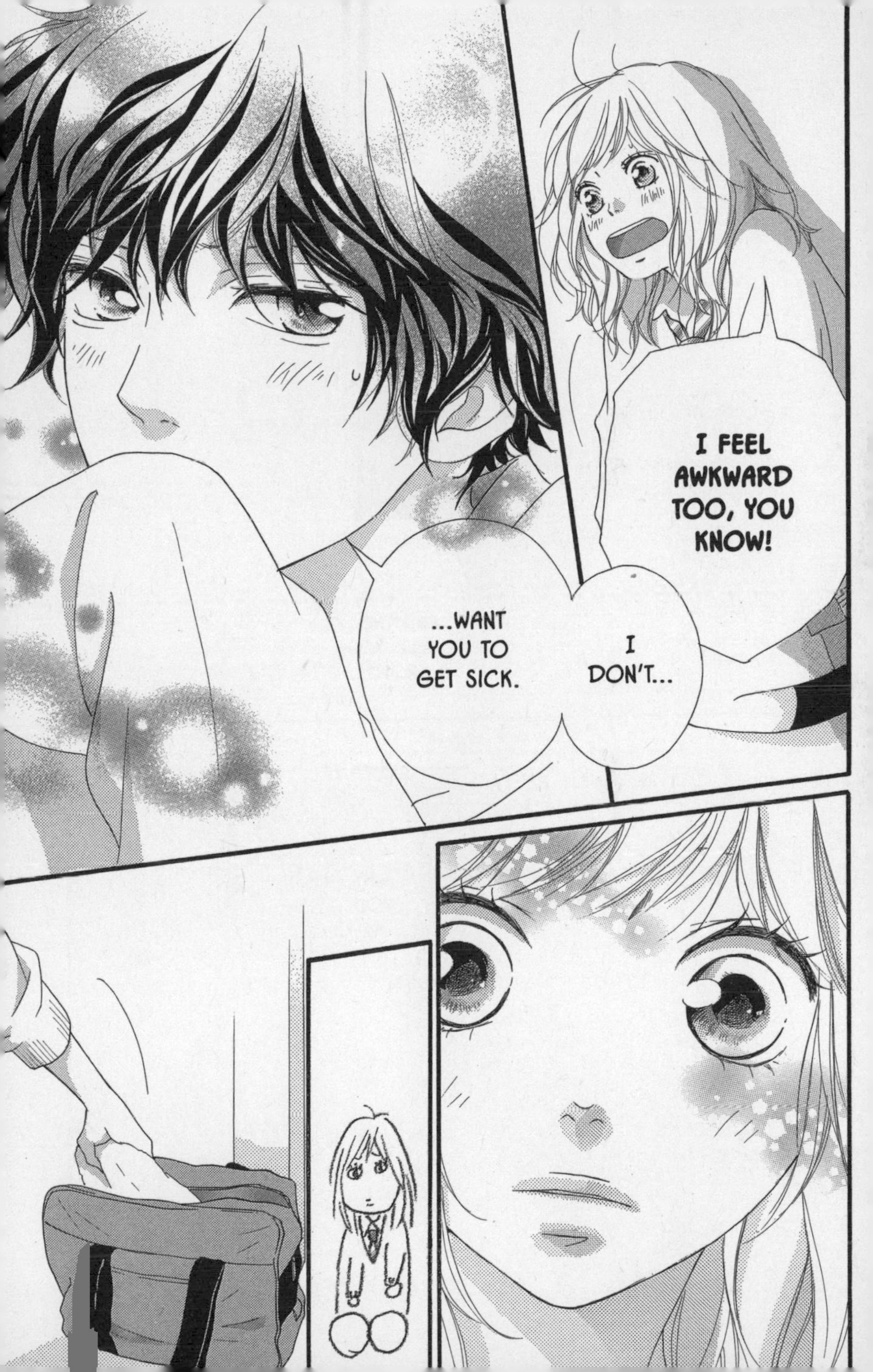
I FEEL AWKWARD TOO, YOU KNOW!
I DON'T...
...WANT YOU TO GET SICK.

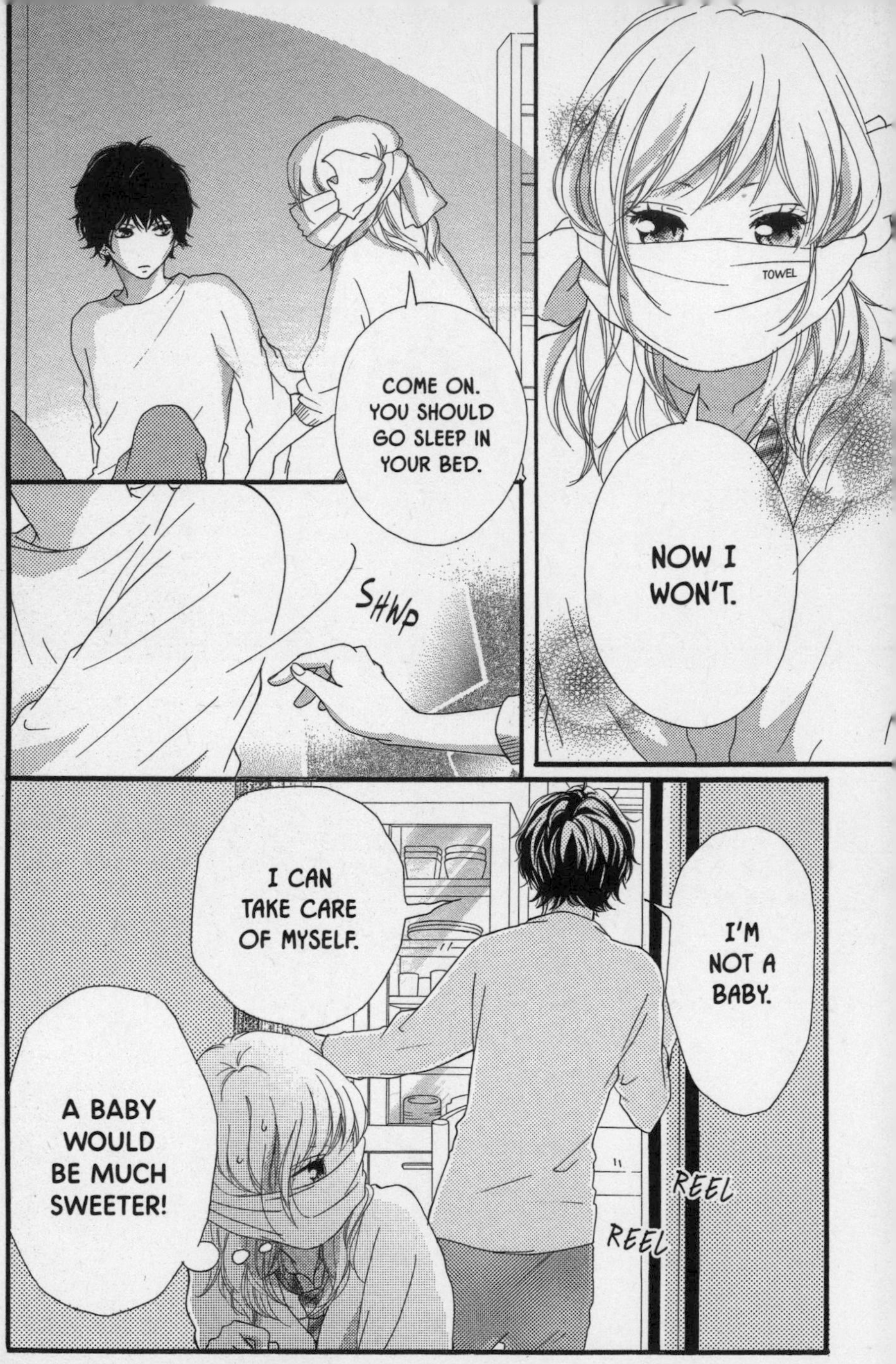
TOWEL
NOW I WON'T.
COME ON. YOU SHOULD GO SLEEP IN YOUR BED.
SHWP
I'M NOT A BABY.
I CAN TAKE CARE OF MYSELF.
REEL
REEL
A BABY WOULD BE MUCH SWEETER!

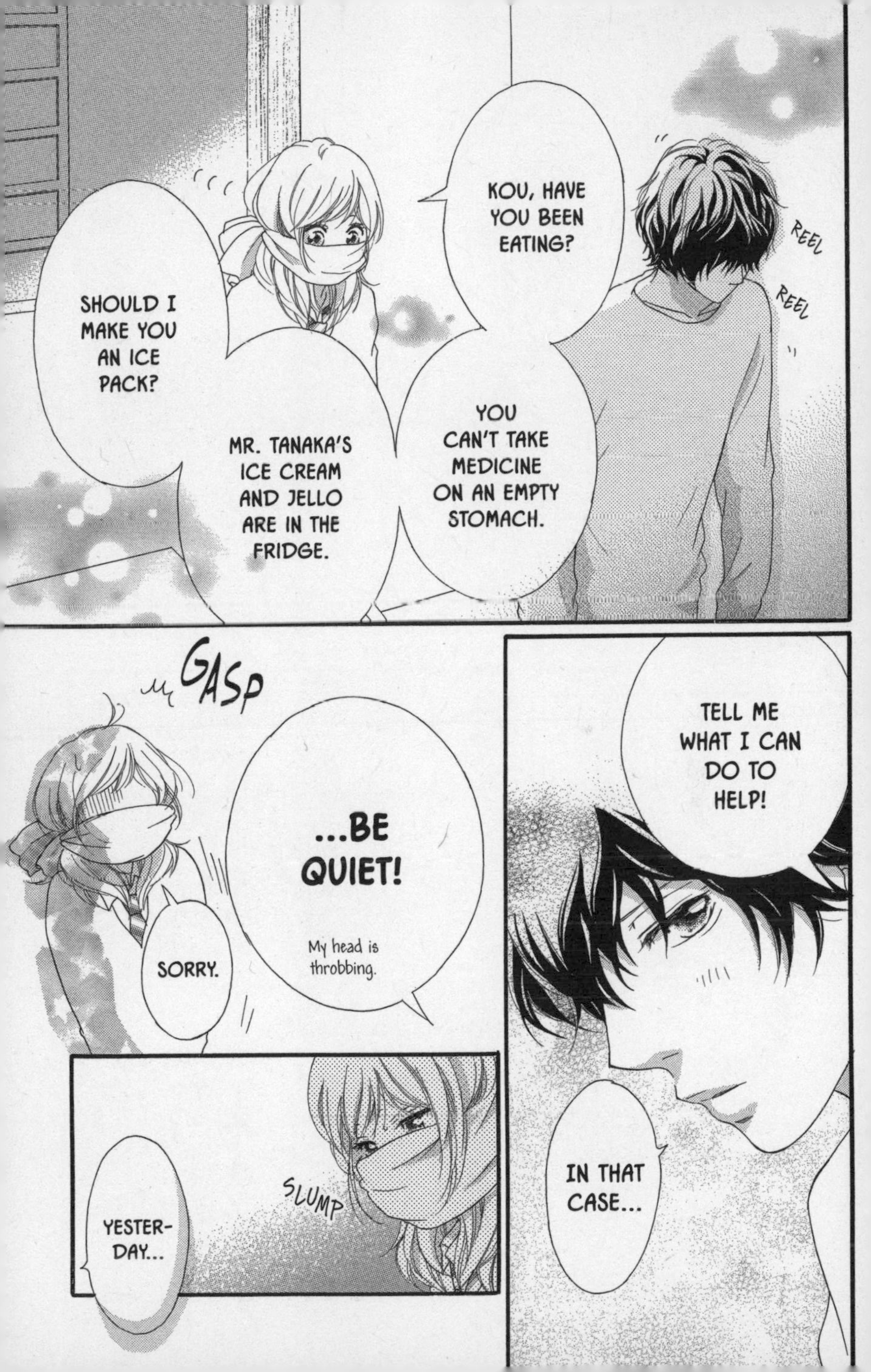
REEL
REEL
KOU, HAVE YOU BEEN EATING?
YOU CAN'T TAKE MEDICINE ON AN EMPTY STOMACH.
MR. TANAKA'S ICE CREAM AND JELLO ARE IN THE FRIDGE.
SHOULD I MAKE YOU AN ICE PACK?
TELL ME WHAT I CAN DO TO HELP!
IN THAT CASE...
GASP
...BE QUIET!
My head is throbbing.
SORRY.
SLUMP
YESTER-DAY...

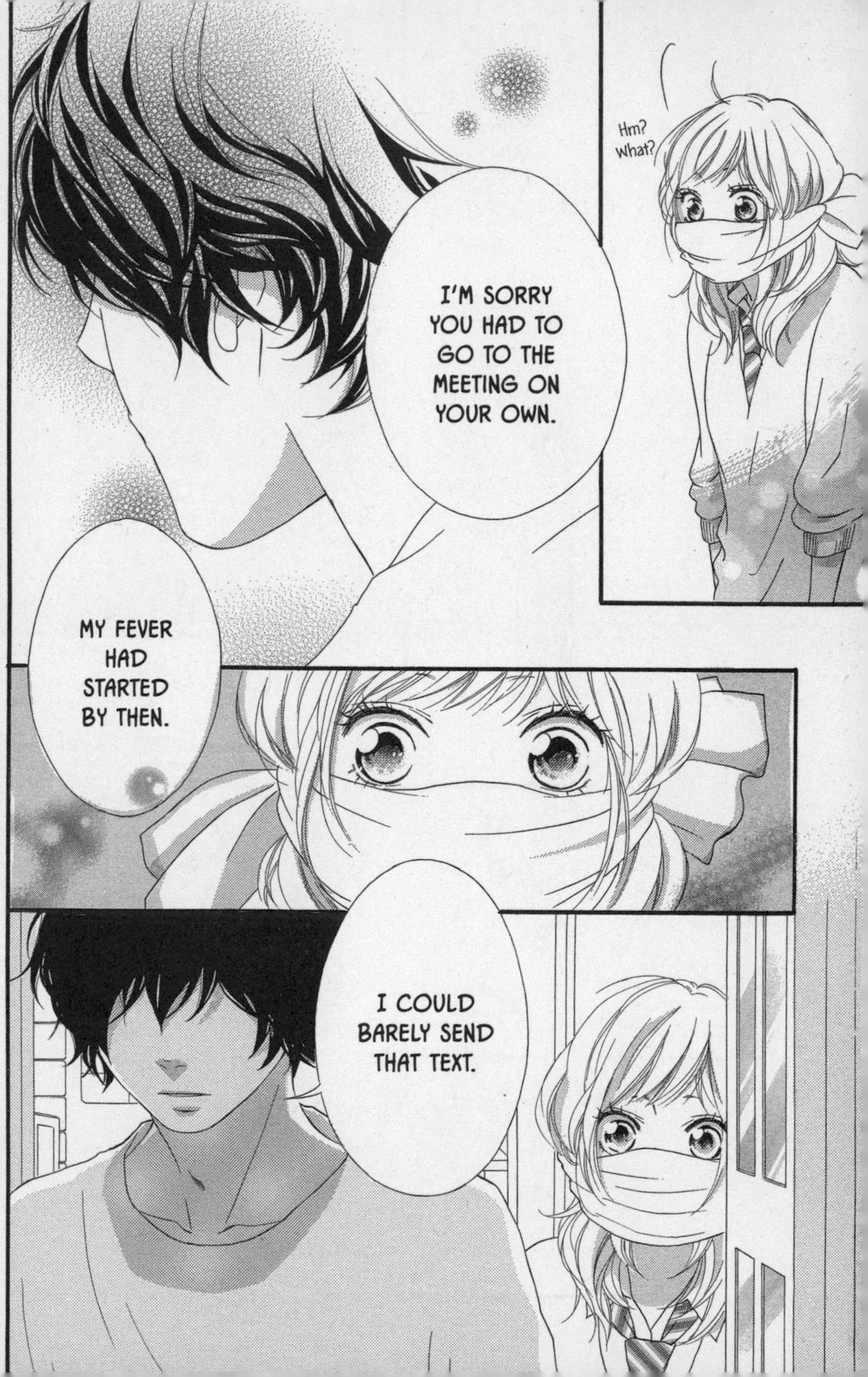
Hm? What?
I'M SORRY YOU HAD TO GO TO THE MEETING ON YOUR OWN.
MY FEVER HAD STARTED BY THEN.
I COULD BARELY SEND THAT TEXT.

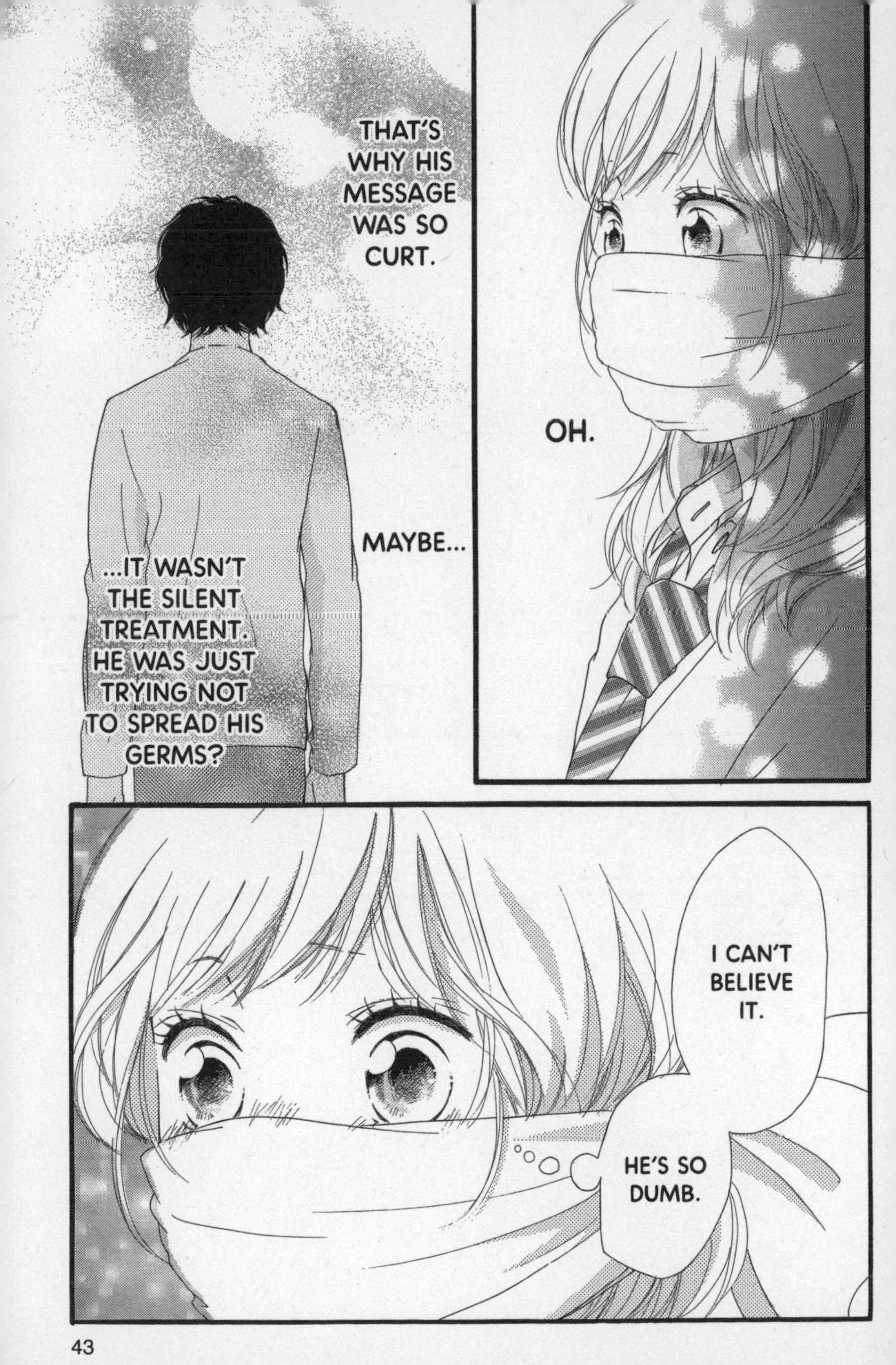
OH.
THAT'S WHY HIS MESSAGE WAS SO CURT.
MAYBE...
...IT WASN'T THE SILENT TREATMENT. HE WAS JUST TRYING NOT TO SPREAD HIS GERMS?
I CAN'T BELIEVE IT.
HE'S SO DUMB.

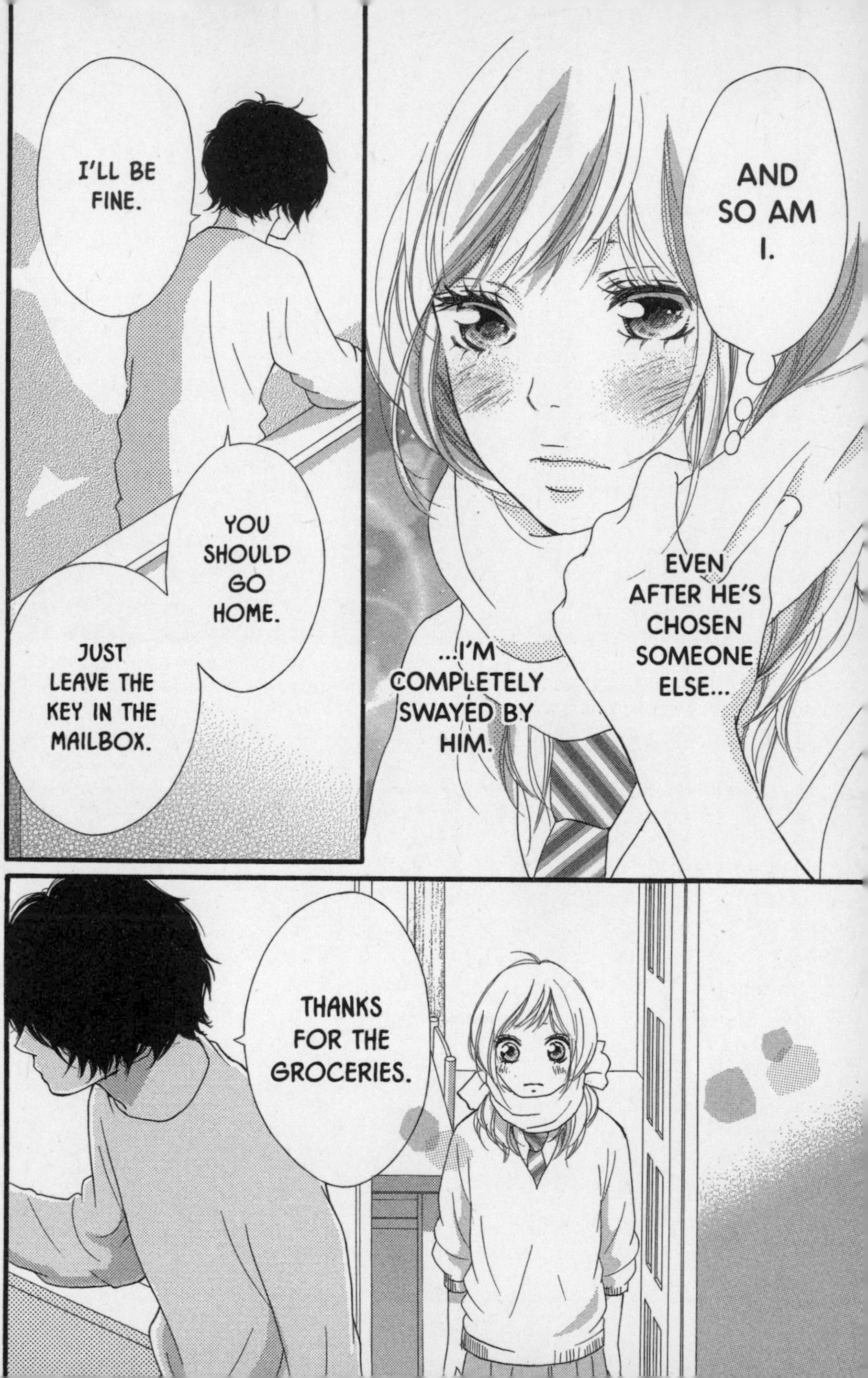
AND SO AM I.
EVEN AFTER HE'S CHOSEN SOMEONE ELSE...
...I'M COMPLETELY SWAYED BY HIM.
I'LL BE FINE.
YOU SHOULD GO HOME.
JUST LEAVE THE KEY IN THE MAILBOX.
THANKS FOR THE GROCERIES.

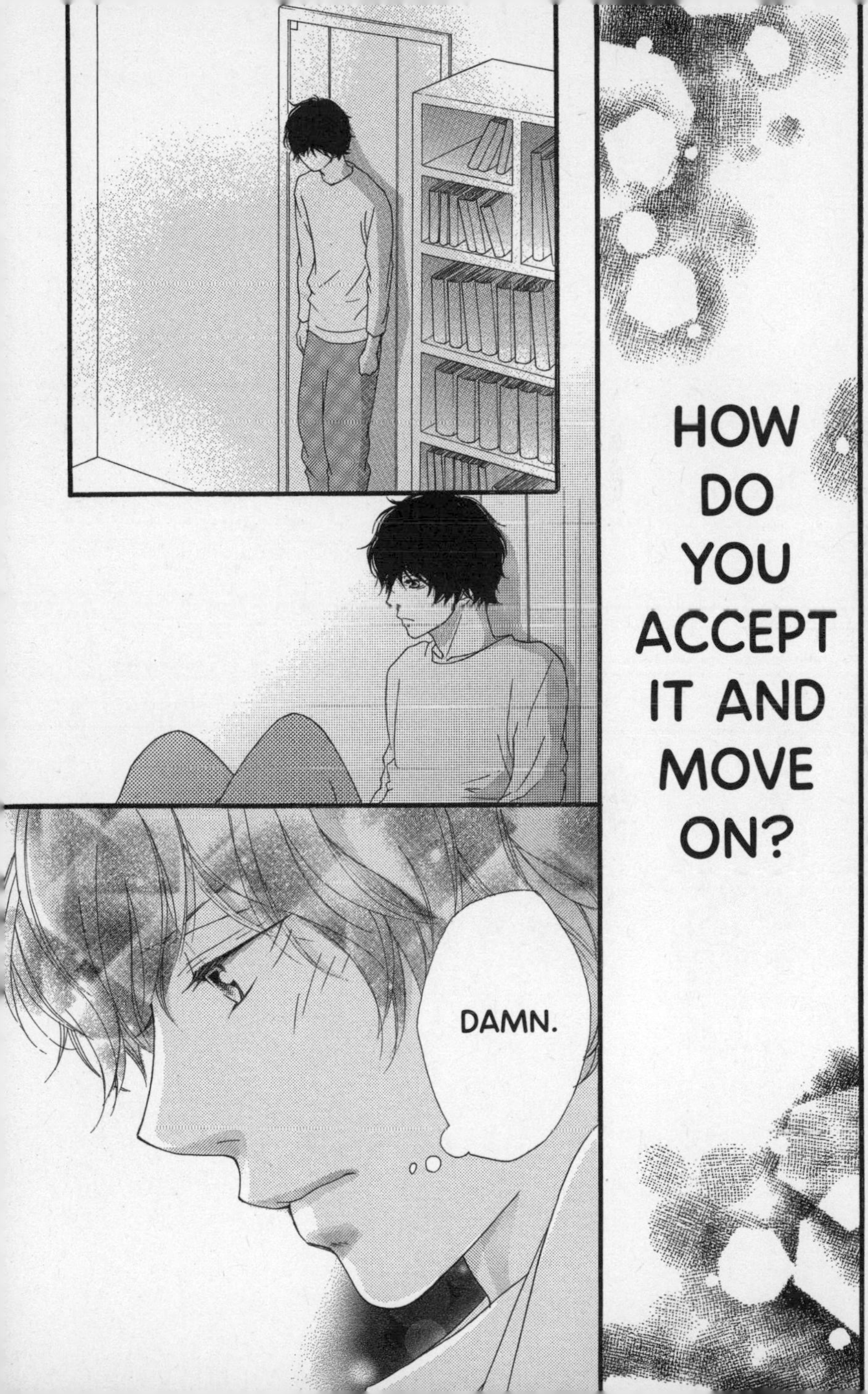
HOW DO YOU ACCEPT IT AND MOVE ON?
DAMN.

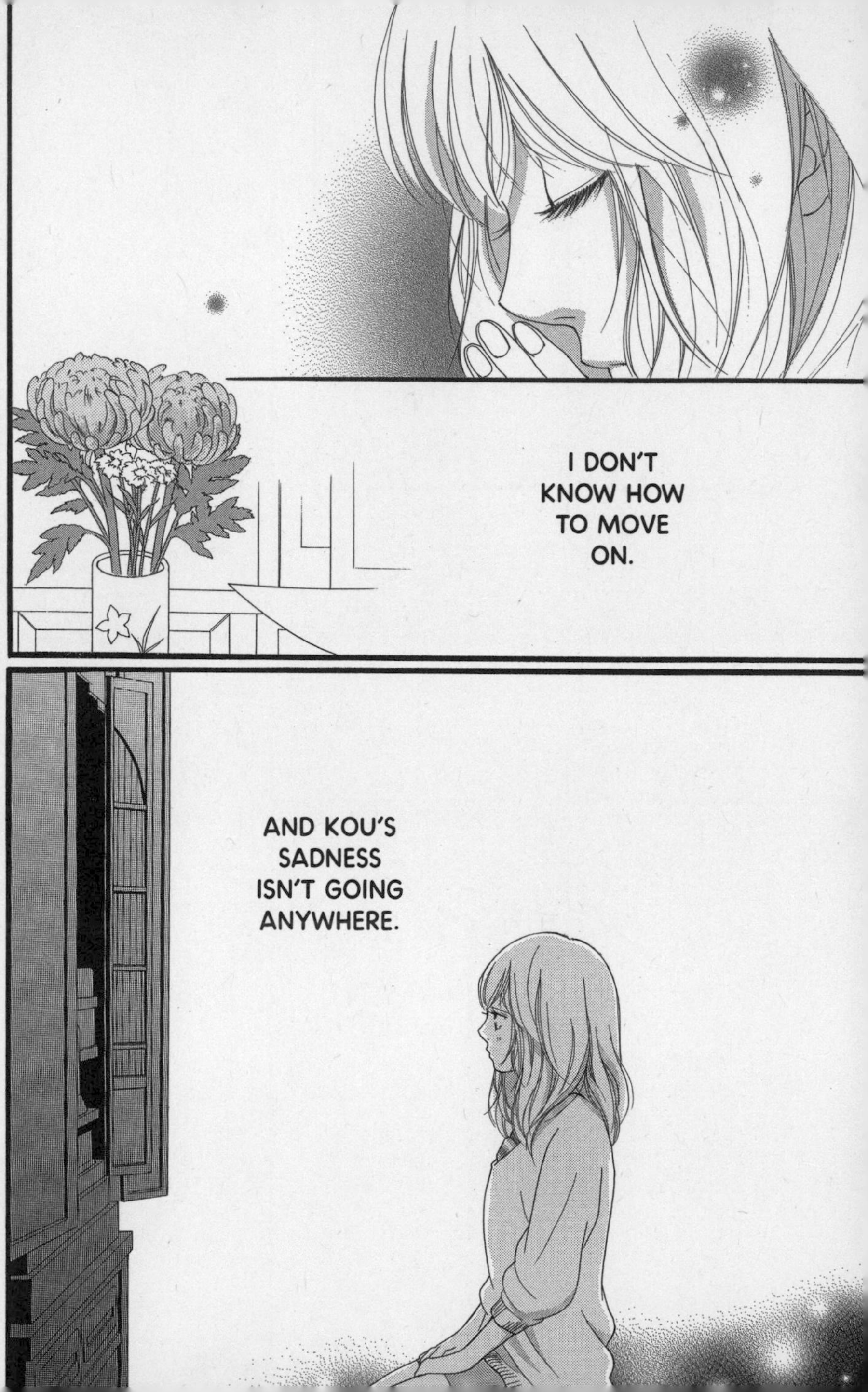
I DON'T KNOW HOW TO MOVE ON.
AND KOU'S SADNESS ISN'T GOING ANYWHERE.

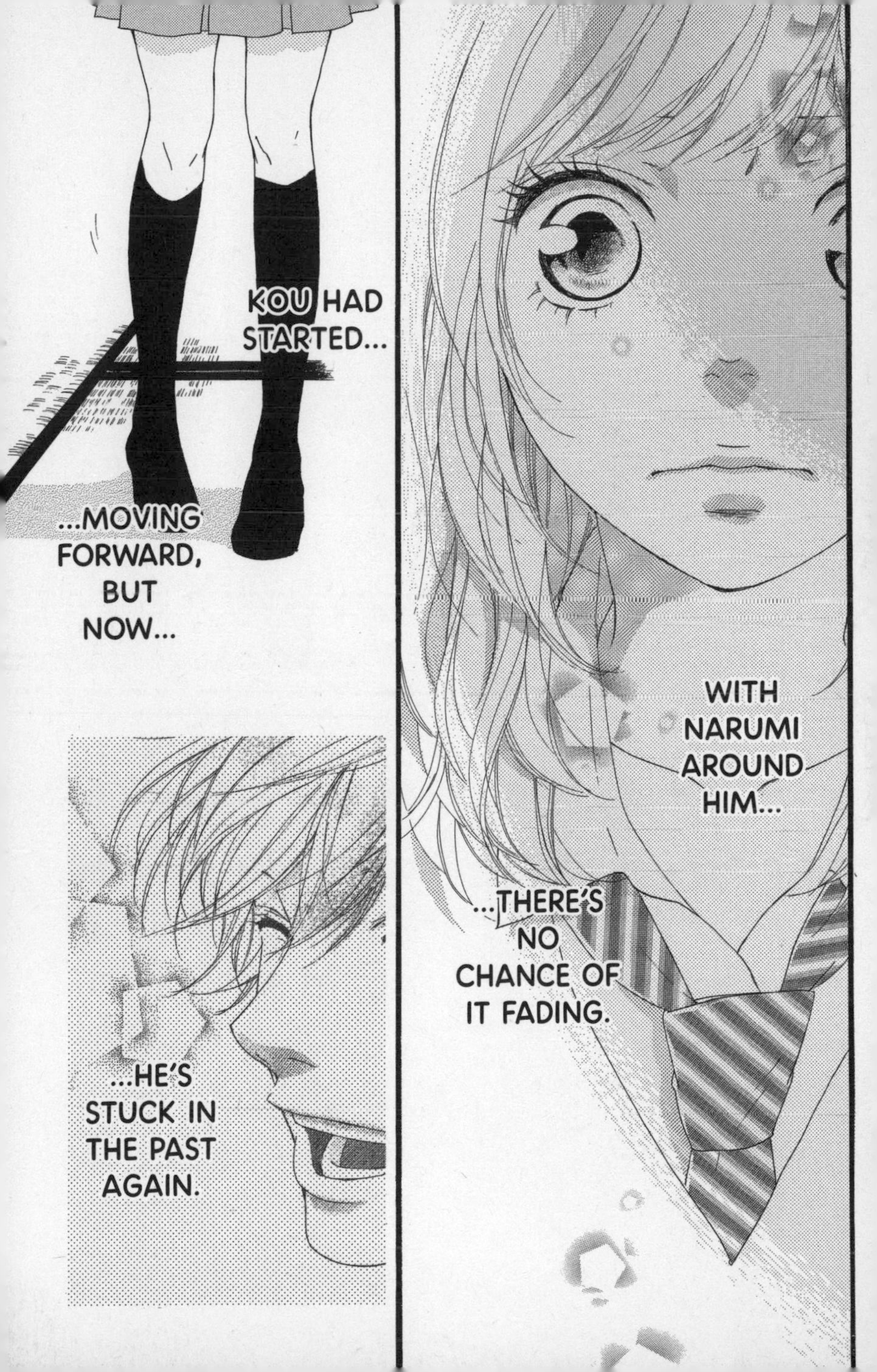
WITH NARUMI AROUND HIM...
...THERE'S NO CHANCE OF IT FADING.
KOU HAD STARTED...
...MOVING FORWARD, BUT NOW...
...HE'S STUCK IN THE PAST AGAIN.

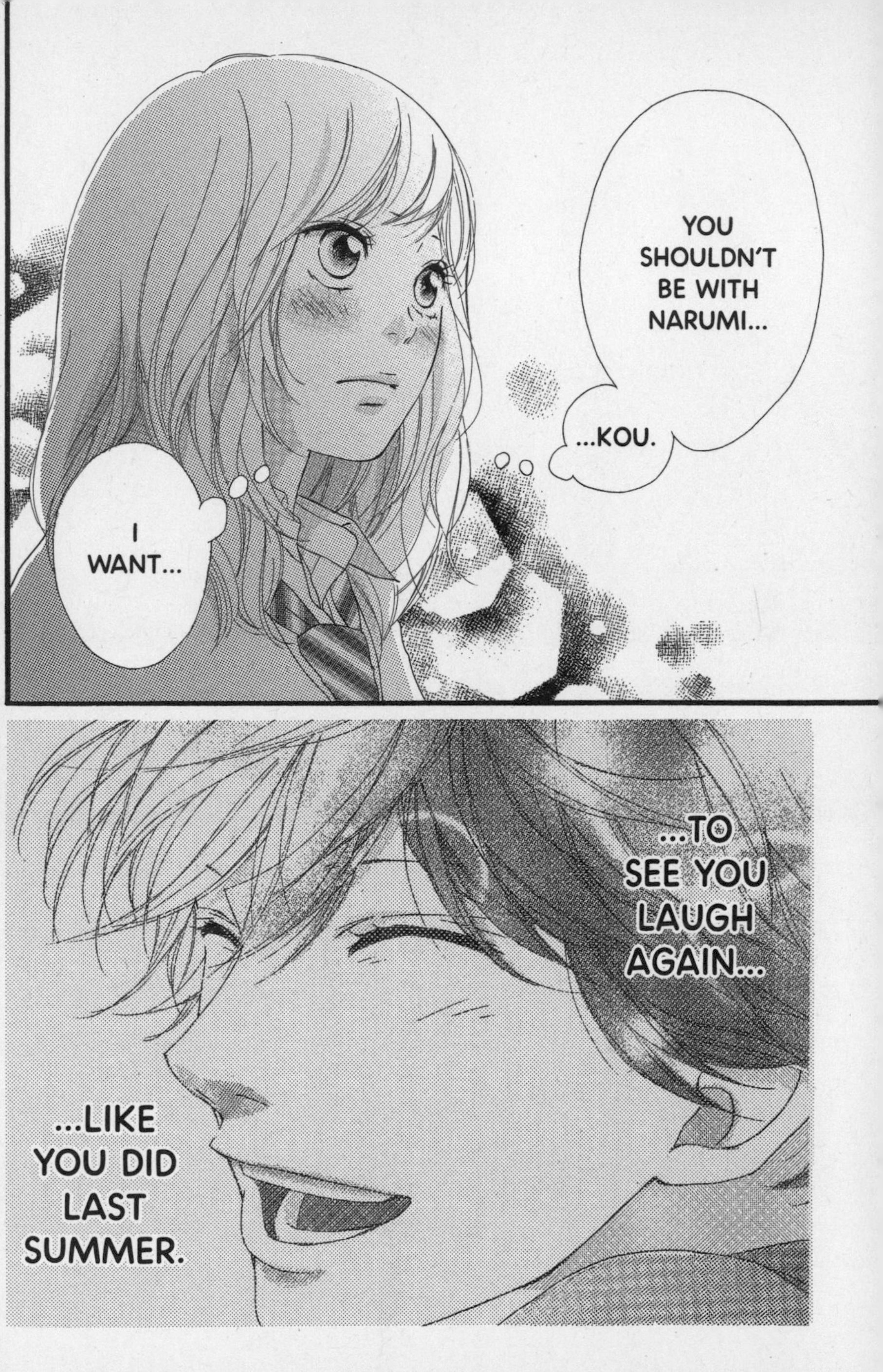
YOU SHOULDN'T BE WITH NARUMI...
...KOU.
I WANT...
...TO SEE YOU LAUGH AGAIN...
...LIKE YOU DID LAST SUMMER.

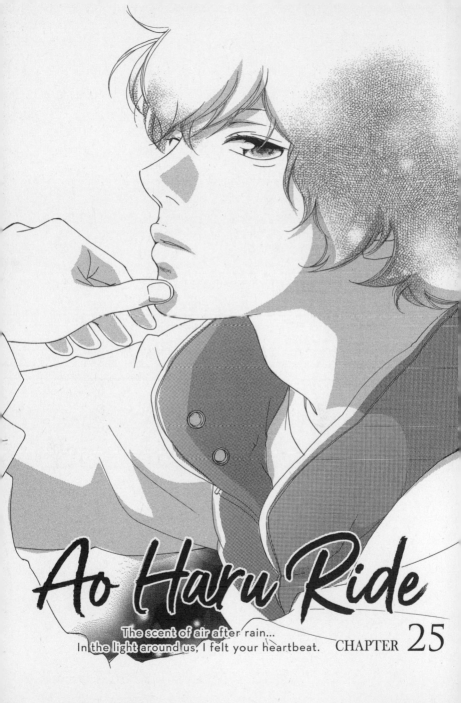

Ao Haru Ride

The scent of air after rain...
In the light around us, I felt your heartbeat. CHAPTER 25

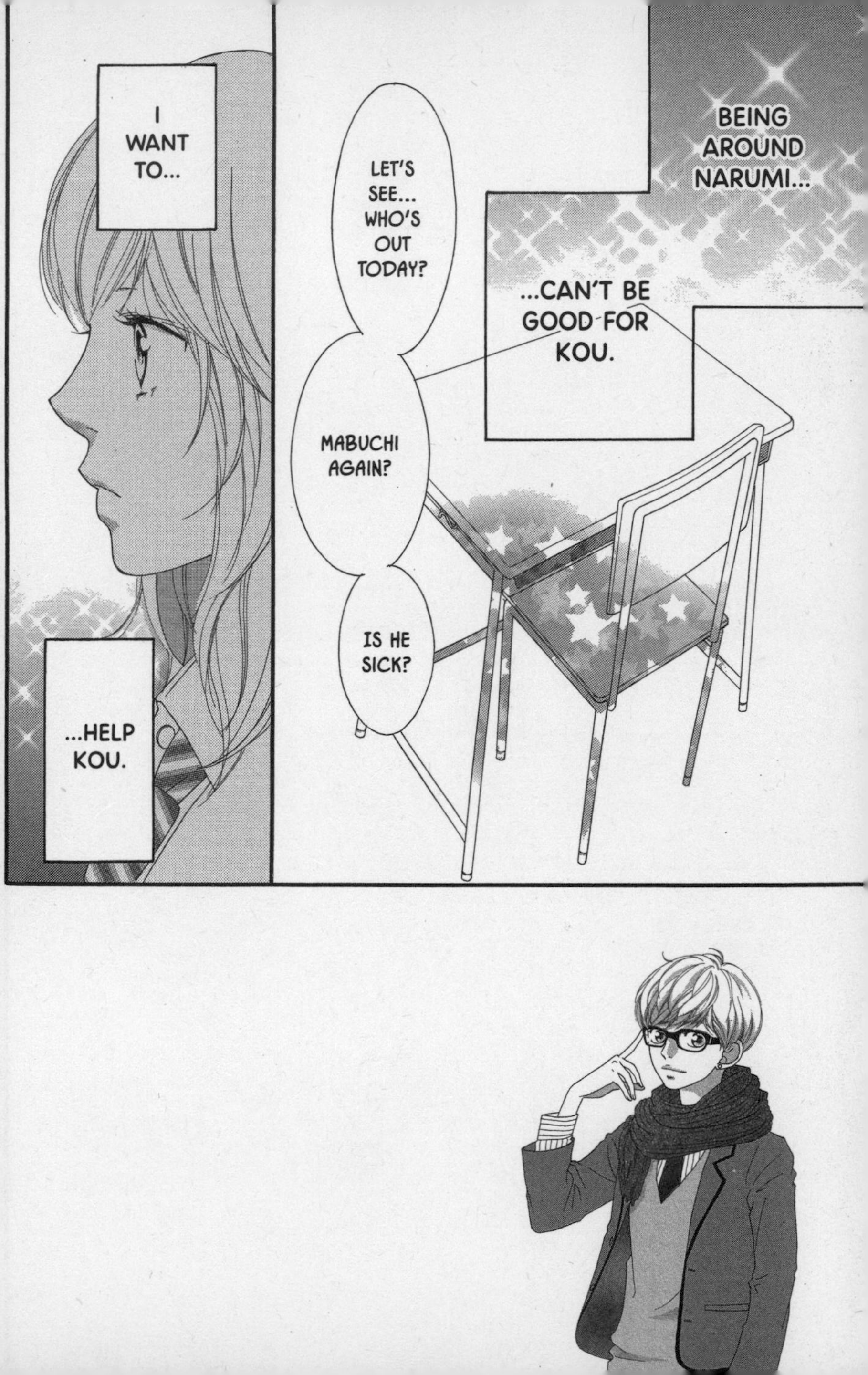
BEING AROUND NARUMI...
...CAN'T BE GOOD FOR KOU.
LET'S SEE... WHO'S OUT TODAY?
MABUCHI AGAIN?
IS HE SICK?
I WANT TO...
...HELP KOU.

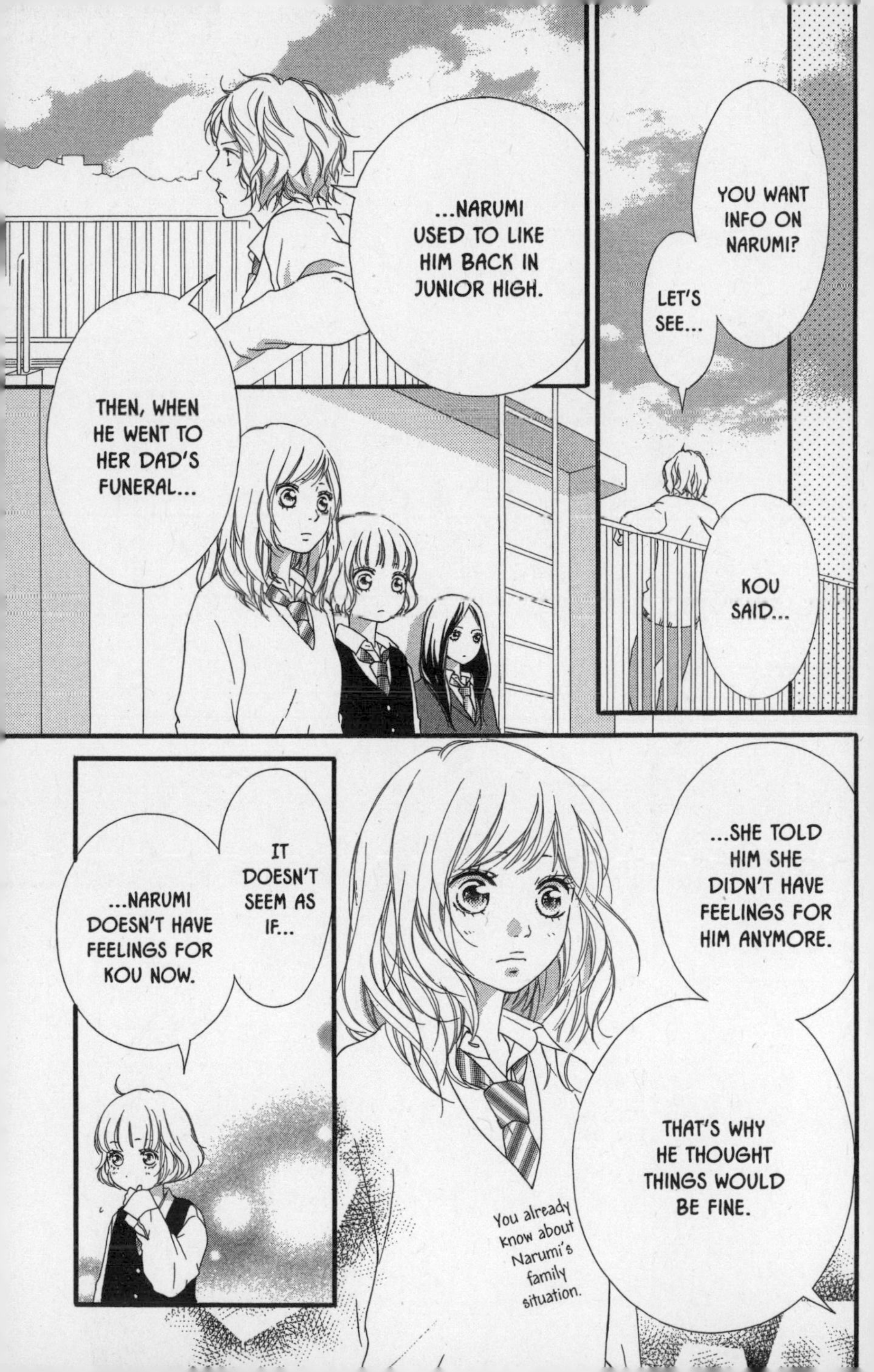
YOU WANT INFO ON NARUMI?
LET'S SEE...
KOU SAID...
...NARUMI USED TO LIKE HIM BACK IN JUNIOR HIGH.
THEN, WHEN HE WENT TO HER DAD'S FUNERAL...
...SHE TOLD HIM SHE DIDN'T HAVE FEELINGS FOR HIM ANYMORE.
THAT'S WHY HE THOUGHT THINGS WOULD BE FINE.
You already know about Narumi's family situation.
IT DOESN'T SEEM AS IF...
...NARUMI DOESN'T HAVE FEELINGS FOR KOU NOW.

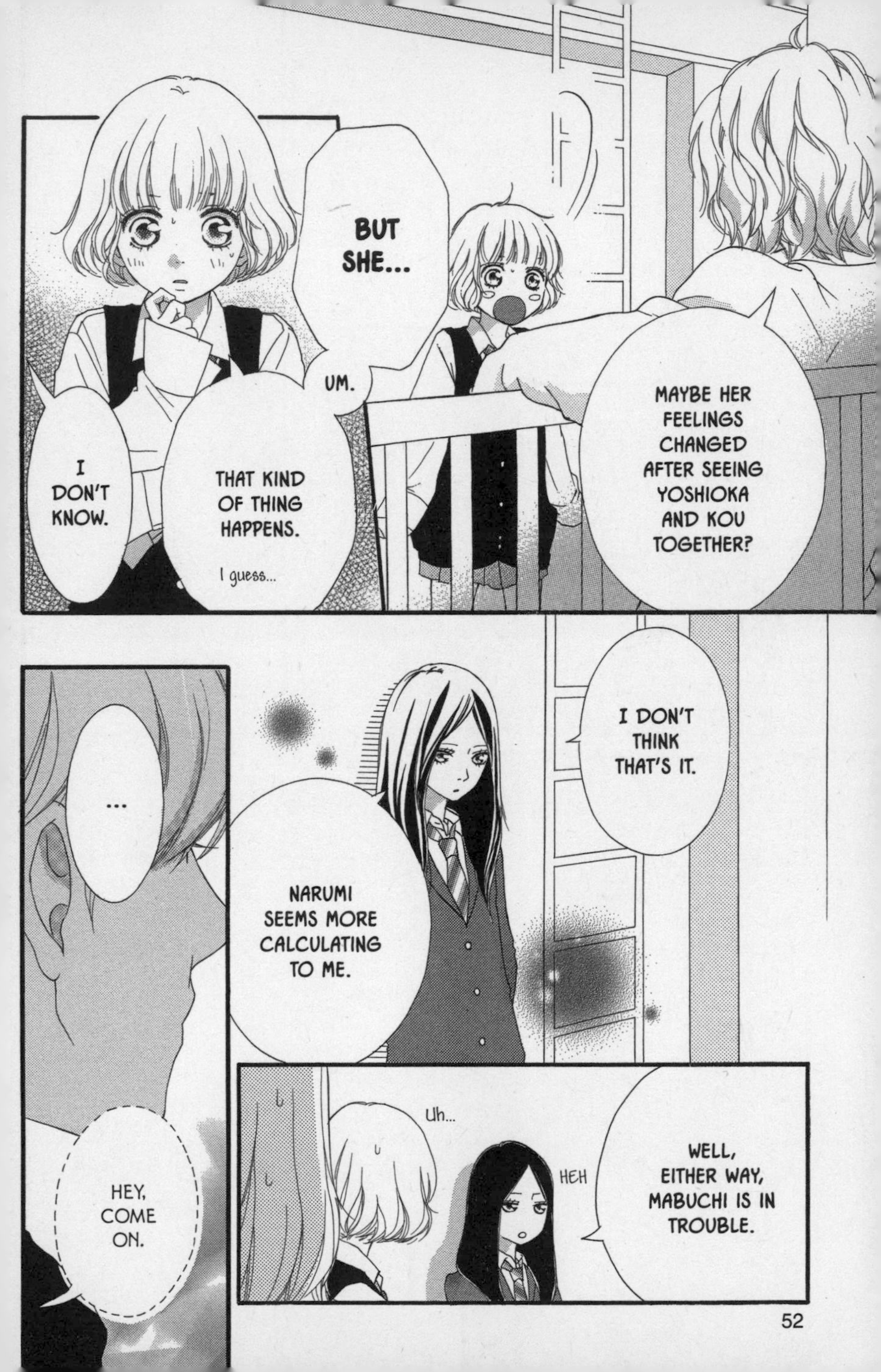
MAYBE HER FEELINGS CHANGED AFTER SEEING YOSHIOKA AND KOU TOGETHER?
BUT SHE...
UM.
THAT KIND OF THING HAPPENS.
I guess...
I DON'T KNOW.
I DON'T THINK THAT'S IT.
NARUMI SEEMS MORE CALCULATING TO ME.
WELL, EITHER WAY, MABUCHI IS IN TROUBLE.
HEH
Uh...
...
HEY, COME ON.

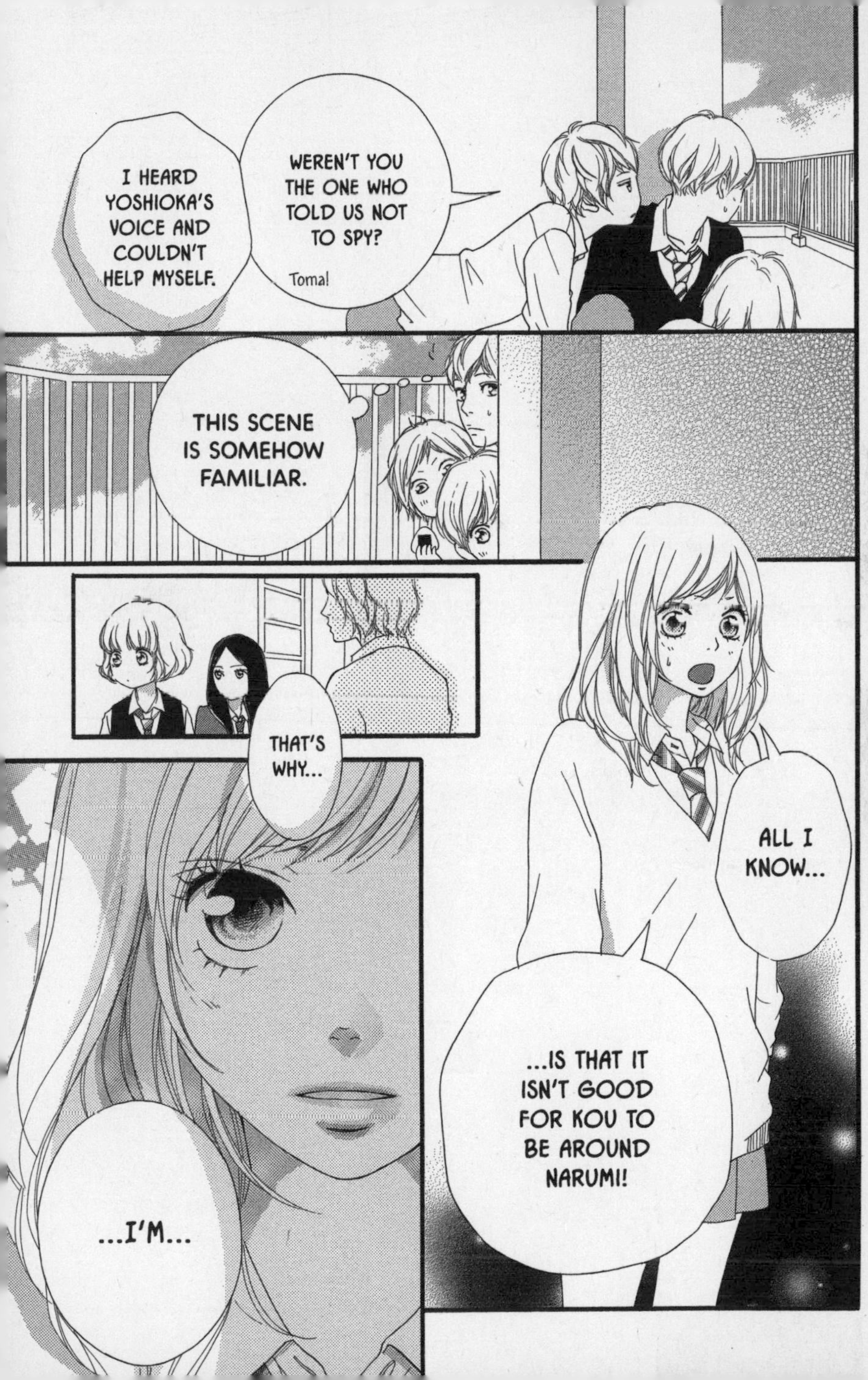
WEREN'T YOU THE ONE WHO TOLD US NOT TO SPY?
Toma!
I HEARD YOSHIOKA'S VOICE AND COULDN'T HELP MYSELF.
THIS SCENE IS SOMEHOW FAMILIAR.
ALL I KNOW...
...IS THAT IT ISN'T GOOD FOR KOU TO BE AROUND NARUMI!
THAT'S WHY...
...I'M...

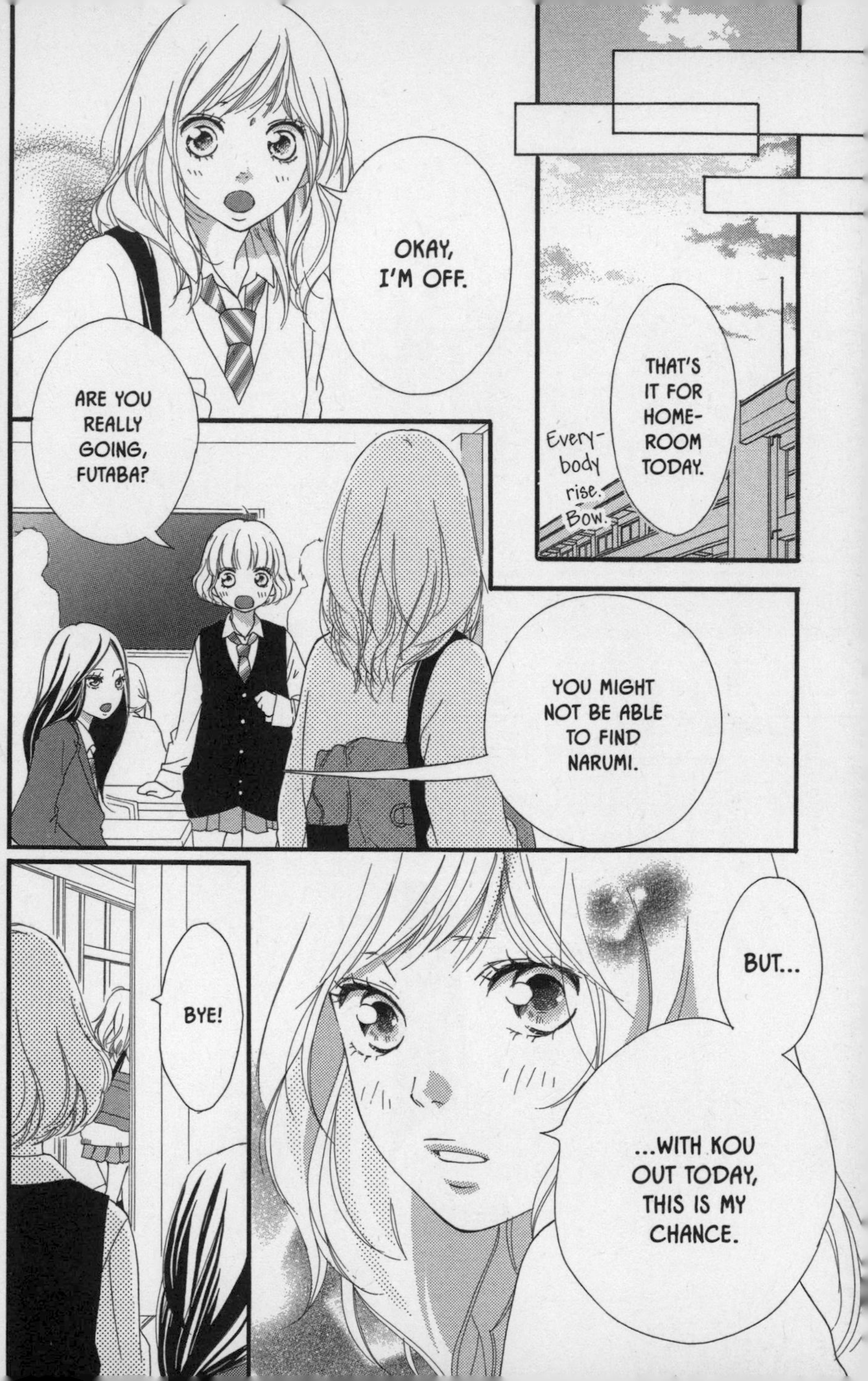
THAT'S IT FOR HOMEROOM TODAY.
Everybody rise. Bow.
OKAY, I'M OFF.
ARE YOU REALLY GOING, FUTABA?
YOU MIGHT NOT BE ABLE TO FIND NARUMI.
BUT...
...WITH KOU OUT TODAY, THIS IS MY CHANCE.
BYE!

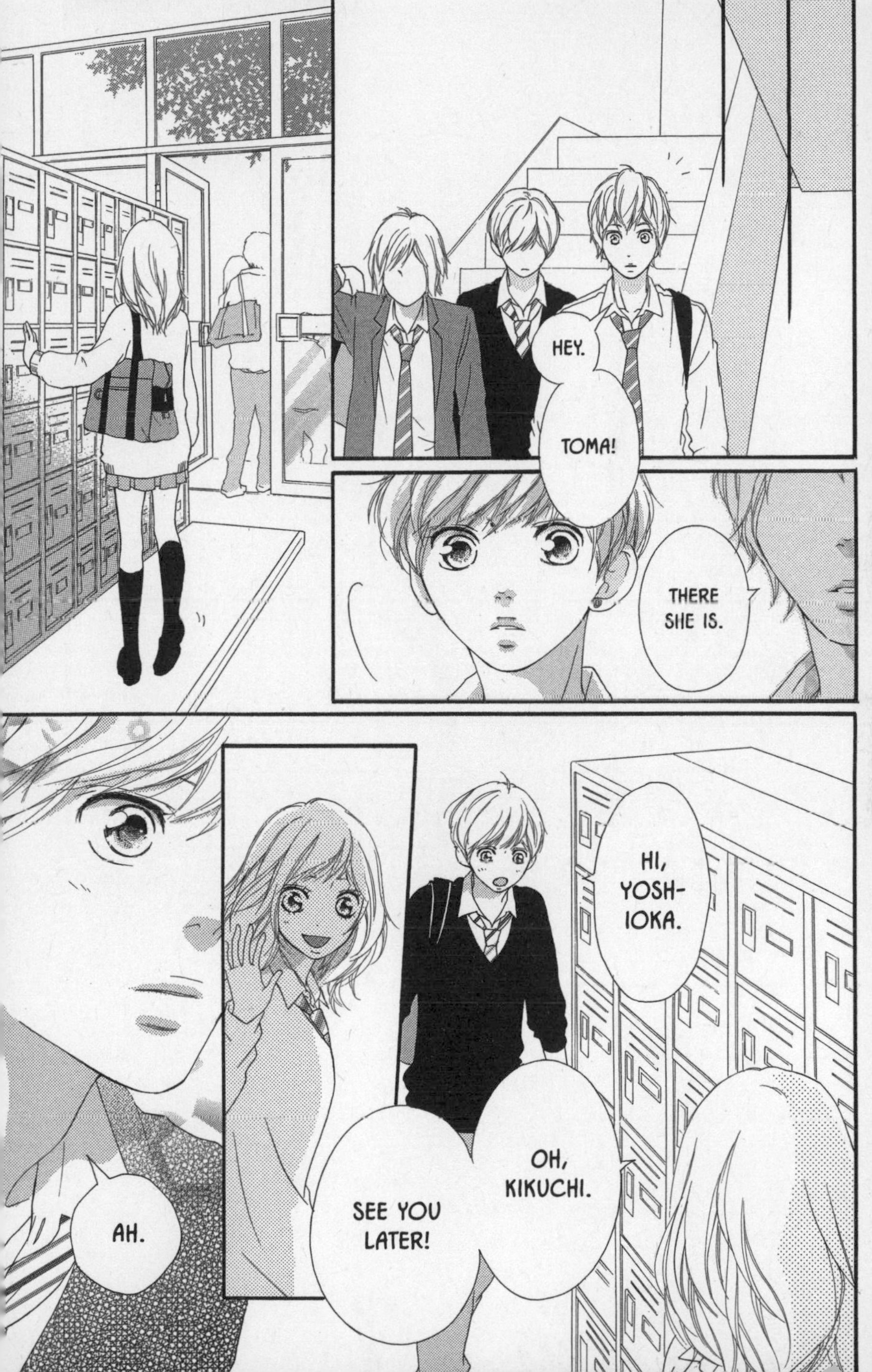
HEY.
TOMA!
THERE SHE IS.
HI, YOSH-IOKA.
OH, KIKUCHI.
SEE YOU LATER!
AH.

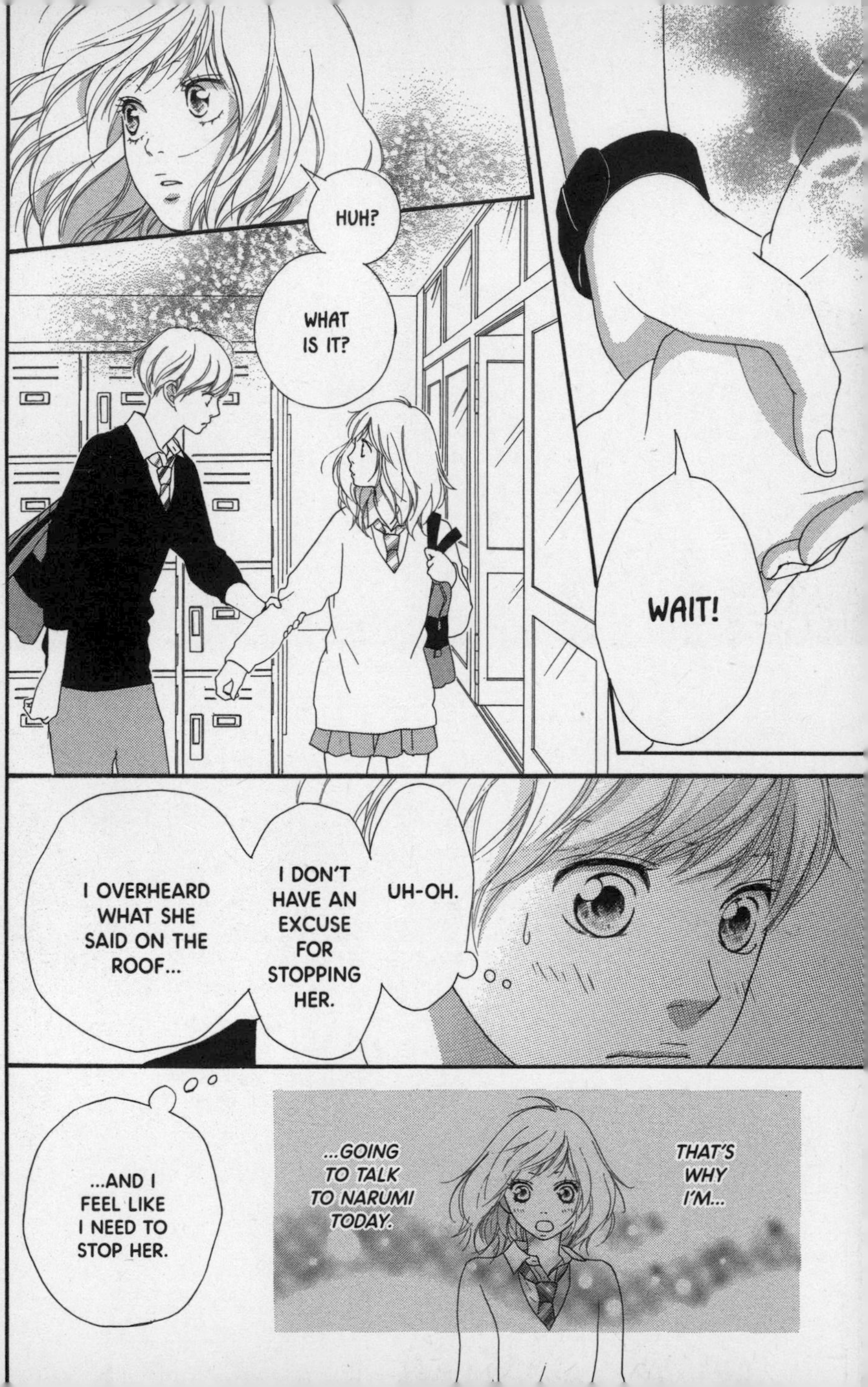
WAIT!
HUH?
WHAT IS IT?
UH-OH.
I DON'T HAVE AN EXCUSE FOR STOPPING HER.
I OVERHEARD WHAT SHE SAID ON THE ROOF...
THAT'S WHY I'M...
...GOING TO TALK TO NARUMI TODAY.
...AND I FEEL LIKE I NEED TO STOP HER.

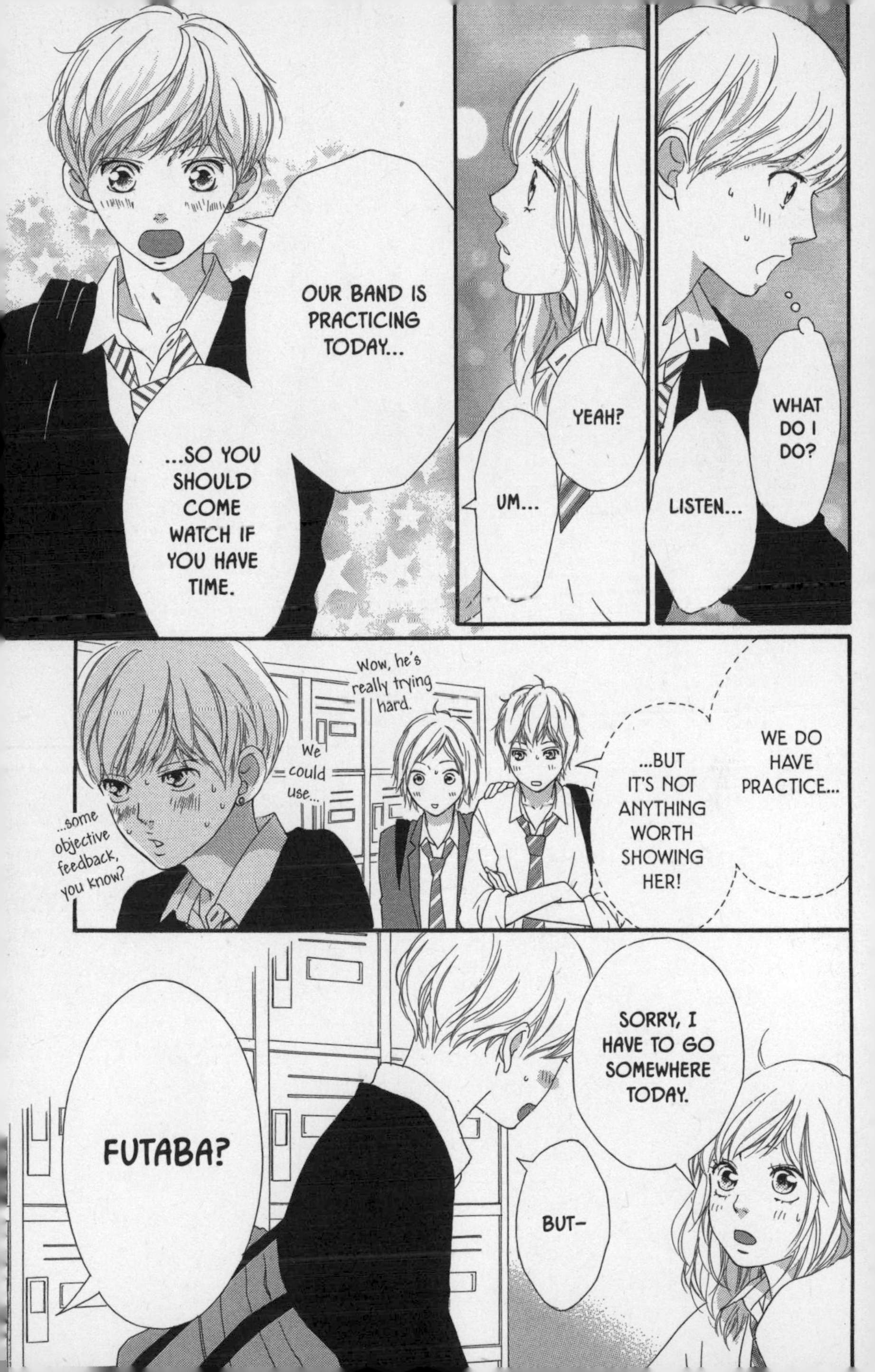
WHAT DO I DO?
LISTEN...
YEAH?
UM...
OUR BAND IS PRACTICING TODAY...
...SO YOU SHOULD COME WATCH IF YOU HAVE TIME.
WE DO HAVE PRACTICE...
...BUT IT'S NOT ANYTHING WORTH SHOWING HER!
Wow, he's really trying hard.
We could use...
...some objective feedback, you know?
SORRY, I HAVE TO GO SOMEWHERE TODAY.
BUT-
FUTABA?

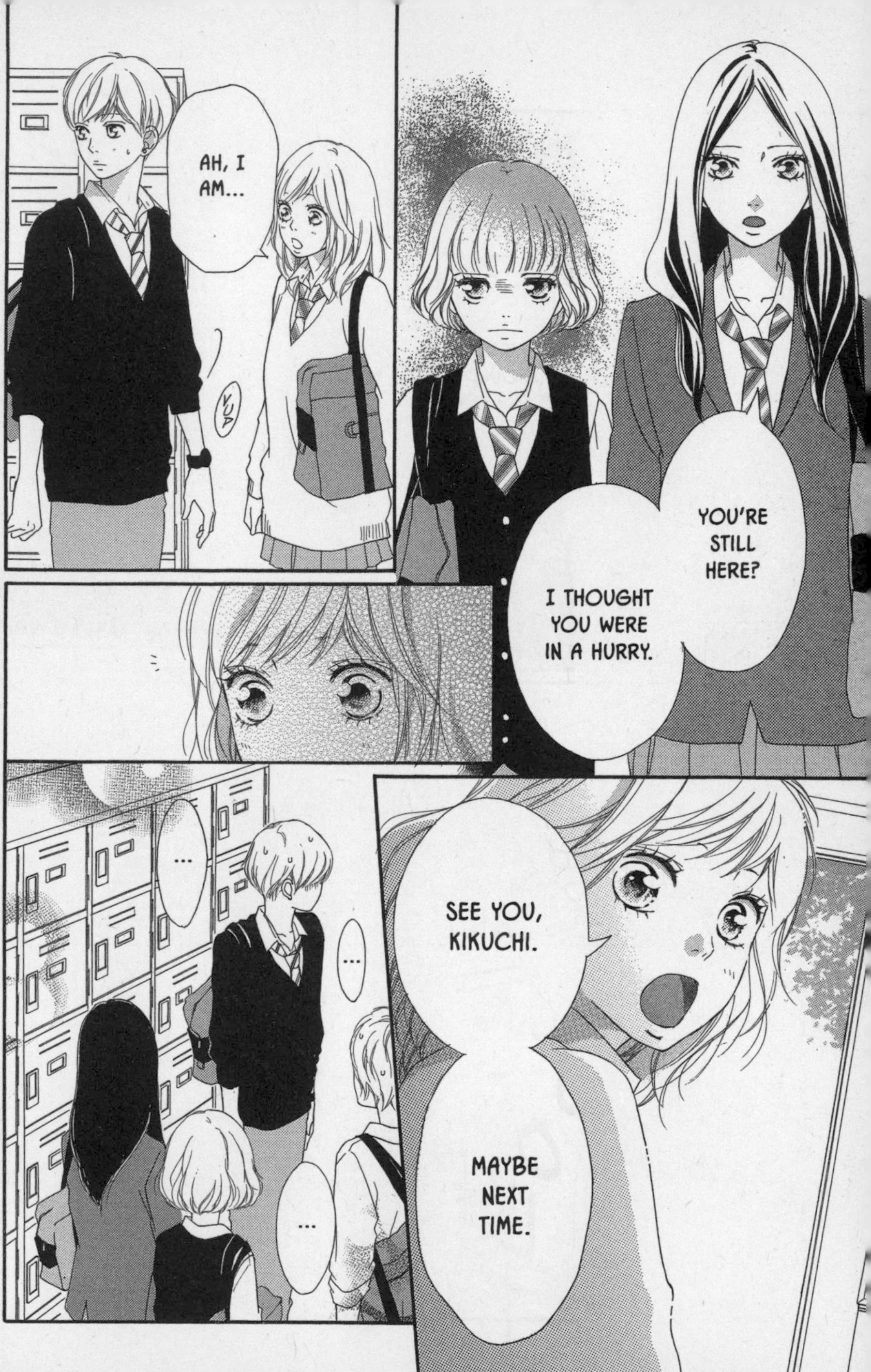
YOU'RE STILL HERE?
I THOUGHT YOU WERE IN A HURRY.
AH, I AM...
SEE YOU, KIKUCHI.
MAYBE NEXT TIME.
...
...
...

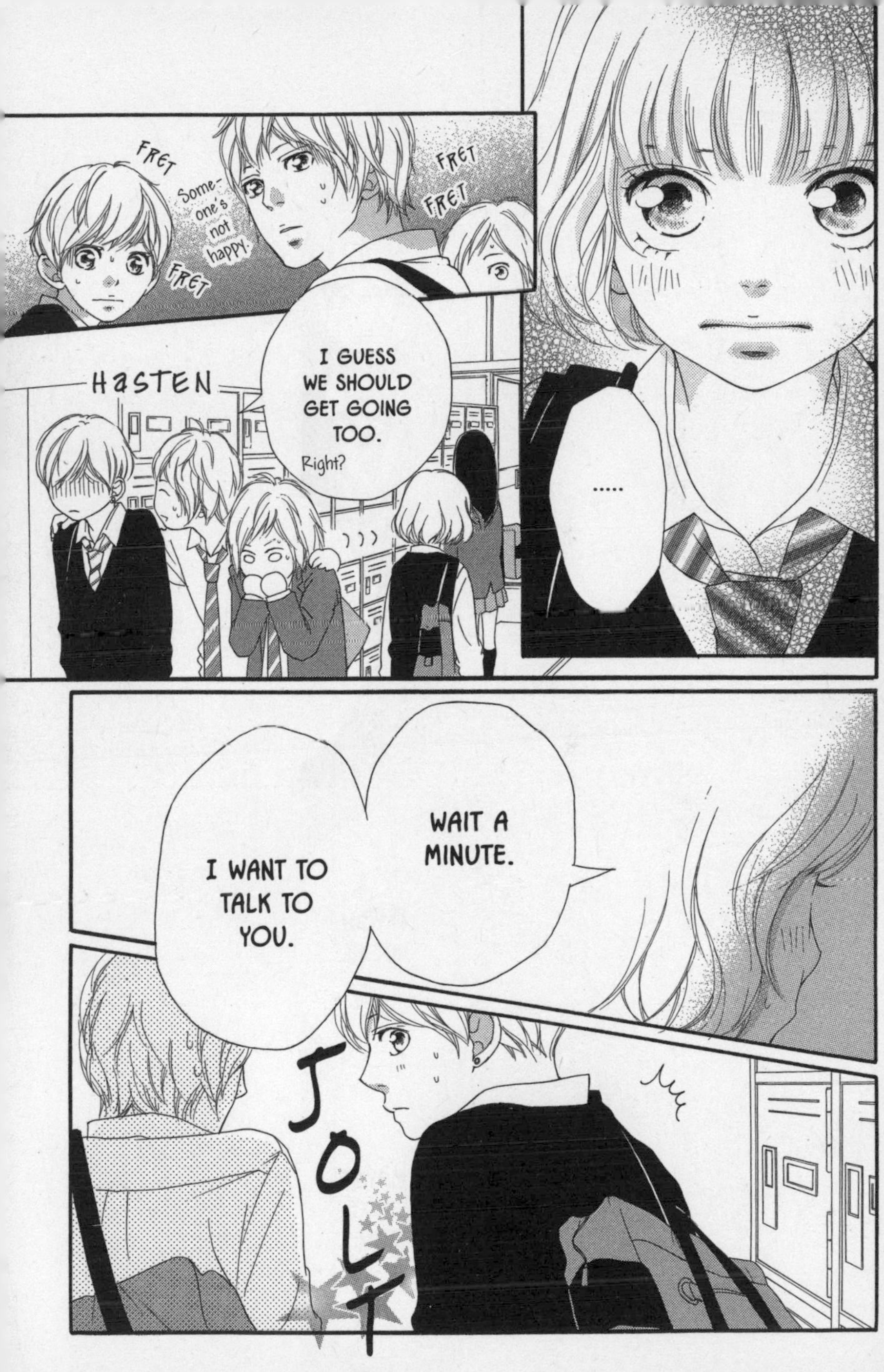
.....
FRET
Some-one's not happy.
FRET
FRET
FRET
HASTEN
I GUESS WE SHOULD GET GOING TOO.
Right?
WAIT A MINUTE.
I WANT TO TALK TO YOU.
JOLT

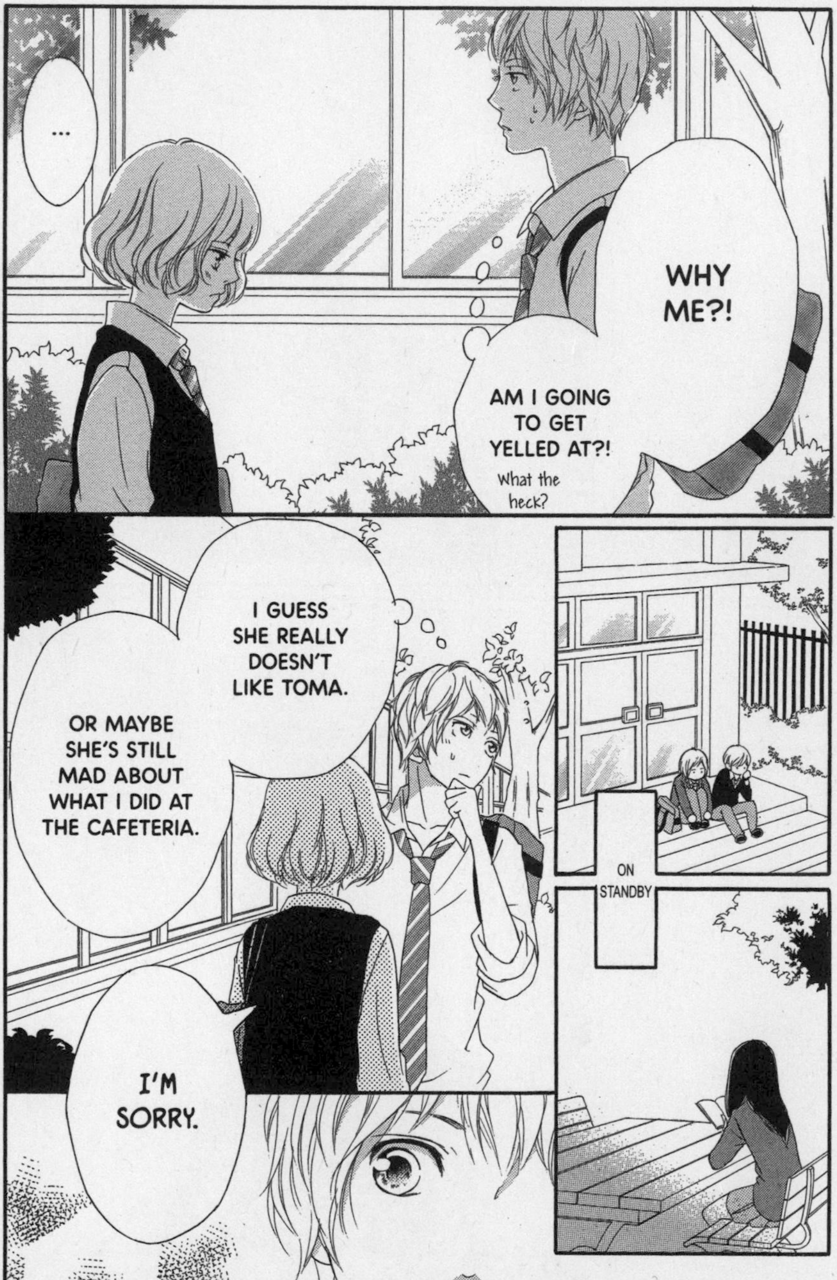
WHY ME?!
AM I GOING TO GET YELLED AT?!
What the heck?
...
ON STANDBY
I GUESS SHE REALLY DOESN'T LIKE TOMA.
OR MAYBE SHE'S STILL MAD ABOUT WHAT I DID AT THE CAFETERIA.
I'M SORRY.

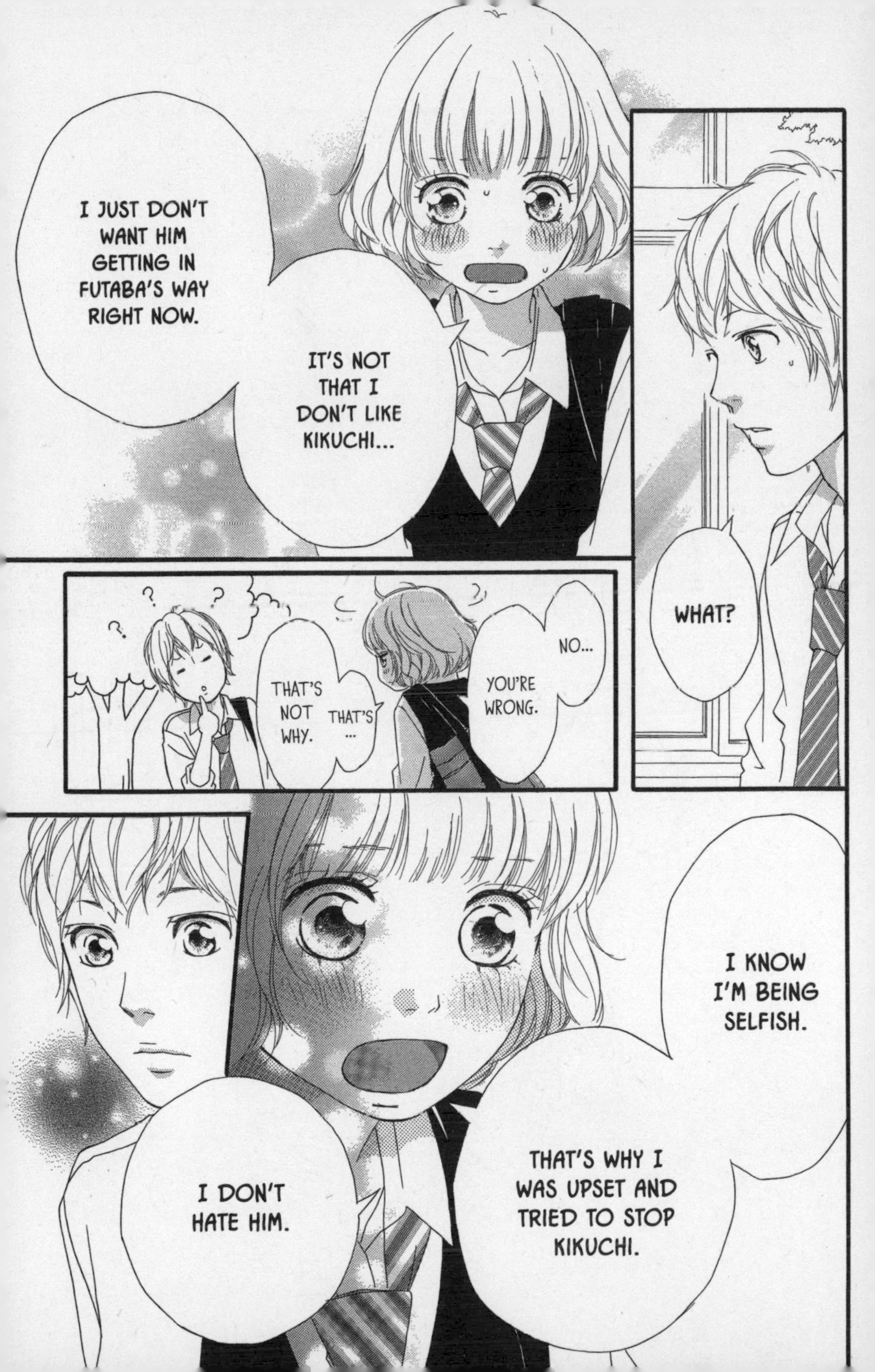
IT'S NOT THAT I DON'T LIKE KIKUCHI...
I JUST DON'T WANT HIM GETTING IN FUTABA'S WAY RIGHT NOW.
WHAT?
NO...
YOU'RE WRONG.
THAT'S ...
THAT'S NOT WHY.
I KNOW I'M BEING SELFISH.
THAT'S WHY I WAS UPSET AND TRIED TO STOP KIKUCHI.
I DON'T HATE HIM.

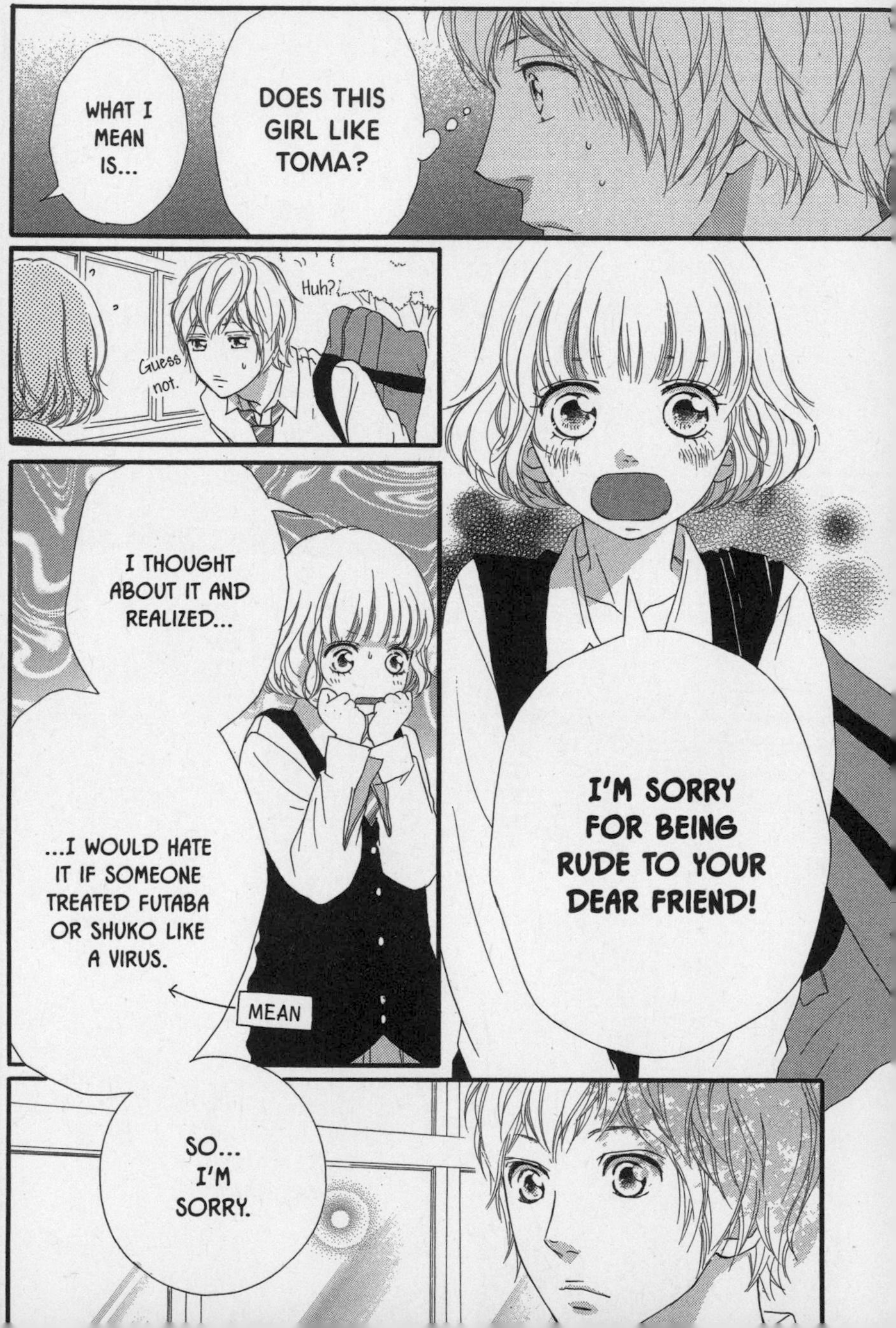
DOES THIS GIRL LIKE TOMA?
WHAT I MEAN IS...
Huh?
Guess not.
I THOUGHT ABOUT IT AND REALIZED...
...I WOULD HATE IT IF SOMEONE TREATED FUTABA OR SHUKO LIKE A VIRUS.
MEAN
I'M SORRY FOR BEING RUDE TO YOUR DEAR FRIEND!
SO... I'M SORRY.

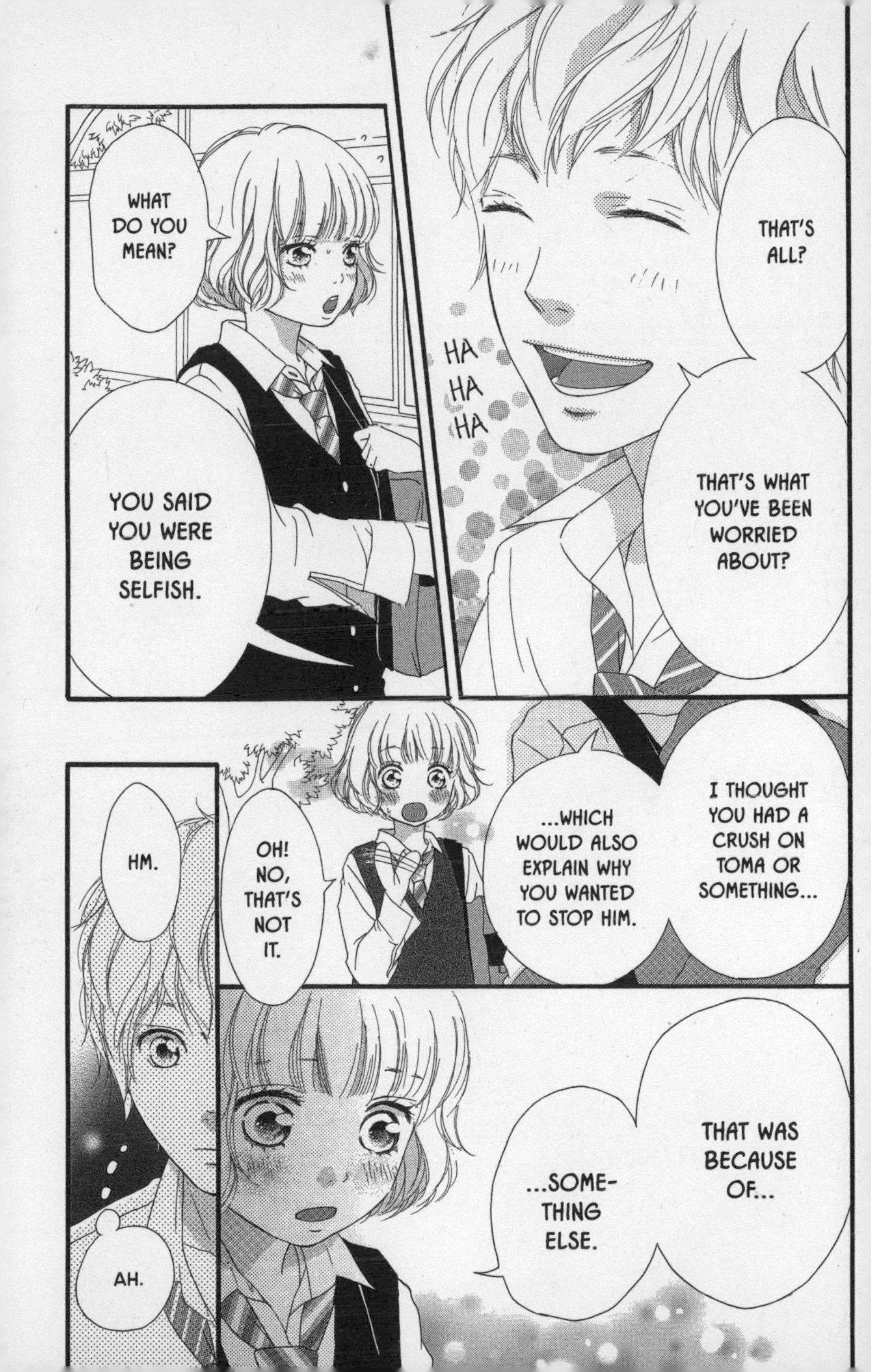
THAT'S ALL?
HA HA HA
THAT'S WHAT YOU'VE BEEN WORRIED ABOUT?
WHAT DO YOU MEAN?
YOU SAID YOU WERE BEING SELFISH.
I THOUGHT YOU HAD A CRUSH ON TOMA OR SOMETHING...
...WHICH WOULD ALSO EXPLAIN WHY YOU WANTED TO STOP HIM.
OH! NO, THAT'S NOT IT.
THAT WAS BECAUSE OF...
...SOME-THING ELSE.
HM.
...
AH.

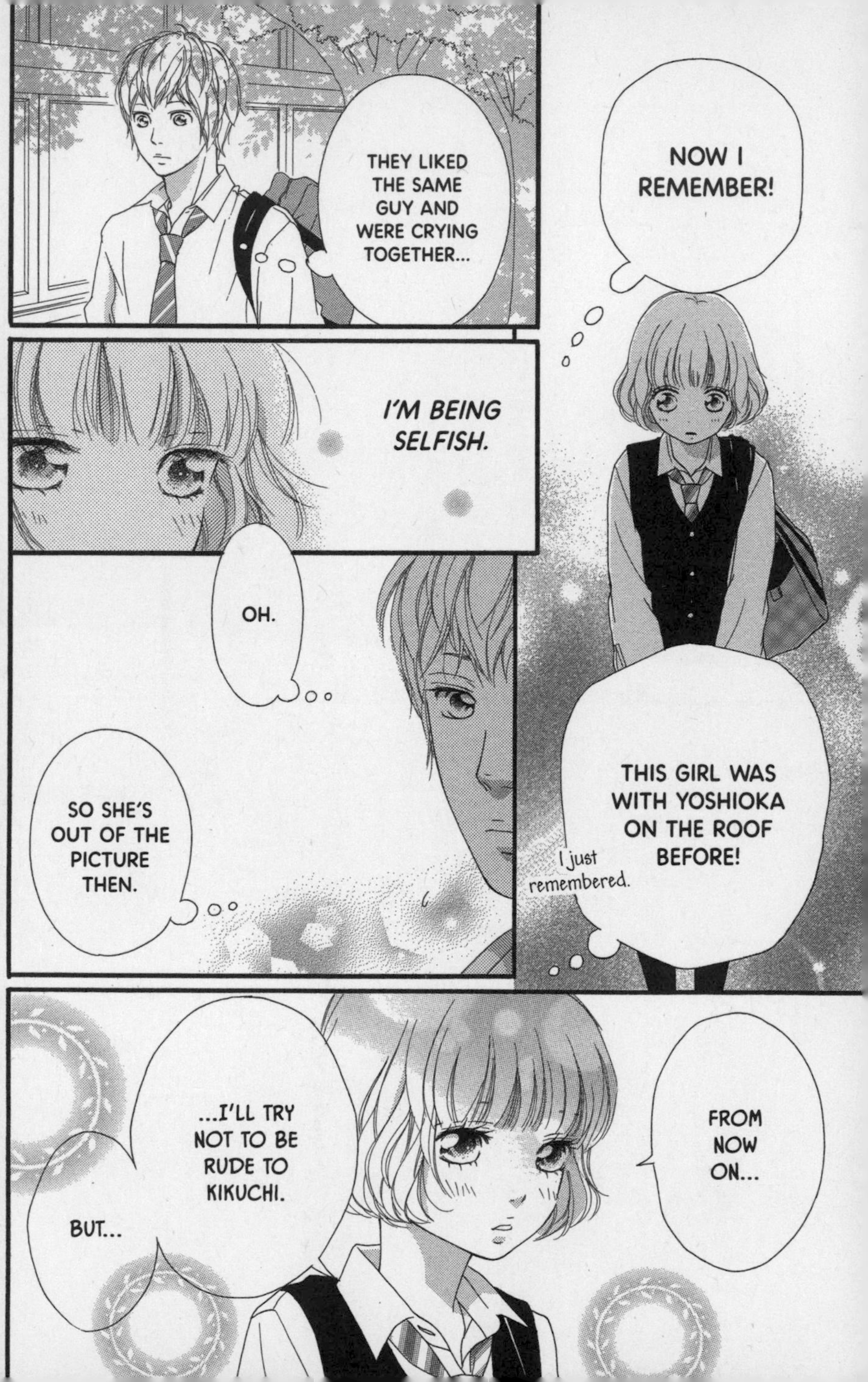
NOW I REMEMBER!
THIS GIRL WAS WITH YOSHIOKA ON THE ROOF BEFORE!
I just remembered.
THEY LIKED THE SAME GUY AND WERE CRYING TOGETHER...
I'M BEING SELFISH.
OH.
SO SHE'S OUT OF THE PICTURE THEN.
FROM NOW ON...
...I'LL TRY NOT TO BE RUDE TO KIKUCHI.
BUT...

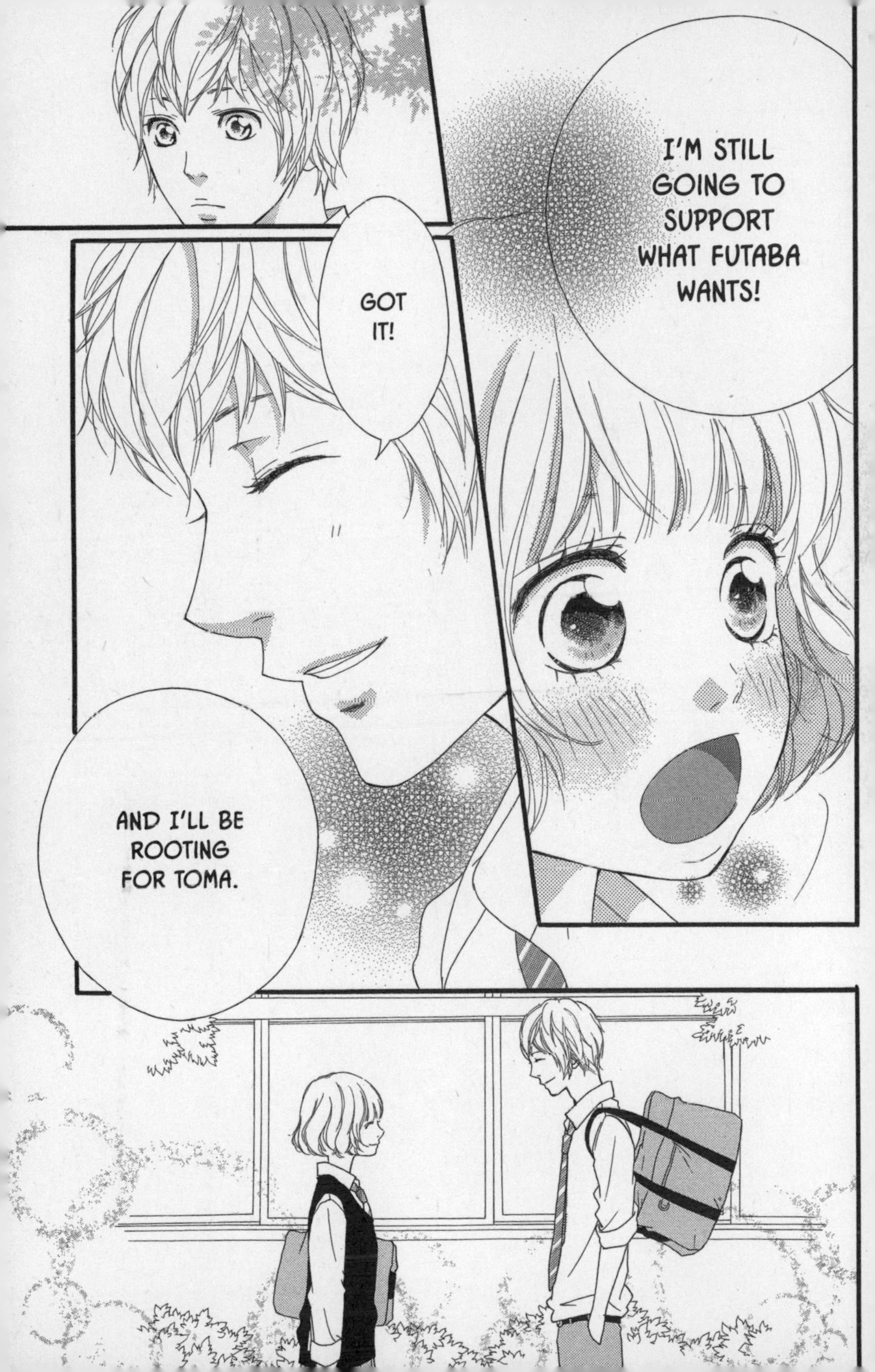
I'M STILL GOING TO SUPPORT WHAT FUTABA WANTS!
GOT IT!
AND I'LL BE ROOTING FOR TOMA.

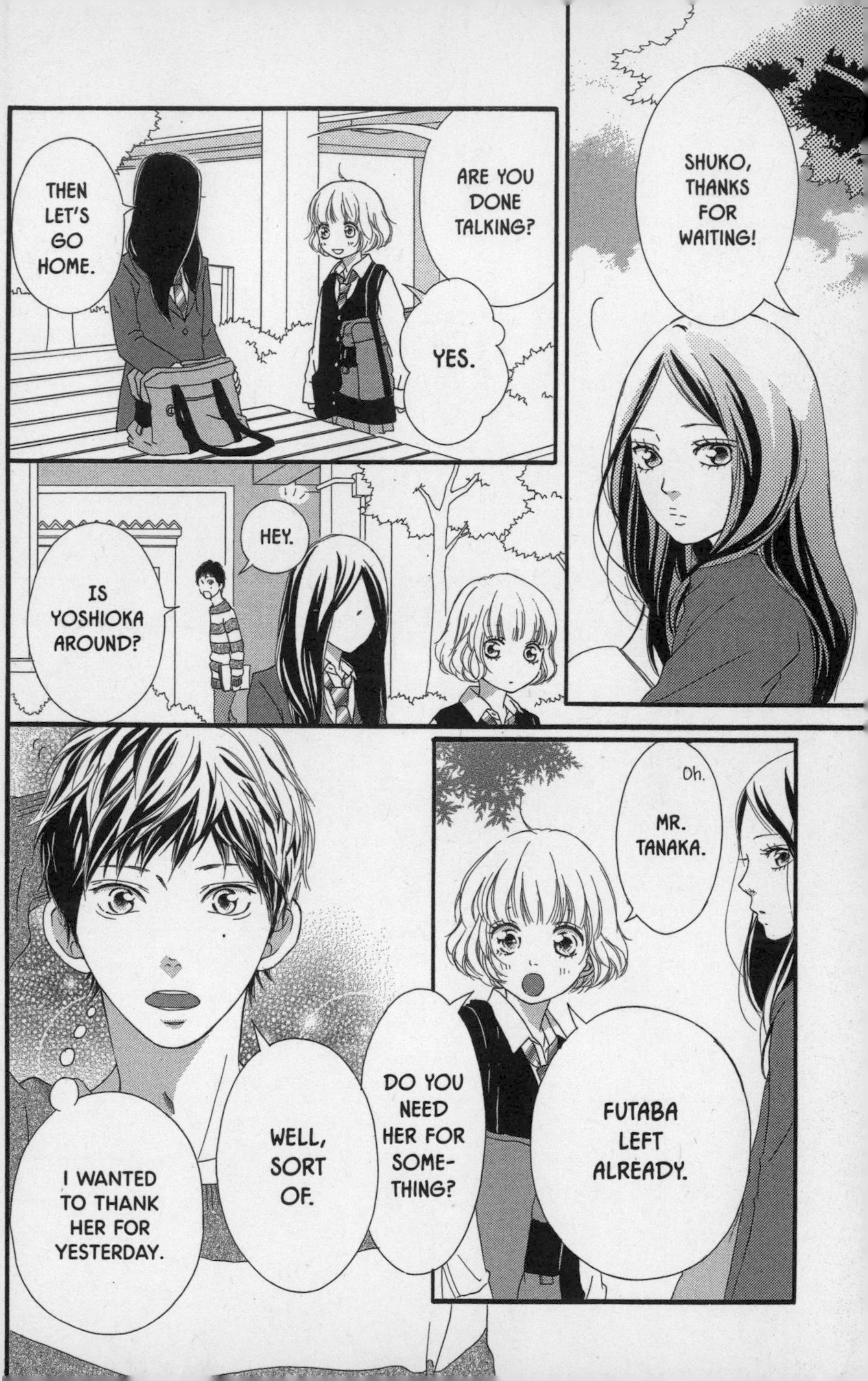
SHUKO, THANKS FOR WAITING!
ARE YOU DONE TALKING?
YES.
THEN LET'S GO HOME.
HEY.
IS YOSHIOKA AROUND?
Oh.
MR. TANAKA.
FUTABA LEFT ALREADY.
DO YOU NEED HER FOR SOME-THING?
WELL, SORT OF.
I WANTED TO THANK HER FOR YESTERDAY.

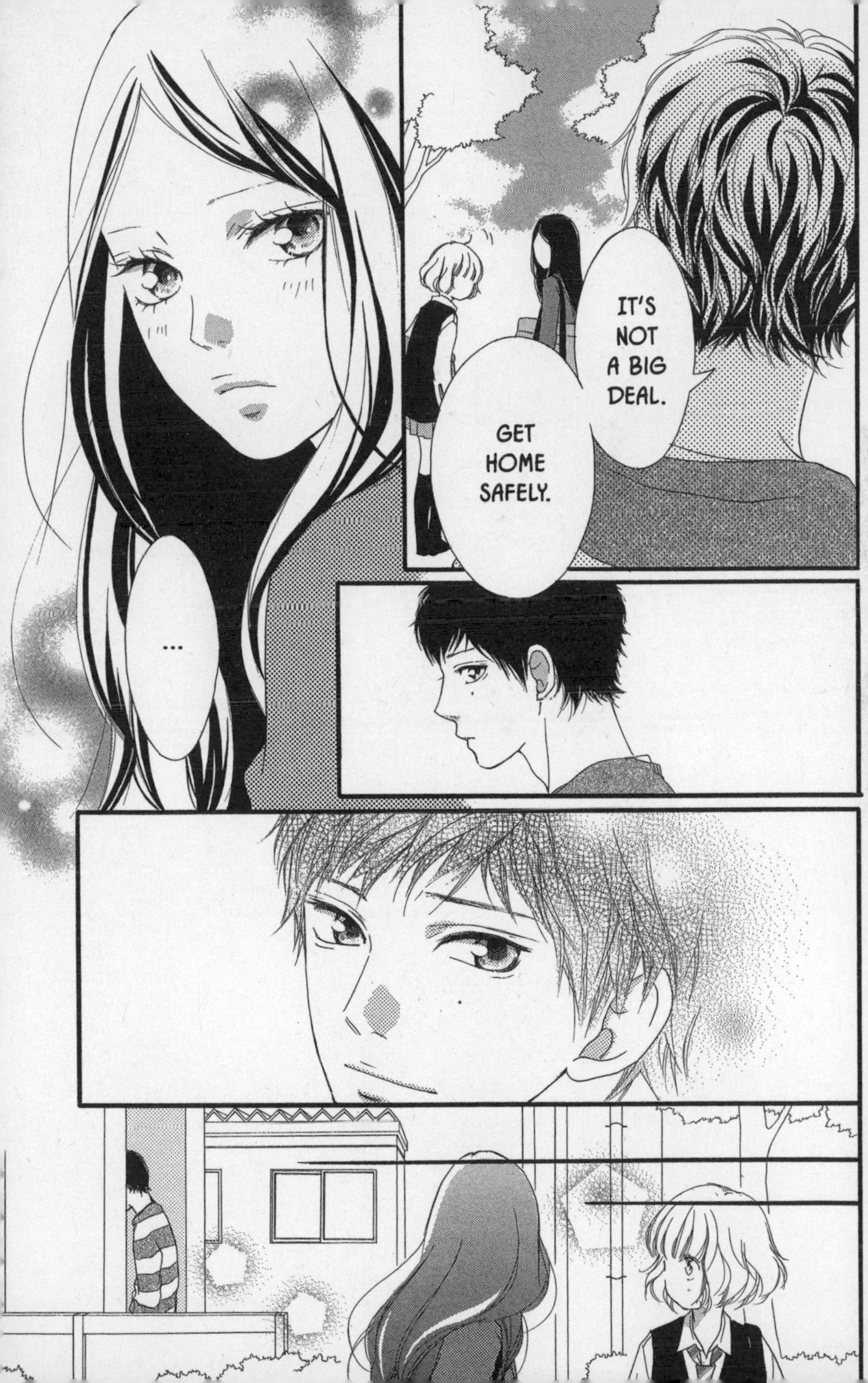
IT'S NOT A BIG DEAL.
GET HOME SAFELY.
...

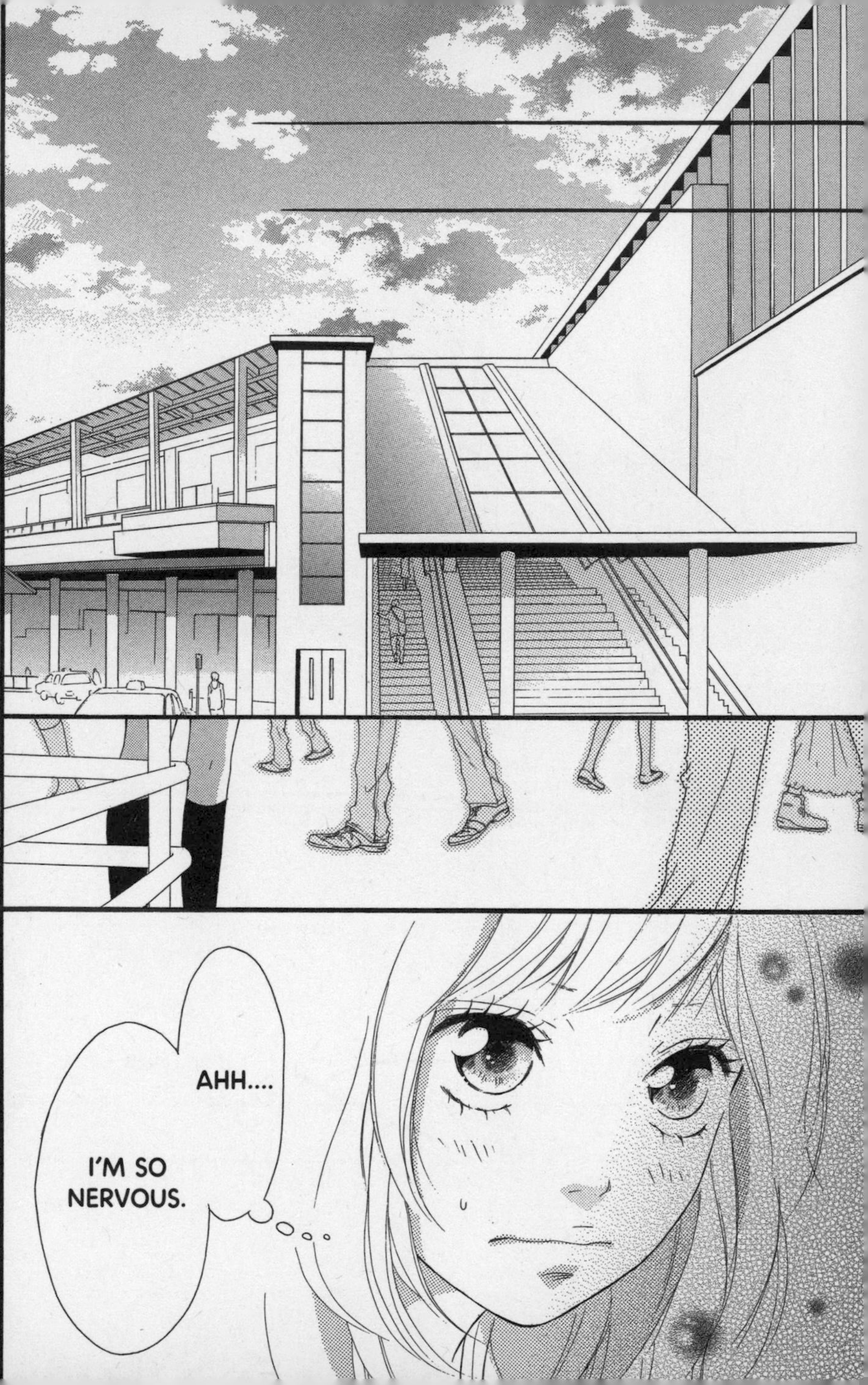
AHH....
I'M SO NERVOUS.

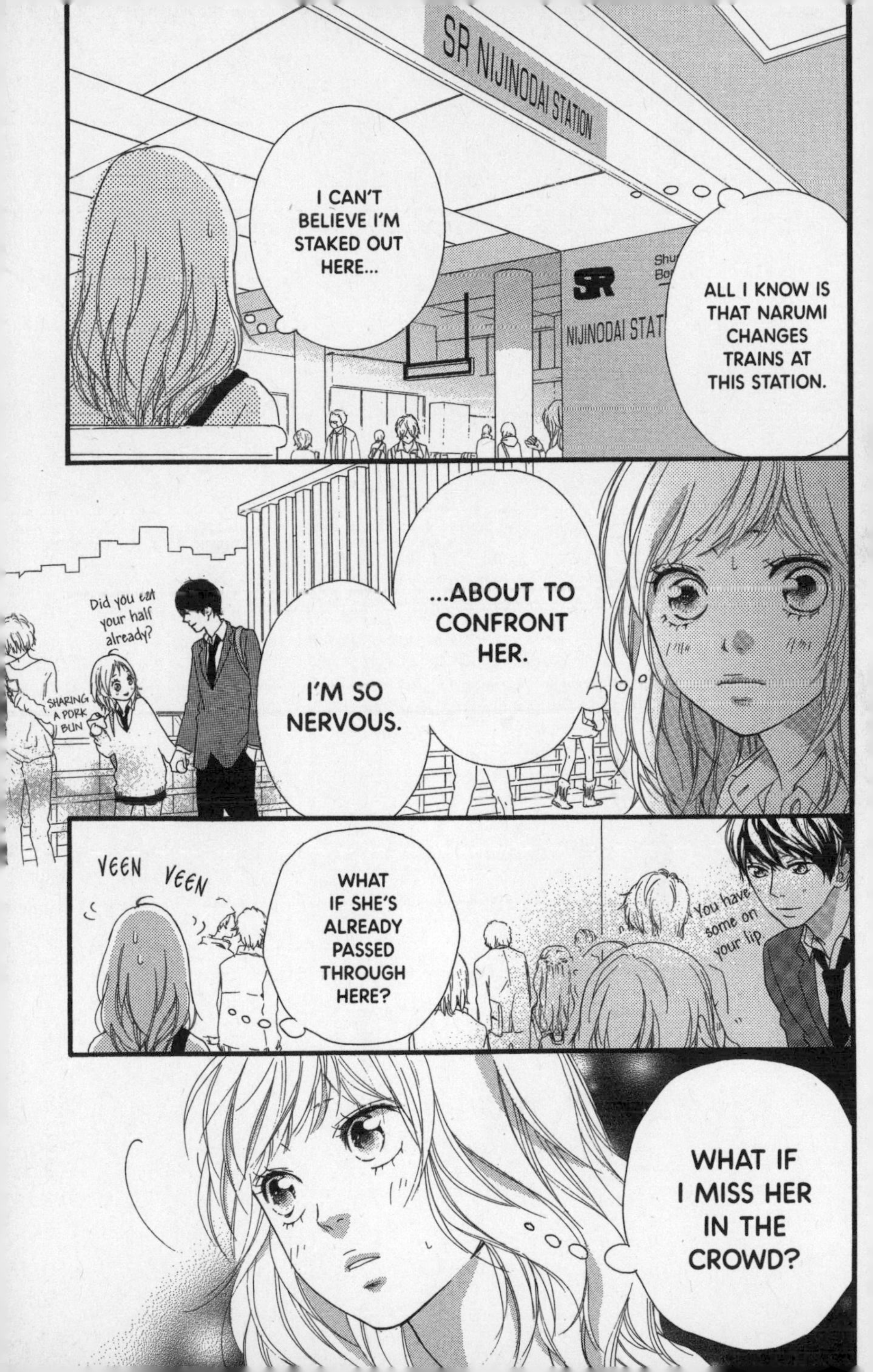
SR NIJINODAI STATION
ALL I KNOW IS THAT NARUMI CHANGES TRAINS AT THIS STATION.
I CAN'T BELIEVE I'M STAKED OUT HERE...
SR
...ABOUT TO CONFRONT HER.
I'M SO NERVOUS.
Did you eat your half already?
SHARING A PORK BUN
You have some on your lip
WHAT IF SHE'S ALREADY PASSED THROUGH HERE?
VEEN VEEN
WHAT IF I MISS HER IN THE CROWD?

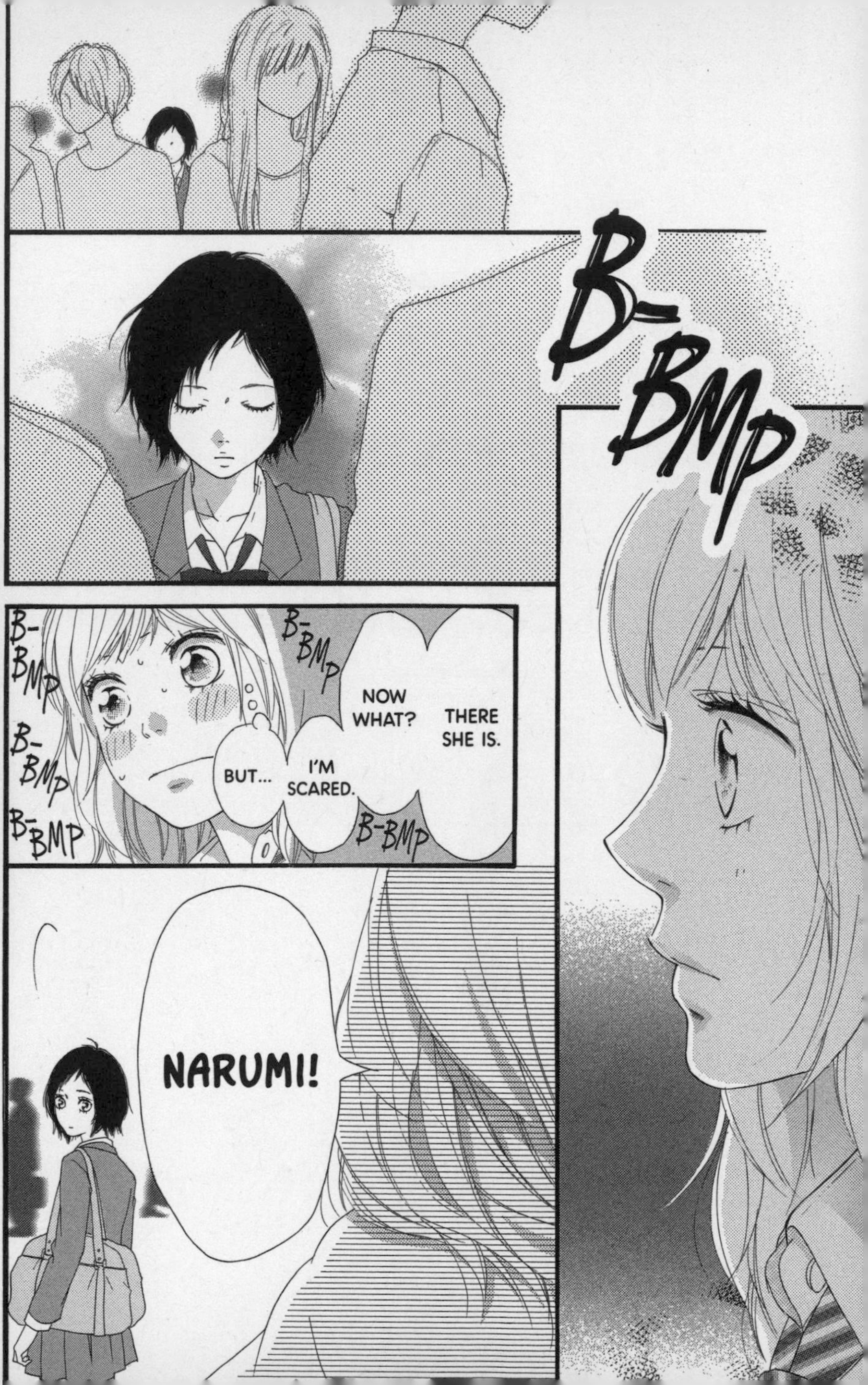
B-BMP
B-BMP
THERE SHE IS.
NOW WHAT?
I'M SCARED.
BUT...
B-BMP
B-BMP
B-BMP
B-BMP
NARUMI!

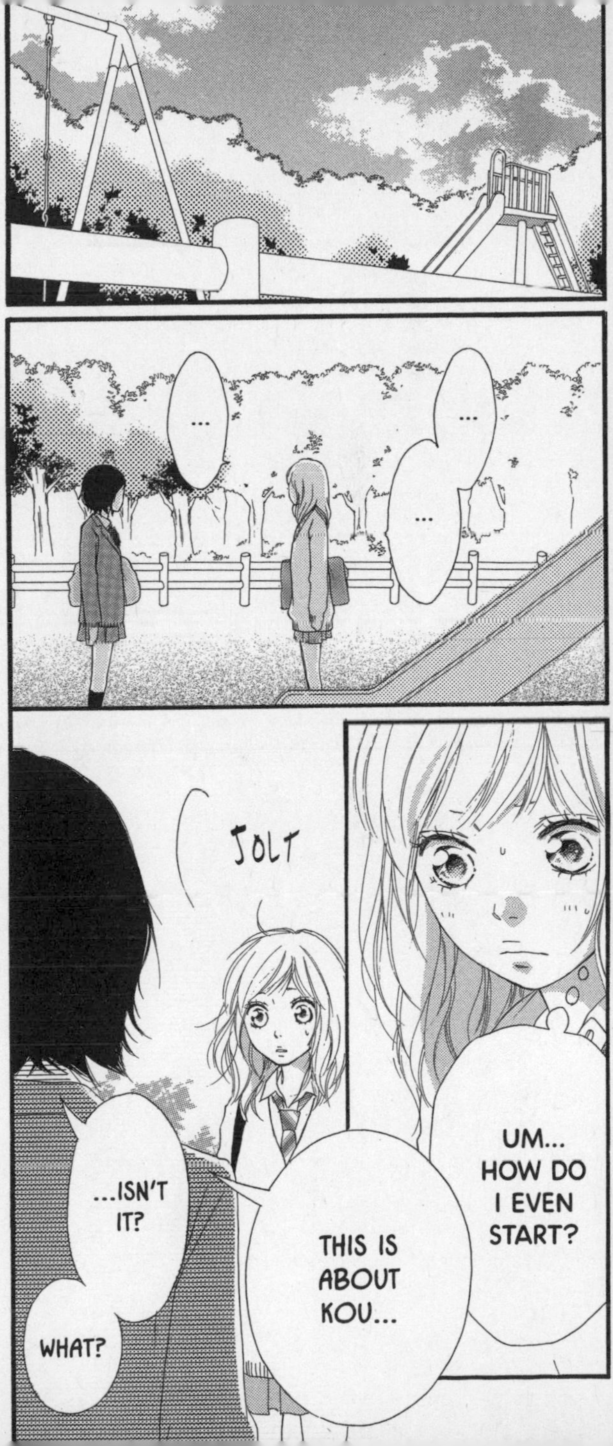
...
...
...
UM... HOW DO I EVEN START?
JOLT
THIS IS ABOUT KOU...
...ISN'T IT?
WHAT?

In middle school, we had to bring lunch from home. During my first year, everybody started bringing in weird lunches for fun. People would pack crackers or stew into their bento boxes, but the one who impressed me the most was the boy who brought *hiyashi chuka* (cold ramen). The noodles were in the bento box, and he had a separate container for the sauce and another container for all the toppings. There was no doubt in my mind that his lunch was the ultimate champion. Or rather, his mother was. And he finished all his room-temperature ramen that day. Midway through he said, "This is gross," but he was probably just feeling self-conscious (or maybe it really was gross...). Anyway, the weird lunch fad didn't last too long. Also, hiyashi chuka is now on sale!! Just kidding. It's not.

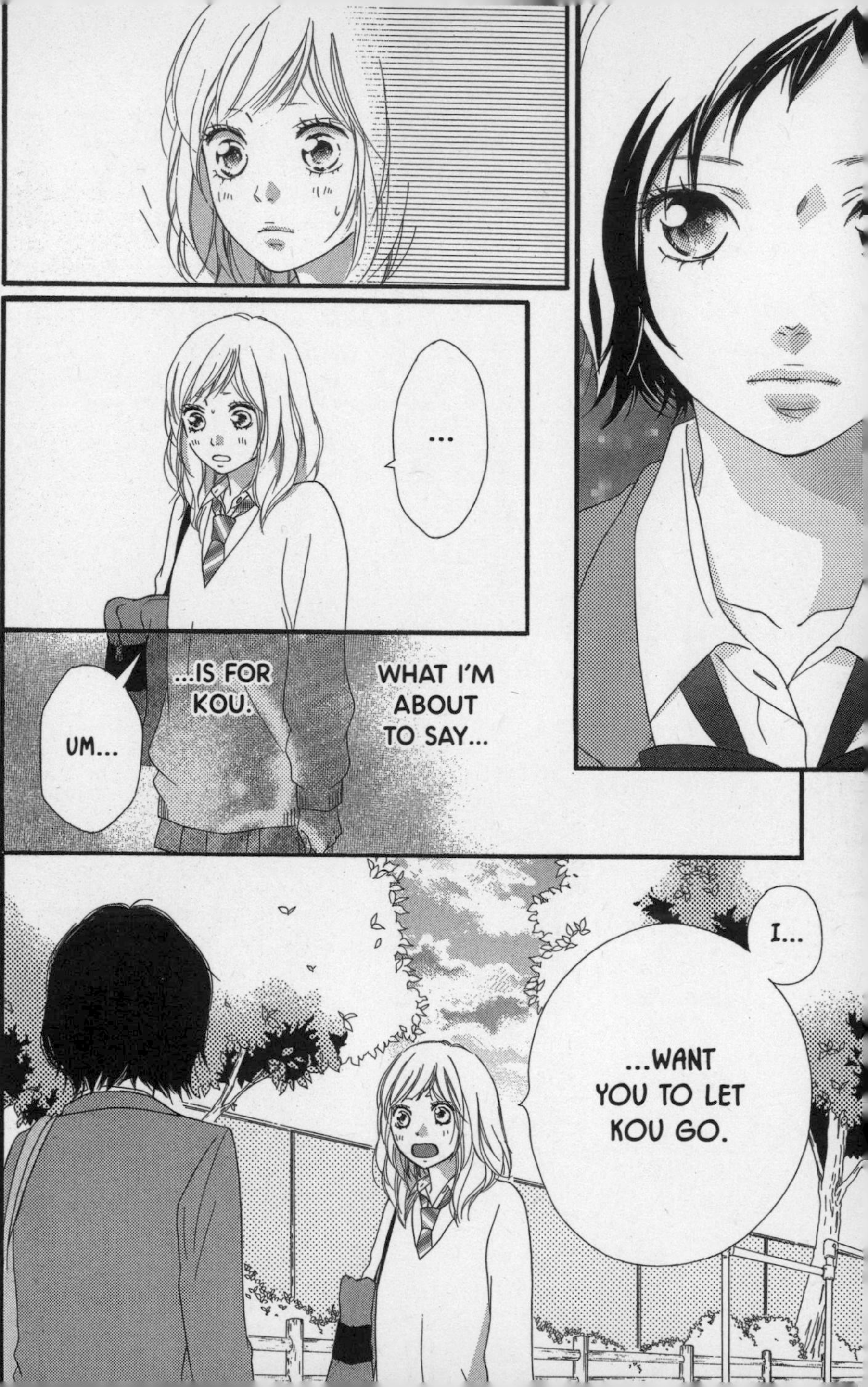
...
WHAT I'M ABOUT TO SAY...
...IS FOR KOU.
UM...
I...
...WANT YOU TO LET KOU GO.

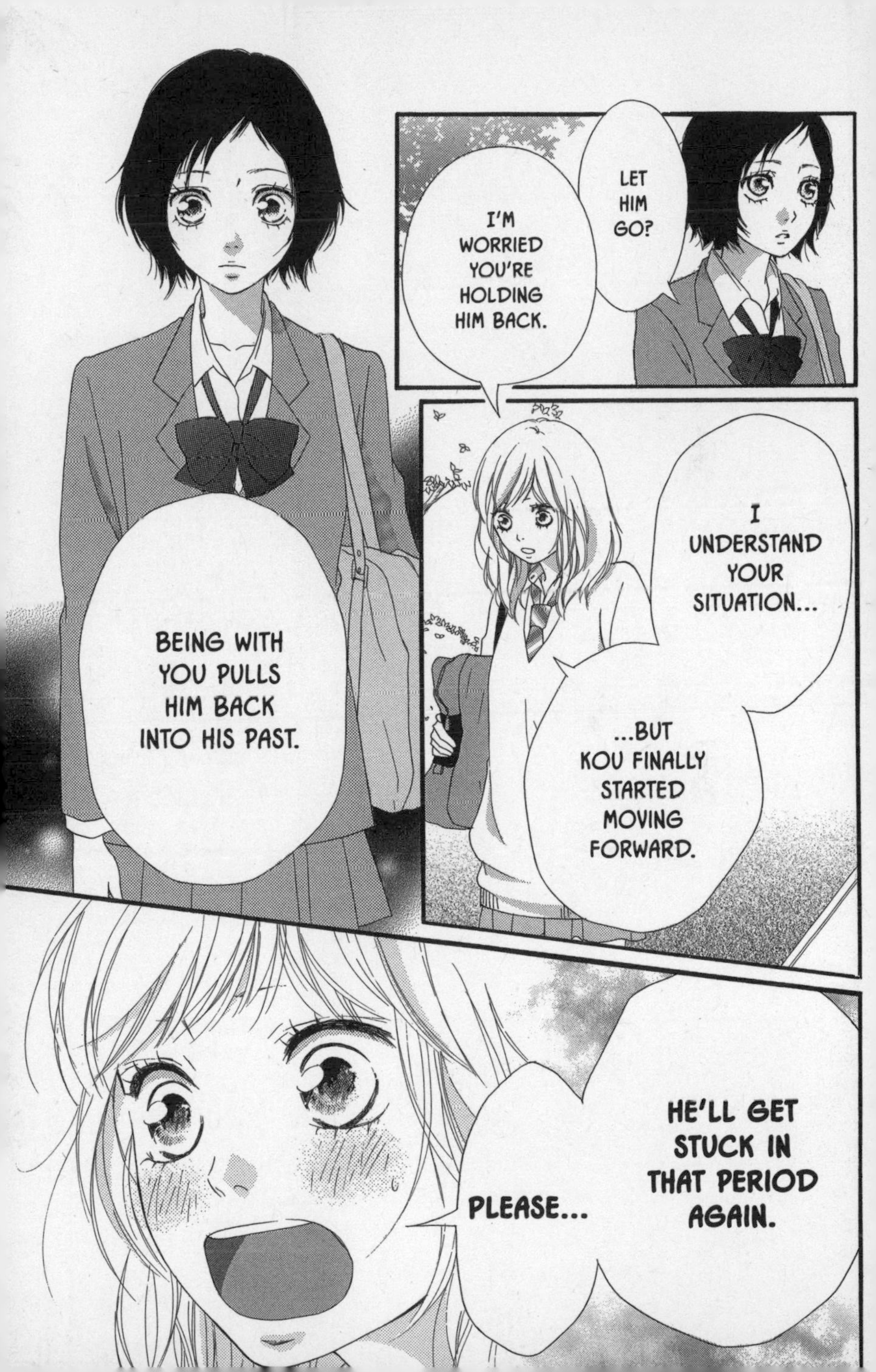
LET HIM GO?
I'M WORRIED YOU'RE HOLDING HIM BACK.
I UNDERSTAND YOUR SITUATION...
...BUT KOU FINALLY STARTED MOVING FORWARD.
BEING WITH YOU PULLS HIM BACK INTO HIS PAST.
HE'LL GET STUCK IN THAT PERIOD AGAIN.
PLEASE...

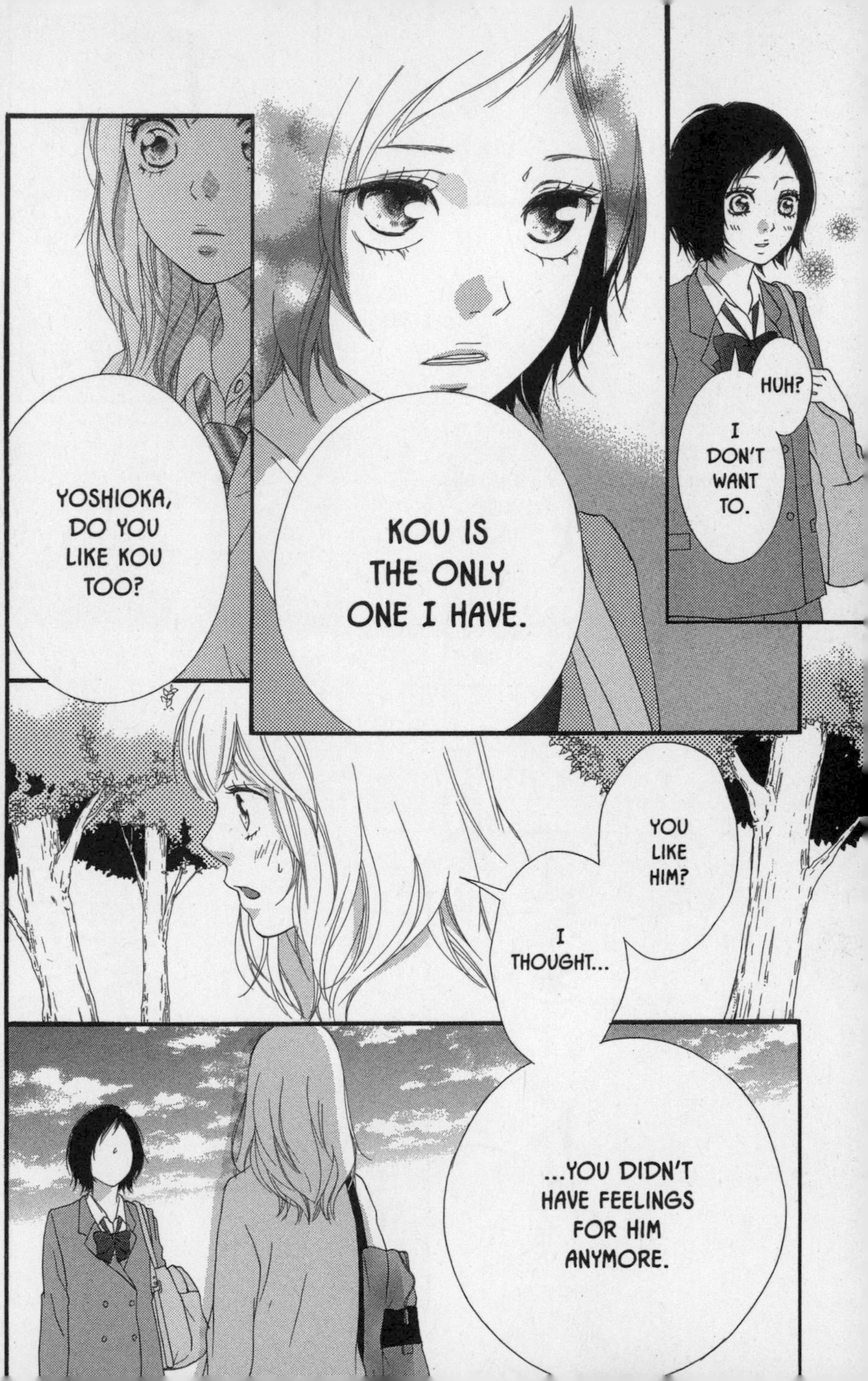
HUH? I DON'T WANT TO.
KOU IS THE ONLY ONE I HAVE.
YOSHIOKA, DO YOU LIKE KOU TOO?
YOU LIKE HIM?
I THOUGHT...
...YOU DIDN'T HAVE FEELINGS FOR HIM ANYMORE.

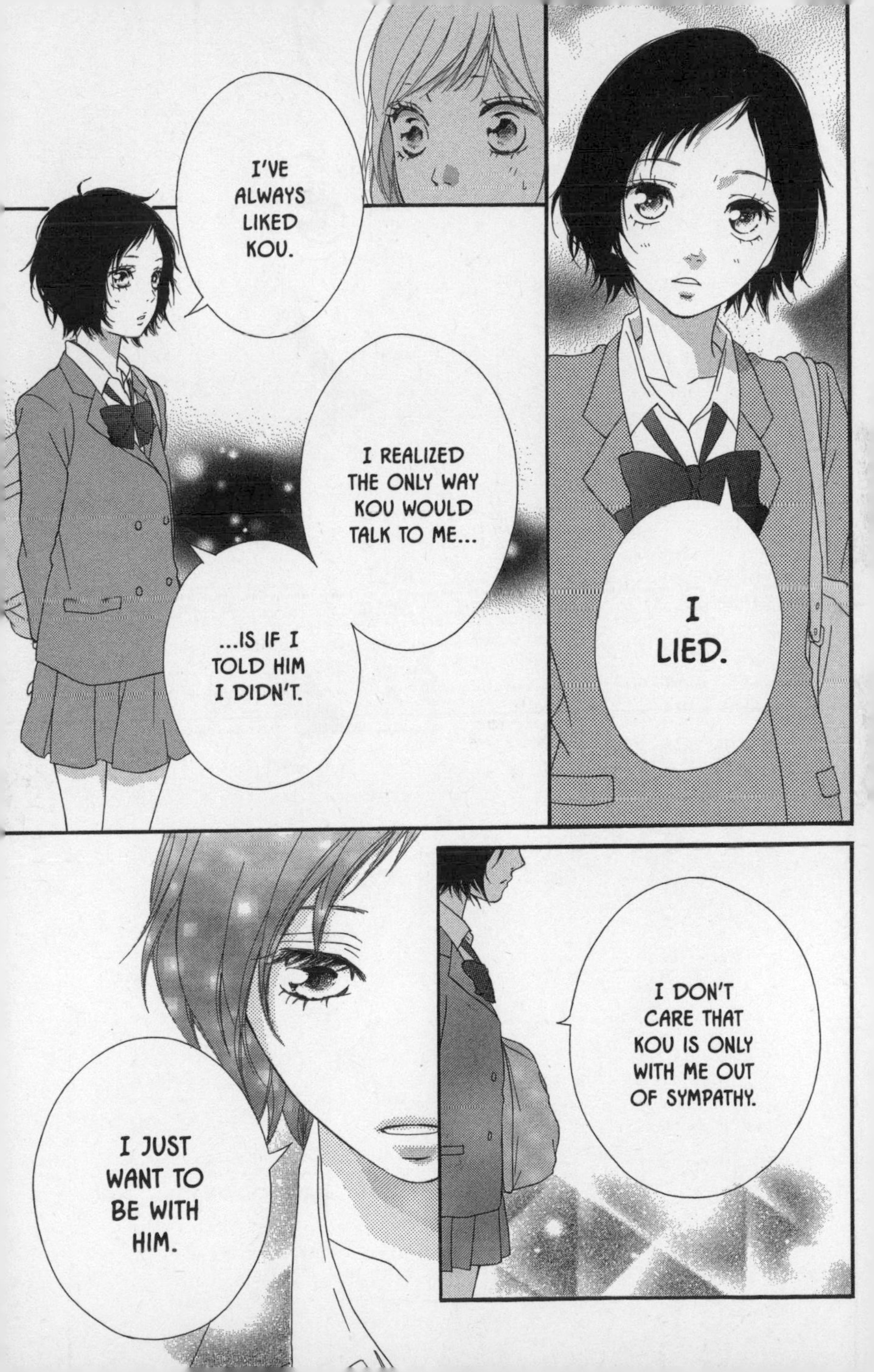
I LIED.
I'VE ALWAYS LIKED KOU.
I REALIZED THE ONLY WAY KOU WOULD TALK TO ME...
...IS IF I TOLD HIM I DIDN'T.
I DON'T CARE THAT KOU IS ONLY WITH ME OUT OF SYMPATHY.
I JUST WANT TO BE WITH HIM.

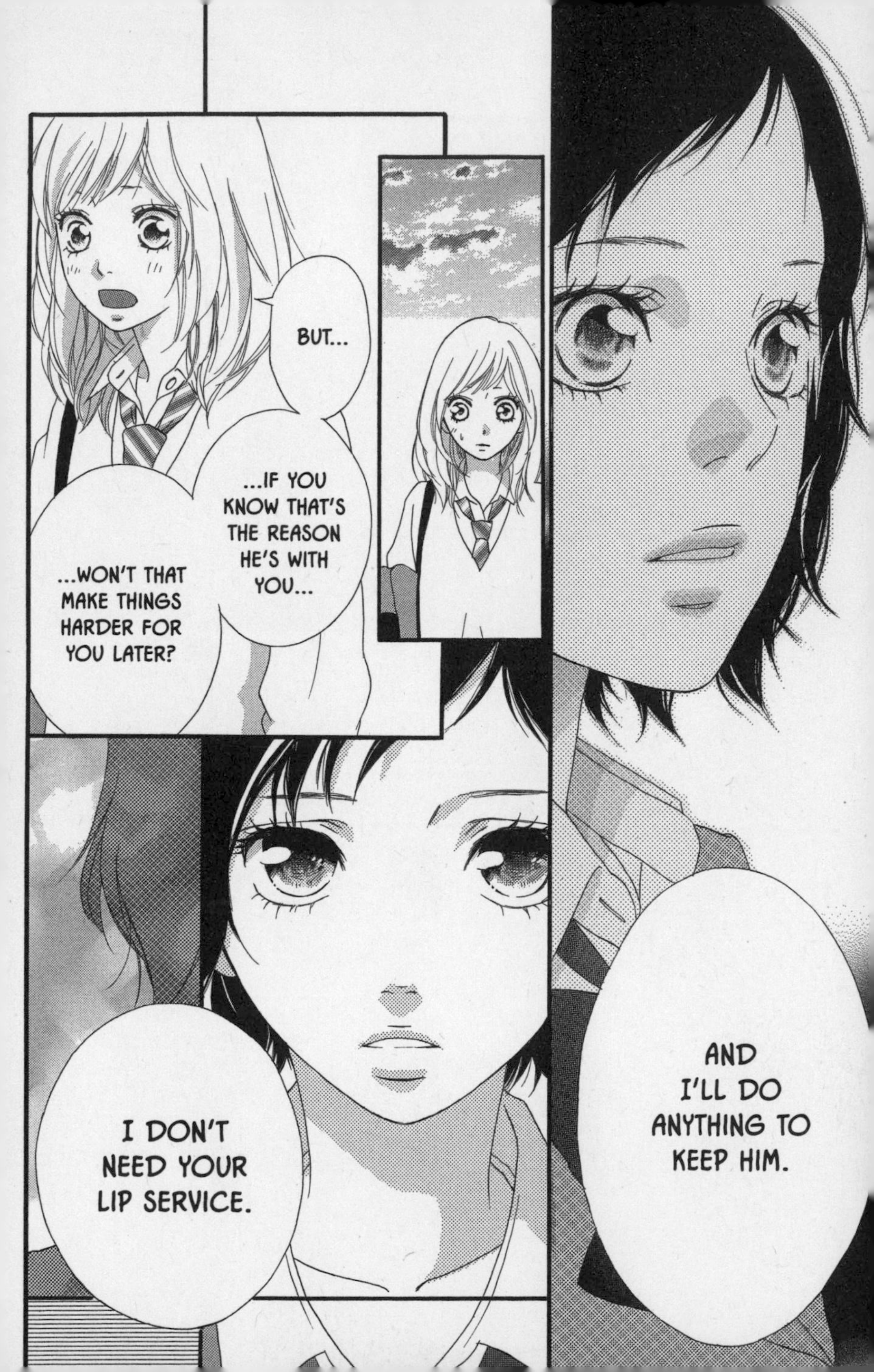
BUT...
...IF YOU KNOW THAT'S THE REASON HE'S WITH YOU...
...WON'T THAT MAKE THINGS HARDER FOR YOU LATER?
I DON'T NEED YOUR LIP SERVICE.
AND I'LL DO ANYTHING TO KEEP HIM.

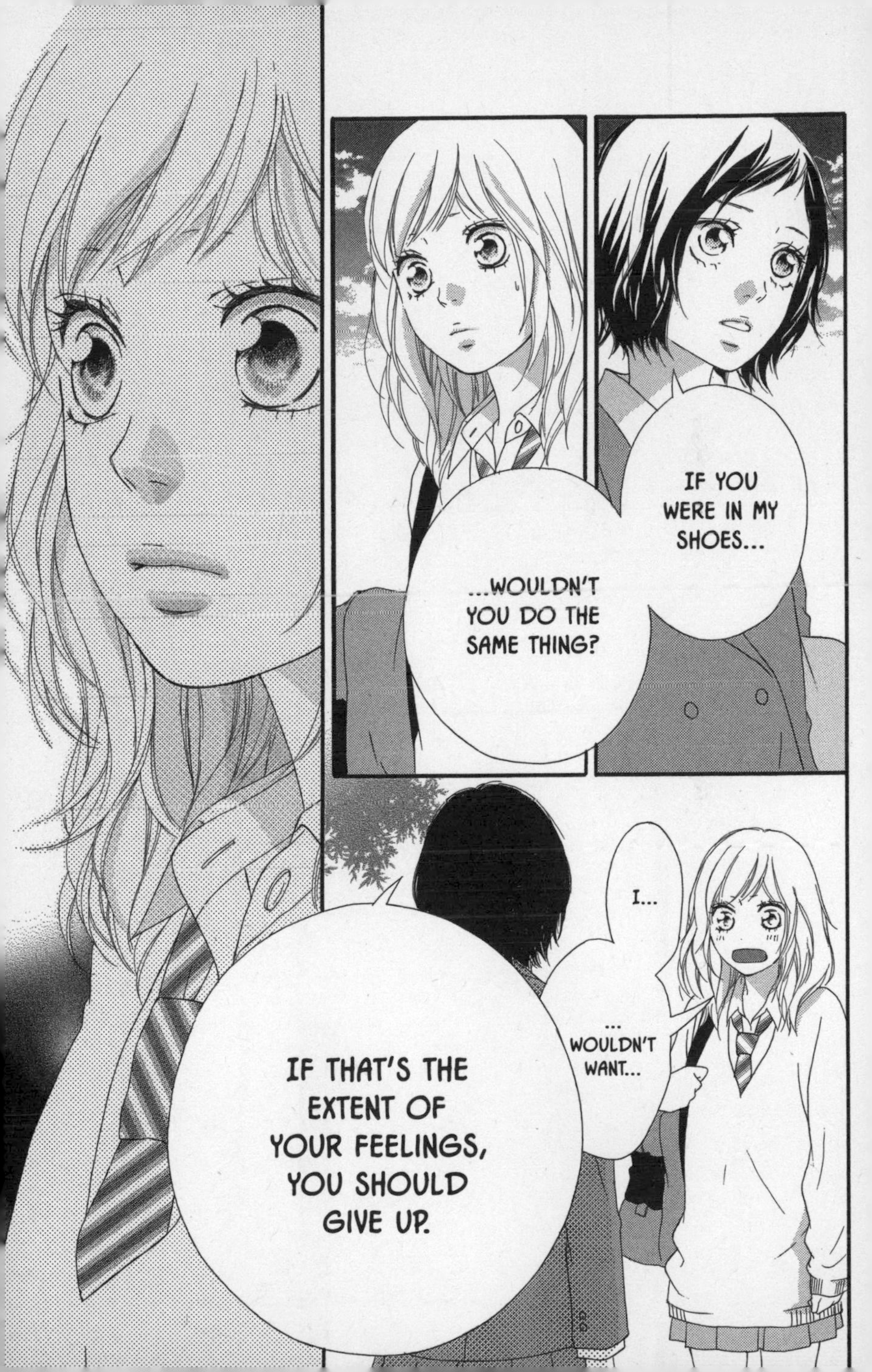
IF YOU WERE IN MY SHOES...
...WOULDN'T YOU DO THE SAME THING?
I...
...WOULDN'T WANT...
IF THAT'S THE EXTENT OF YOUR FEELINGS, YOU SHOULD GIVE UP.

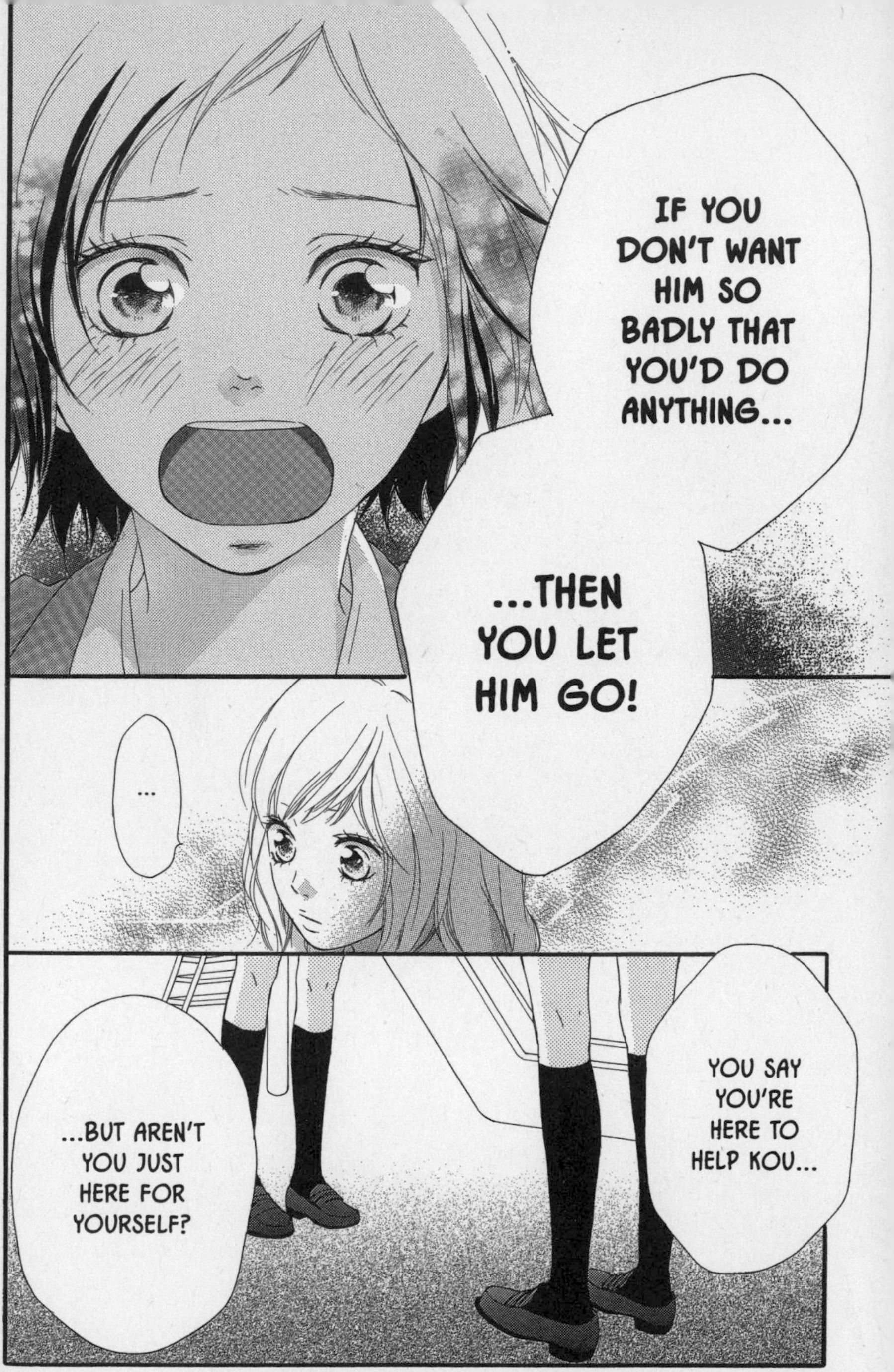
IF YOU DON'T WANT HIM SO BADLY THAT YOU'D DO ANYTHING...
...THEN YOU LET HIM GO!
...
YOU SAY YOU'RE HERE TO HELP KOU...
...BUT AREN'T YOU JUST HERE FOR YOURSELF?

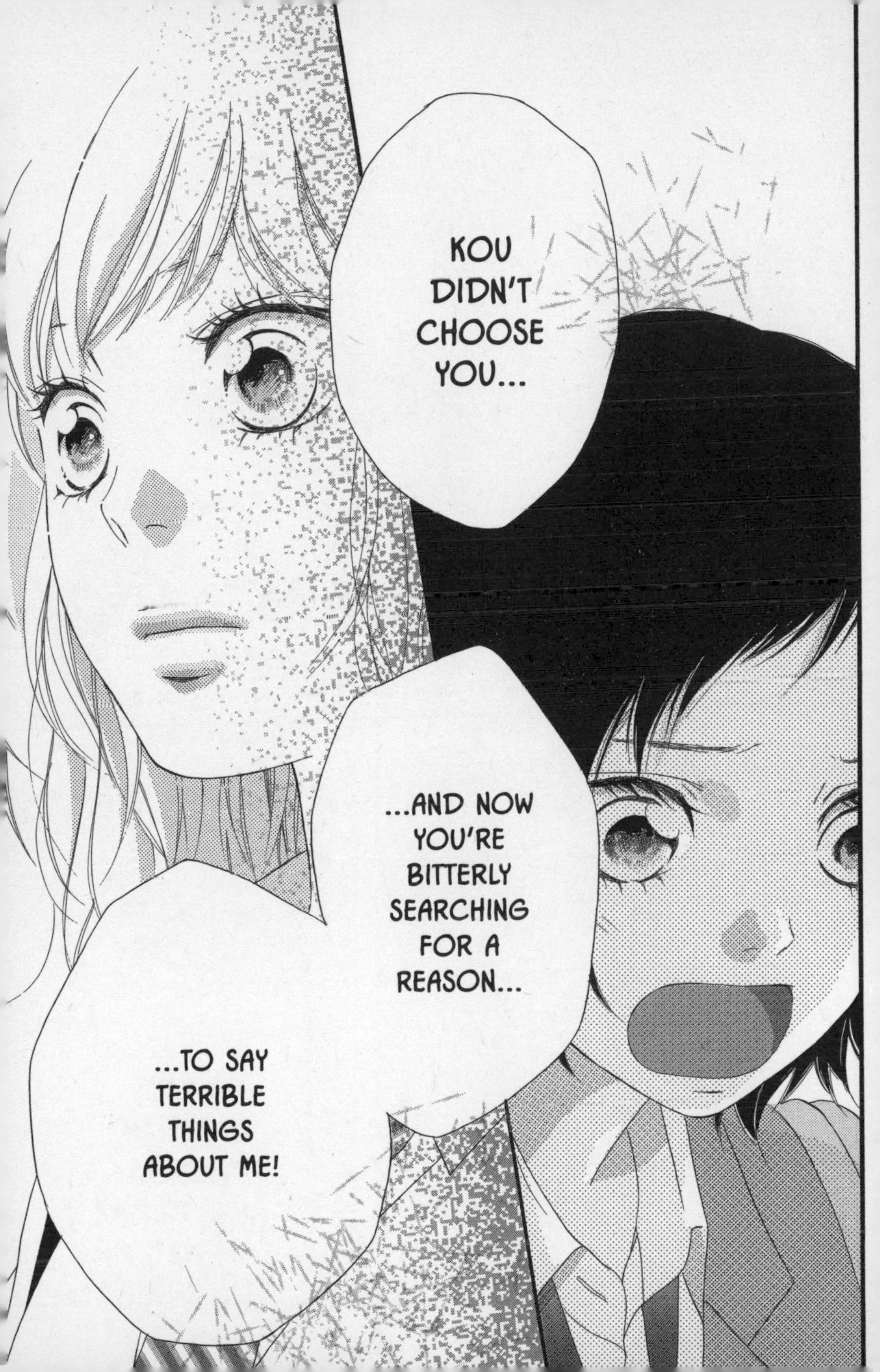
KOU DIDN'T CHOOSE YOU...
...AND NOW YOU'RE BITTERLY SEARCHING FOR A REASON...
...TO SAY TERRIBLE THINGS ABOUT ME!

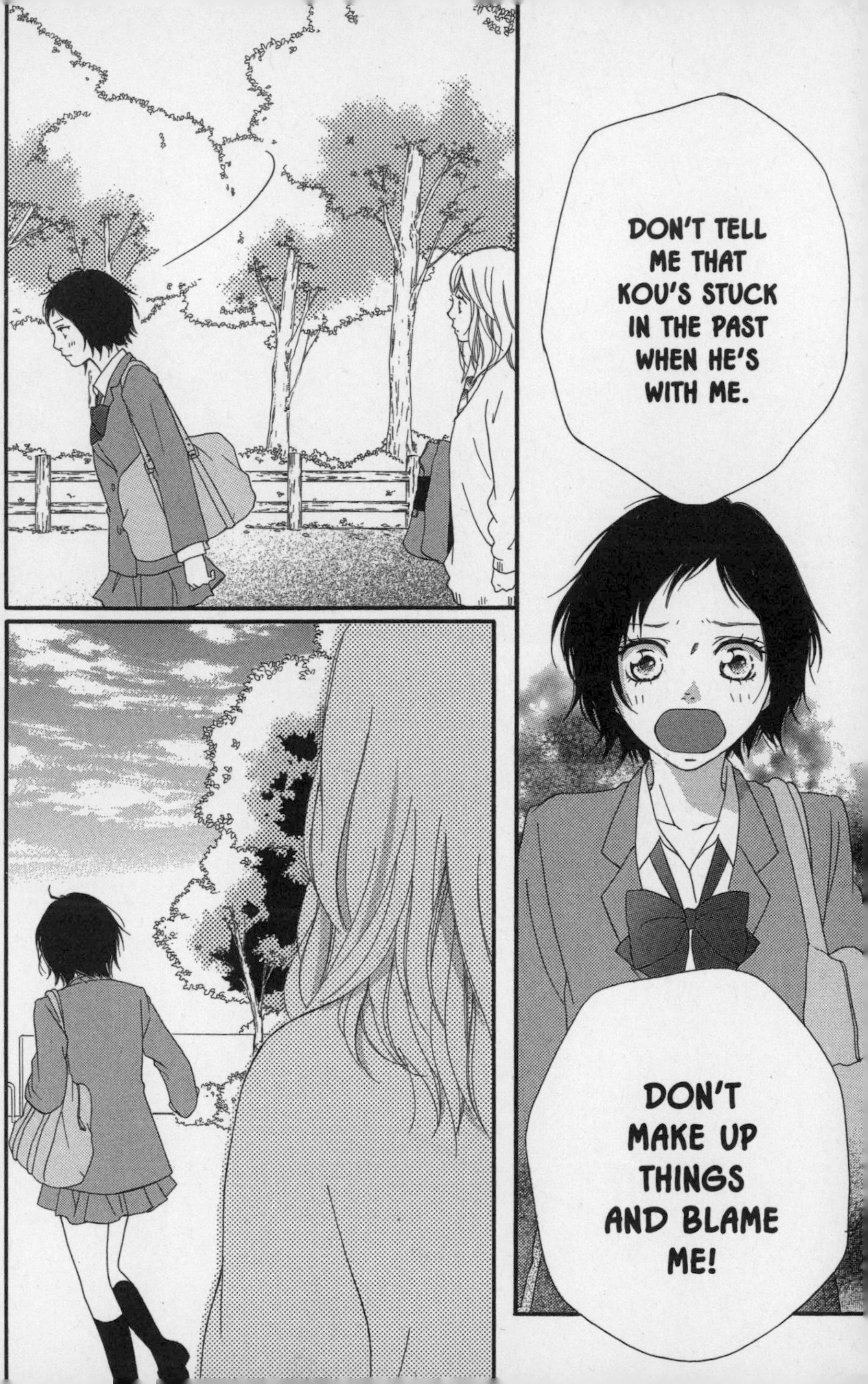
DON'T TELL ME THAT KOU'S STUCK IN THE PAST WHEN HE'S WITH ME.
DON'T MAKE UP THINGS AND BLAME ME!

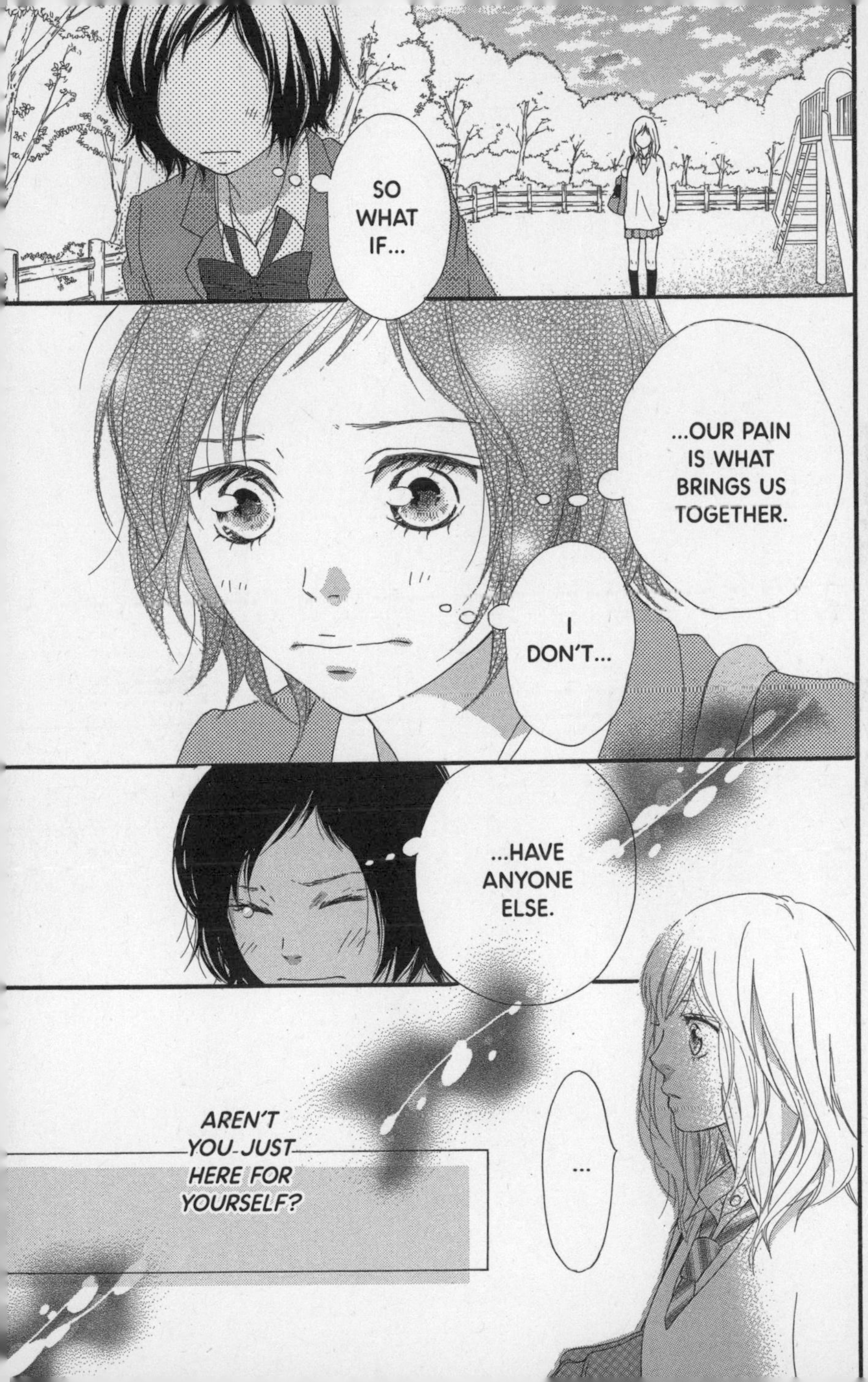
SO WHAT IF...
...OUR PAIN IS WHAT BRINGS US TOGETHER.
I DON'T...
...HAVE ANYONE ELSE.
...
AREN'T YOU JUST HERE FOR YOURSELF?

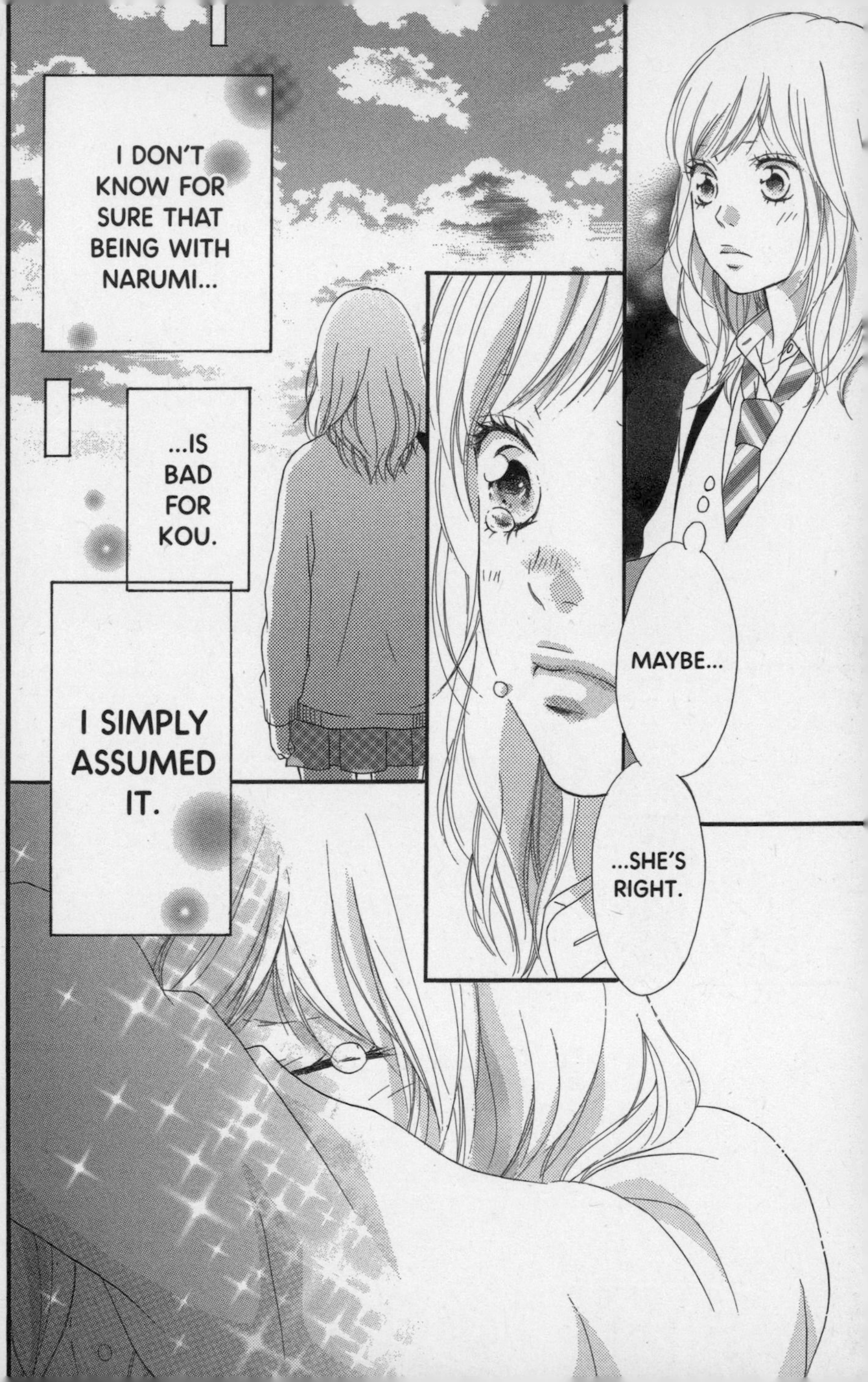
MAYBE...
...SHE'S RIGHT.
I DON'T KNOW FOR SURE THAT BEING WITH NARUMI...
...IS BAD FOR KOU.
I SIMPLY ASSUMED IT.

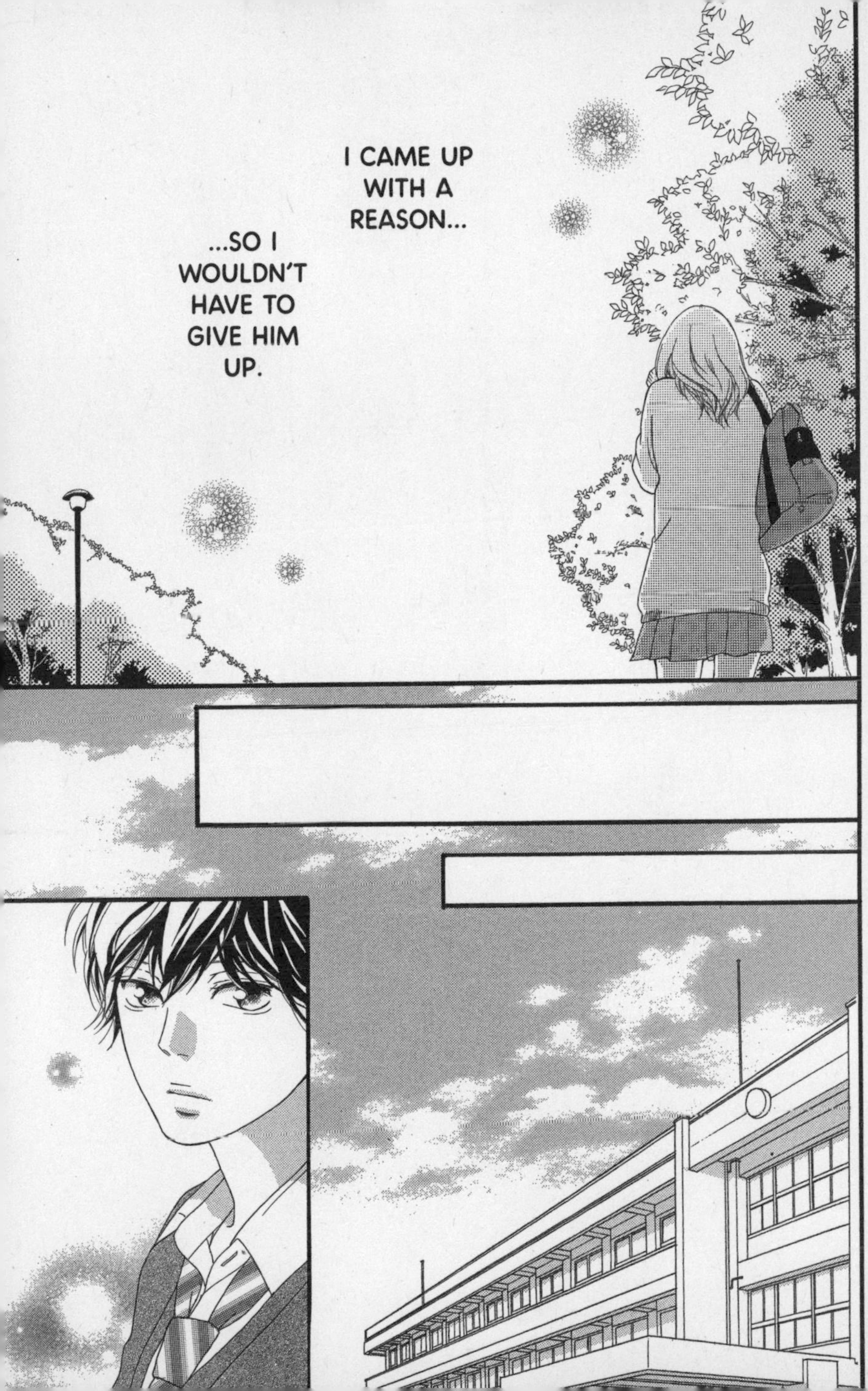
I CAME UP WITH A REASON...
...SO I WOULDN'T HAVE TO GIVE HIM UP.

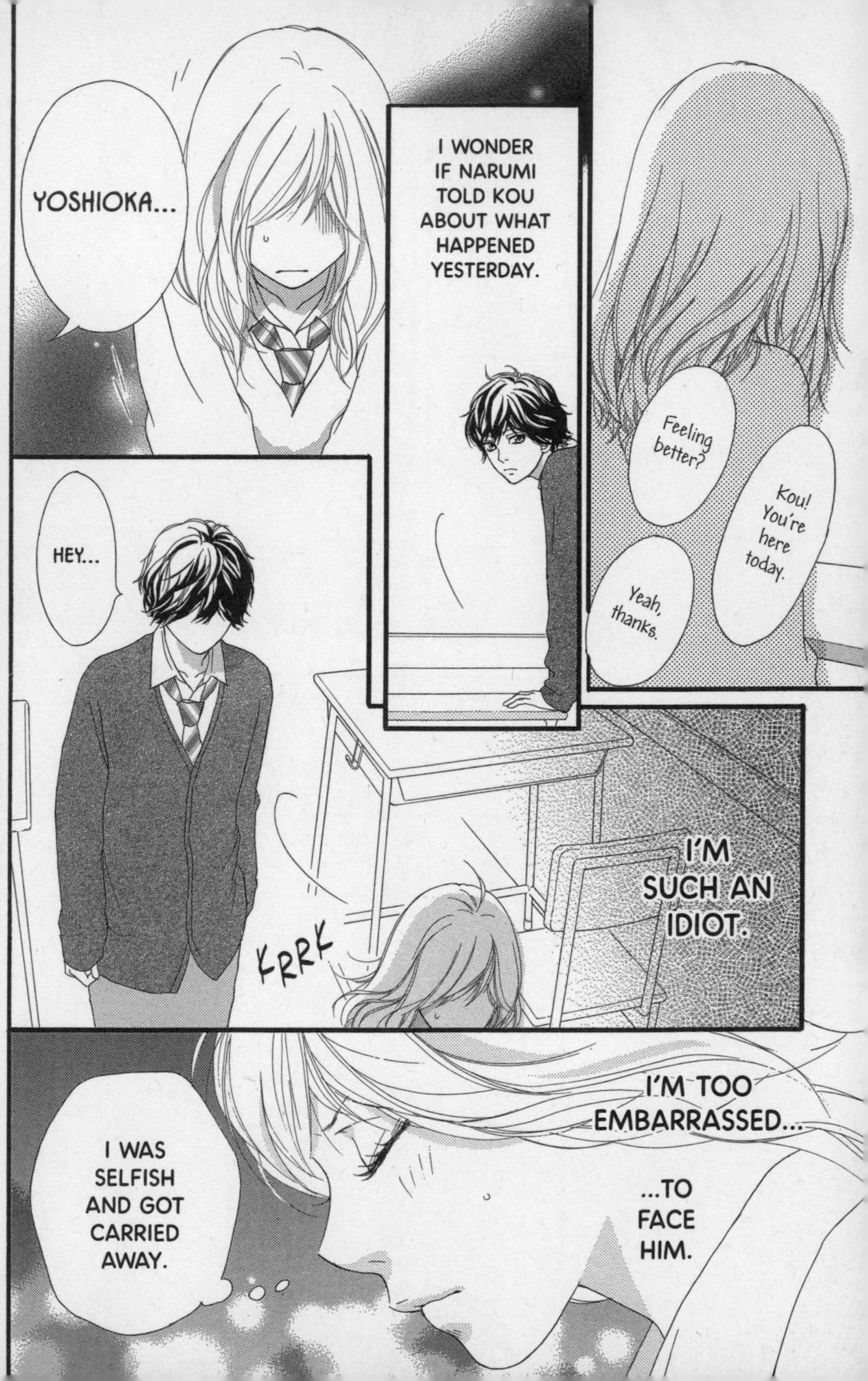
Kou! You're here today.
Feeling better?
Yeah, thanks.
I WONDER IF NARUMI TOLD KOU ABOUT WHAT HAPPENED YESTERDAY.
YOSHIOKA...
HEY...
KRRK
I'M SUCH AN IDIOT.
I'M TOO EMBARRASSED...
...TO FACE HIM.
I WAS SELFISH AND GOT CARRIED AWAY.

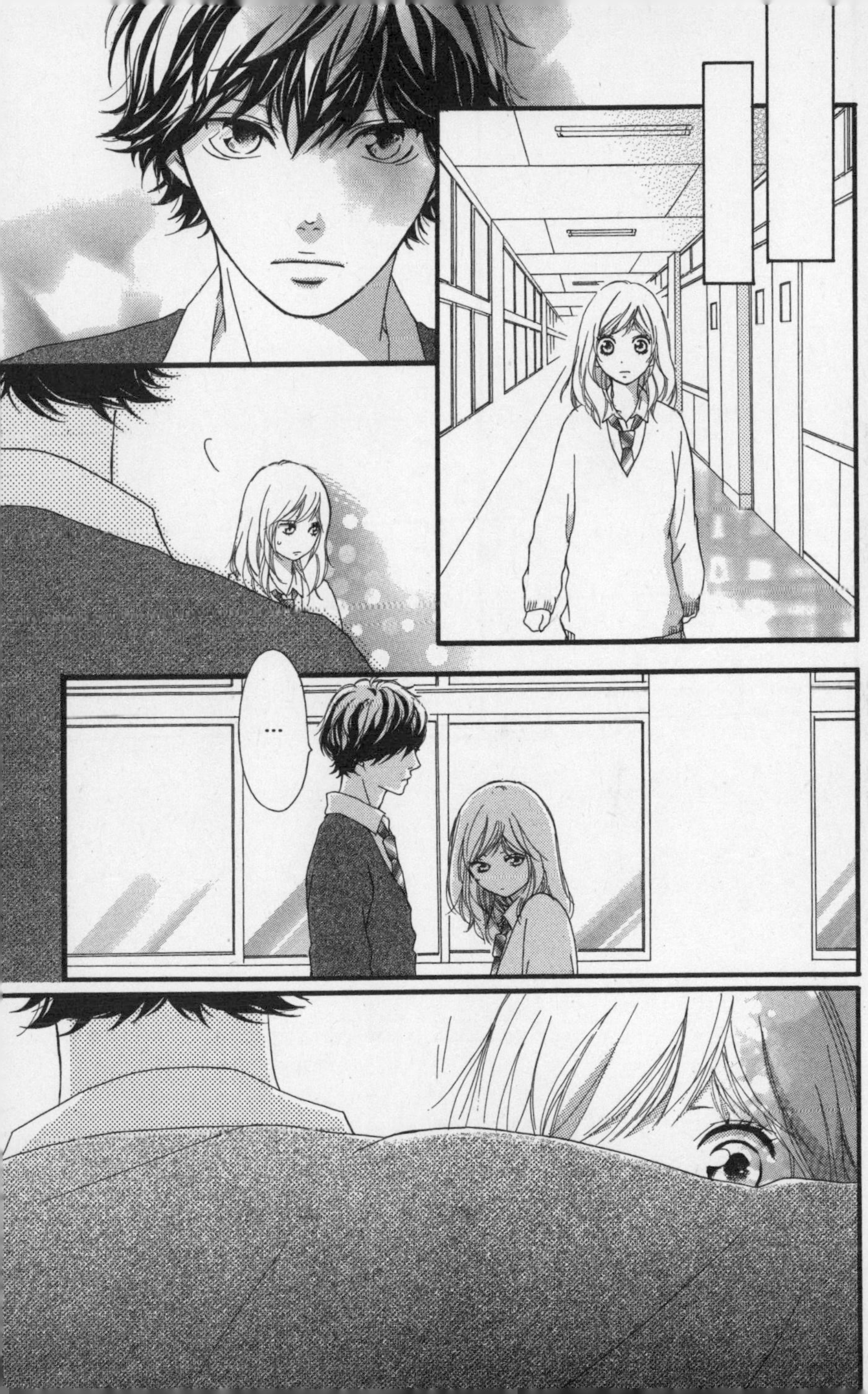
...

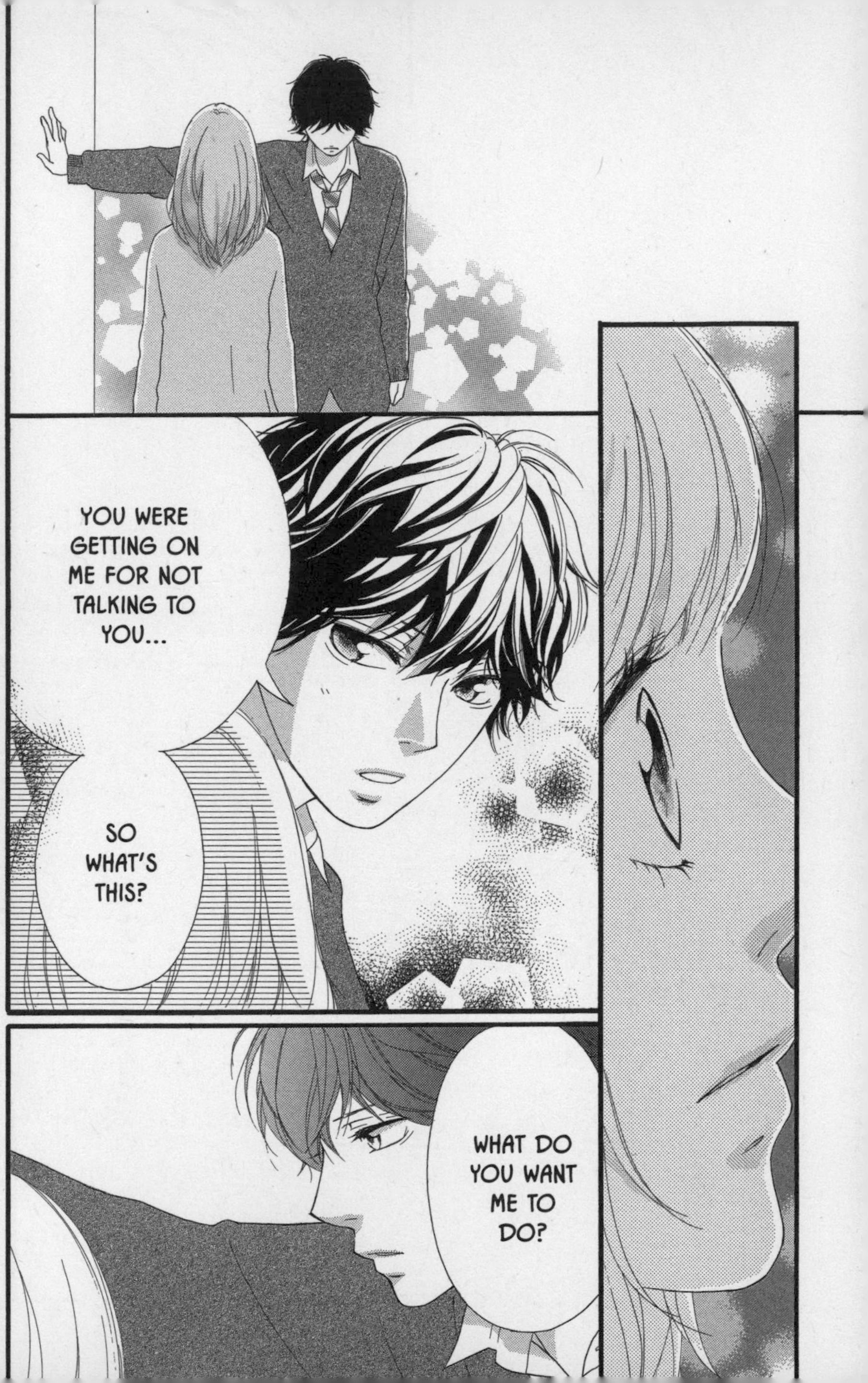
YOU WERE GETTING ON ME FOR NOT TALKING TO YOU...
SO WHAT'S THIS?
WHAT DO YOU WANT ME TO DO?

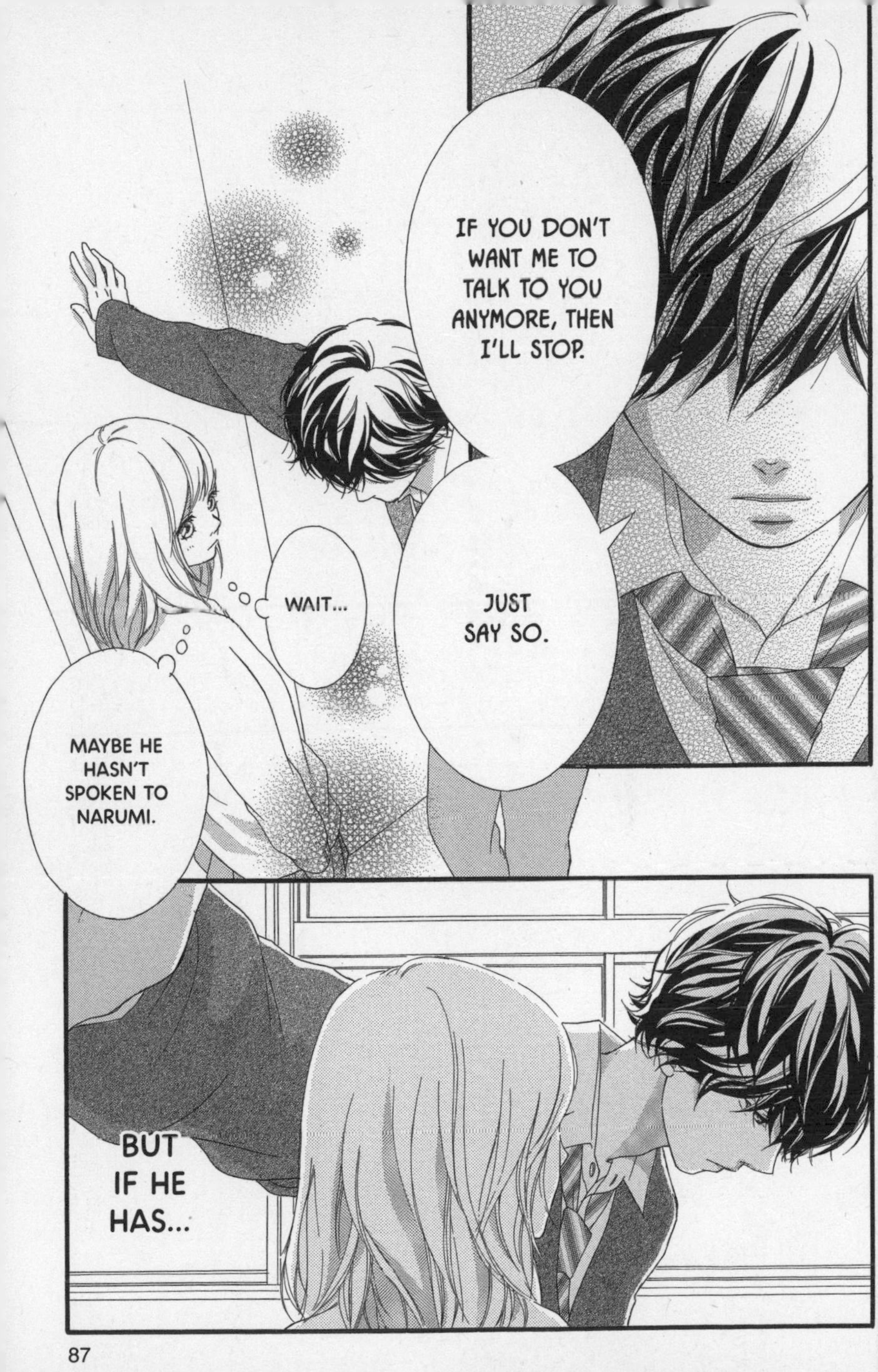
IF YOU DON'T WANT ME TO TALK TO YOU ANYMORE, THEN I'LL STOP.
JUST SAY SO.
WAIT...
MAYBE HE HASN'T SPOKEN TO NARUMI.
BUT IF HE HAS...

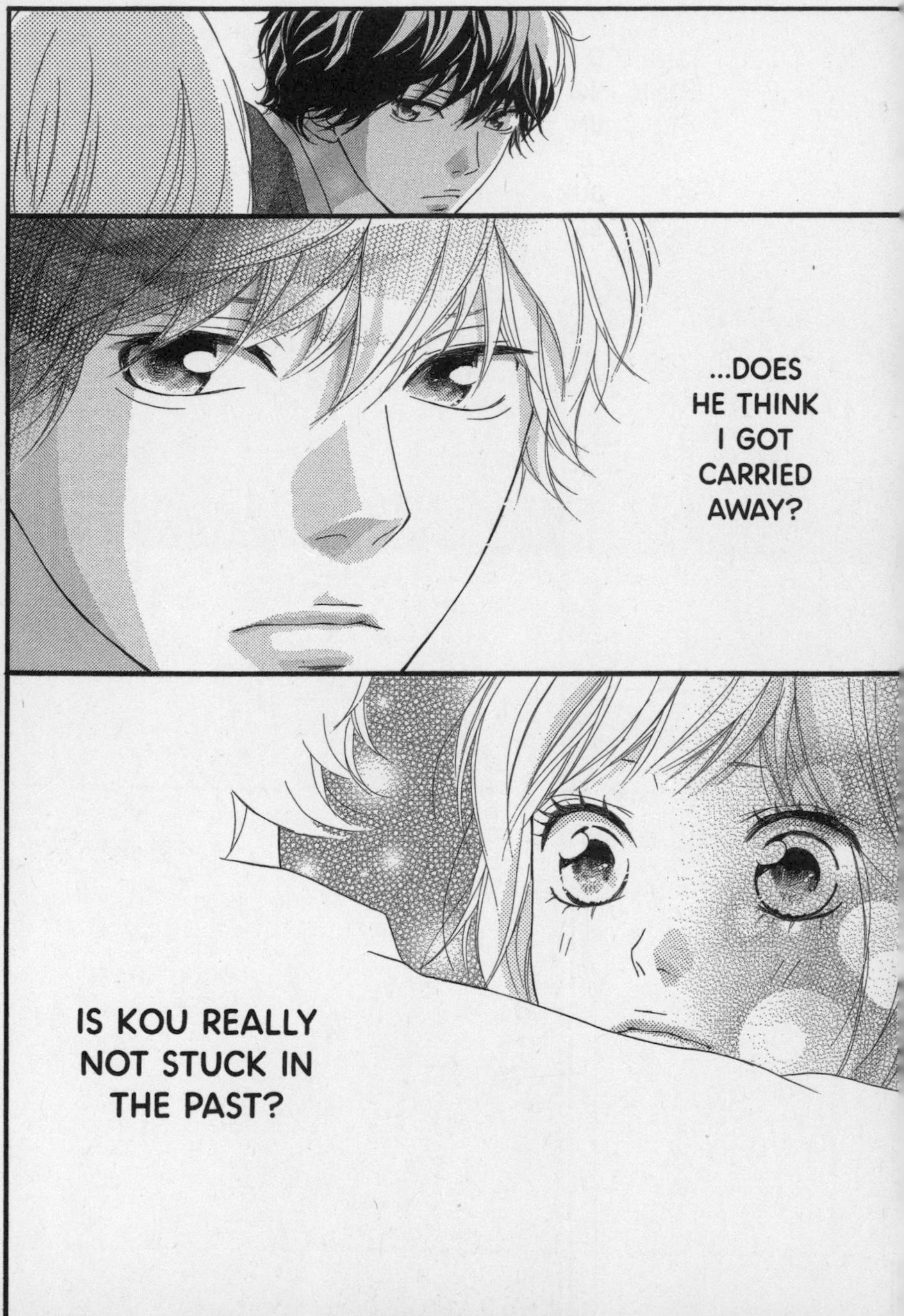
...DOES HE THINK I GOT CARRIED AWAY?
IS KOU REALLY NOT STUCK IN THE PAST?

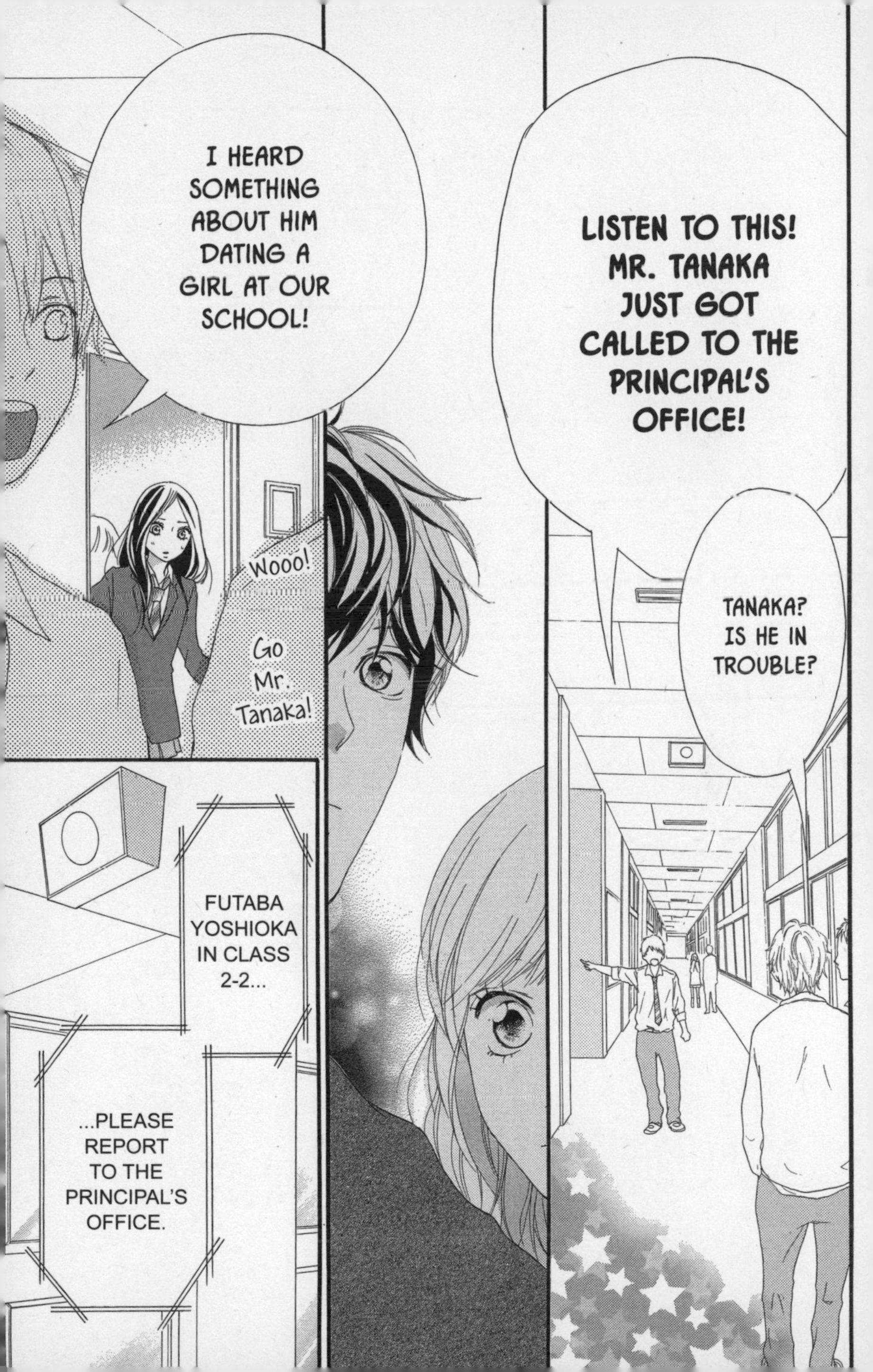
LISTEN TO THIS! MR. TANAKA JUST GOT CALLED TO THE PRINCIPAL'S OFFICE!
TANAKA? IS HE IN TROUBLE?
I HEARD SOMETHING ABOUT HIM DATING A GIRL AT OUR SCHOOL!
Wooo!
Go Mr. Tanaka!
FUTABA YOSHIOKA IN CLASS 2-2...
...PLEASE REPORT TO THE PRINCIPAL'S OFFICE.

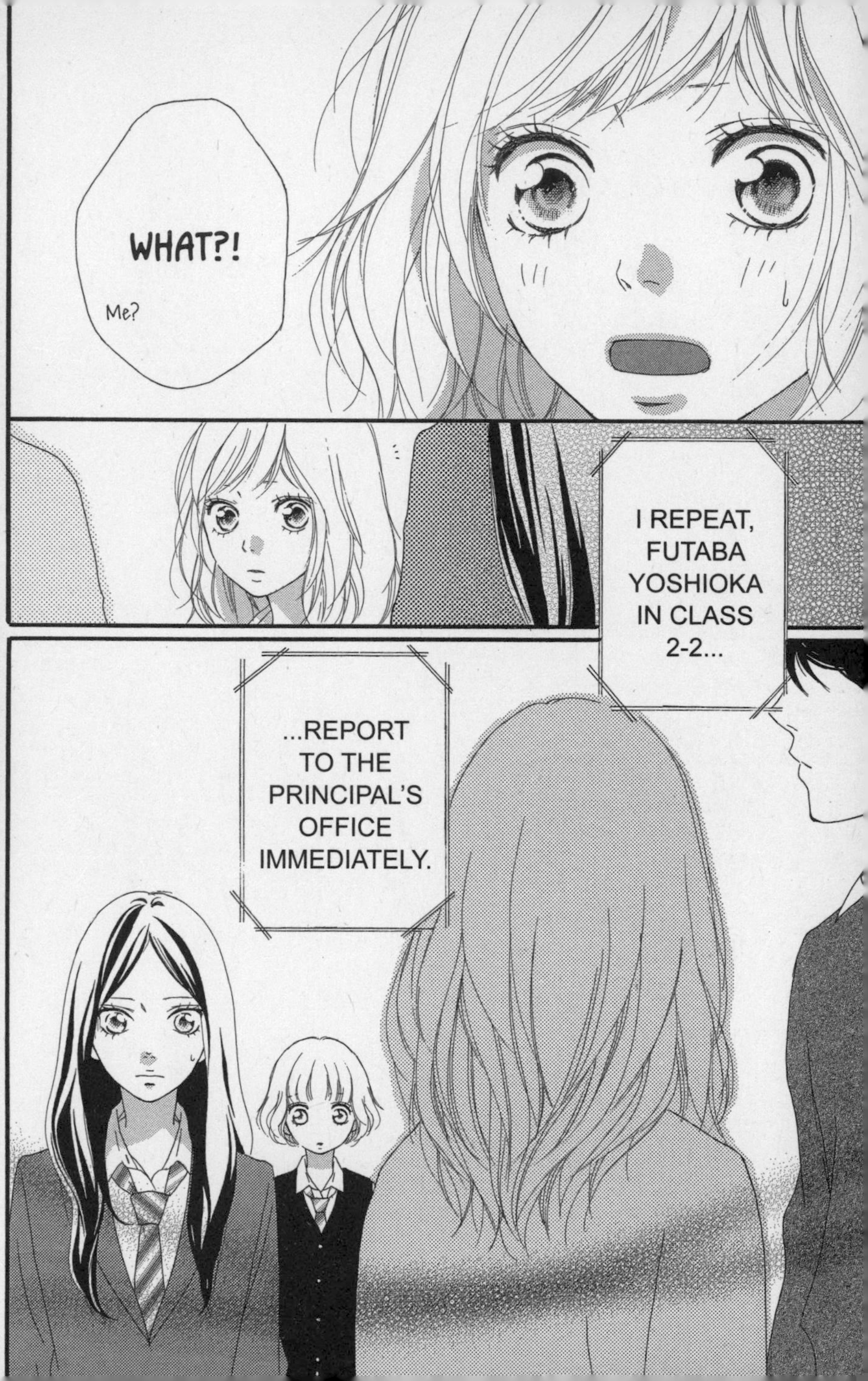
WHAT?!
Me?
I REPEAT, FUTABA YOSHIOKA IN CLASS 2-2...
...REPORT TO THE PRINCIPAL'S OFFICE IMMEDIATELY.

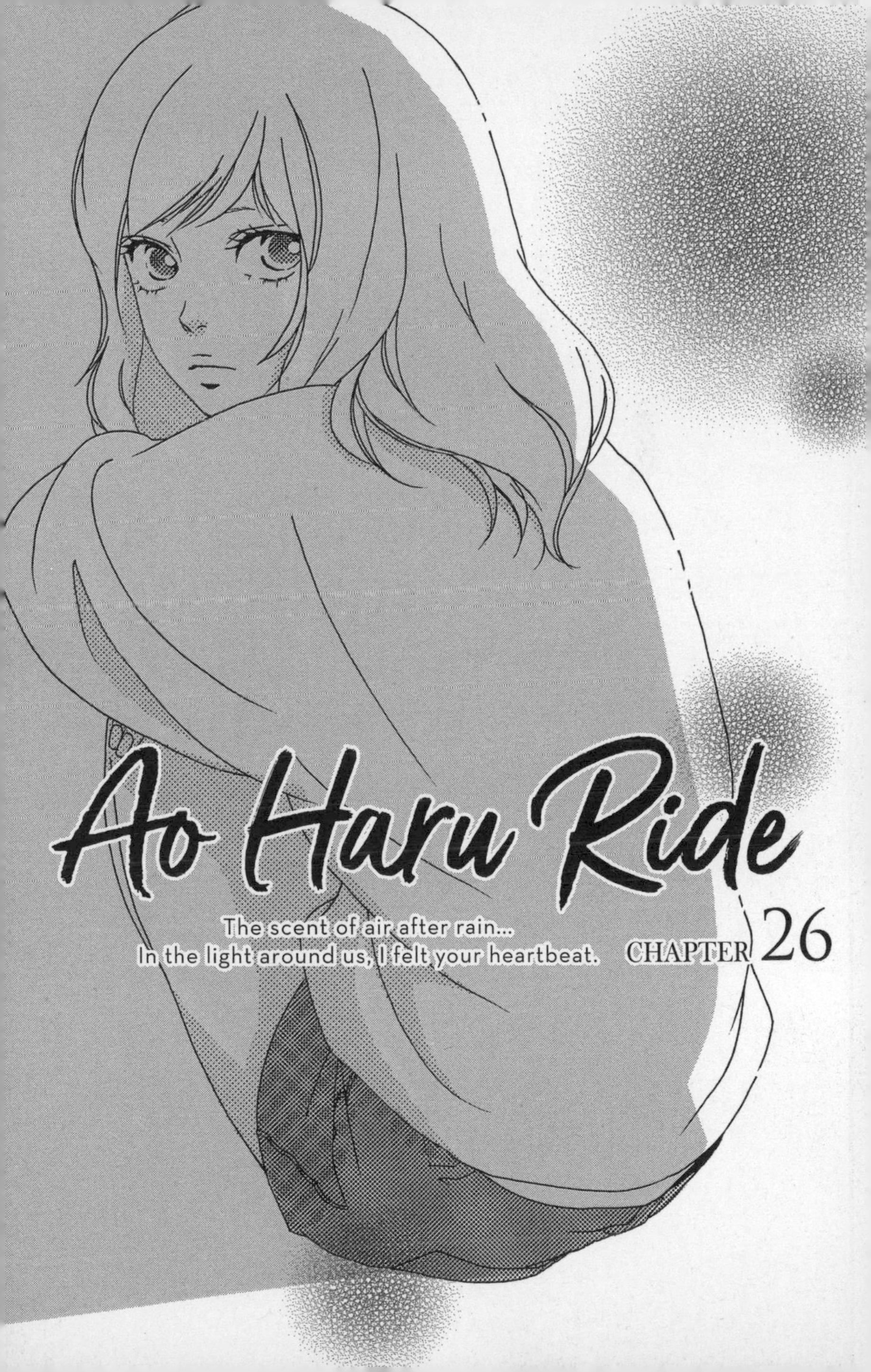
Ao Haru Ride
The scent of air after rain...
In the light around us, I felt your heartbeat.
CHAPTER 26

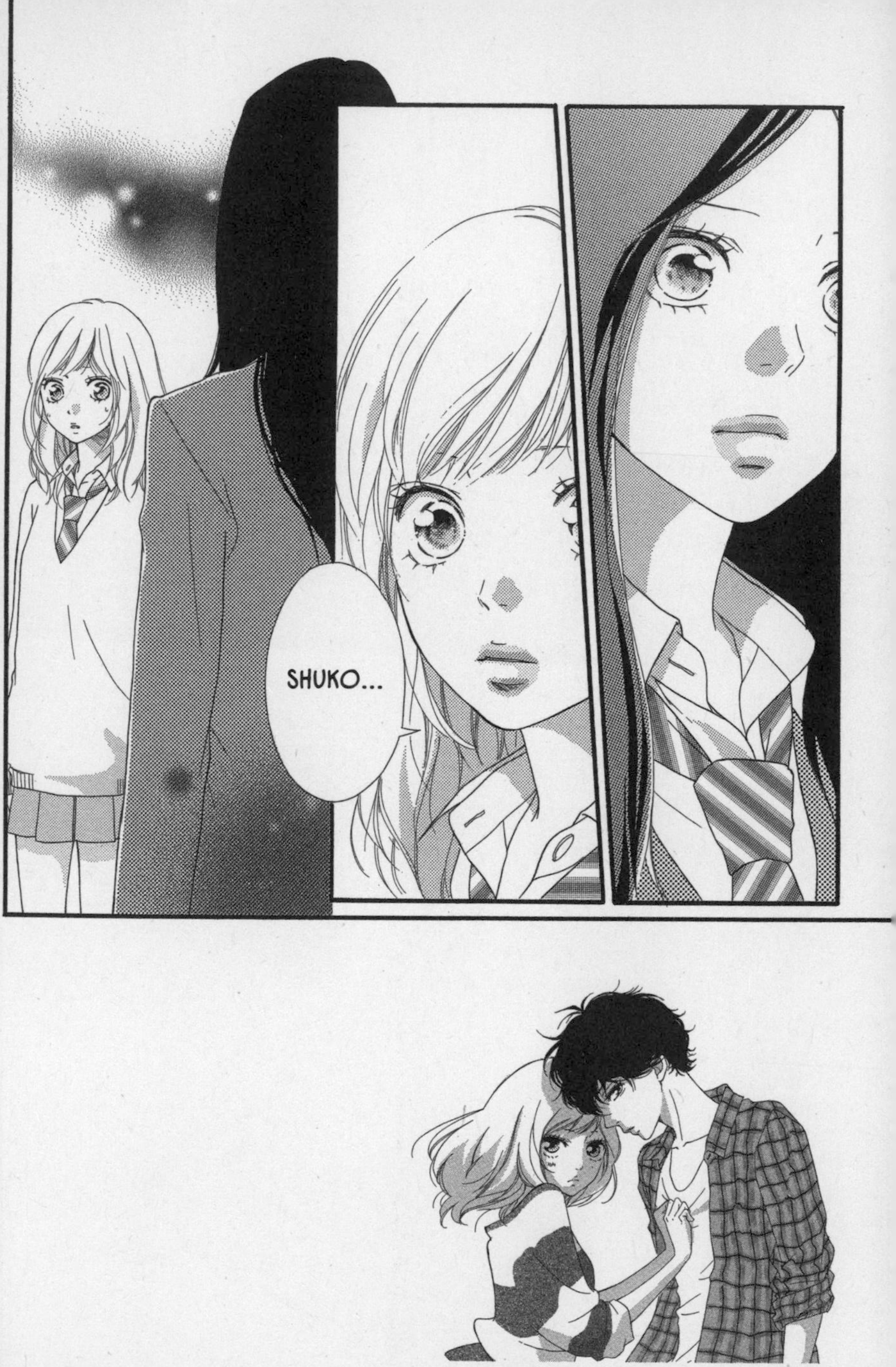
SHUKO...

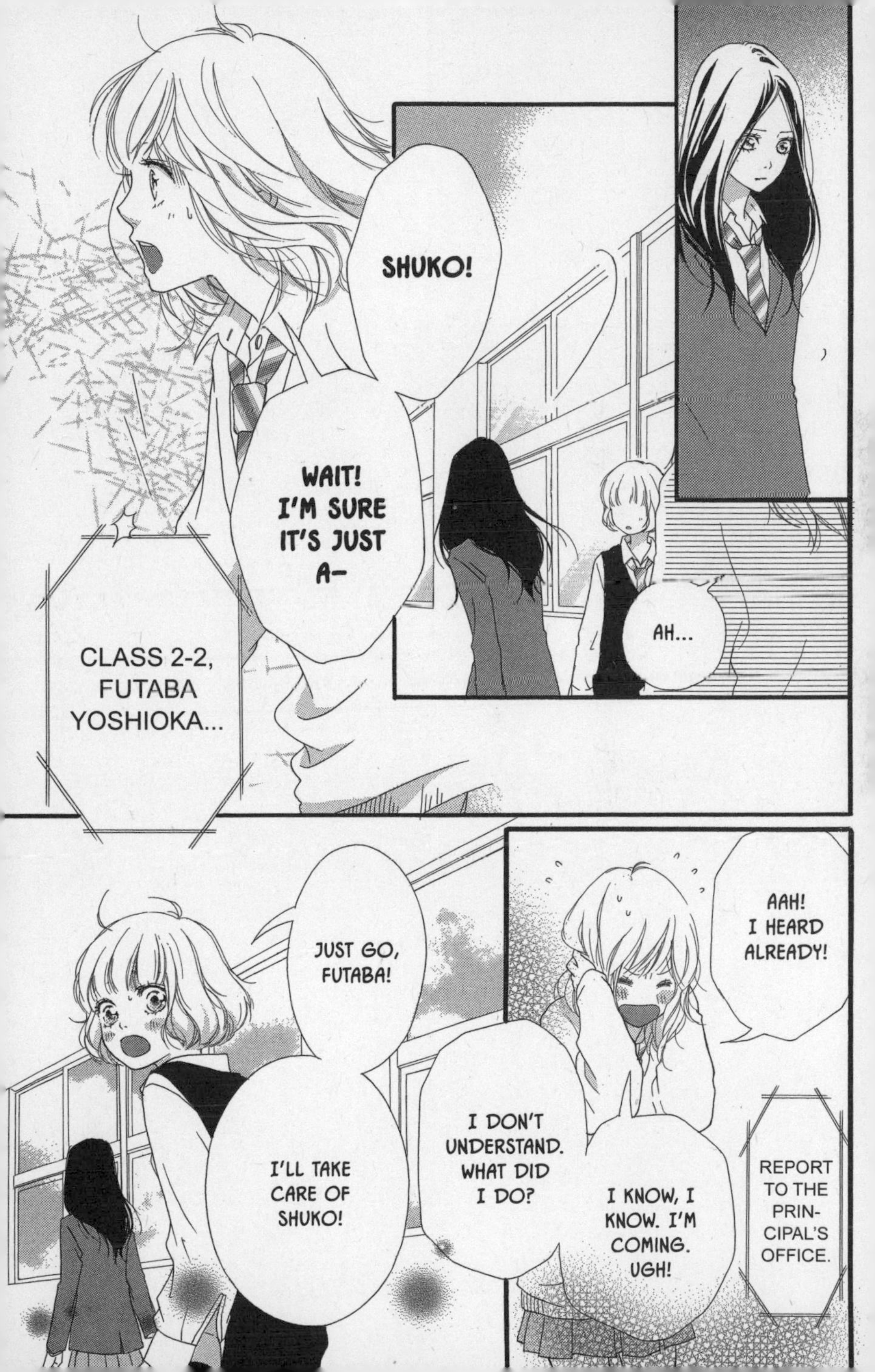
AH...
SHUKO!
WAIT! I'M SURE IT'S JUST A–
CLASS 2-2, FUTABA YOSHIOKA...
AAH! I HEARD ALREADY!
REPORT TO THE PRIN-CIPAL'S OFFICE.
I KNOW, I KNOW. I'M COMING. UGH!
I DON'T UNDERSTAND. WHAT DID I DO?
JUST GO, FUTABA!
I'LL TAKE CARE OF SHUKO!

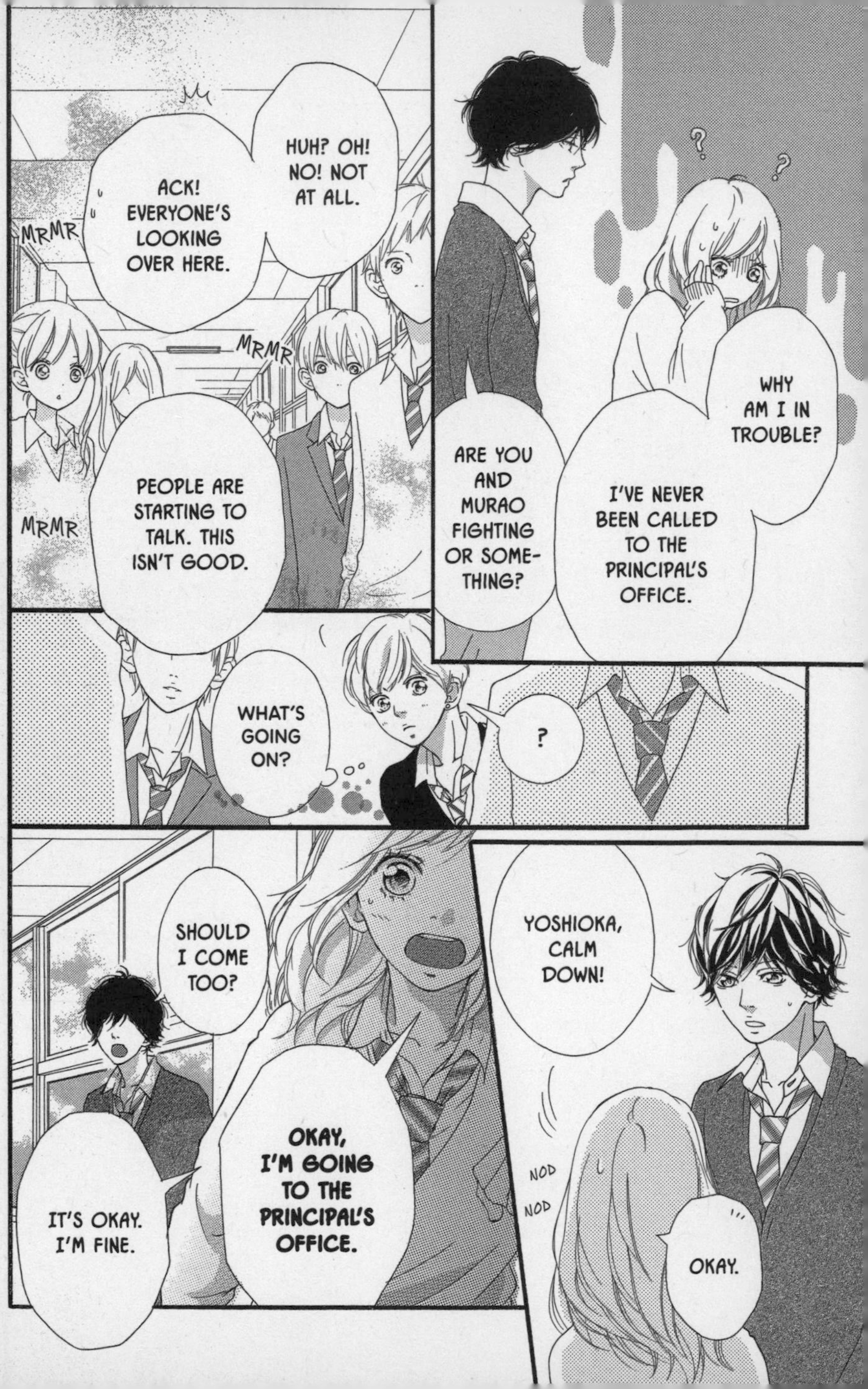
WHY AM I IN TROUBLE?
I'VE NEVER BEEN CALLED TO THE PRINCIPAL'S OFFICE.
ARE YOU AND MURAO FIGHTING OR SOME-THING?
HUH? OH! NO! NOT AT ALL.
ACK! EVERYONE'S LOOKING OVER HERE.
MRMR
MRMR
PEOPLE ARE STARTING TO TALK. THIS ISN'T GOOD.
MRMR
?
WHAT'S GOING ON?
YOSHIOKA, CALM DOWN!
NOD NOD
OKAY.
SHOULD I COME TOO?
OKAY, I'M GOING TO THE PRINCIPAL'S OFFICE.
IT'S OKAY. I'M FINE.

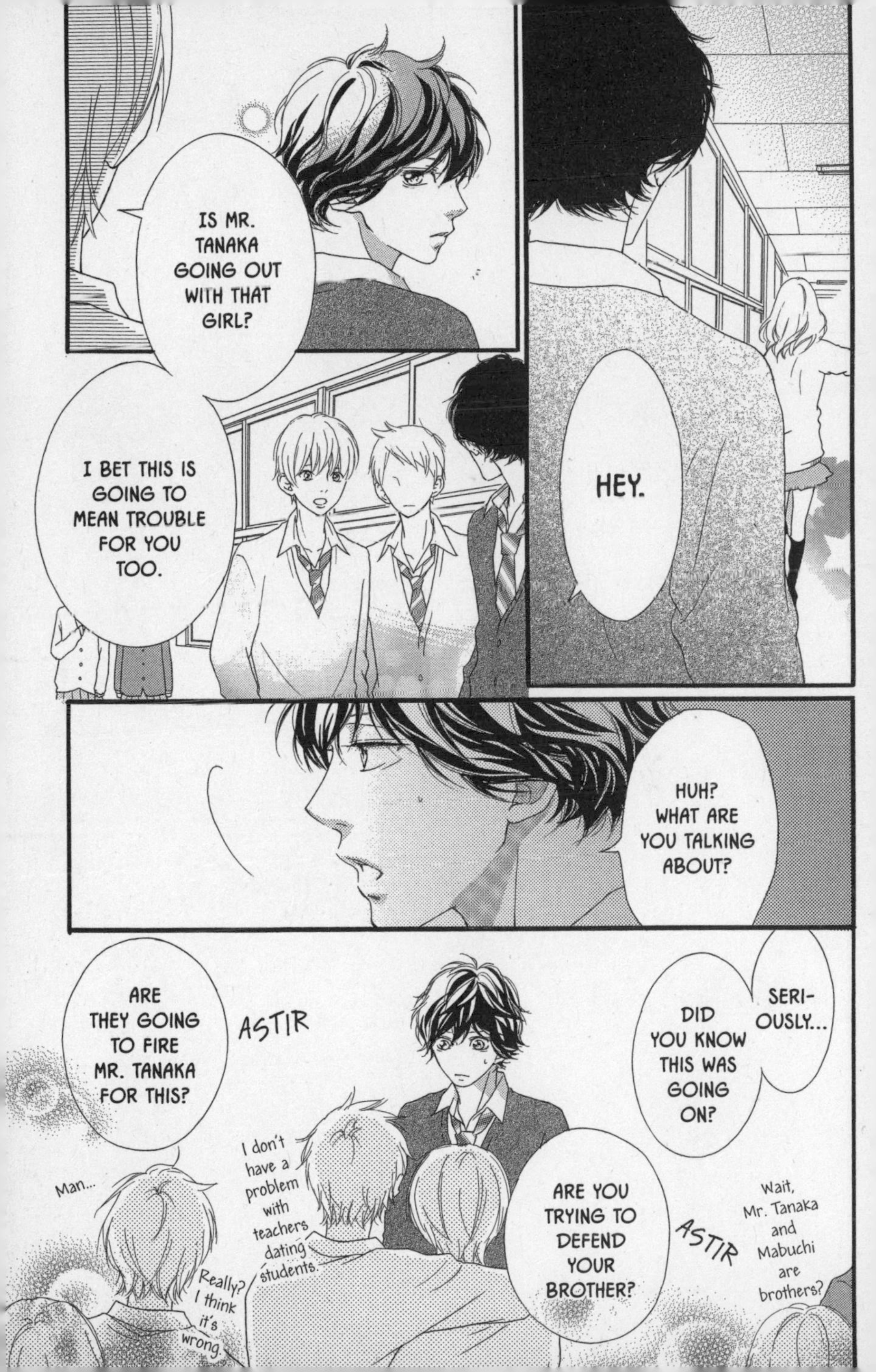
HEY.
IS MR. TANAKA GOING OUT WITH THAT GIRL?
I BET THIS IS GOING TO MEAN TROUBLE FOR YOU TOO.
HUH? WHAT ARE YOU TALKING ABOUT?
SERI-OUSLY...
DID YOU KNOW THIS WAS GOING ON?
ARE THEY GOING TO FIRE MR. TANAKA FOR THIS?
ASTIR
Wait, Mr. Tanaka and Mabuchi are brothers?
ASTIR
ARE YOU TRYING TO DEFEND YOUR BROTHER?
I don't have a problem with teachers dating students.
Man...
Really? I think it's wrong.

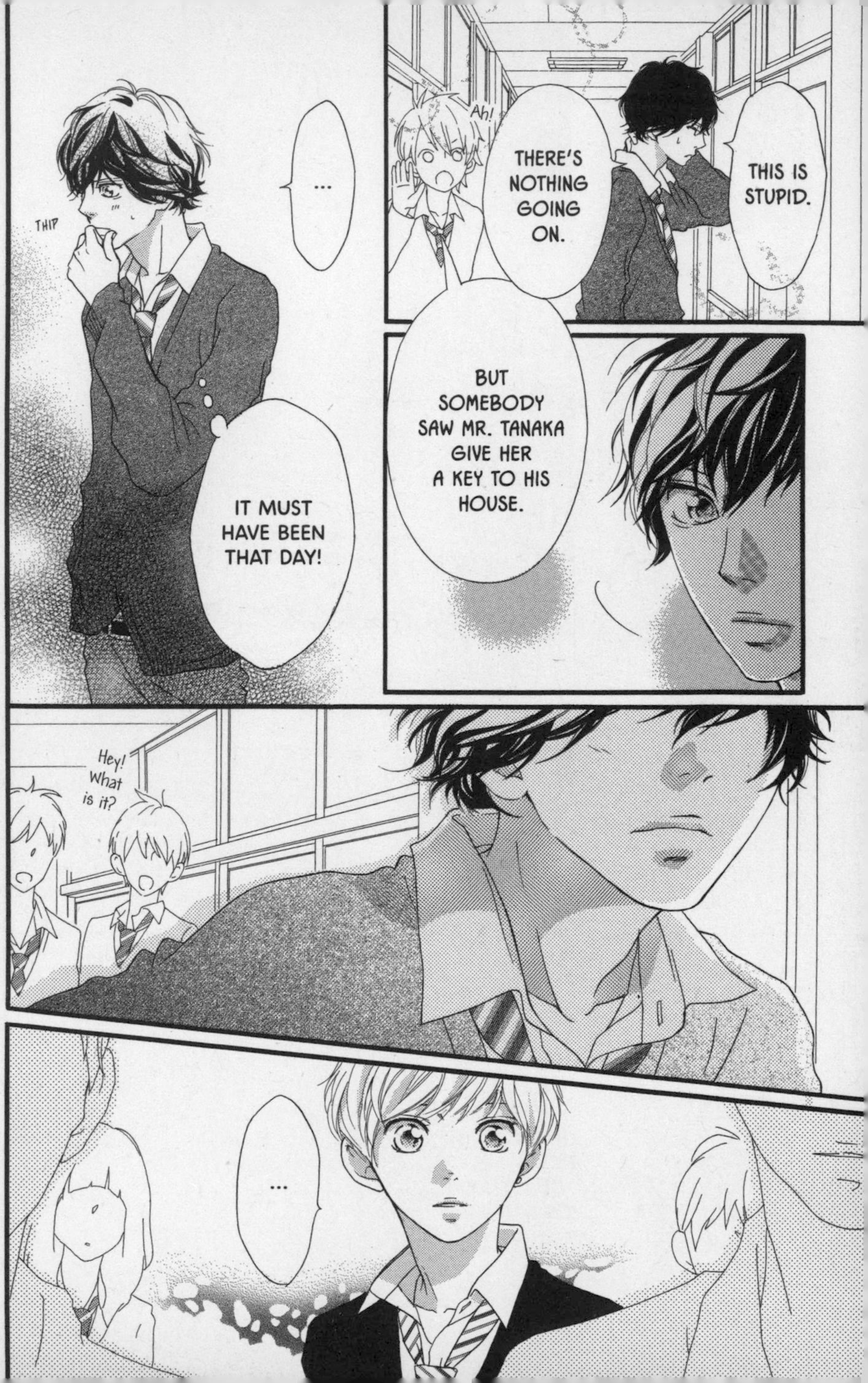
THIS IS STUPID.
Ah!
THERE'S NOTHING GOING ON.
BUT SOMEBODY SAW MR. TANAKA GIVE HER A KEY TO HIS HOUSE.
...
THIP
IT MUST HAVE BEEN THAT DAY!
Hey! What is it?
...

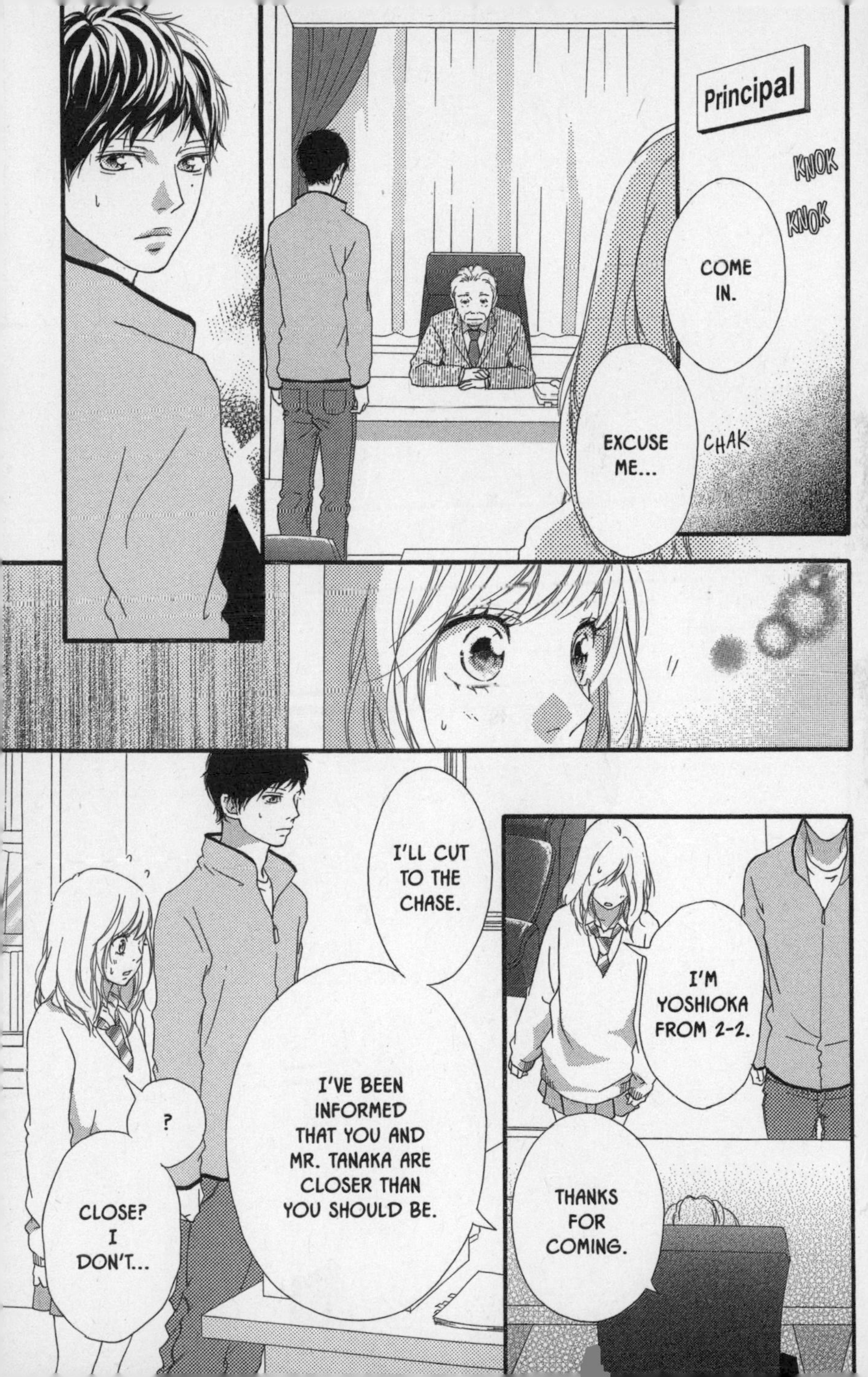
Principal
KNOK KNOK
COME IN.
CHAK
EXCUSE ME...
I'M YOSHIOKA FROM 2-2.
THANKS FOR COMING.
I'LL CUT TO THE CHASE.
I'VE BEEN INFORMED THAT YOU AND MR. TANAKA ARE CLOSER THAN YOU SHOULD BE.
?
CLOSE? I DON'T...

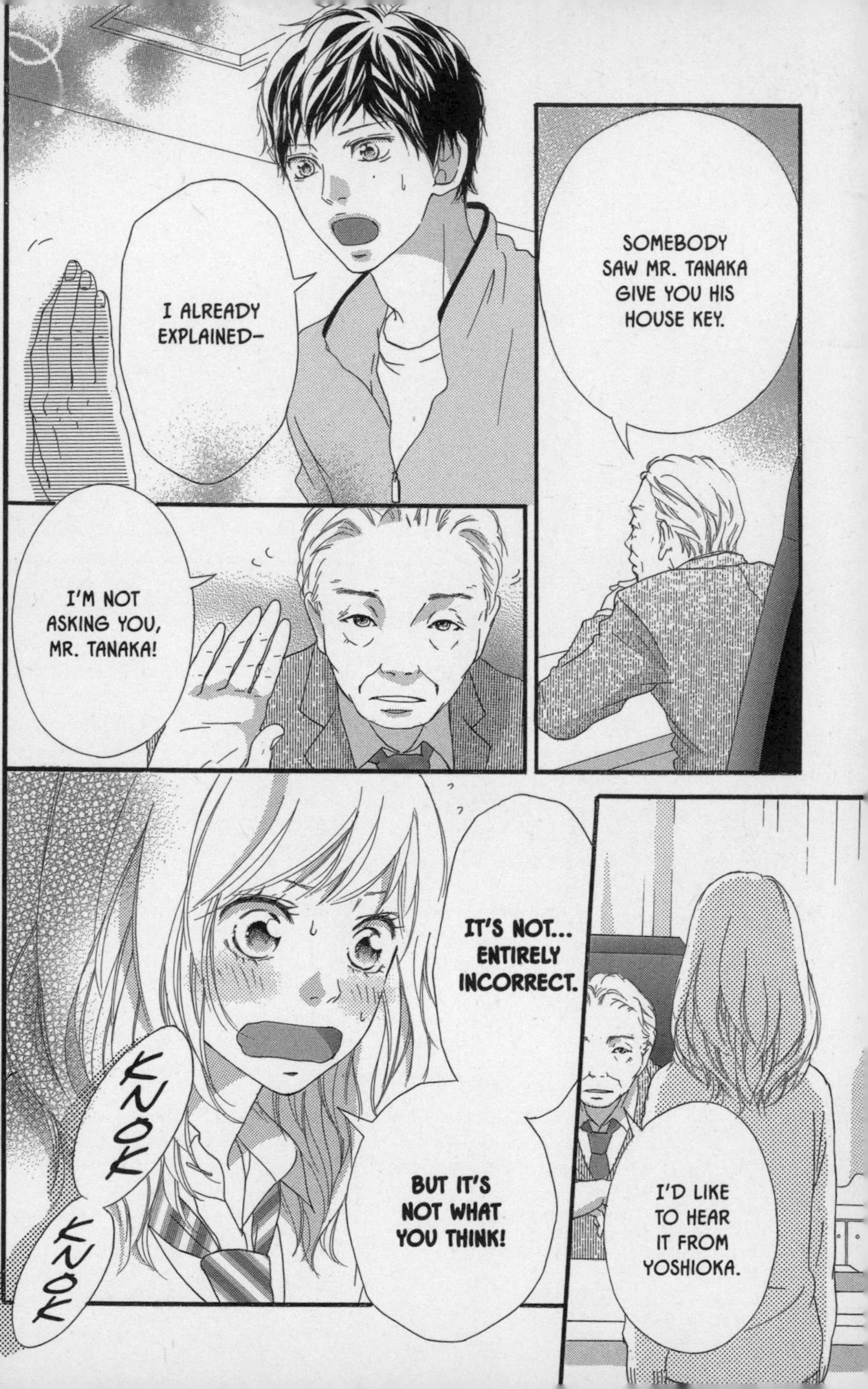
SOMEBODY SAW MR. TANAKA GIVE YOU HIS HOUSE KEY.
I ALREADY EXPLAINED—
I'M NOT ASKING YOU, MR. TANAKA!
I'D LIKE TO HEAR IT FROM YOSHIOKA.
IT'S NOT... ENTIRELY INCORRECT.
BUT IT'S NOT WHAT YOU THINK!
KNOK
KNOK

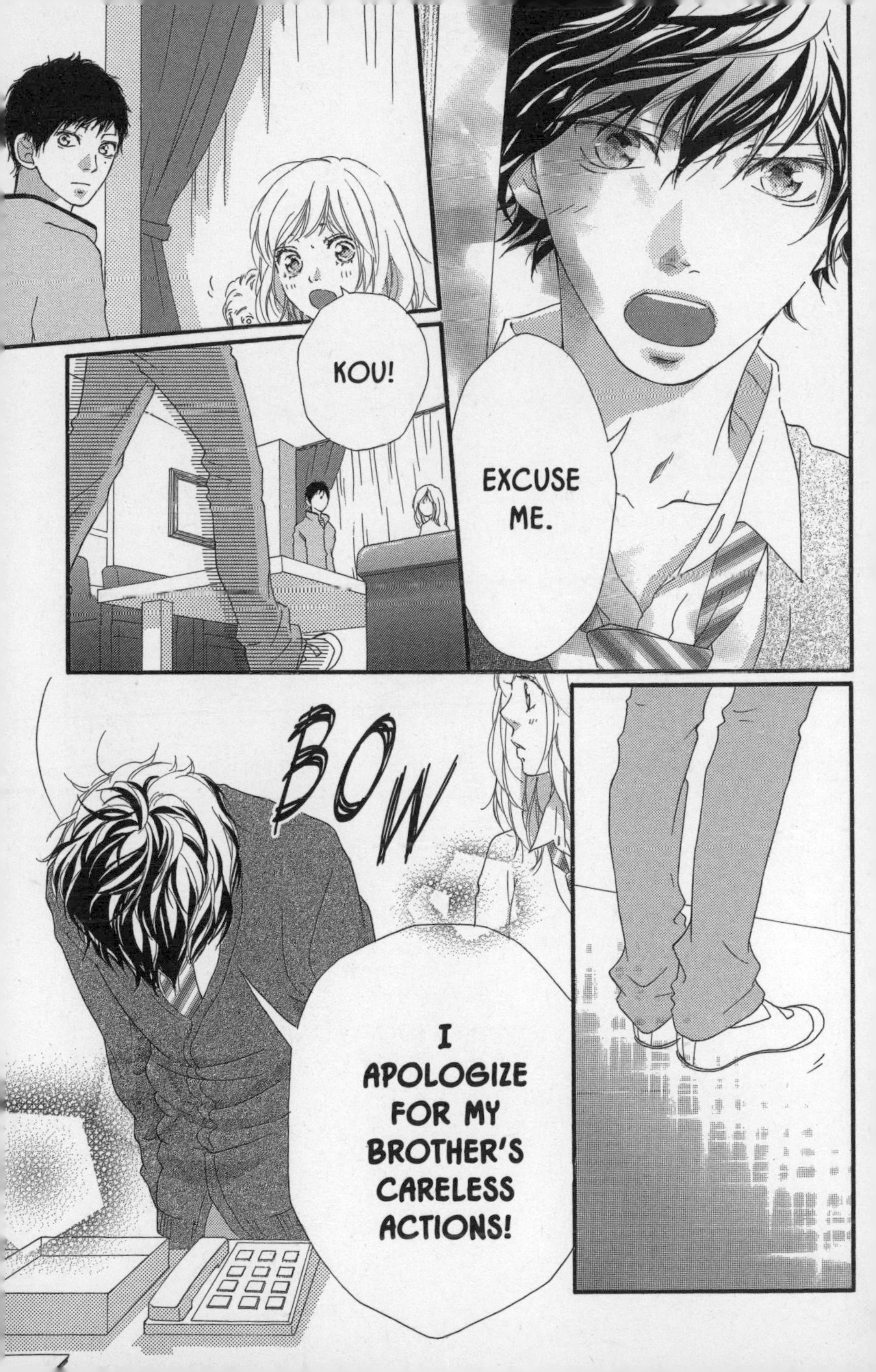
EXCUSE ME.
KOU!
BOW
I APOLOGIZE FOR MY BROTHER'S CARELESS ACTIONS!

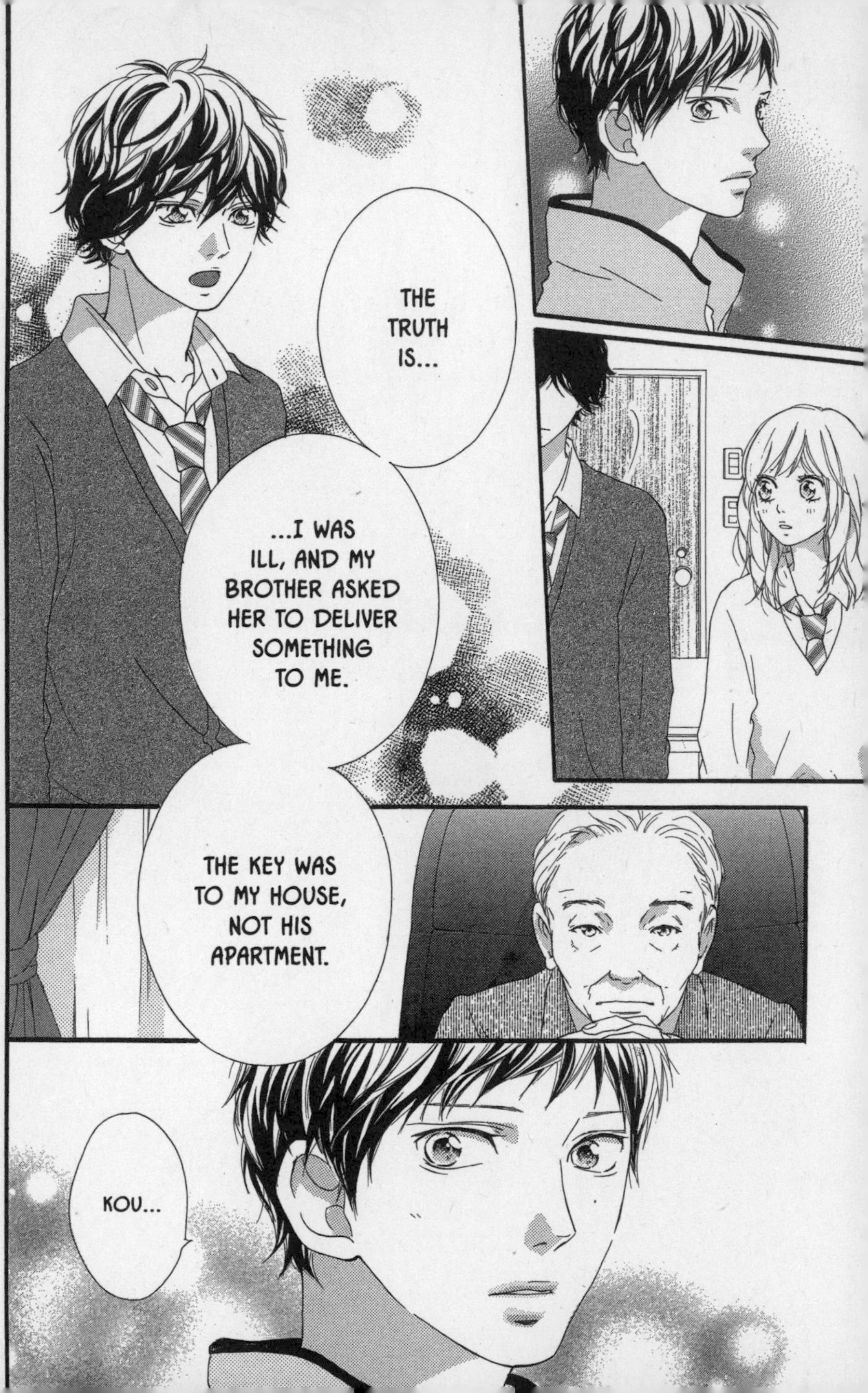
THE TRUTH IS...
...I WAS ILL, AND MY BROTHER ASKED HER TO DELIVER SOMETHING TO ME.
THE KEY WAS TO MY HOUSE, NOT HIS APARTMENT.
KOU...

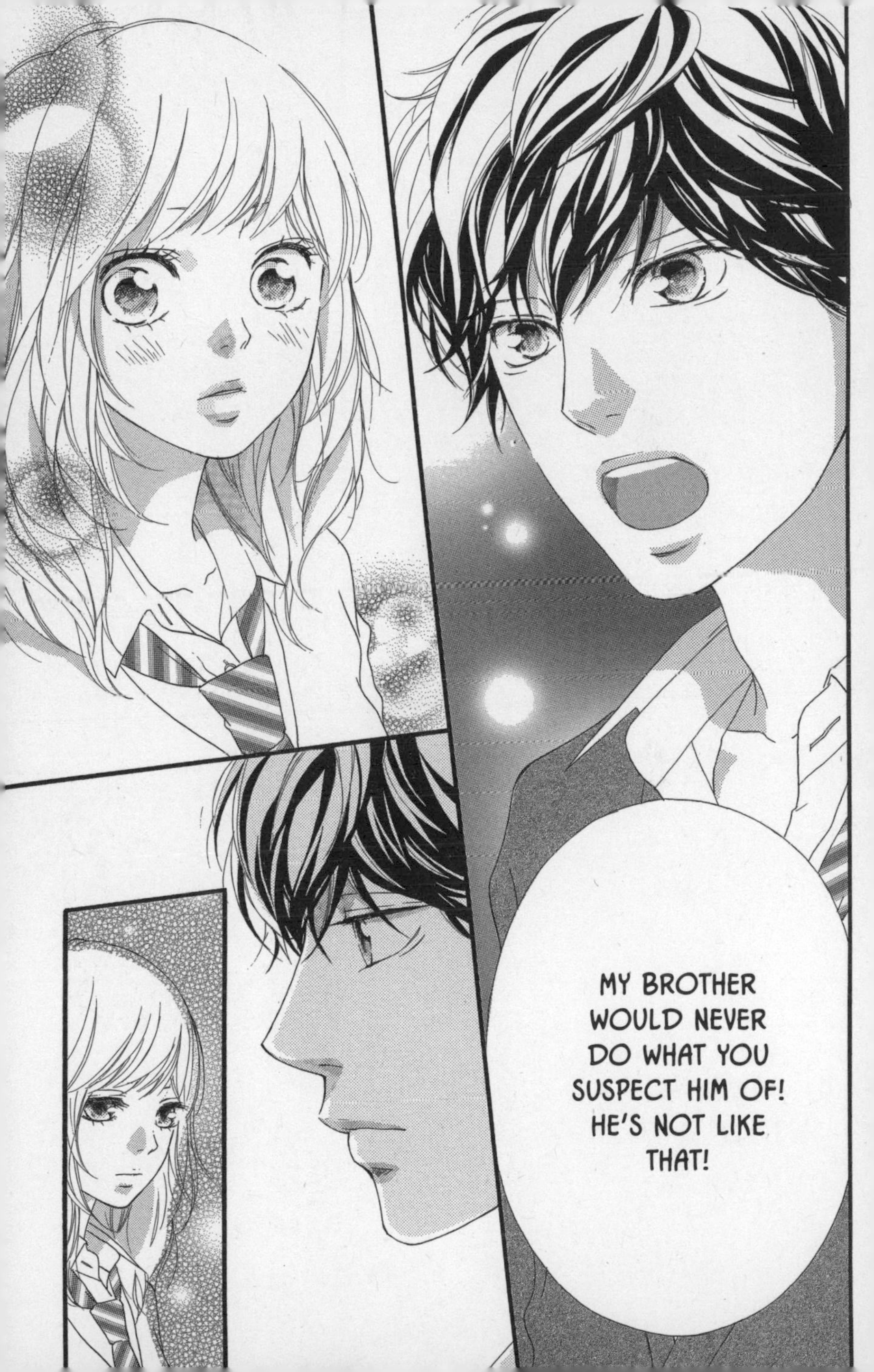
MY BROTHER WOULD NEVER DO WHAT YOU SUSPECT HIM OF! HE'S NOT LIKE THAT!

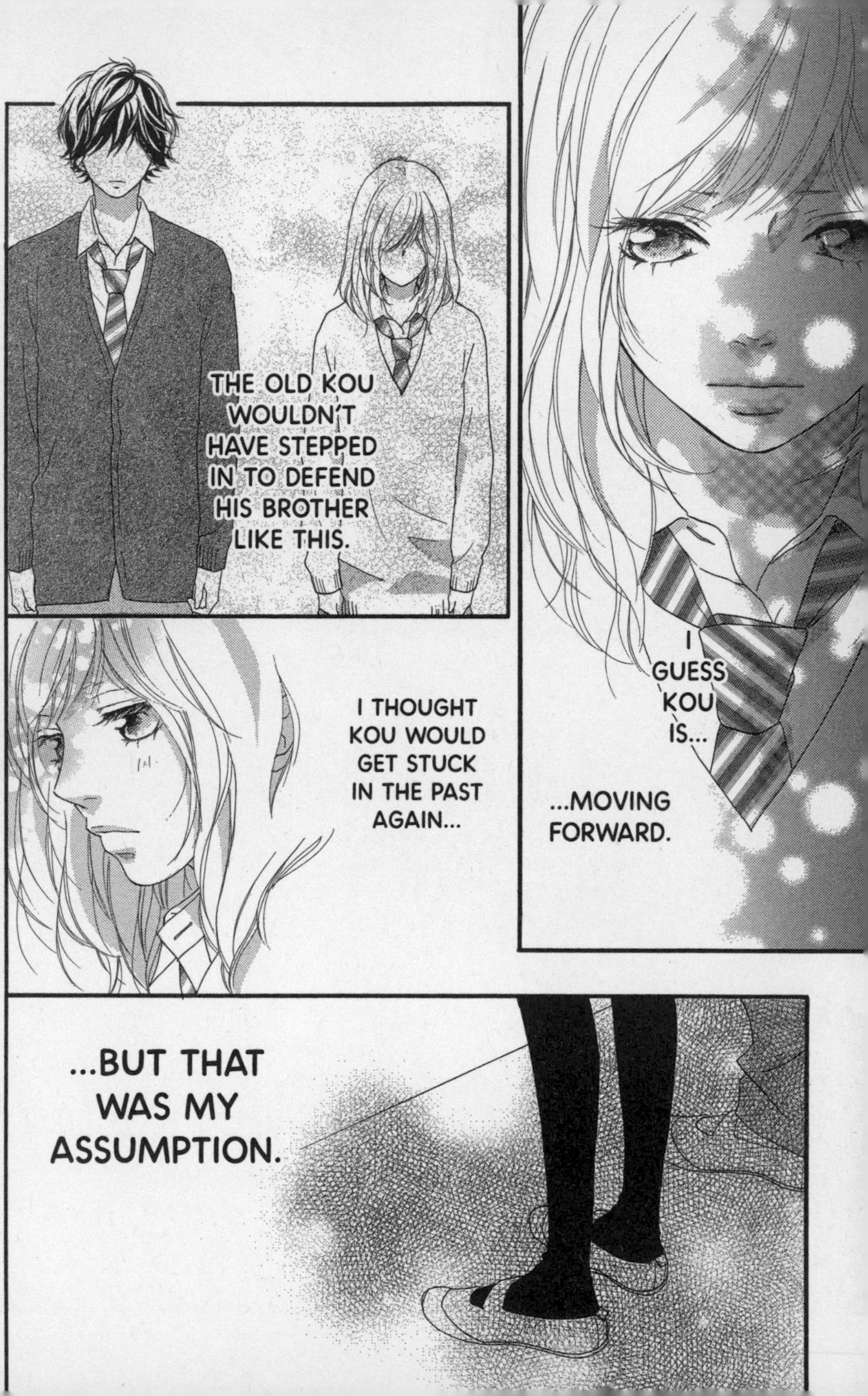
I GUESS KOU IS...
...MOVING FORWARD.
THE OLD KOU WOULDN'T HAVE STEPPED IN TO DEFEND HIS BROTHER LIKE THIS.
I THOUGHT KOU WOULD GET STUCK IN THE PAST AGAIN...
...BUT THAT WAS MY ASSUMPTION.

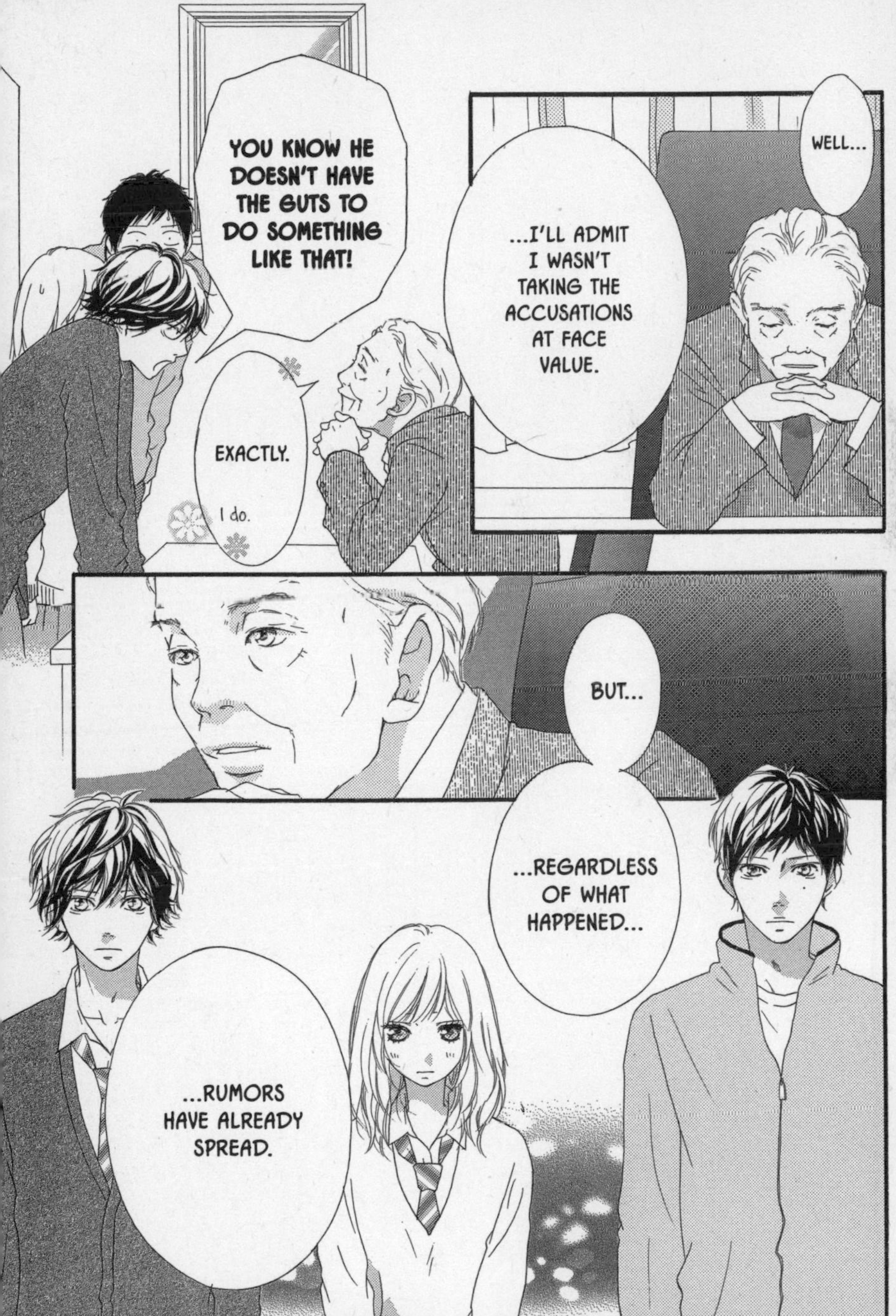
YOU KNOW HE DOESN'T HAVE THE GUTS TO DO SOMETHING LIKE THAT!
EXACTLY.
I do.
WELL...
...I'LL ADMIT I WASN'T TAKING THE ACCUSATIONS AT FACE VALUE.
BUT...
...REGARDLESS OF WHAT HAPPENED...
...RUMORS HAVE ALREADY SPREAD.

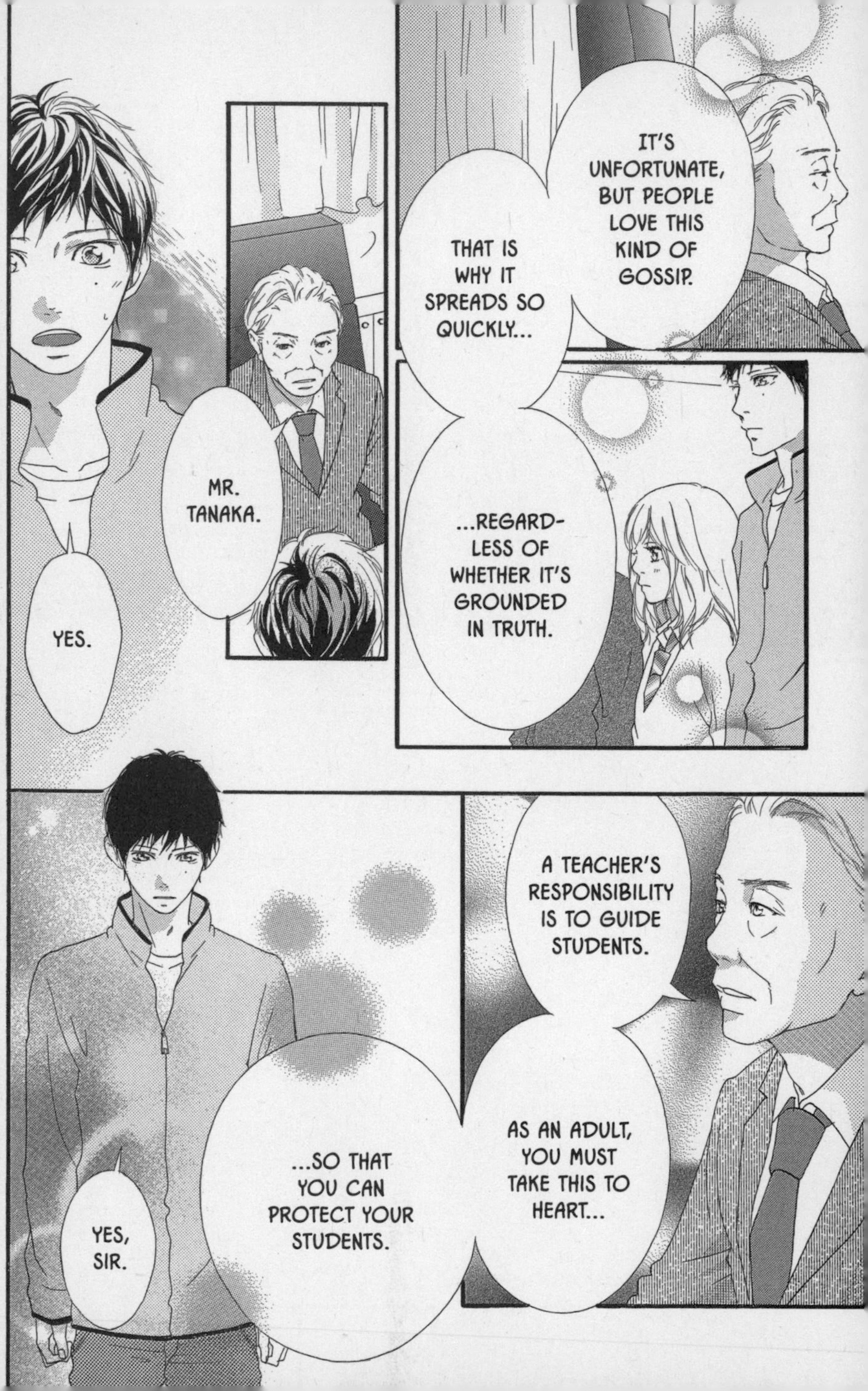
IT'S UNFORTUNATE, BUT PEOPLE LOVE THIS KIND OF GOSSIP.
THAT IS WHY IT SPREADS SO QUICKLY...
...REGARD-LESS OF WHETHER IT'S GROUNDED IN TRUTH.
MR. TANAKA.
YES.
A TEACHER'S RESPONSIBILITY IS TO GUIDE STUDENTS.
AS AN ADULT, YOU MUST TAKE THIS TO HEART...
...SO THAT YOU CAN PROTECT YOUR STUDENTS.
YES, SIR.

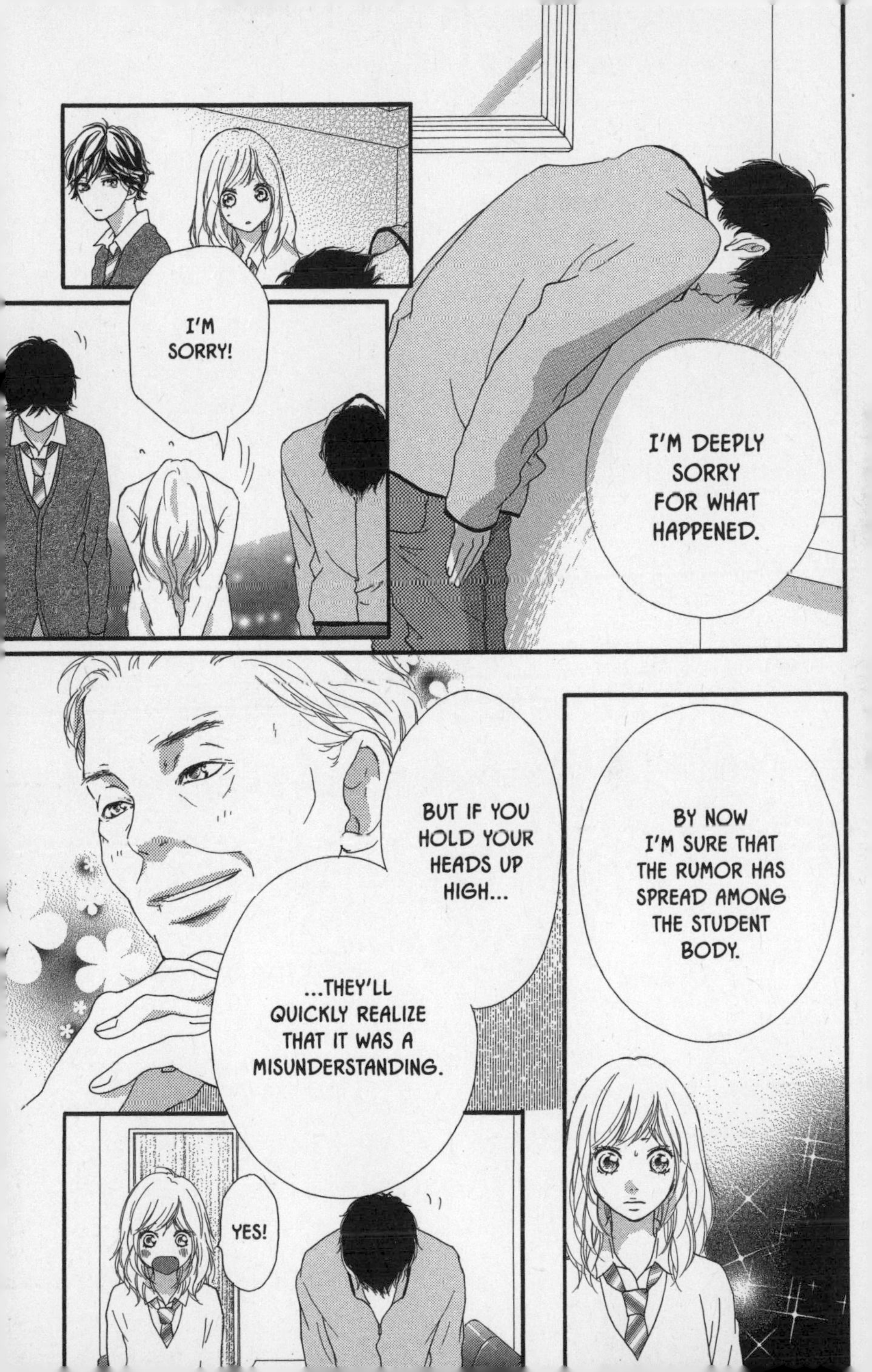
I'M DEEPLY SORRY FOR WHAT HAPPENED.
I'M SORRY!
BY NOW I'M SURE THAT THE RUMOR HAS SPREAD AMONG THE STUDENT BODY.
BUT IF YOU HOLD YOUR HEADS UP HIGH...
...THEY'LL QUICKLY REALIZE THAT IT WAS A MISUNDERSTANDING.
YES!

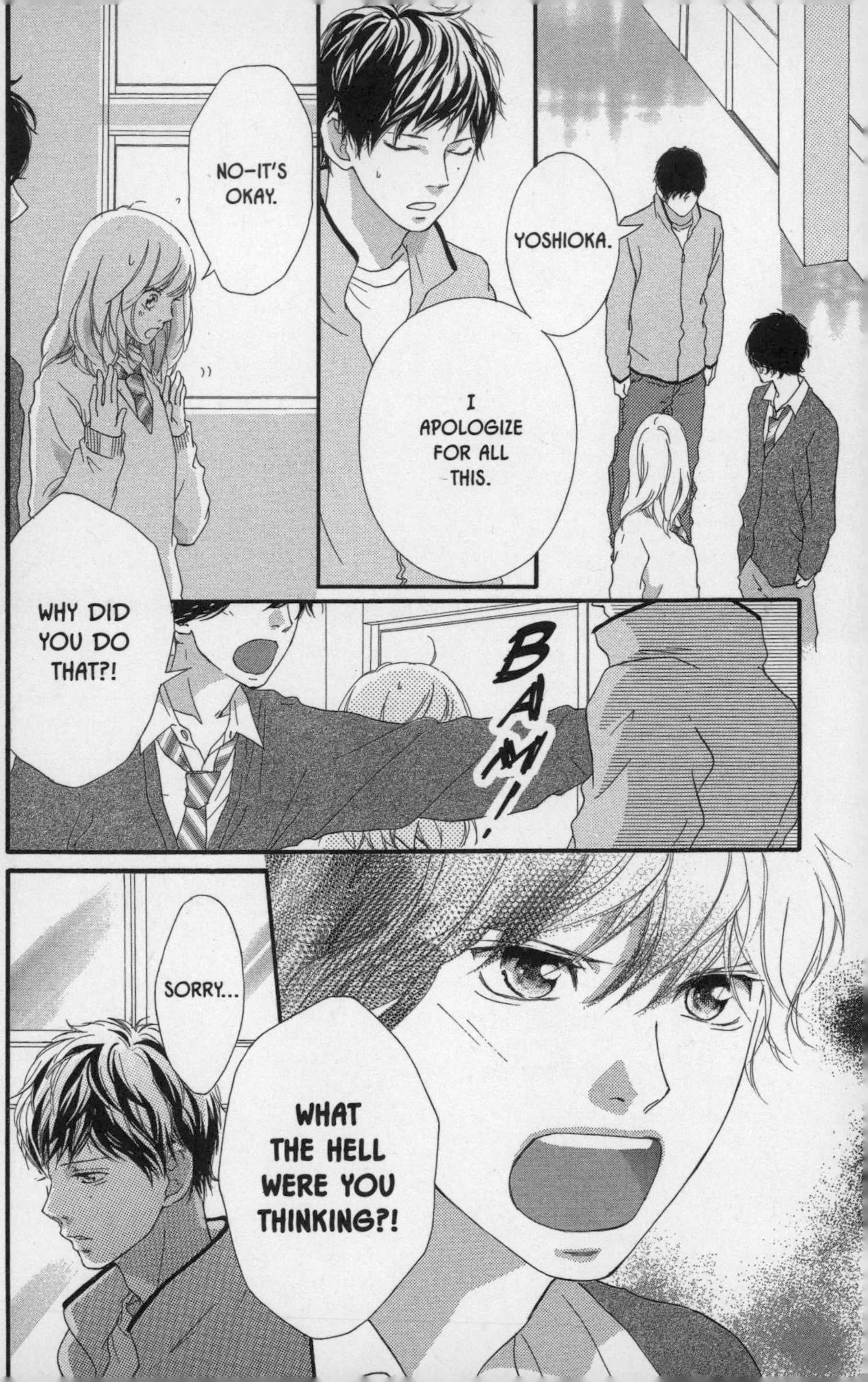
YOSHIOKA.
I APOLOGIZE FOR ALL THIS.
NO—IT'S OKAY.
BAM!
WHY DID YOU DO THAT?!
WHAT THE HELL WERE YOU THINKING?!
SORRY...

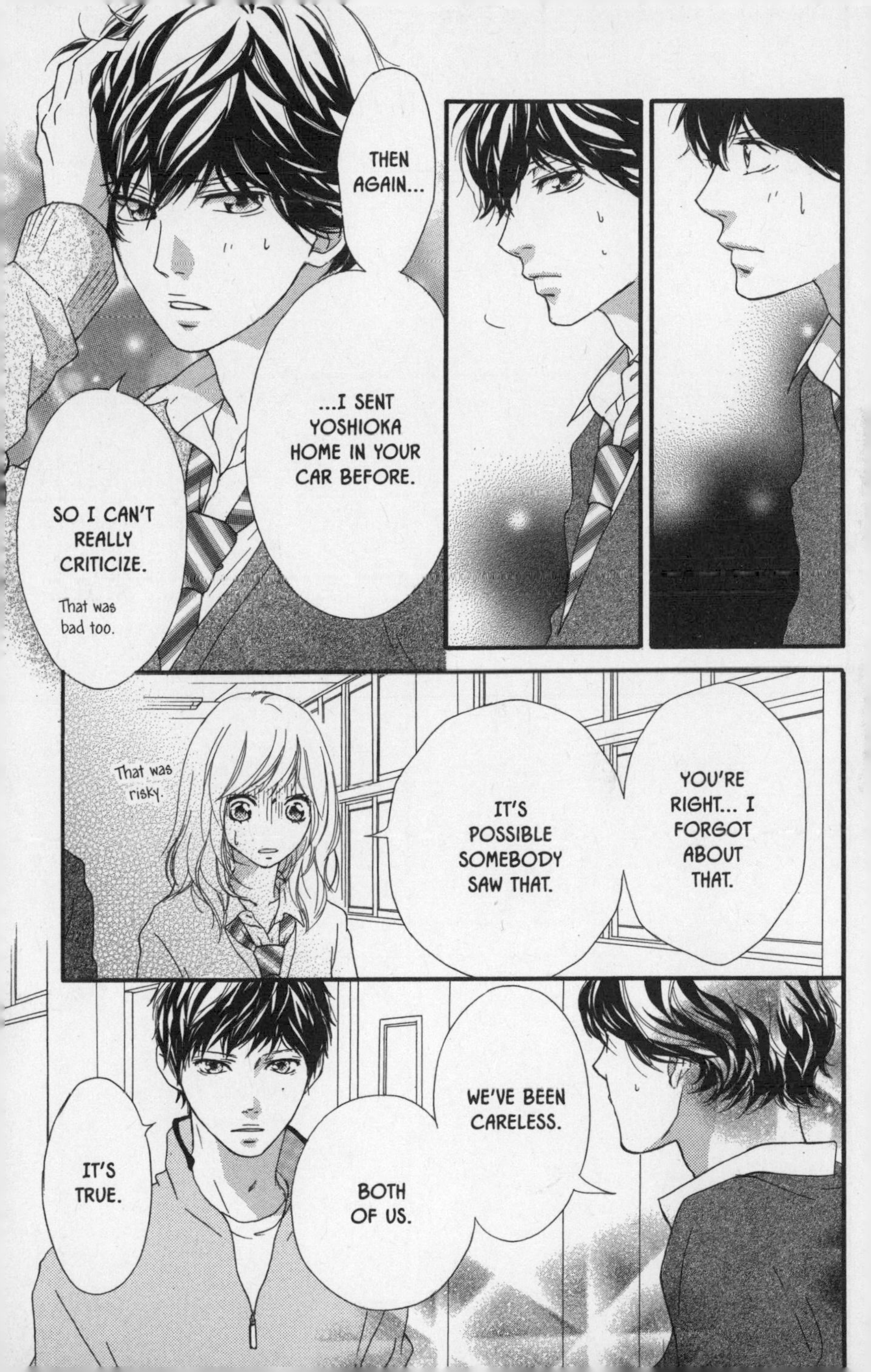
THEN AGAIN...
...I SENT YOSHIOKA HOME IN YOUR CAR BEFORE.
SO I CAN'T REALLY CRITICIZE.
That was bad too.
YOU'RE RIGHT... I FORGOT ABOUT THAT.
IT'S POSSIBLE SOMEBODY SAW THAT.
That was risky.
WE'VE BEEN CARELESS.
BOTH OF US.
IT'S TRUE.

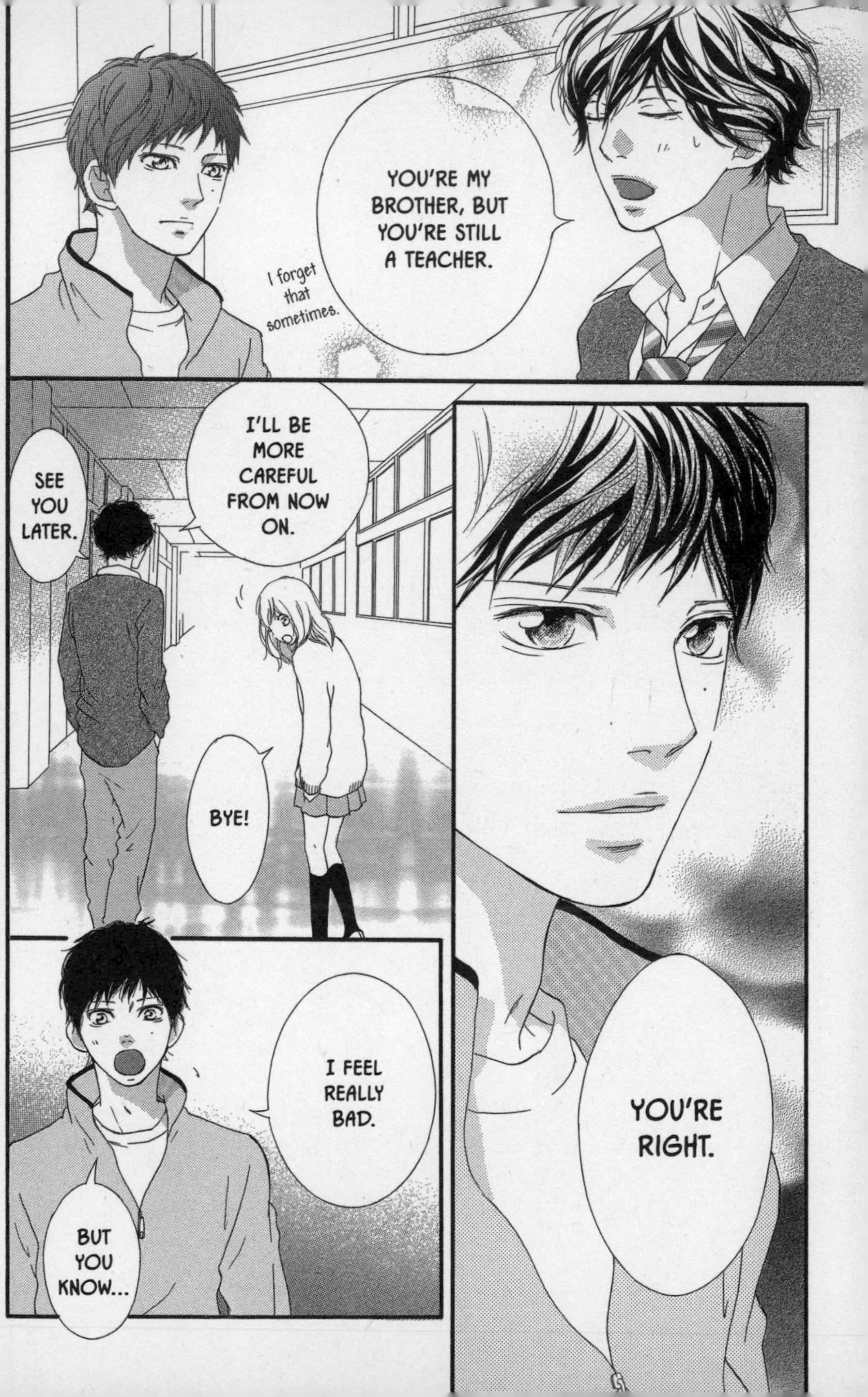
YOU'RE MY BROTHER, BUT YOU'RE STILL A TEACHER.
I forget that sometimes.
YOU'RE RIGHT.
I'LL BE MORE CAREFUL FROM NOW ON.
SEE YOU LATER.
BYE!
I FEEL REALLY BAD.
BUT YOU KNOW...

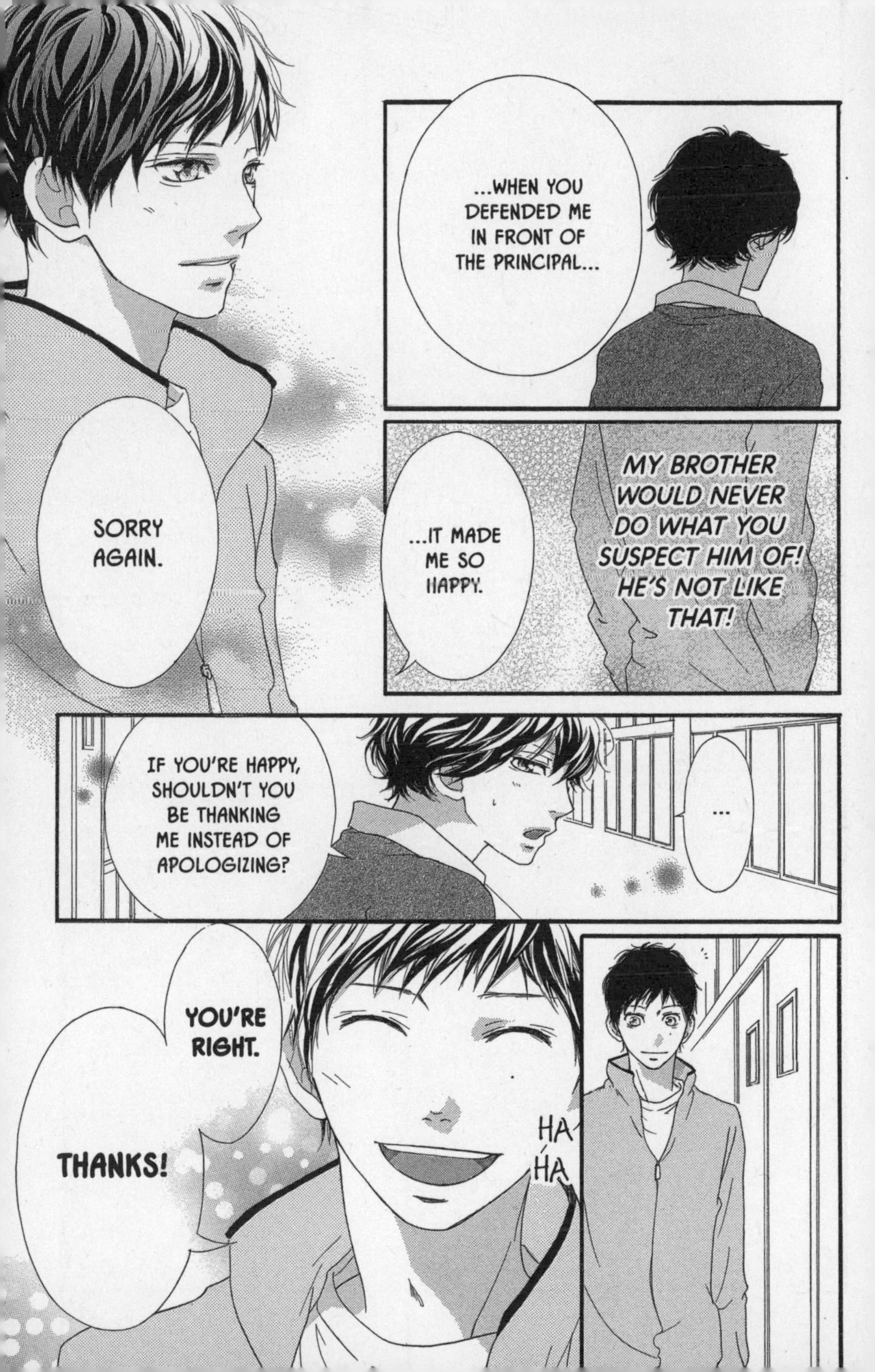
...WHEN YOU DEFENDED ME IN FRONT OF THE PRINCIPAL...
MY BROTHER WOULD NEVER DO WHAT YOU SUSPECT HIM OF! HE'S NOT LIKE THAT!
...IT MADE ME SO HAPPY.
SORRY AGAIN.
...
IF YOU'RE HAPPY, SHOULDN'T YOU BE THANKING ME INSTEAD OF APOLOGIZING?
YOU'RE RIGHT.
HA HA
THANKS!

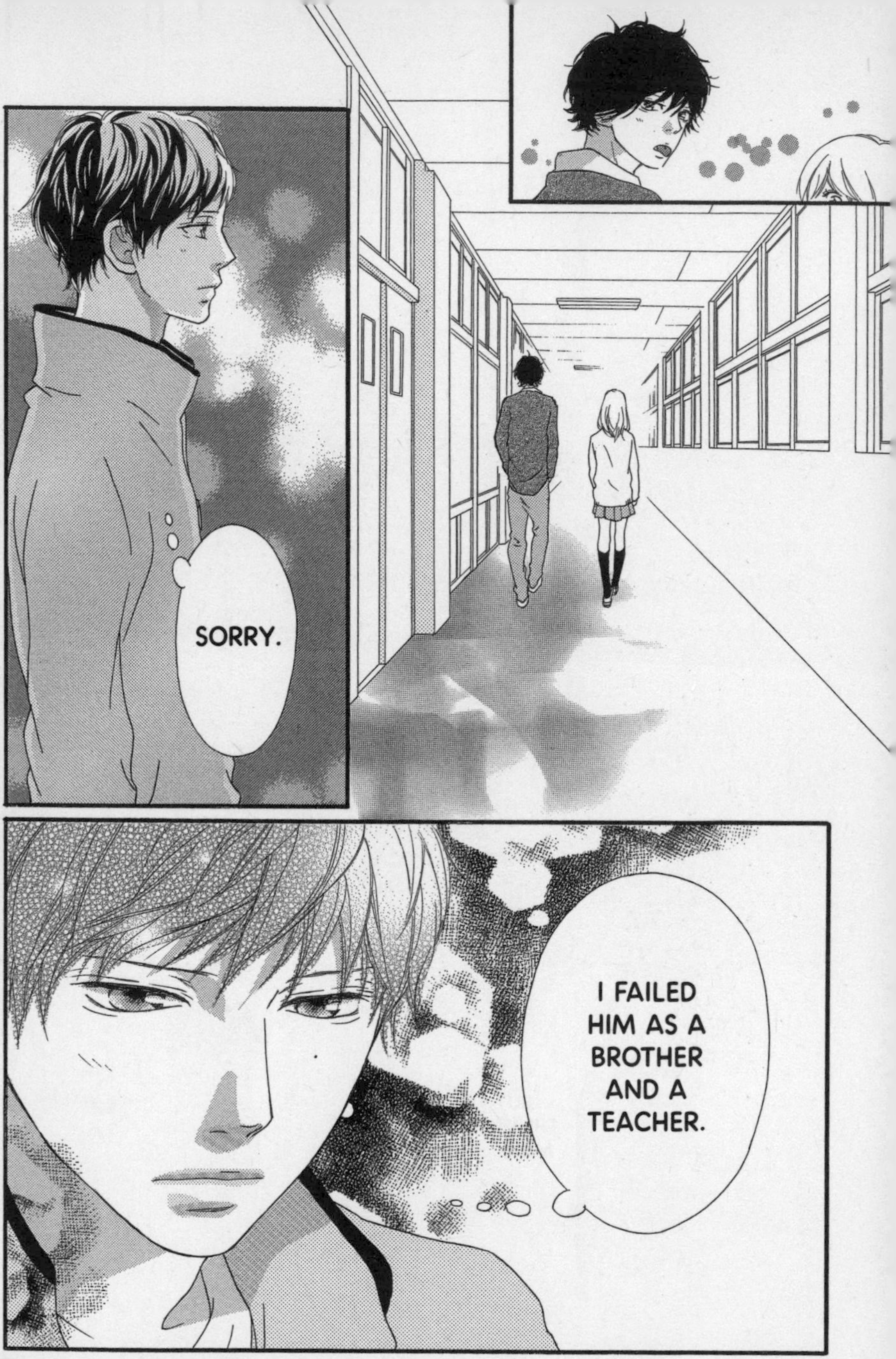
SORRY.
I FAILED HIM AS A BROTHER AND A TEACHER.

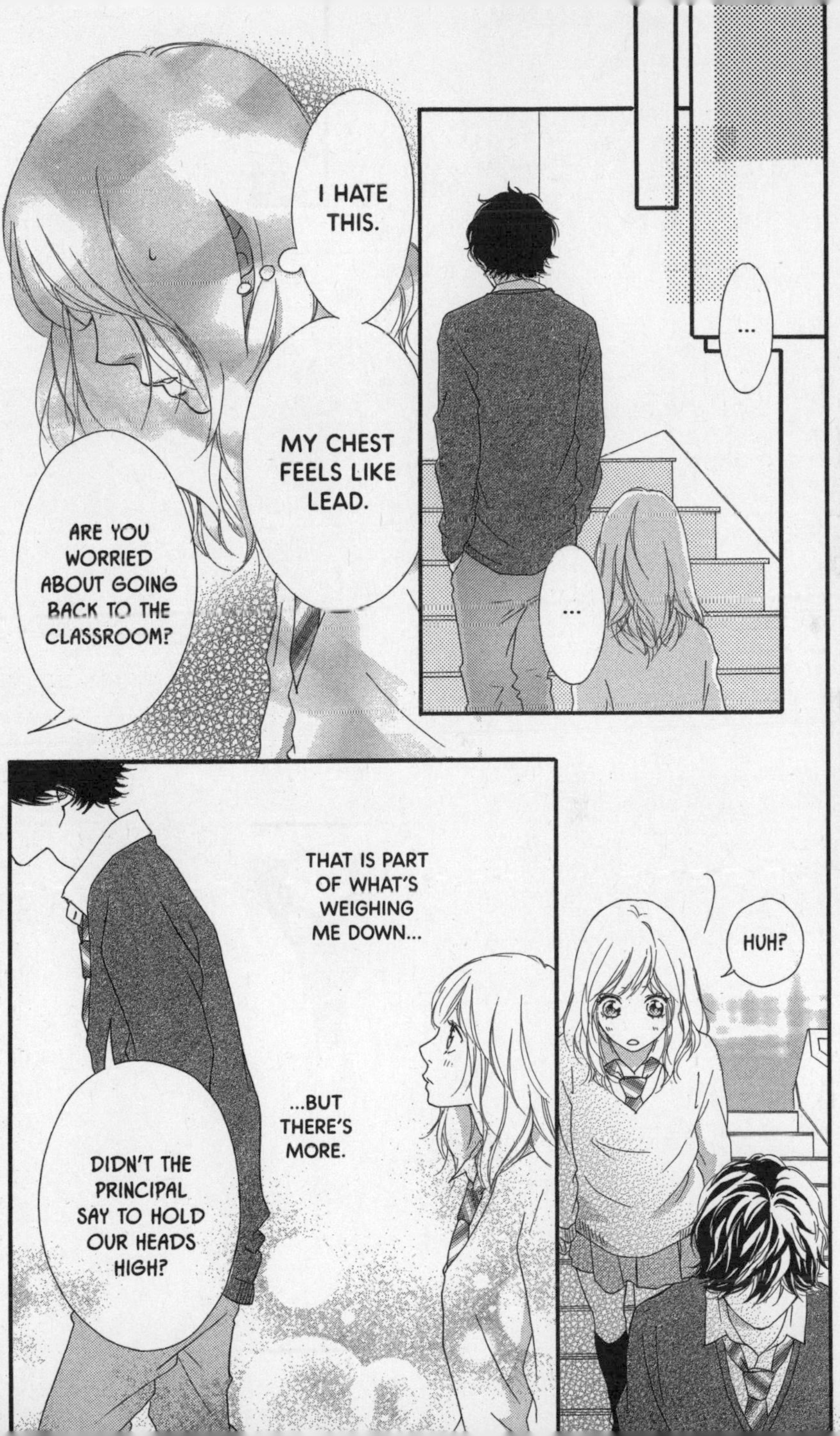
...
...
I HATE THIS.
MY CHEST FEELS LIKE LEAD.
ARE YOU WORRIED ABOUT GOING BACK TO THE CLASSROOM?
HUH?
THAT IS PART OF WHAT'S WEIGHING ME DOWN...
...BUT THERE'S MORE.
DIDN'T THE PRINCIPAL SAY TO HOLD OUR HEADS HIGH?

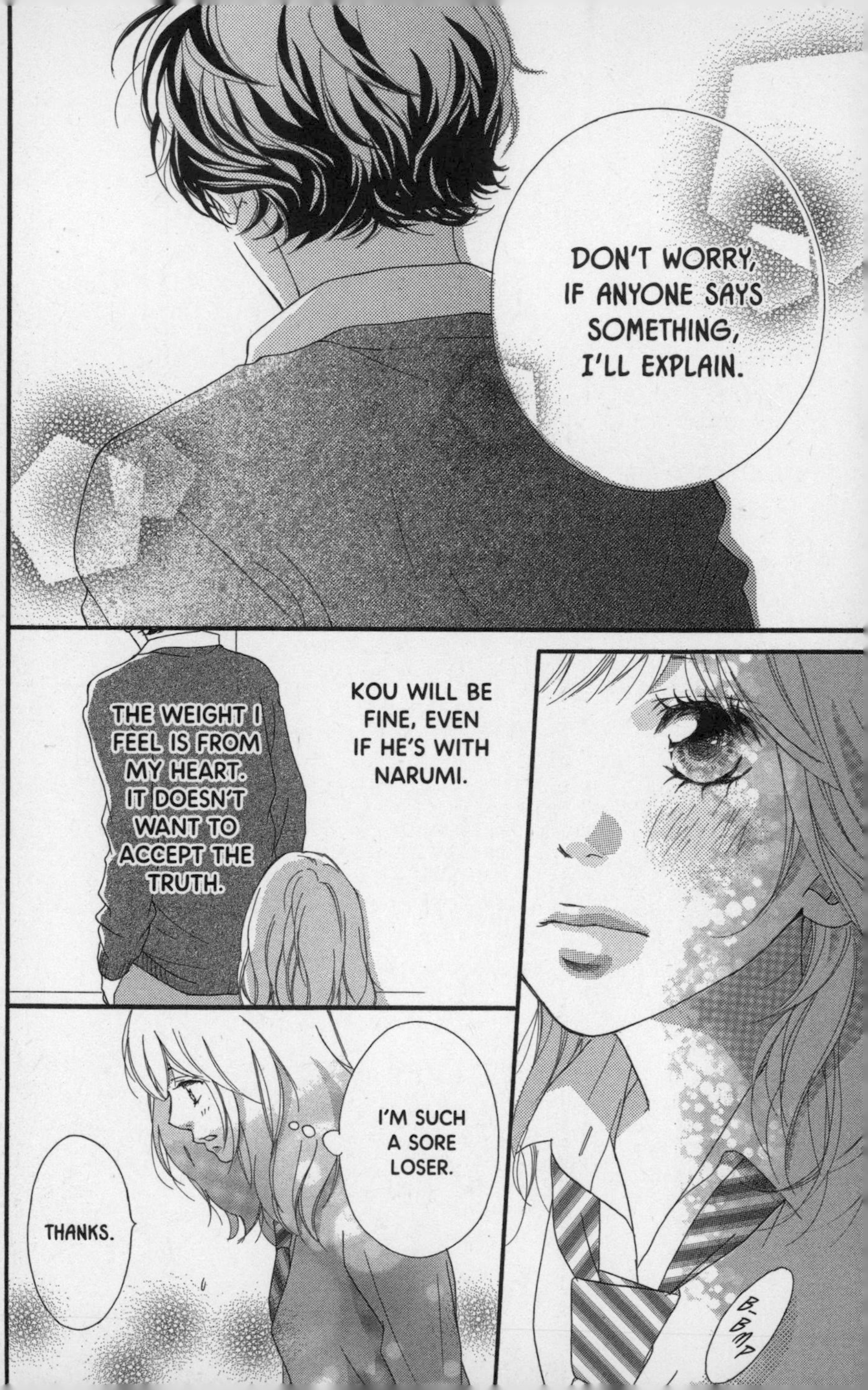
DON'T WORRY, IF ANYONE SAYS SOMETHING, I'LL EXPLAIN.
B-BMP
KOU WILL BE FINE, EVEN IF HE'S WITH NARUMI.
THE WEIGHT I FEEL IS FROM MY HEART. IT DOESN'T WANT TO ACCEPT THE TRUTH.
I'M SUCH A SORE LOSER.
THANKS.

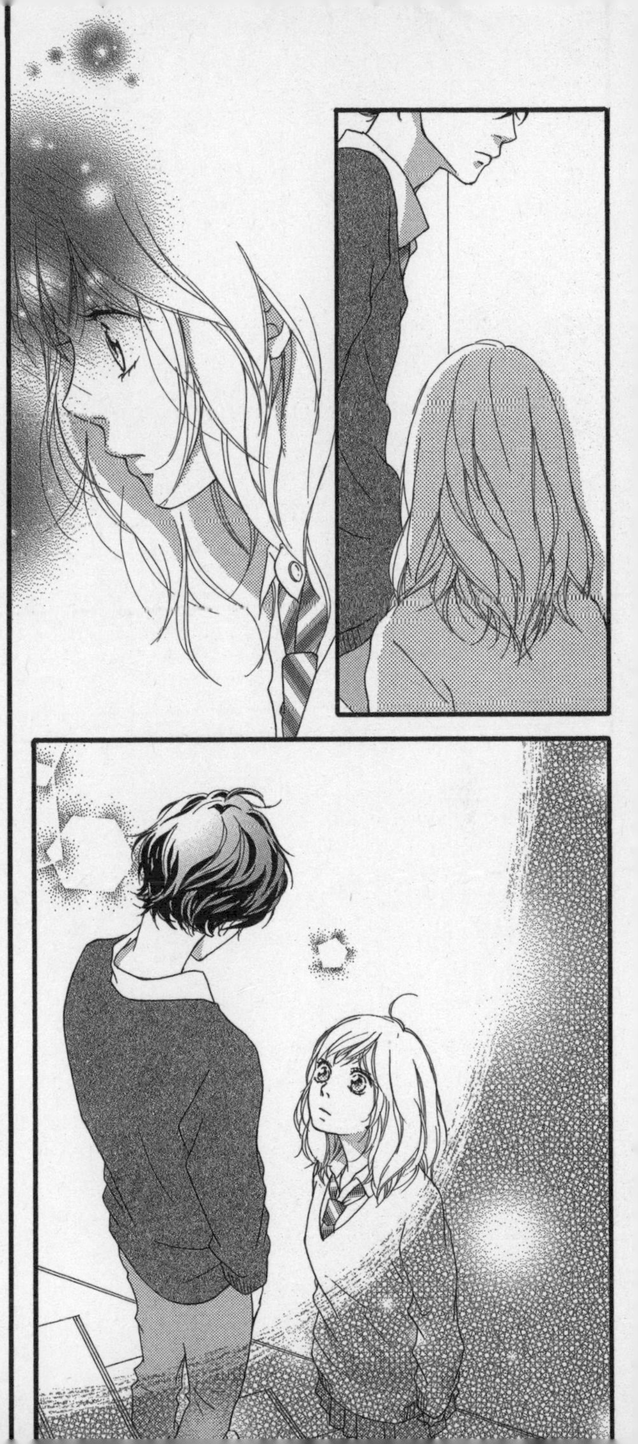

I had the opportunity to create the character designs for the original anime *Hal*, and amidst the confusion(?) I got to visit the production company—WIT STUDIO! I imagined production companies to be tense and full of ragged warriors who never sleep. But when I visited, it was still in the early days of production, and the studio was lovely. It was full of fresh-faced people. I got to see some of the storyboards too, but geez, there were so many that I couldn't keep up. There were enough to make your right hand fall off if you drew them all... I don't understand how they piece together snippets that are just a few seconds long and manage to tell a story! The whole time I was there, I just kept saying "wow." Each anime is the culmination of so many meticulous tasks!

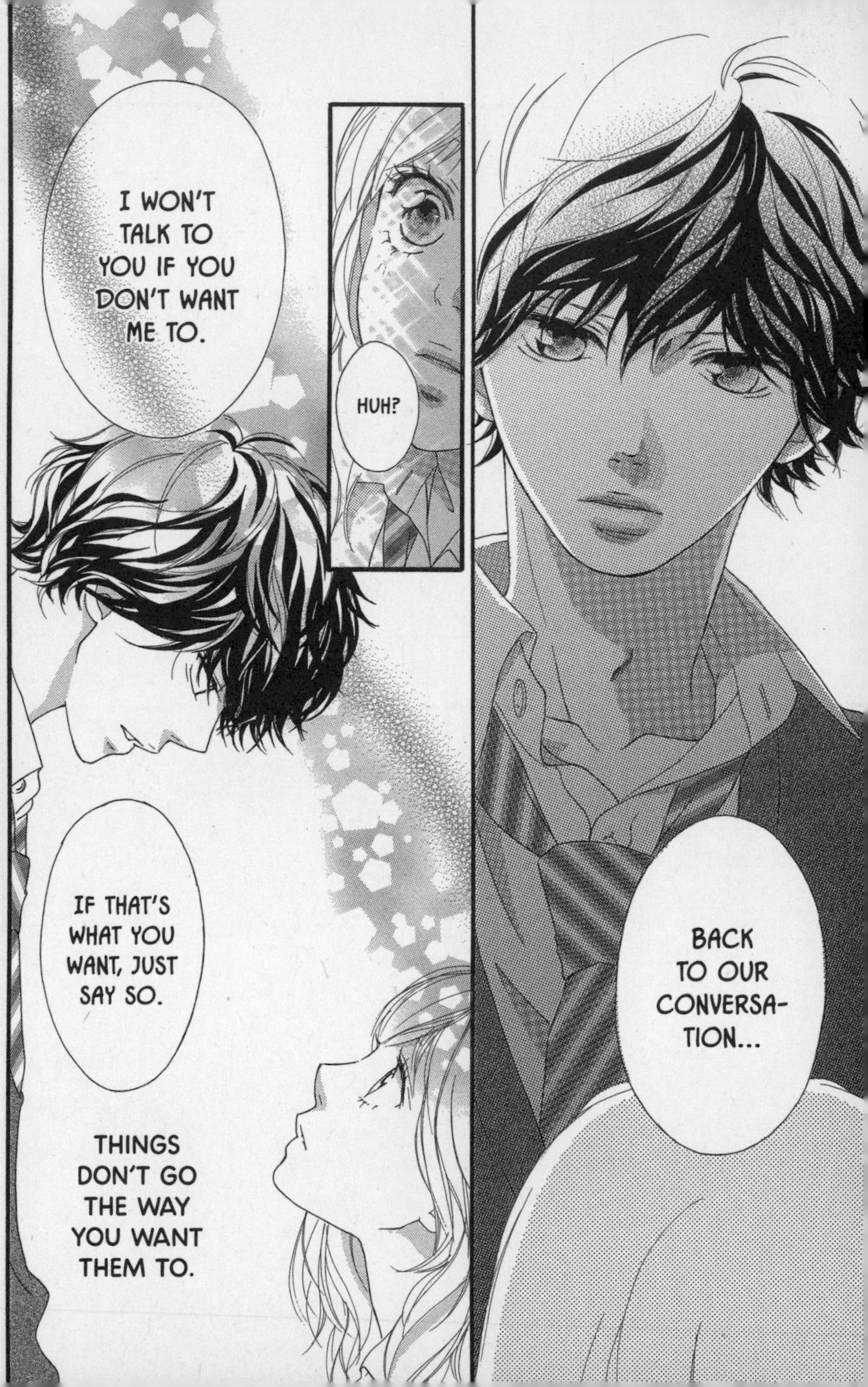
BACK TO OUR CONVERSA-TION...
I WON'T TALK TO YOU IF YOU DON'T WANT ME TO.
HUH?
IF THAT'S WHAT YOU WANT, JUST SAY SO.
THINGS DON'T GO THE WAY YOU WANT THEM TO.

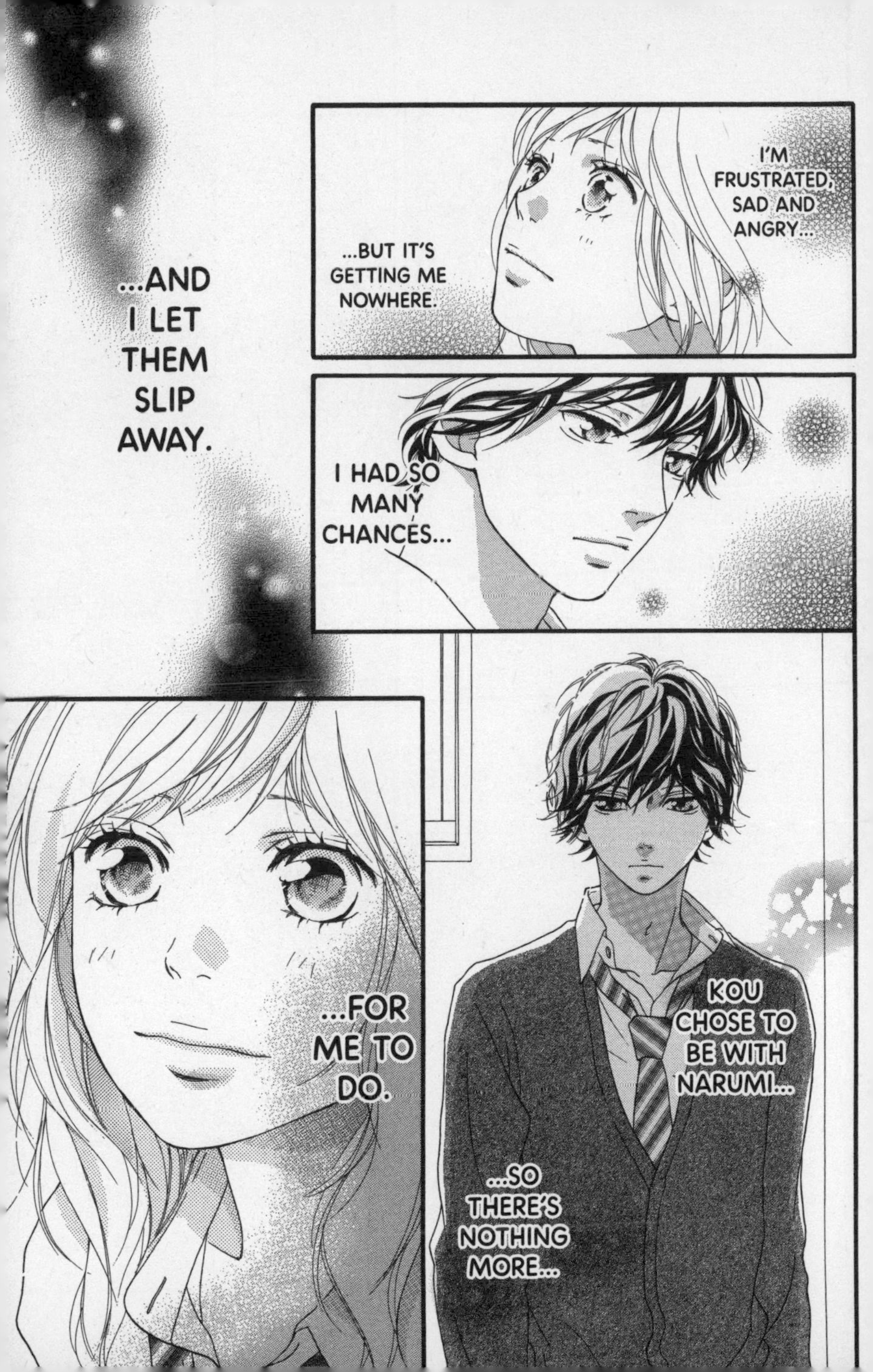
I'M FRUSTRATED, SAD AND ANGRY...
...BUT IT'S GETTING ME NOWHERE.
I HAD SO MANY CHANCES...
...AND I LET THEM SLIP AWAY.
KOU CHOSE TO BE WITH NARUMI...
...SO THERE'S NOTHING MORE...
...FOR ME TO DO.

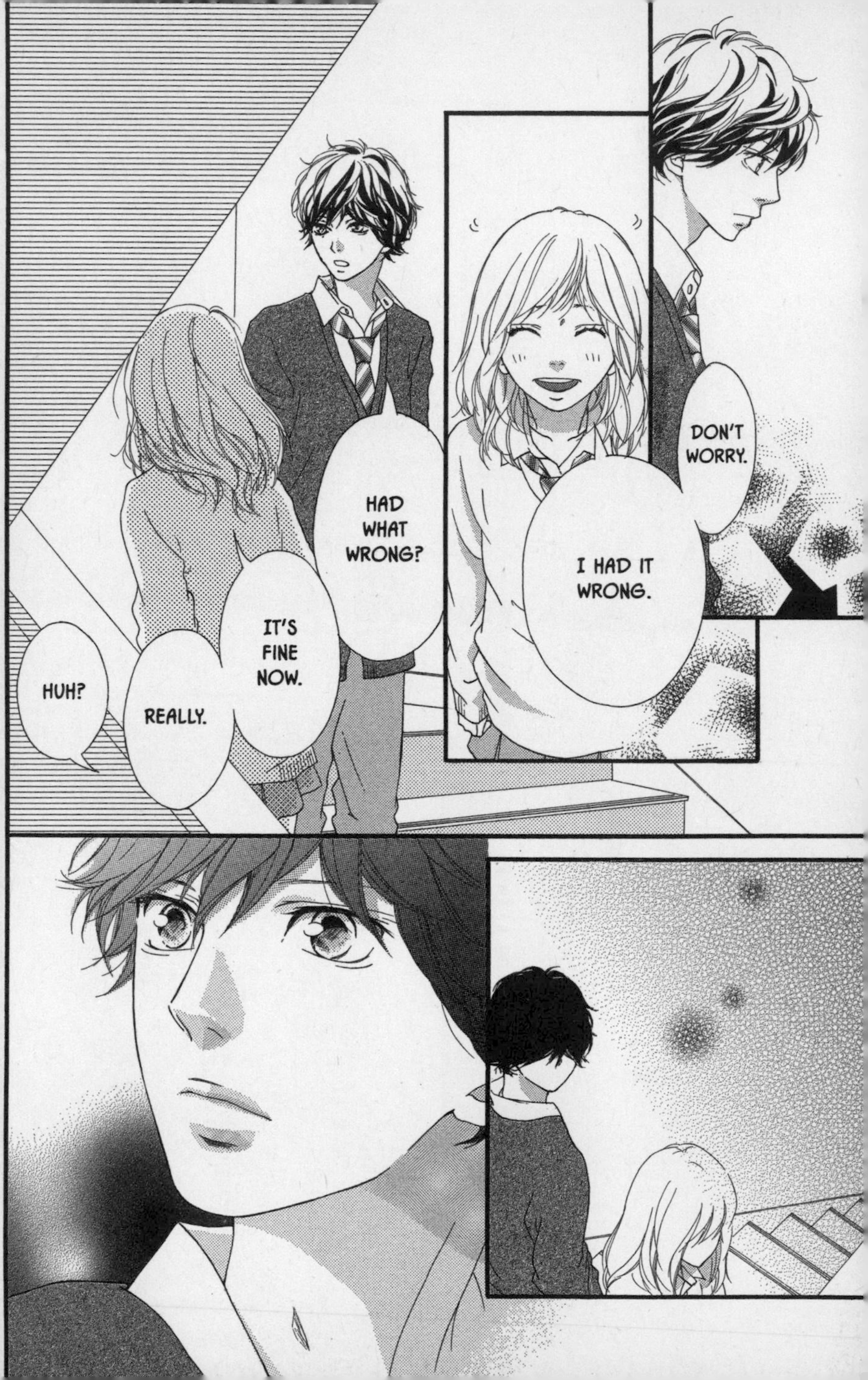
DON'T WORRY.
I HAD IT WRONG.
HAD WHAT WRONG?
IT'S FINE NOW.
REALLY.
HUH?

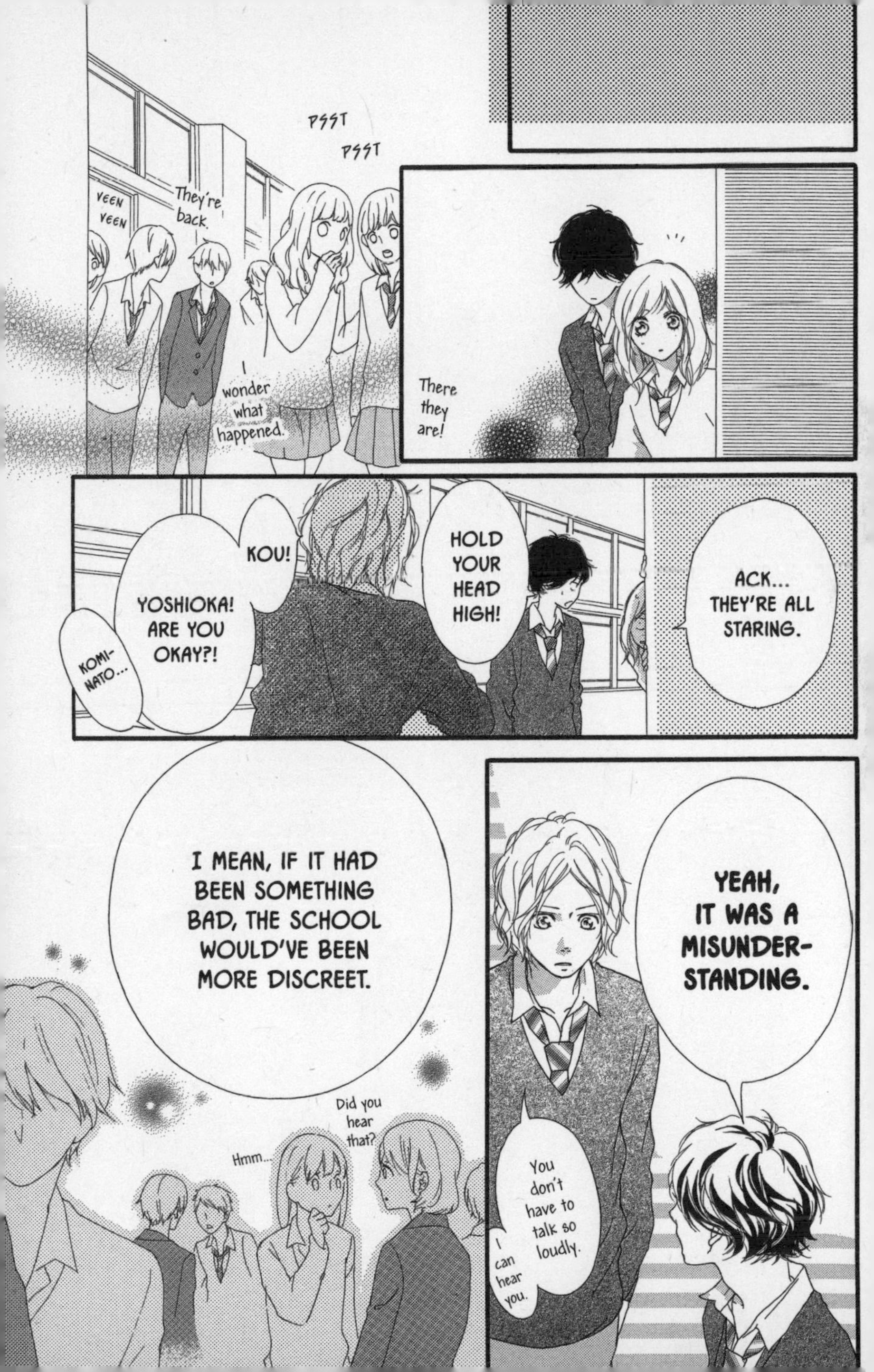
There they are!
PSST
PSST
They're back.
VEEN VEEN
I wonder what happened.
ACK... THEY'RE ALL STARING.
HOLD YOUR HEAD HIGH!
KOU!
YOSHIOKA! ARE YOU OKAY?!
KOMINATO...
YEAH, IT WAS A MISUNDERSTANDING.
You don't have to talk so loudly.
I can hear you.
I MEAN, IF IT HAD BEEN SOMETHING BAD, THE SCHOOL WOULD'VE BEEN MORE DISCREET.
Did you hear that?
Hmm...

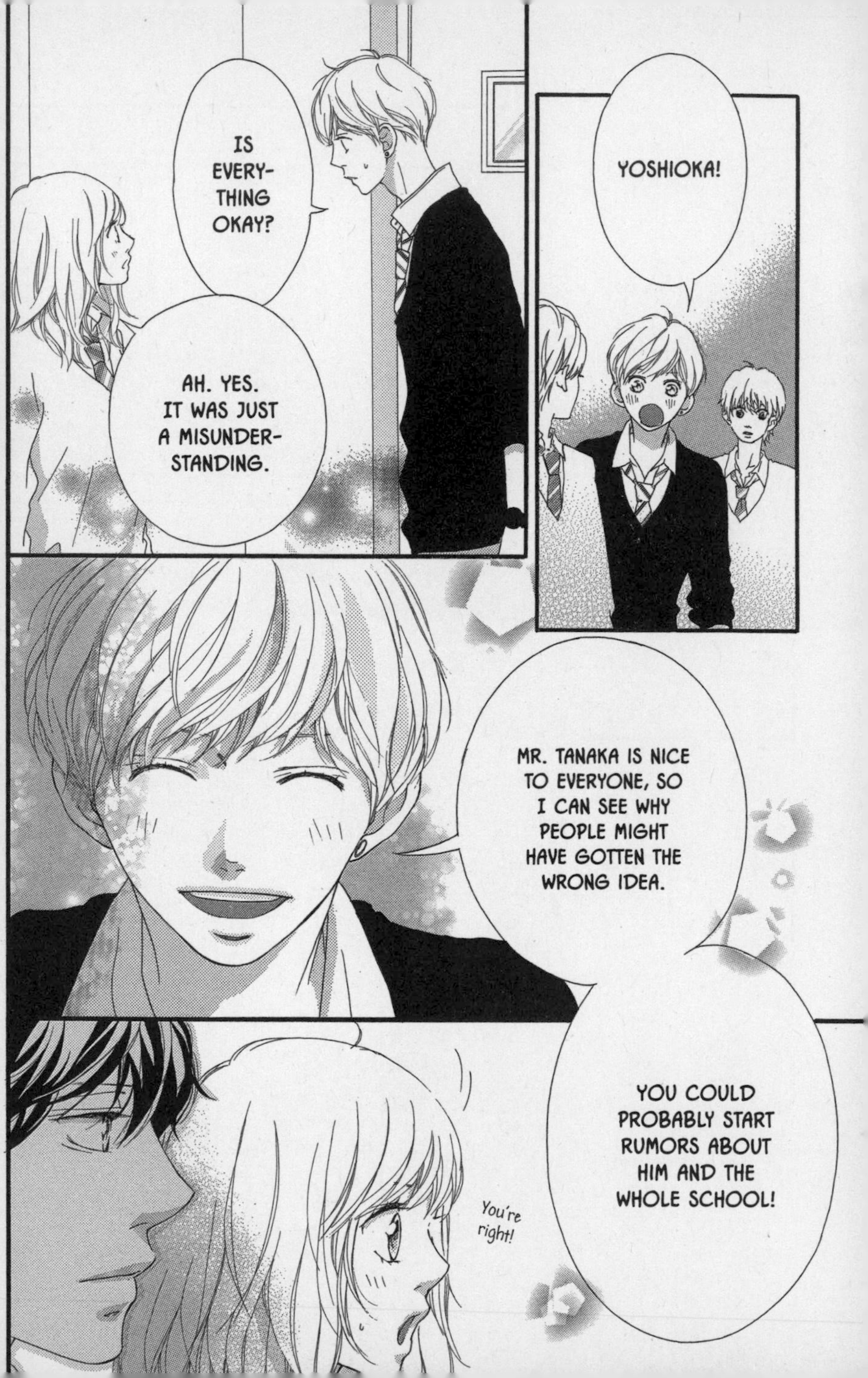
YOSHIOKA!
IS EVERY-THING OKAY?
AH. YES. IT WAS JUST A MISUNDER-STANDING.
MR. TANAKA IS NICE TO EVERYONE, SO I CAN SEE WHY PEOPLE MIGHT HAVE GOTTEN THE WRONG IDEA.
YOU COULD PROBABLY START RUMORS ABOUT HIM AND THE WHOLE SCHOOL!
You're right!

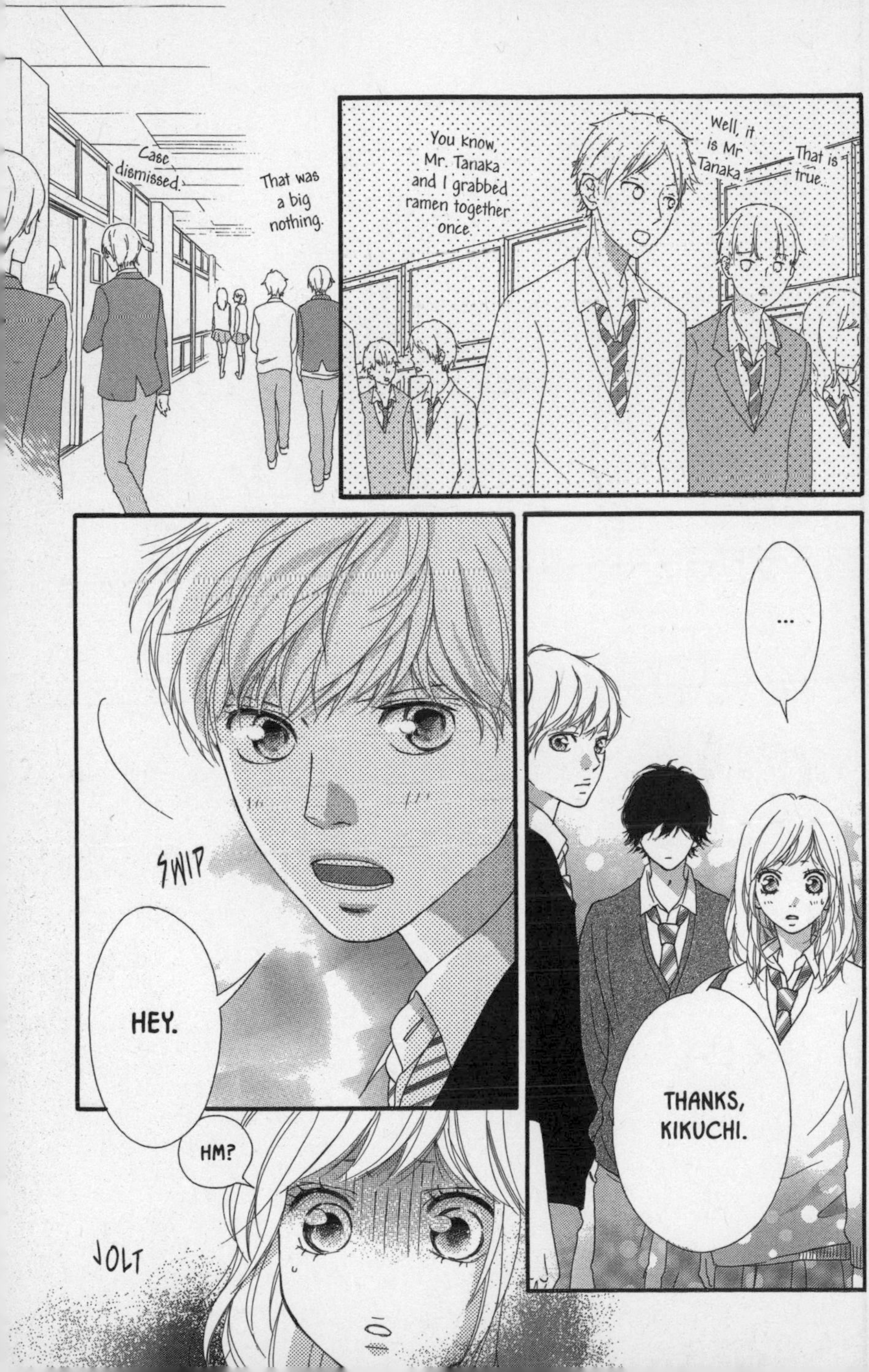
You know, Mr. Tanaka and I grabbed ramen together once.
Well, it is Mr. Tanaka.
That is true...
Case dismissed.
That was a big nothing.
...
THANKS, KIKUCHI.
SWIP
HEY.
HM?
JOLT

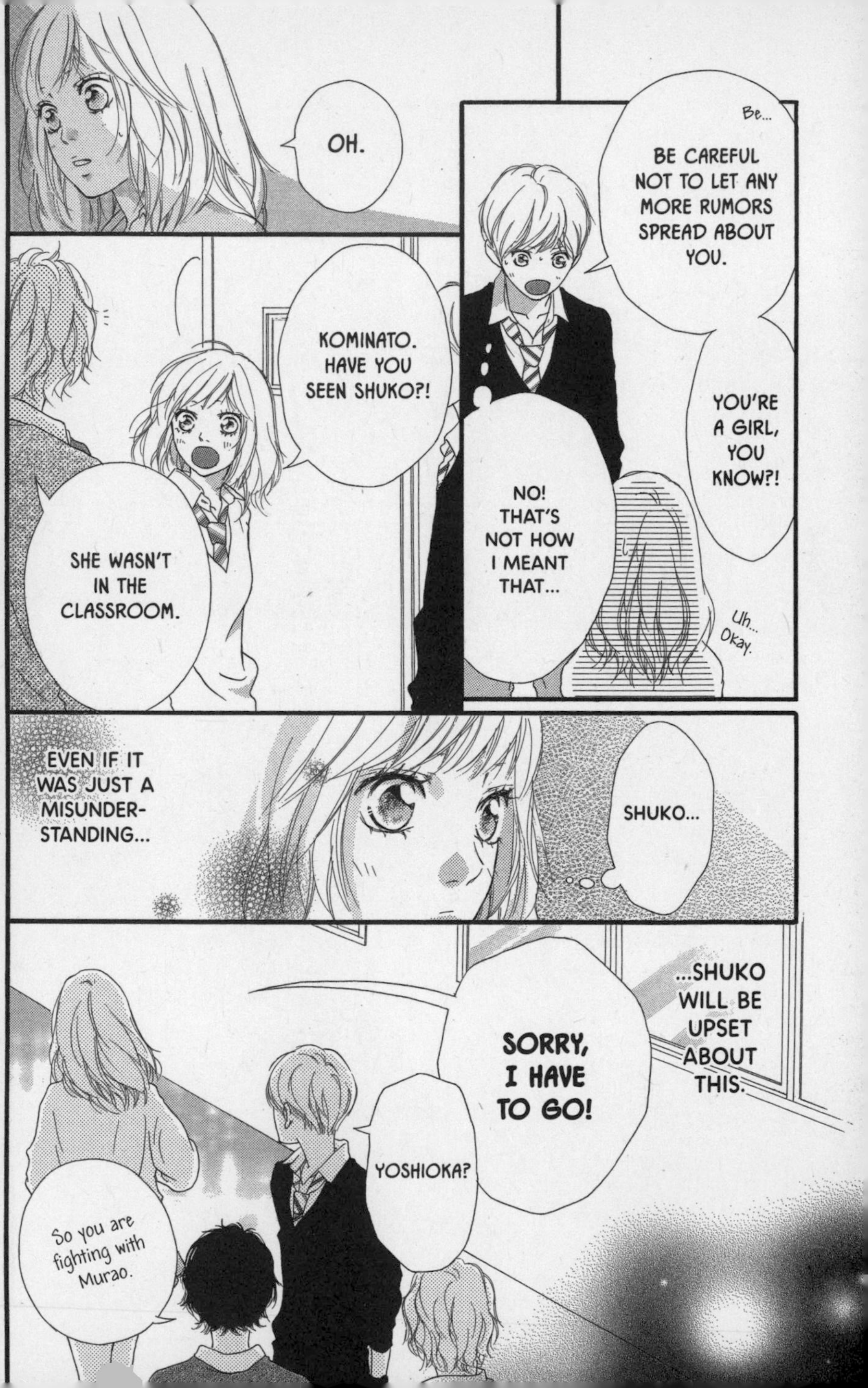
Be...
BE CAREFUL NOT TO LET ANY MORE RUMORS SPREAD ABOUT YOU.
YOU'RE A GIRL, YOU KNOW?!
NO! THAT'S NOT HOW I MEANT THAT...
Uh... Okay.
OH.
KOMINATO. HAVE YOU SEEN SHUKO?!
SHE WASN'T IN THE CLASSROOM.
SHUKO...
EVEN IF IT WAS JUST A MISUNDER-STANDING...
...SHUKO WILL BE UPSET ABOUT THIS.
SORRY, I HAVE TO GO!
YOSHIOKA?
So you are fighting with Murao.

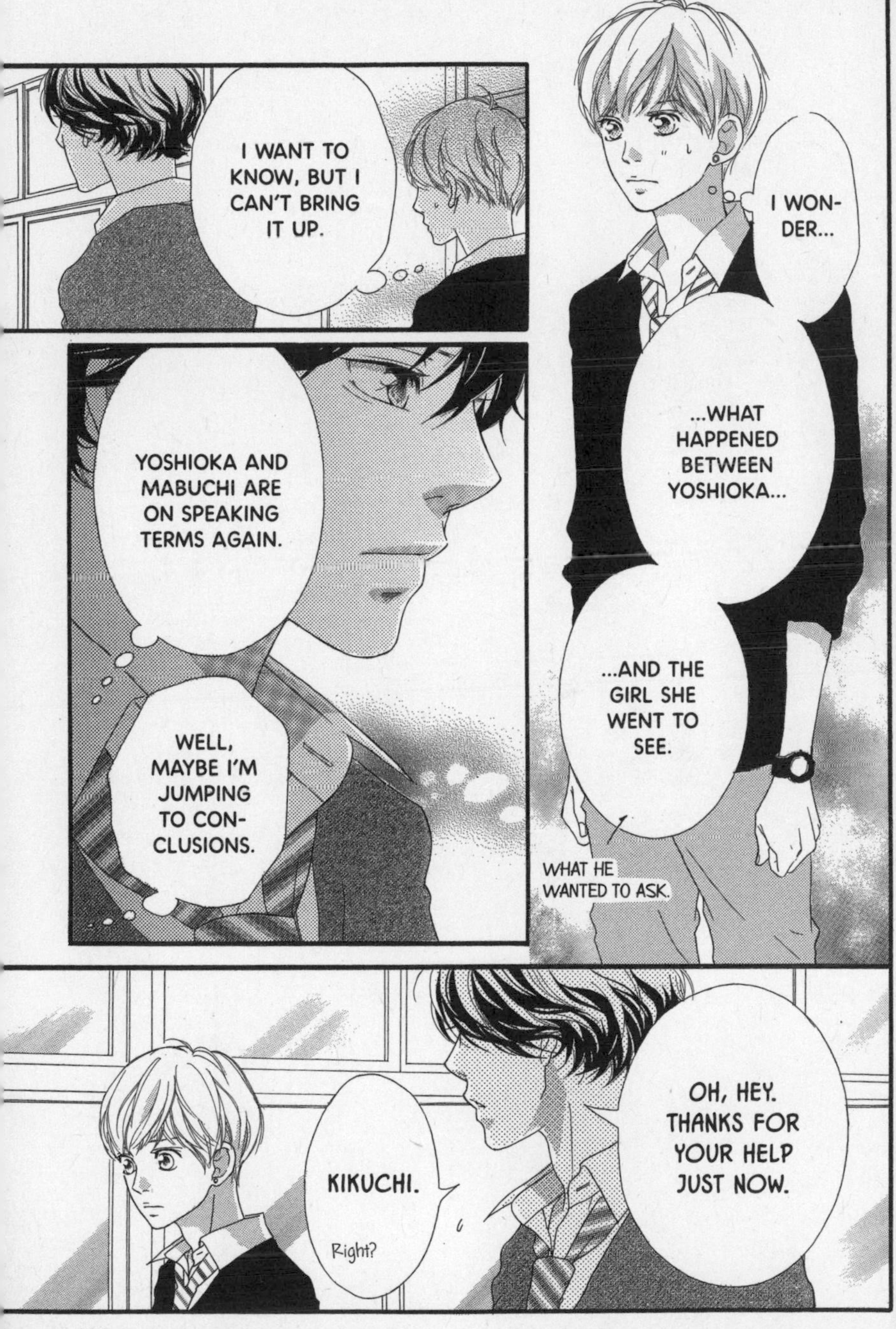
I WON-DER...
...WHAT HAPPENED BETWEEN YOSHIOKA...
...AND THE GIRL SHE WENT TO SEE.
WHAT HE WANTED TO ASK.
I WANT TO KNOW, BUT I CAN'T BRING IT UP.
YOSHIOKA AND MABUCHI ARE ON SPEAKING TERMS AGAIN.
WELL, MAYBE I'M JUMPING TO CON-CLUSIONS.
OH, HEY. THANKS FOR YOUR HELP JUST NOW.
KIKUCHI.
Right?

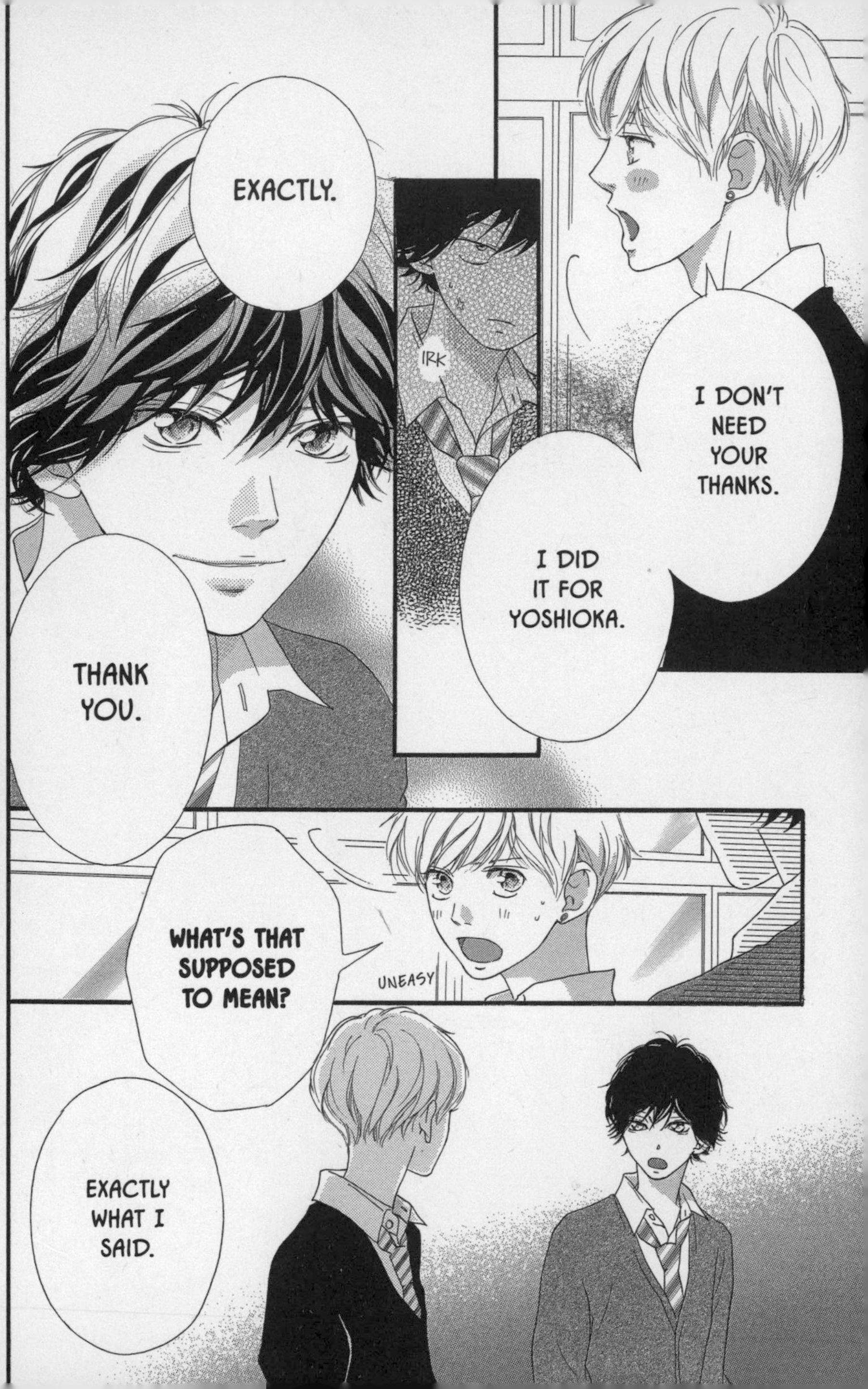
I DON'T NEED YOUR THANKS.
I DID IT FOR YOSHIOKA.
IRK
EXACTLY.
THANK YOU.
UNEASY
WHAT'S THAT SUPPOSED TO MEAN?
EXACTLY WHAT I SAID.

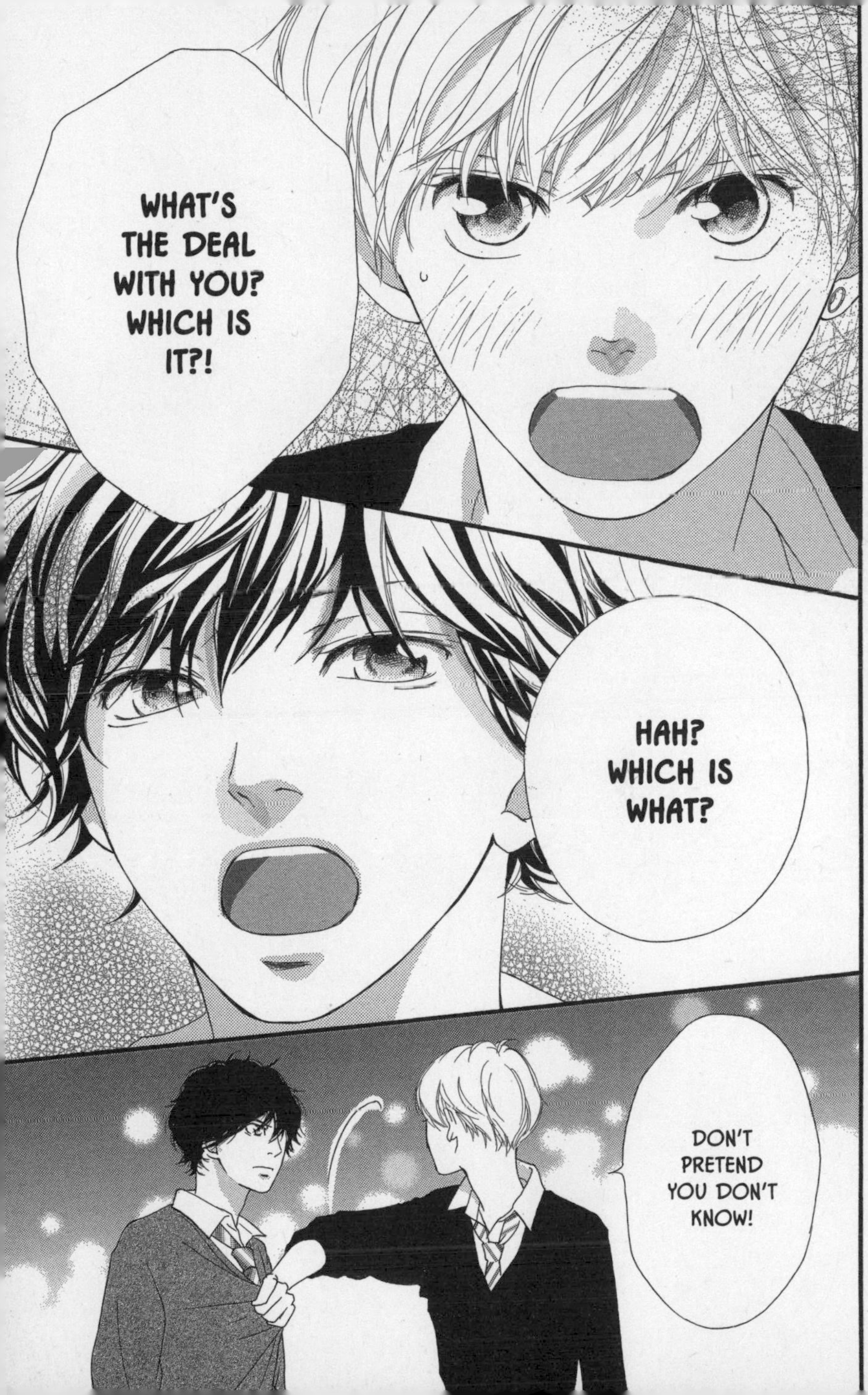
WHAT'S THE DEAL WITH YOU? WHICH IS IT?!
HAH? WHICH IS WHAT?
DON'T PRETEND YOU DON'T KNOW!

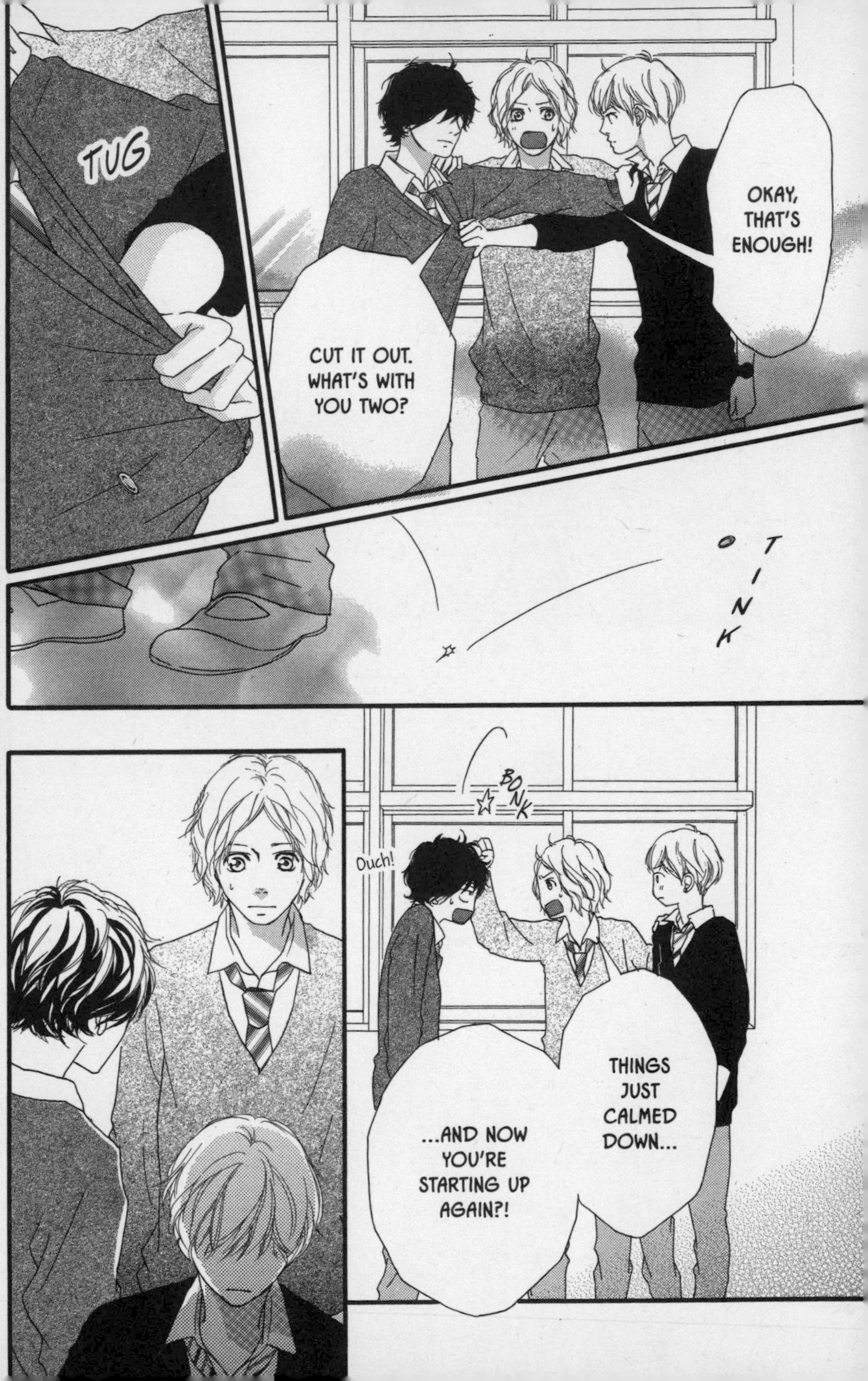
OKAY, THAT'S ENOUGH!
CUT IT OUT. WHAT'S WITH YOU TWO?
TUG
TINK
BONK
Ouch!
THINGS JUST CALMED DOWN...
...AND NOW YOU'RE STARTING UP AGAIN?!

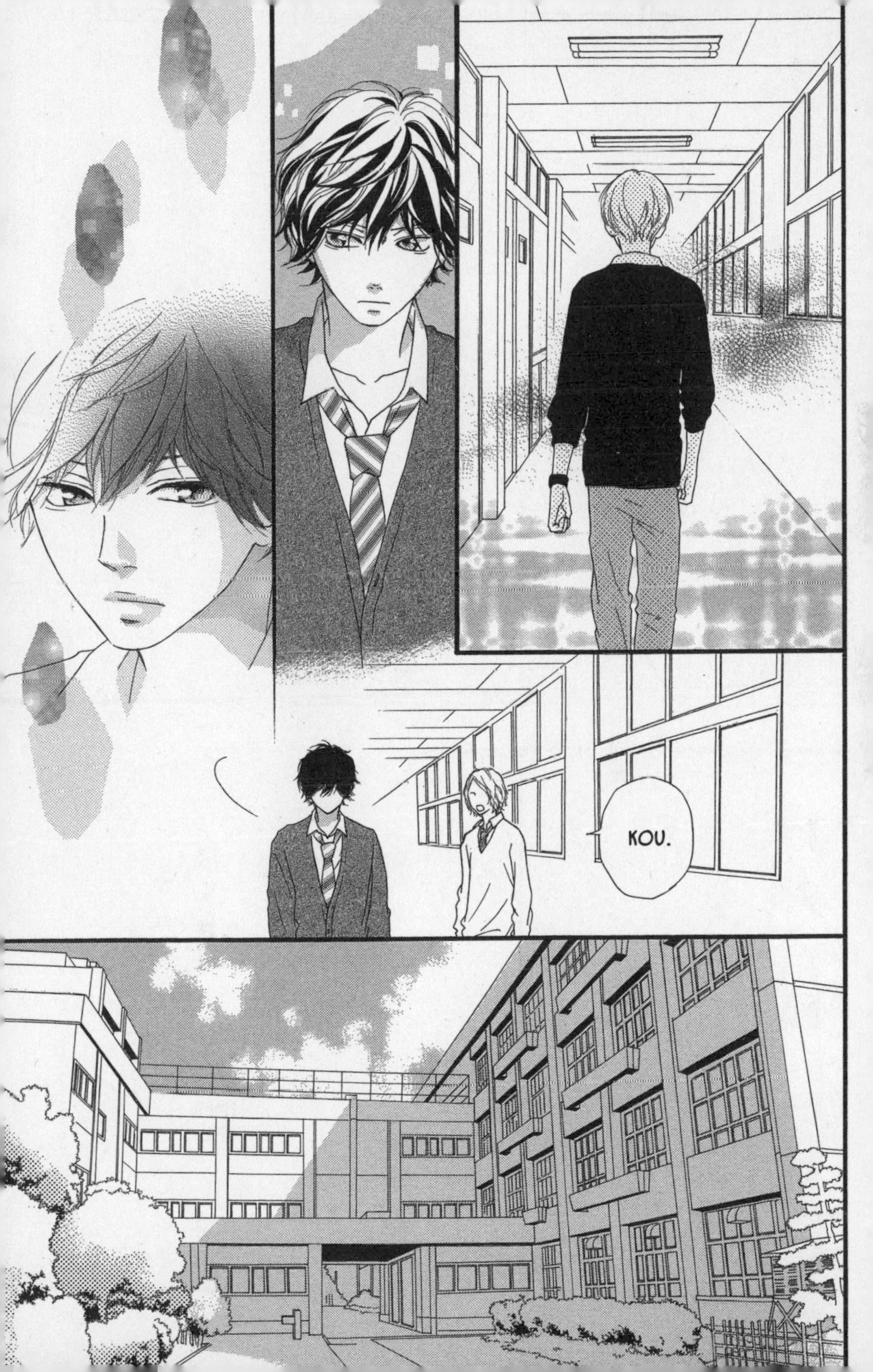
KOU.

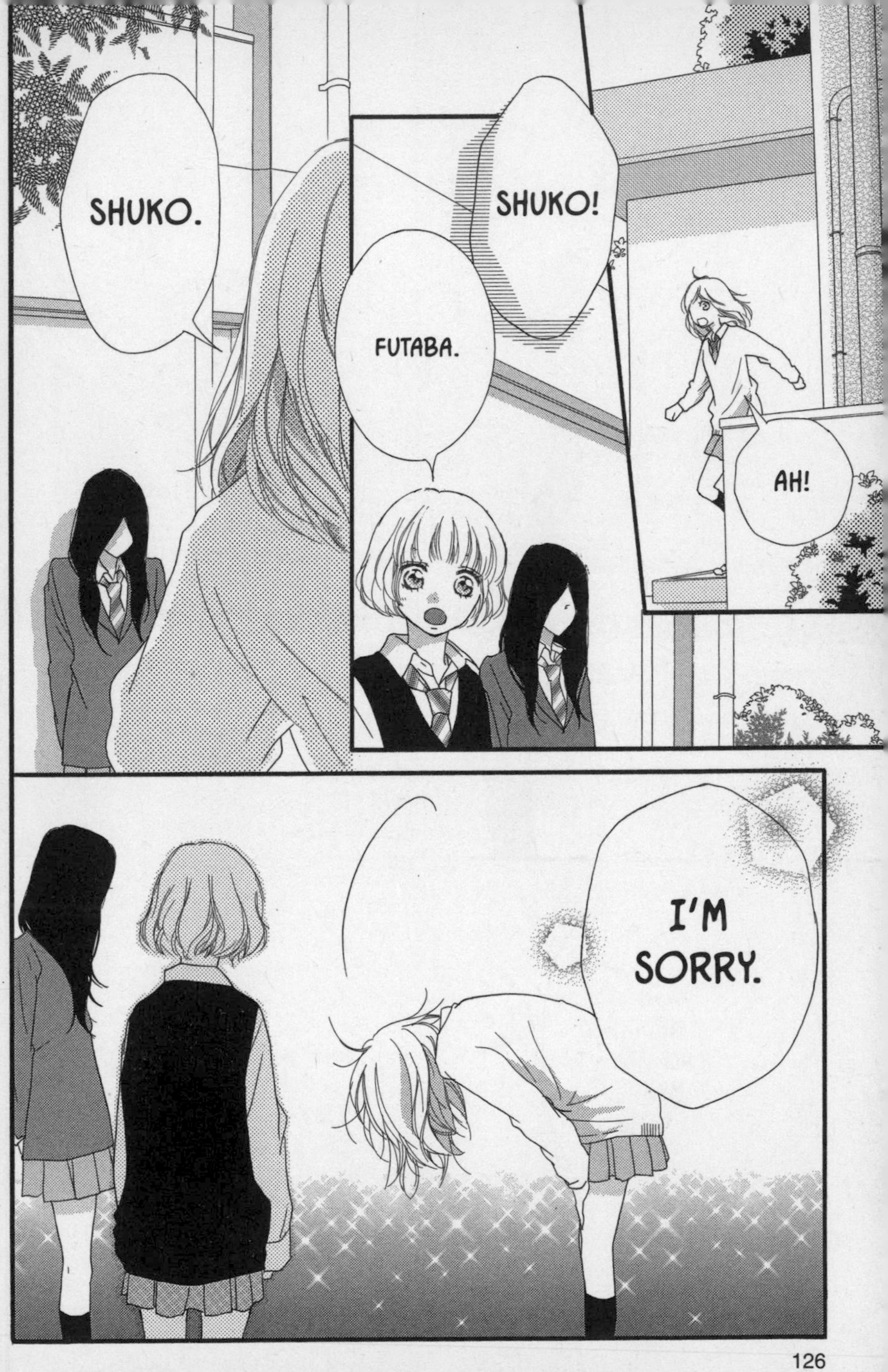
SHUKO!
AH!
FUTABA.
SHUKO.
I'M SORRY.

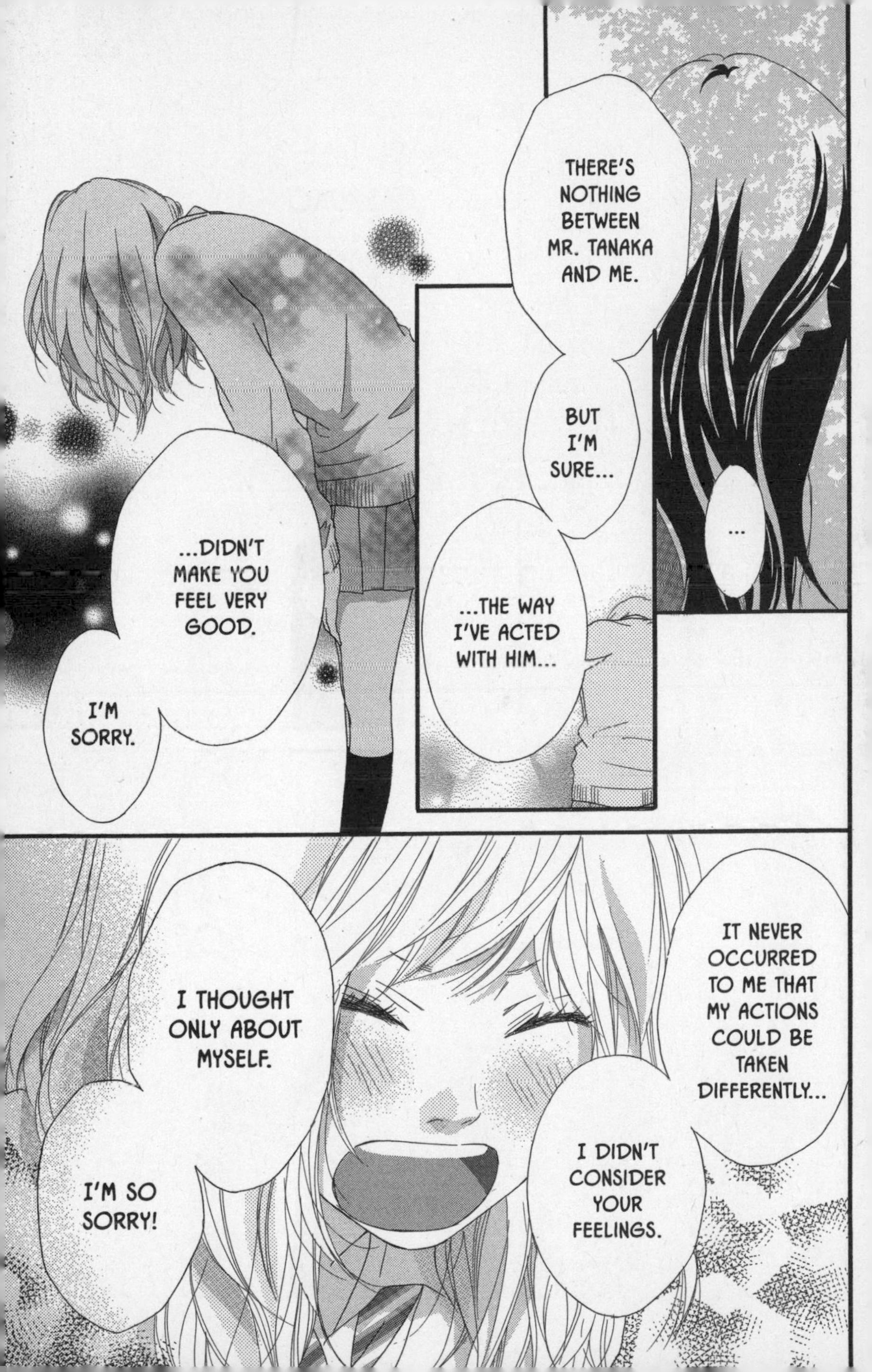
THERE'S NOTHING BETWEEN MR. TANAKA AND ME.
BUT I'M SURE...
...
...THE WAY I'VE ACTED WITH HIM...
...DIDN'T MAKE YOU FEEL VERY GOOD.
I'M SORRY.
IT NEVER OCCURRED TO ME THAT MY ACTIONS COULD BE TAKEN DIFFERENTLY...
I DIDN'T CONSIDER YOUR FEELINGS.
I THOUGHT ONLY ABOUT MYSELF.
I'M SO SORRY!

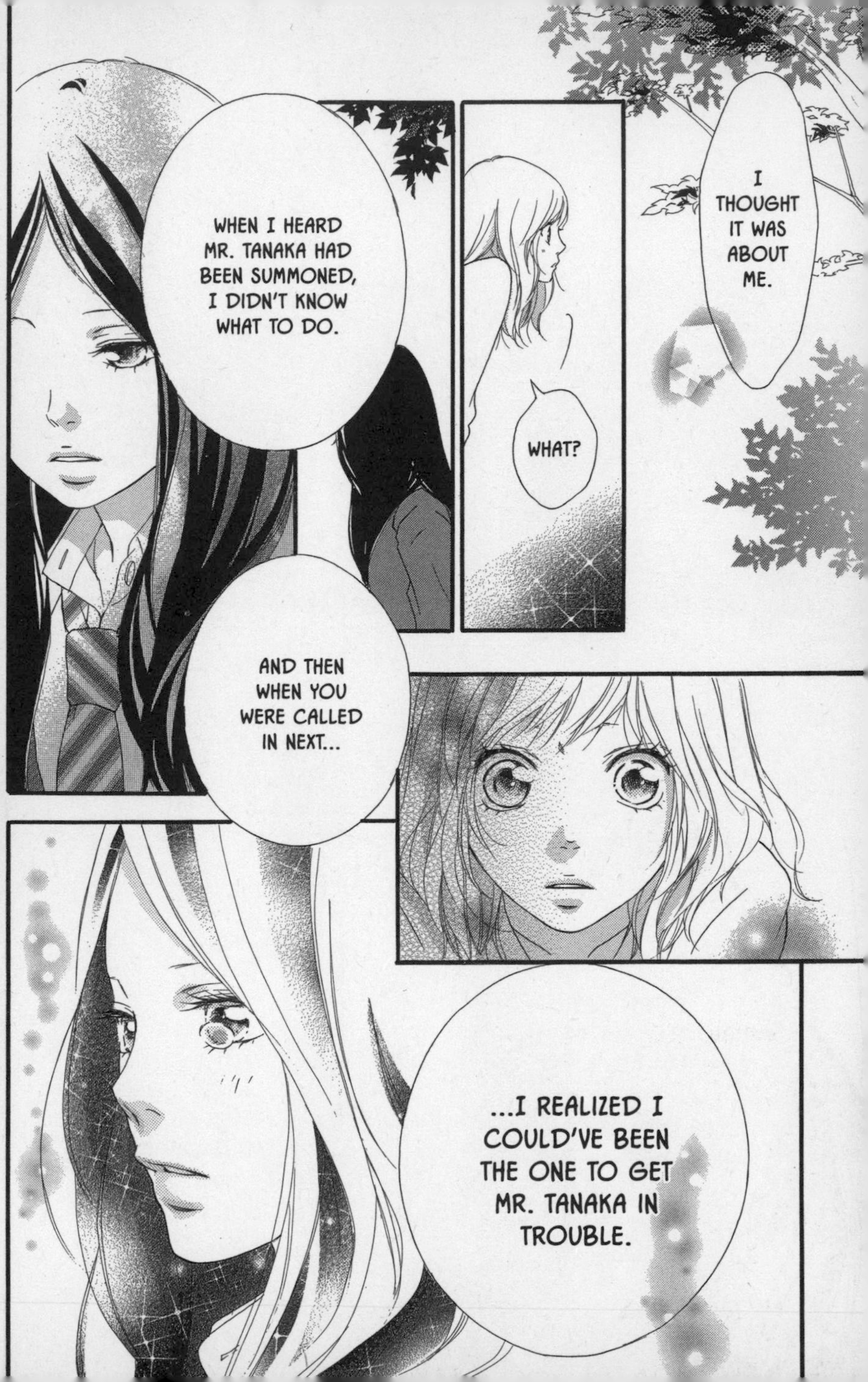
I THOUGHT IT WAS ABOUT ME.
WHAT?
WHEN I HEARD MR. TANAKA HAD BEEN SUMMONED, I DIDN'T KNOW WHAT TO DO.
AND THEN WHEN YOU WERE CALLED IN NEXT...
...I REALIZED I COULD'VE BEEN THE ONE TO GET MR. TANAKA IN TROUBLE.

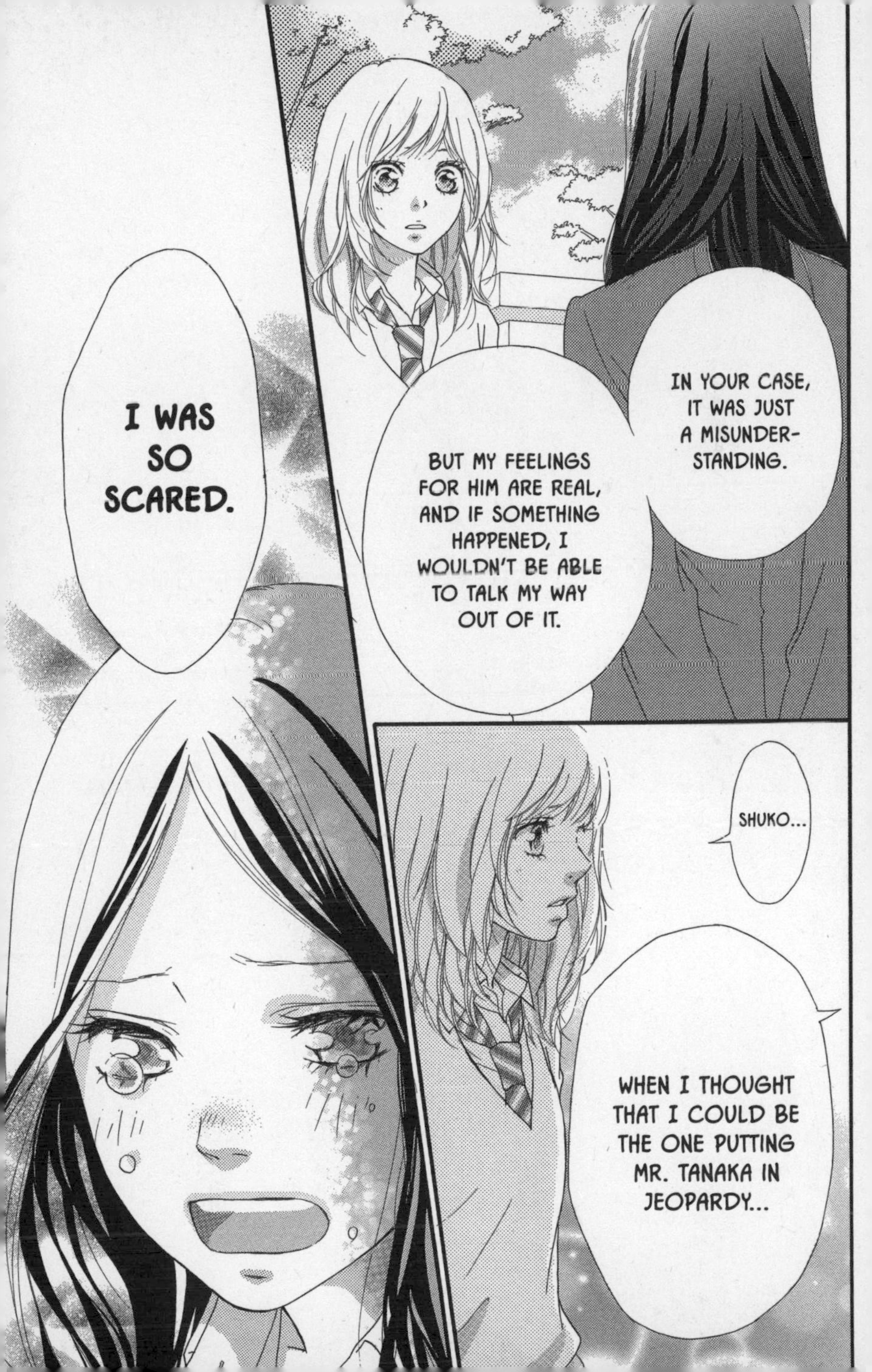
IN YOUR CASE, IT WAS JUST A MISUNDER-STANDING.
BUT MY FEELINGS FOR HIM ARE REAL, AND IF SOMETHING HAPPENED, I WOULDN'T BE ABLE TO TALK MY WAY OUT OF IT.
SHUKO...
WHEN I THOUGHT THAT I COULD BE THE ONE PUTTING MR. TANAKA IN JEOPARDY...
I WAS SO SCARED.

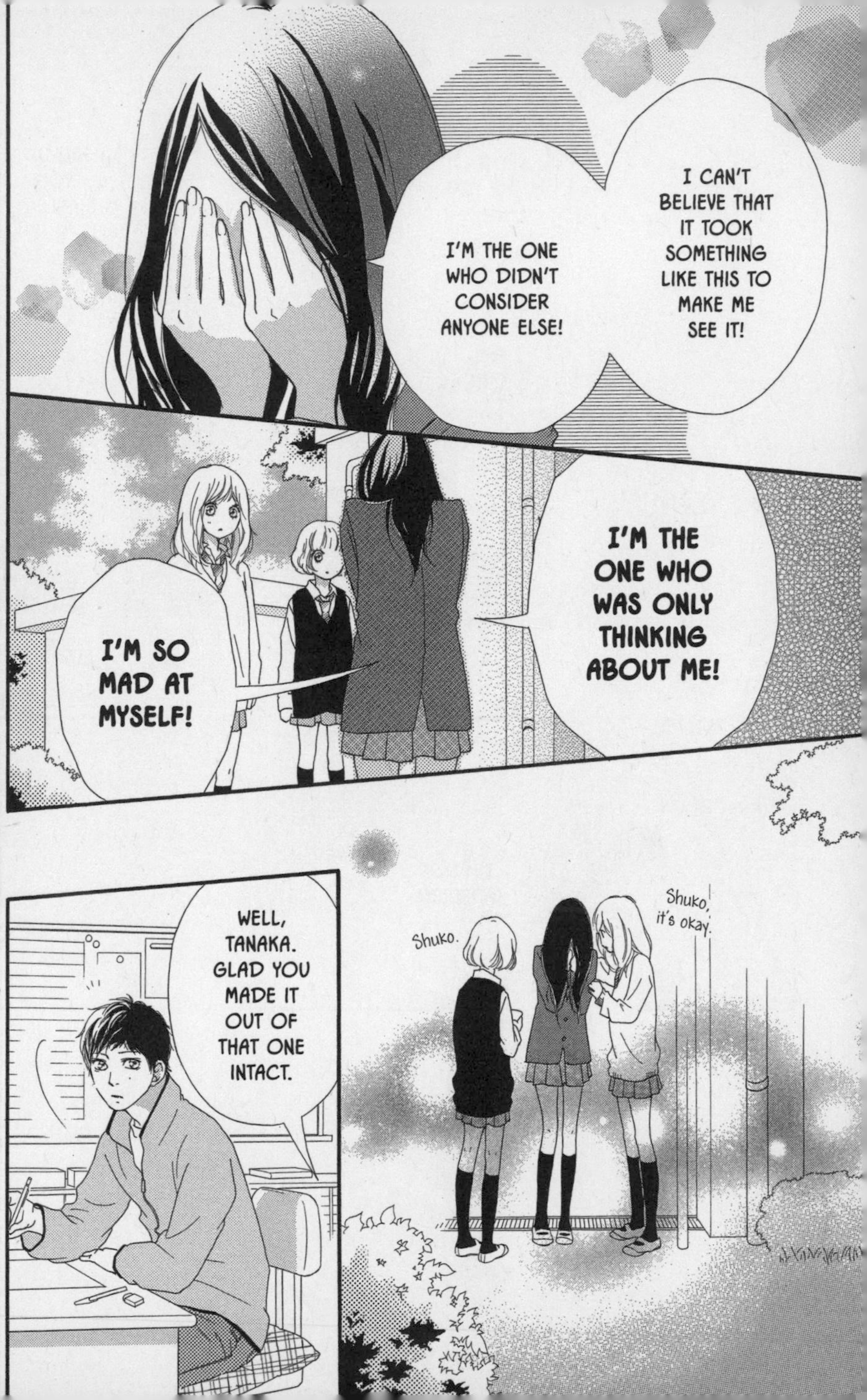
I CAN'T BELIEVE THAT IT TOOK SOMETHING LIKE THIS TO MAKE ME SEE IT!
I'M THE ONE WHO DIDN'T CONSIDER ANYONE ELSE!
I'M THE ONE WHO WAS ONLY THINKING ABOUT ME!
I'M SO MAD AT MYSELF!
Shuko, it's okay.
Shuko.
WELL, TANAKA. GLAD YOU MADE IT OUT OF THAT ONE INTACT.

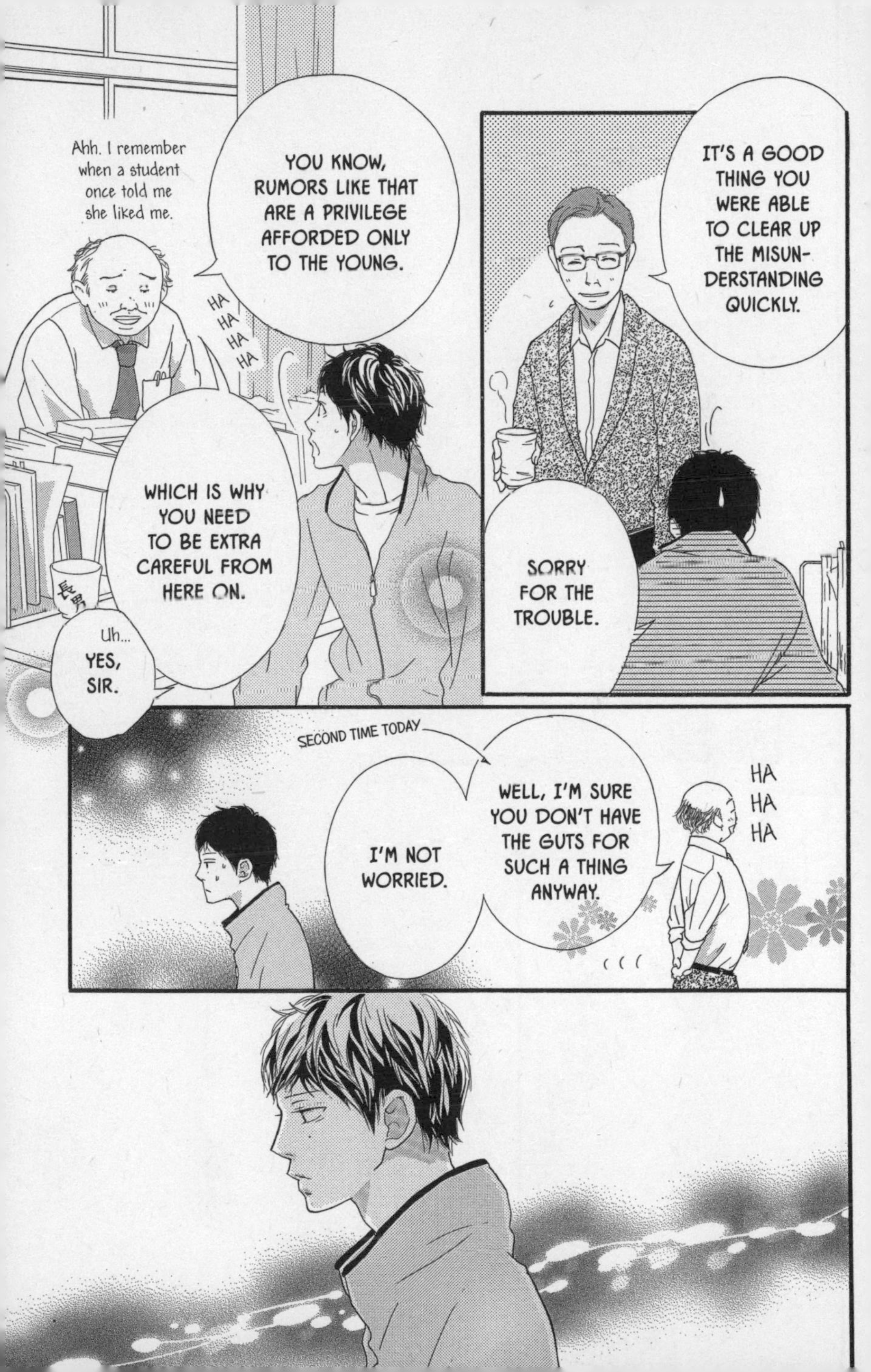
IT'S A GOOD THING YOU WERE ABLE TO CLEAR UP THE MISUNDERSTANDING QUICKLY.
SORRY FOR THE TROUBLE.
YOU KNOW, RUMORS LIKE THAT ARE A PRIVILEGE AFFORDED ONLY TO THE YOUNG.
Ahh. I remember when a student once told me she liked me.
HA HA HA HA
WHICH IS WHY YOU NEED TO BE EXTRA CAREFUL FROM HERE ON.
長男
Uh... YES, SIR.
HA HA HA
WELL, I'M SURE YOU DON'T HAVE THE GUTS FOR SUCH A THING ANYWAY.
SECOND TIME TODAY
I'M NOT WORRIED.

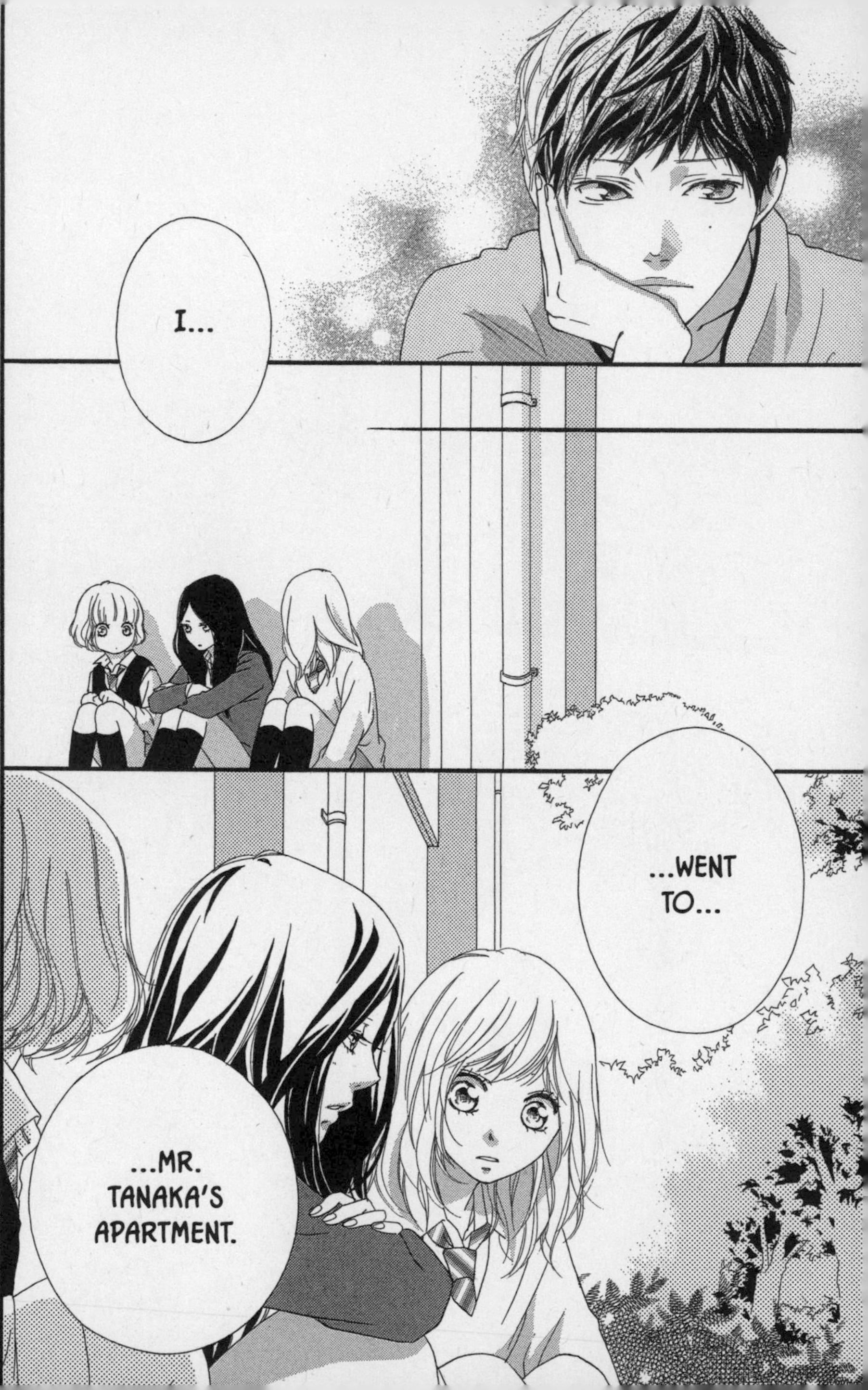
I...
...WENT TO...
...MR. TANAKA'S APARTMENT.

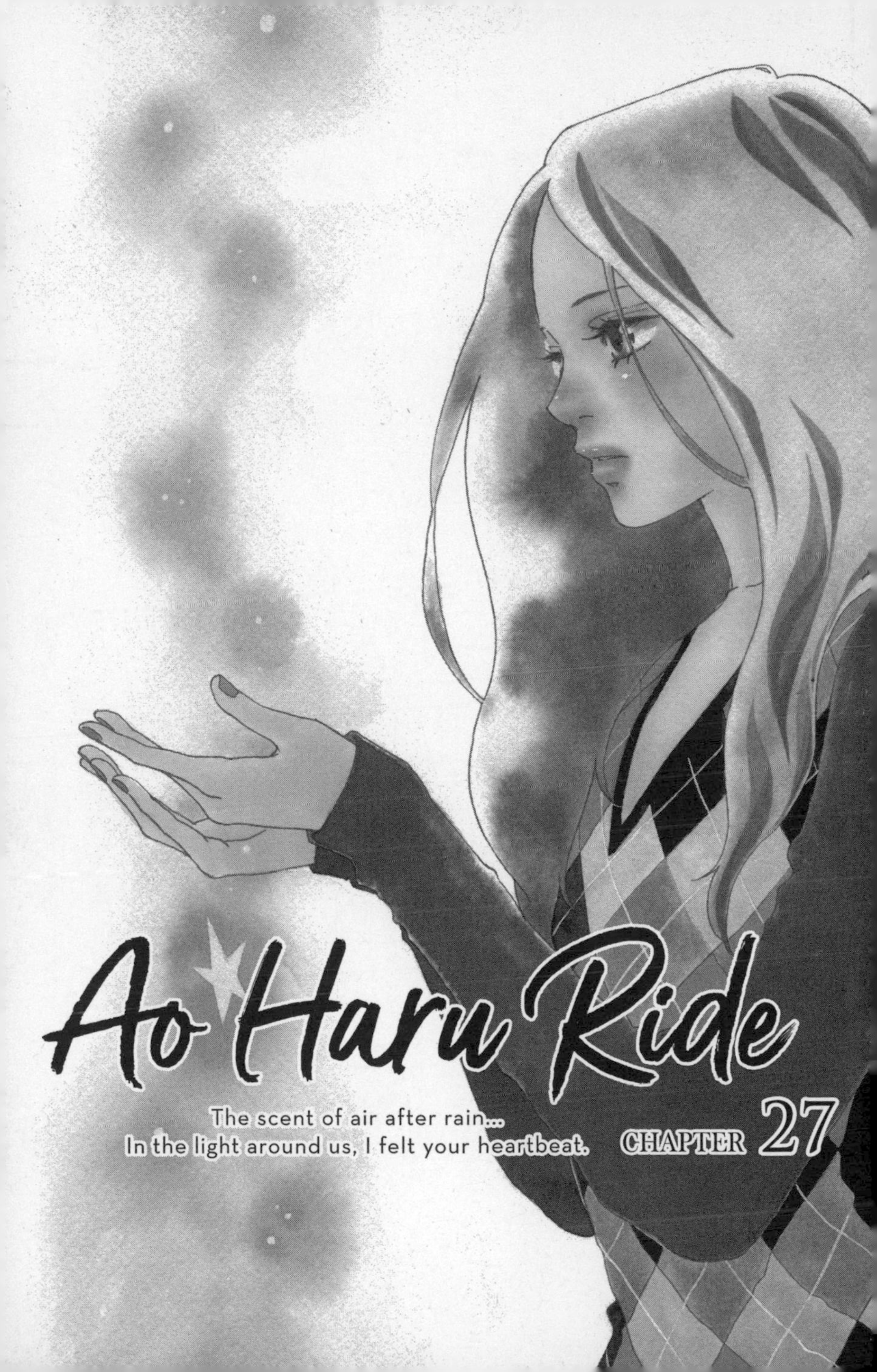
Ao Haru Ride
The scent of air after rain...
In the light around us, I felt your heartbeat.
CHAPTER 27

Yui Narumi

Birthday:
August 7

Astrological Sign, Blood Type:
Leo, type B

Height, Weight:
5'2", 101 lbs.

Favorite Subject in School:
Math

Least Favorite Subject in School:
English

Favorite Food:
Fried chicken

Least Favorite Food:
Peanuts

Favorite Music:
Etsuko Yakushimaru

Siblings:
Only child

Age When First Crush Happened:
First year of junior high

Fun Fact:
Formerly left-handed

Favorite Snack:
DARS Biscuits

Favorite Drink:
Jasmine tea

Favorite Color:
Aqua

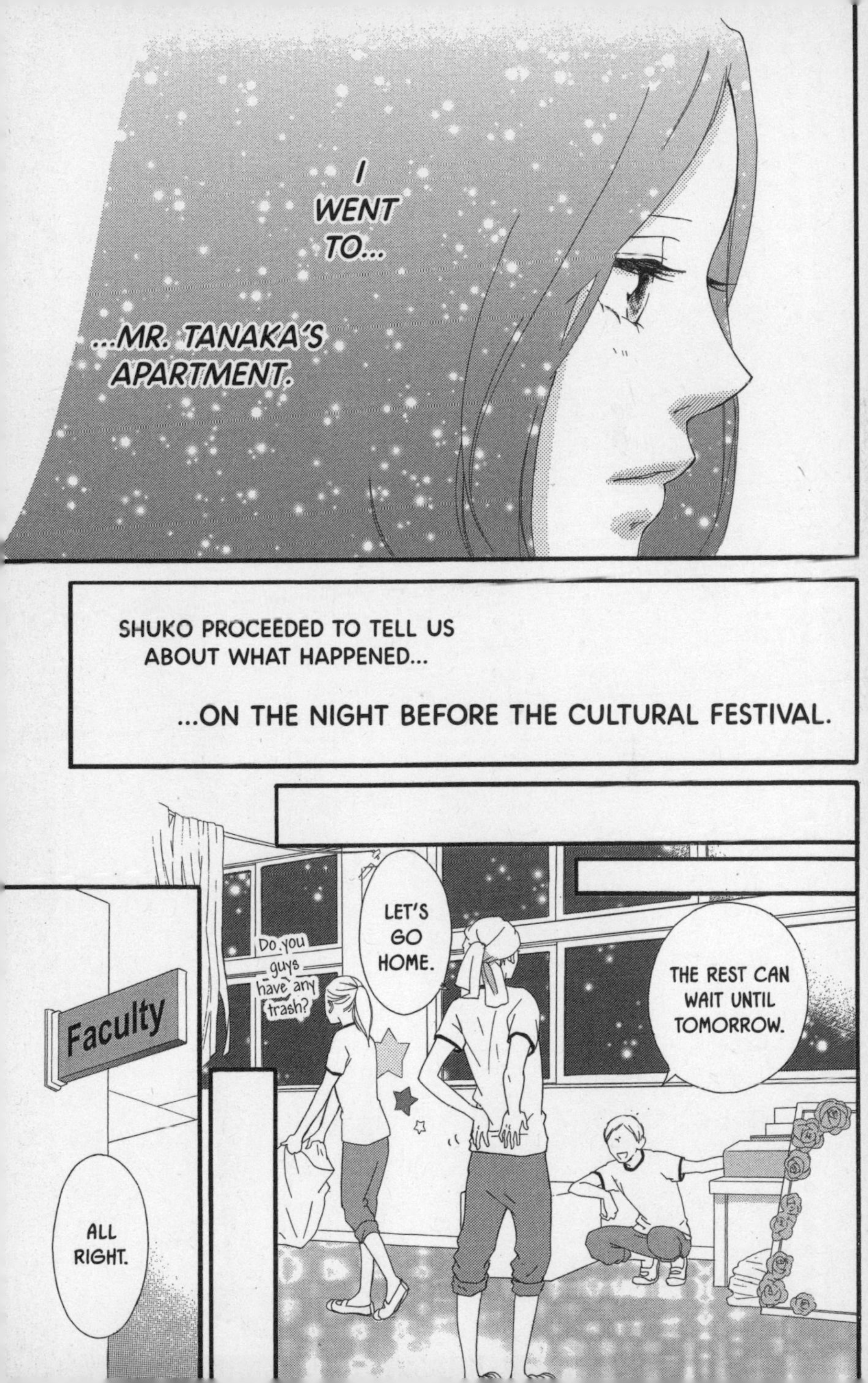
I WENT TO...
...MR. TANAKA'S APARTMENT.
SHUKO PROCEEDED TO TELL US ABOUT WHAT HAPPENED...
...ON THE NIGHT BEFORE THE CULTURAL FESTIVAL.
THE REST CAN WAIT UNTIL TOMORROW.
LET'S GO HOME.
Do you guys have any trash?
Faculty
ALL RIGHT.

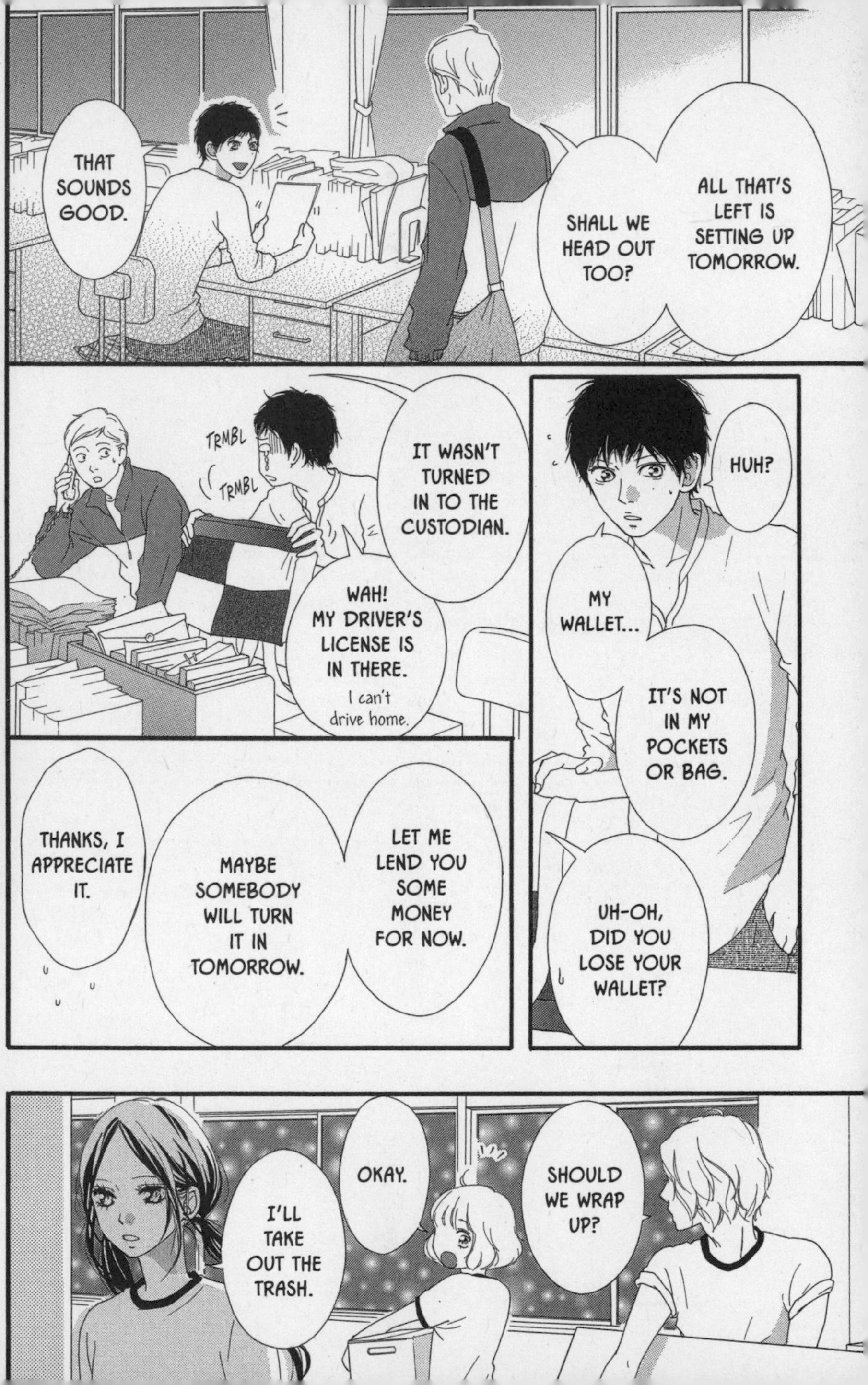
ALL THAT'S LEFT IS SETTING UP TOMORROW.
SHALL WE HEAD OUT TOO?
THAT SOUNDS GOOD.
HUH?
MY WALLET...
IT'S NOT IN MY POCKETS OR BAG.
UH-OH, DID YOU LOSE YOUR WALLET?
IT WASN'T TURNED IN TO THE CUSTODIAN.
TRMBL
TRMBL
WAH! MY DRIVER'S LICENSE IS IN THERE.
I can't drive home.
LET ME LEND YOU SOME MONEY FOR NOW.
MAYBE SOMEBODY WILL TURN IT IN TOMORROW.
THANKS, I APPRECIATE IT.
SHOULD WE WRAP UP?
OKAY.
I'LL TAKE OUT THE TRASH.

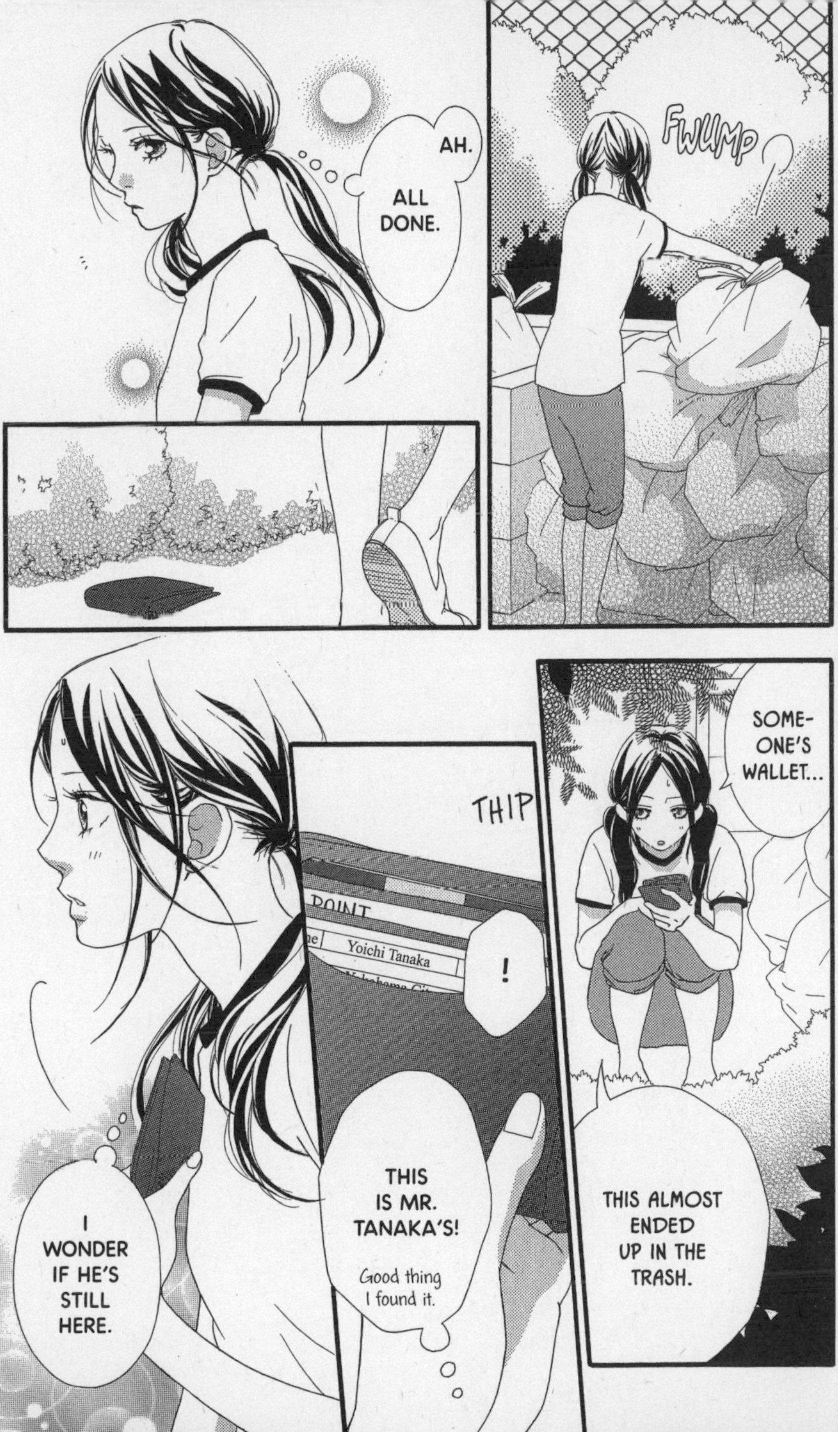
FWUMP
AH.
ALL DONE.
SOME-ONE'S WALLET...
THIS ALMOST ENDED UP IN THE TRASH.
THIP
POINT
Yoichi Tanaka
!
THIS IS MR. TANAKA'S!
Good thing I found it.
I WONDER IF HE'S STILL HERE.

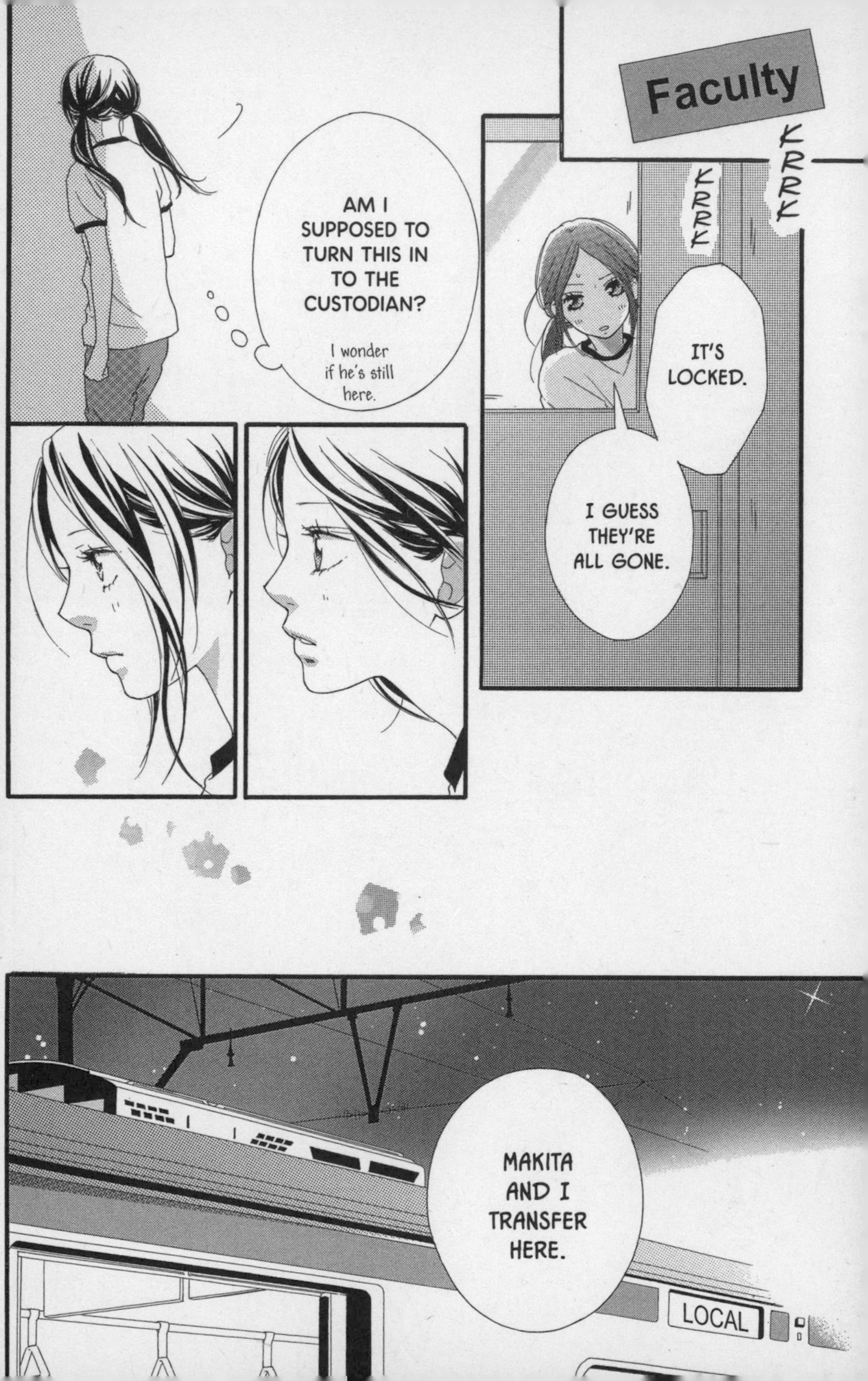
Faculty
KRRK
KRRK
IT'S LOCKED.
I GUESS THEY'RE ALL GONE.
AM I SUPPOSED TO TURN THIS IN TO THE CUSTODIAN?
I wonder if he's still here.
MAKITA AND I TRANSFER HERE.
LOCAL

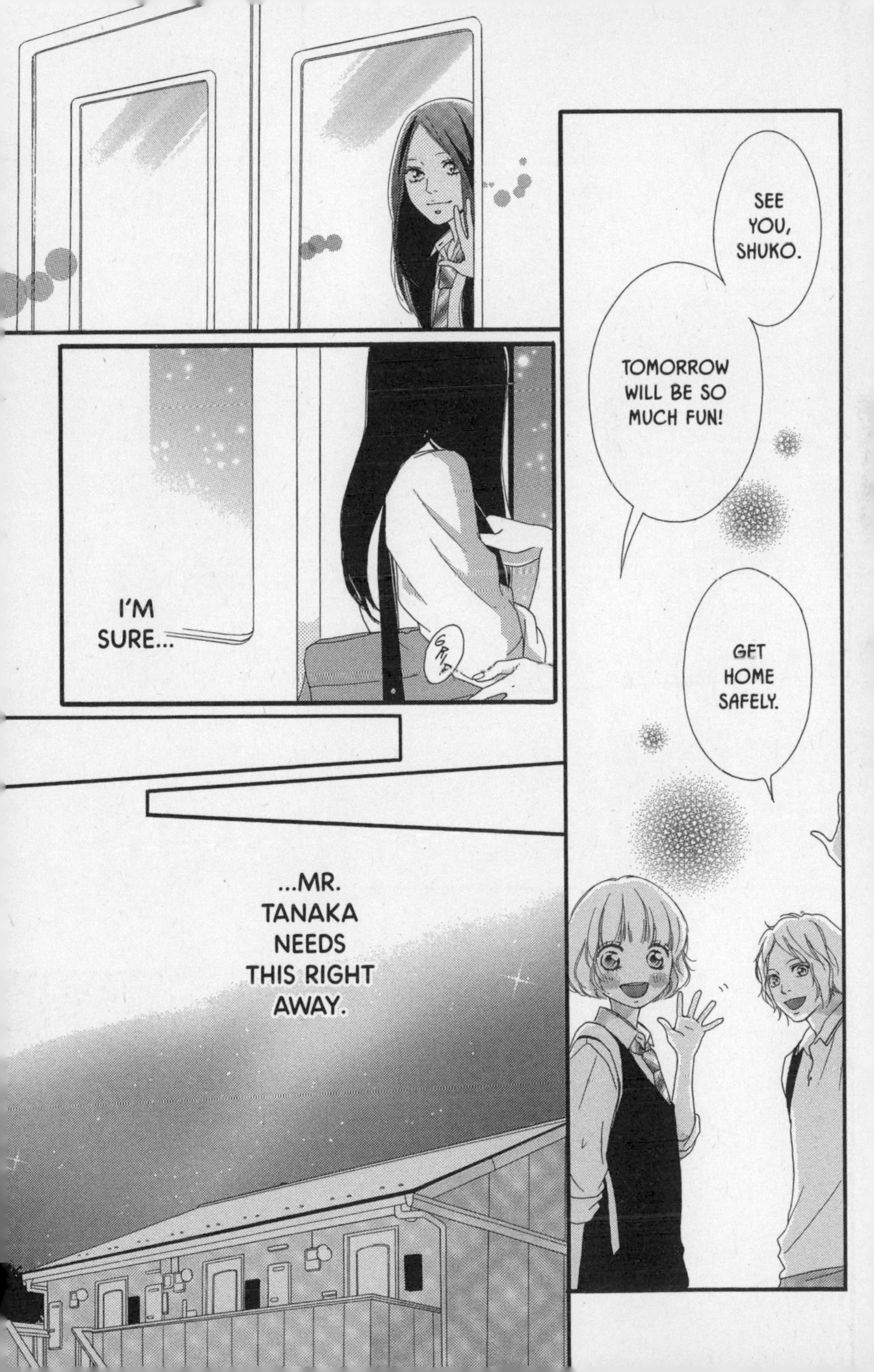
SEE YOU, SHUKO.
TOMORROW WILL BE SO MUCH FUN!
GET HOME SAFELY.
I'M SURE...
...MR. TANAKA NEEDS THIS RIGHT AWAY.

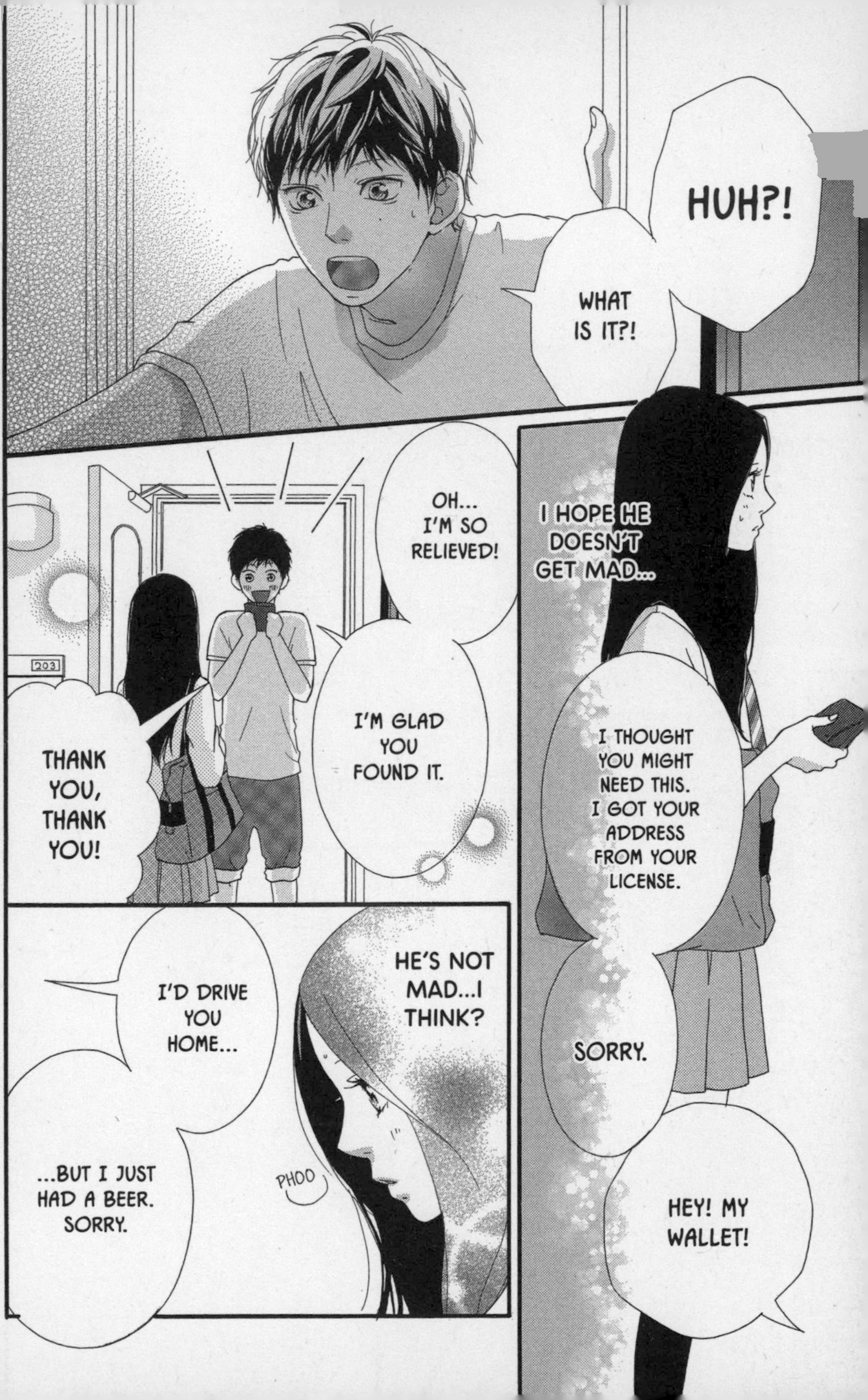
HUH?!
WHAT IS IT?!
I HOPE HE DOESN'T GET MAD...
I THOUGHT YOU MIGHT NEED THIS. I GOT YOUR ADDRESS FROM YOUR LICENSE.
SORRY.
HEY! MY WALLET!
OH... I'M SO RELIEVED!
I'M GLAD YOU FOUND IT.
203
THANK YOU, THANK YOU!
HE'S NOT MAD...I THINK?
PHOO
I'D DRIVE YOU HOME...
...BUT I JUST HAD A BEER. SORRY.

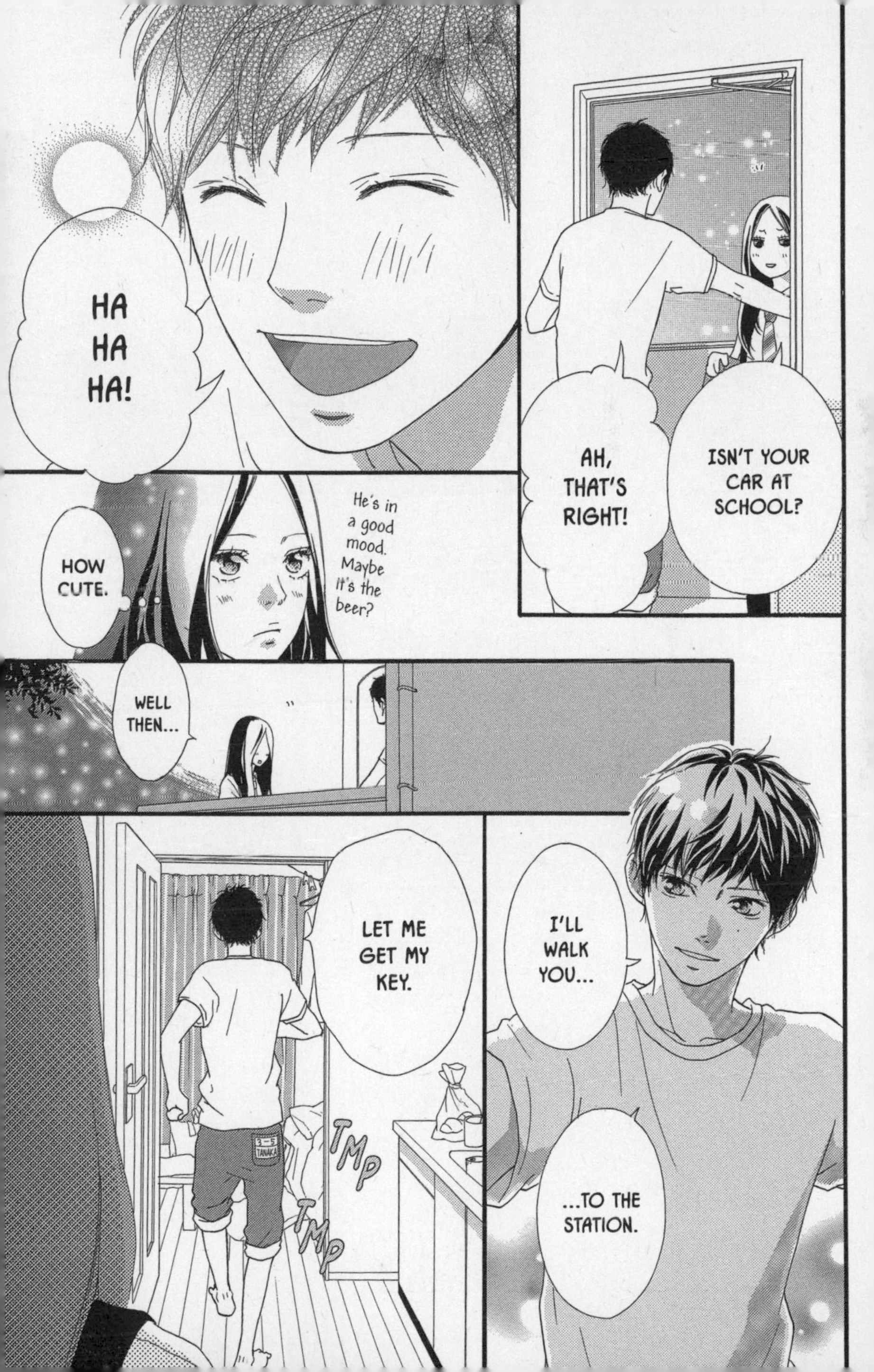
ISN'T YOUR CAR AT SCHOOL?
AH, THAT'S RIGHT!
HA HA HA!
He's in a good mood. Maybe it's the beer?
HOW CUTE.
WELL THEN...
I'LL WALK YOU...
...TO THE STATION.
LET ME GET MY KEY.
3-5 TANAKA
TMP
TMP

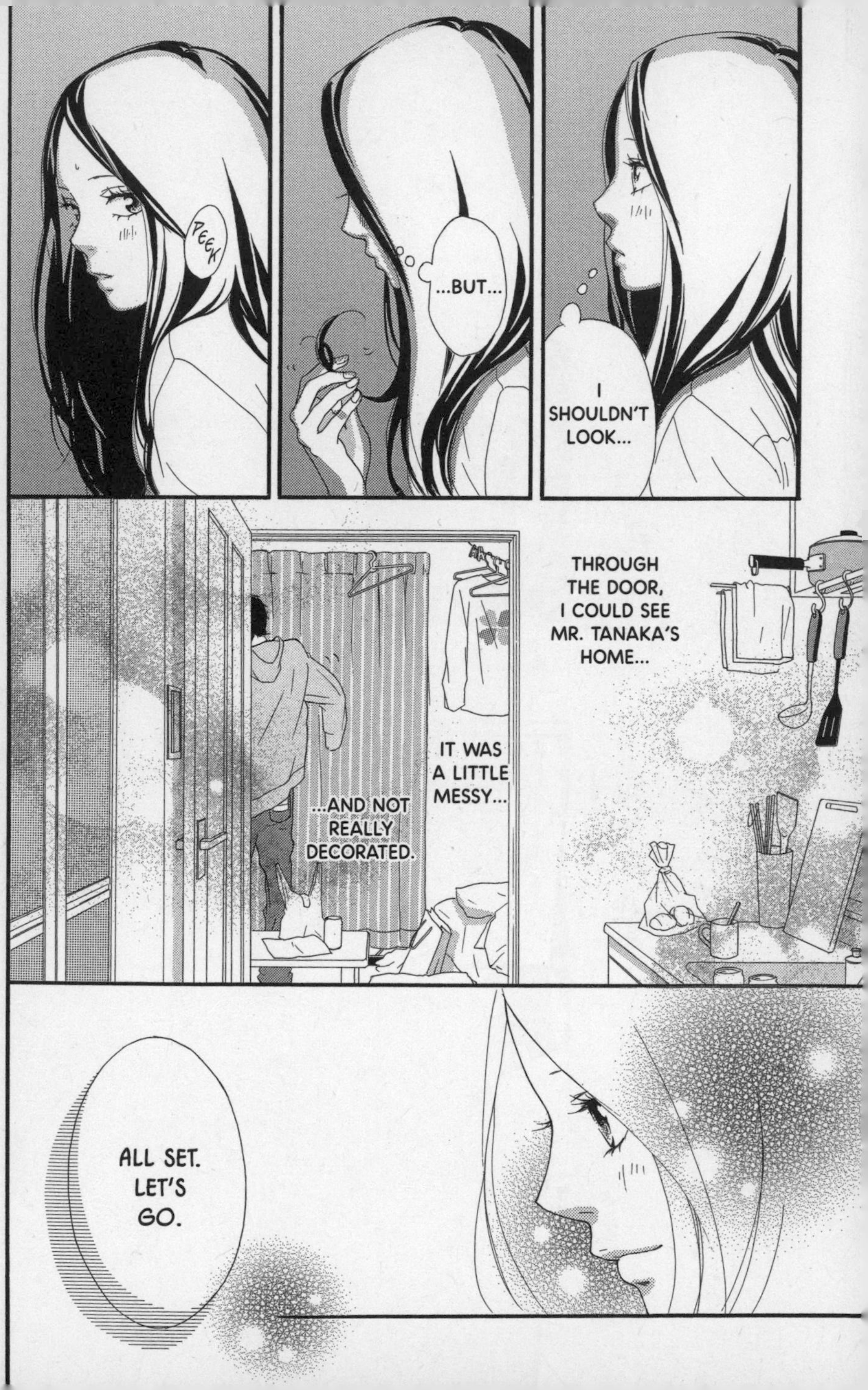
I SHOULDN'T LOOK...
...BUT...
PEEK
THROUGH THE DOOR, I COULD SEE MR. TANAKA'S HOME...
IT WAS A LITTLE MESSY...
...AND NOT REALLY DECORATED.
ALL SET. LET'S GO.

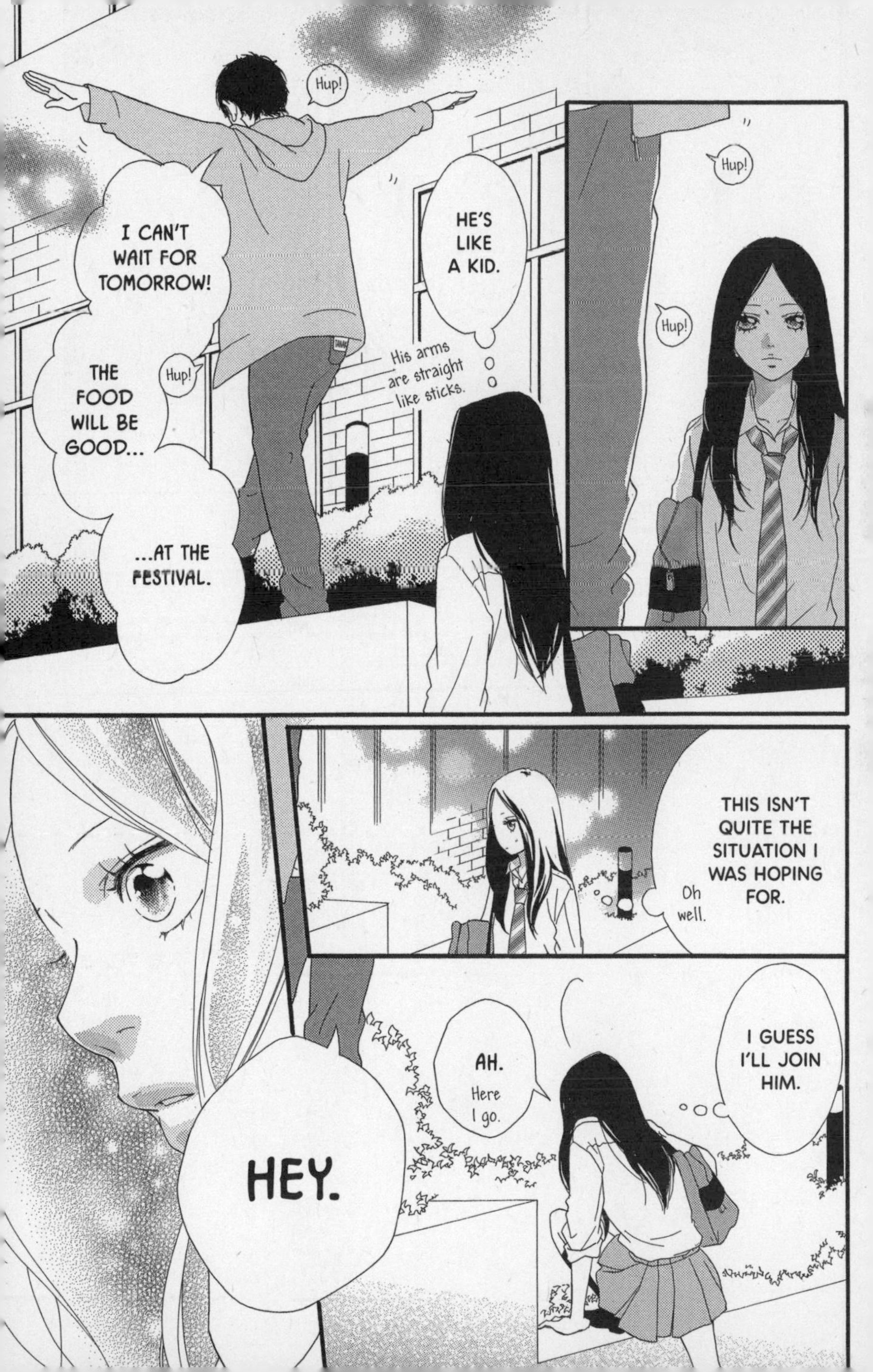
Hup!
Hup!
Hup!
HE'S LIKE A KID.
His arms are straight like sticks.
I CAN'T WAIT FOR TOMORROW!
Hup!
THE FOOD WILL BE GOOD...
...AT THE FESTIVAL.
THIS ISN'T QUITE THE SITUATION I WAS HOPING FOR.
Oh well.
I GUESS I'LL JOIN HIM.
AH.
Here I go.
HEY.

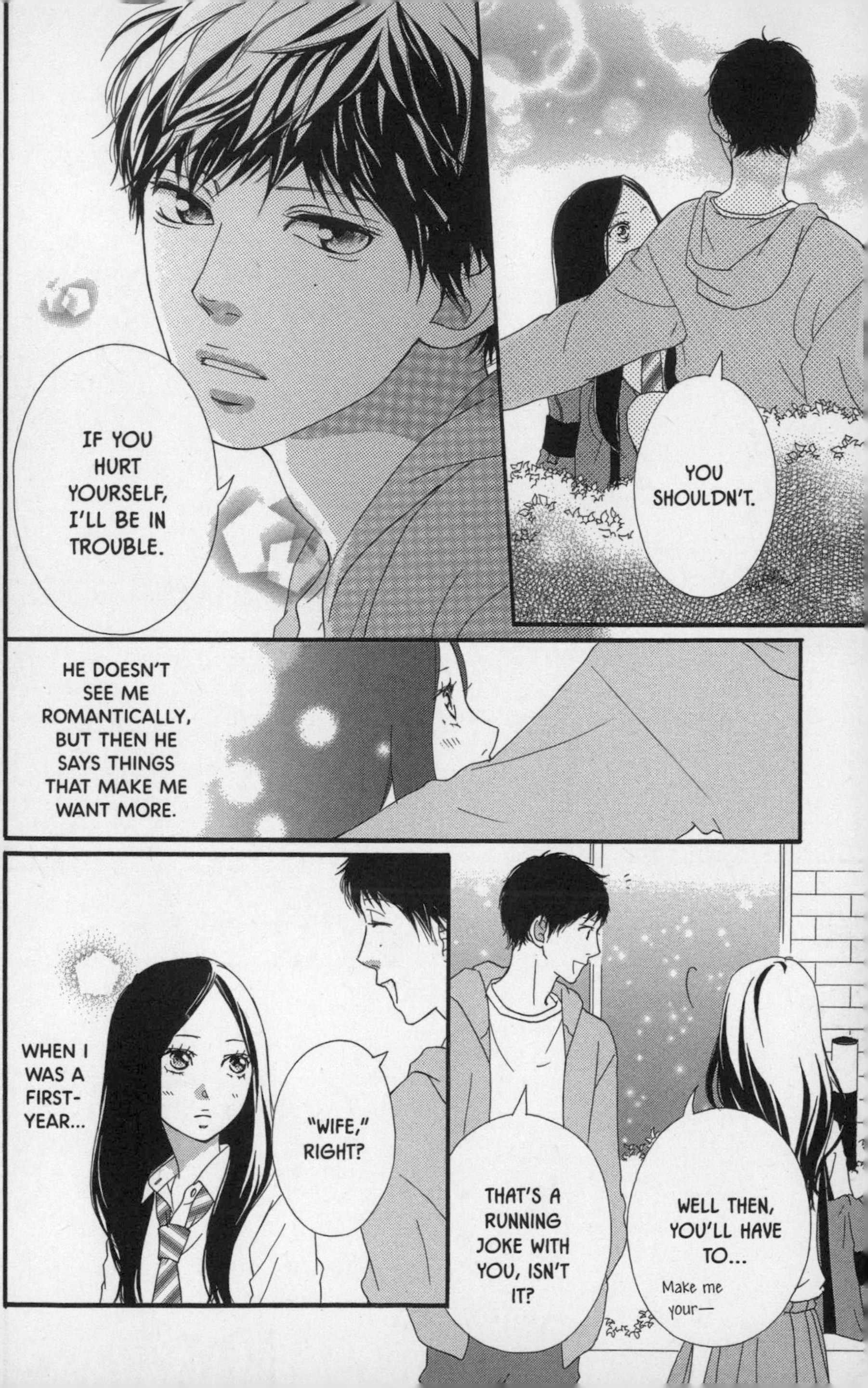
YOU SHOULDN'T.
IF YOU HURT YOURSELF, I'LL BE IN TROUBLE.
HE DOESN'T SEE ME ROMANTICALLY, BUT THEN HE SAYS THINGS THAT MAKE ME WANT MORE.
WELL THEN, YOU'LL HAVE TO...
Make me your—
THAT'S A RUNNING JOKE WITH YOU, ISN'T IT?
"WIFE," RIGHT?
WHEN I WAS A FIRST-YEAR...

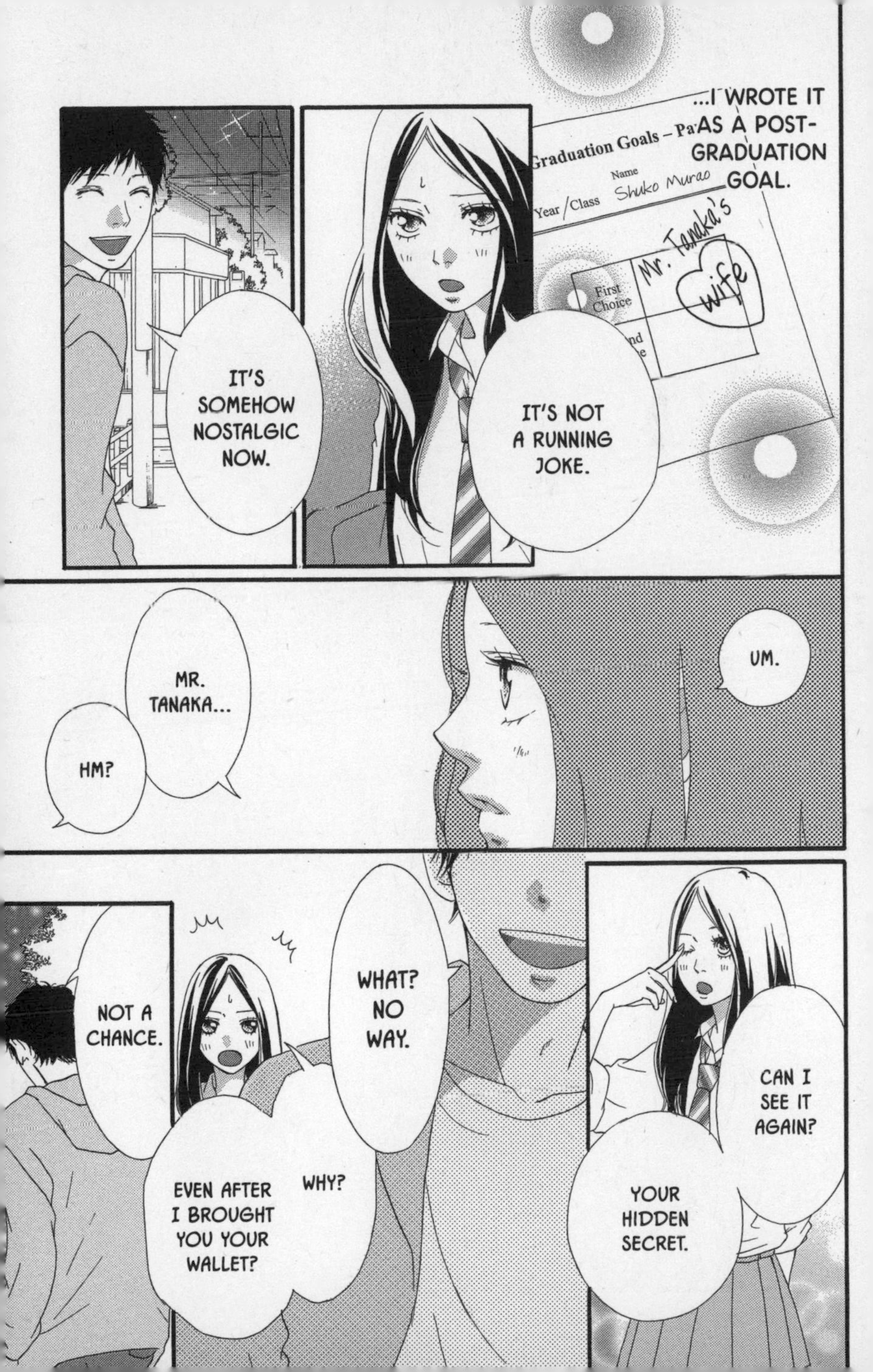
...I WROTE IT AS A POST-GRADUATION GOAL.
Graduation Goals – Pa
Name
Shuko Murao
Year / Class
First Choice
Mr. Tanaka's wife
IT'S NOT A RUNNING JOKE.
IT'S SOMEHOW NOSTALGIC NOW.
UM.
MR. TANAKA...
HM?
CAN I SEE IT AGAIN?
YOUR HIDDEN SECRET.
WHAT? NO WAY.
WHY?
EVEN AFTER I BROUGHT YOU YOUR WALLET?
NOT A CHANCE.

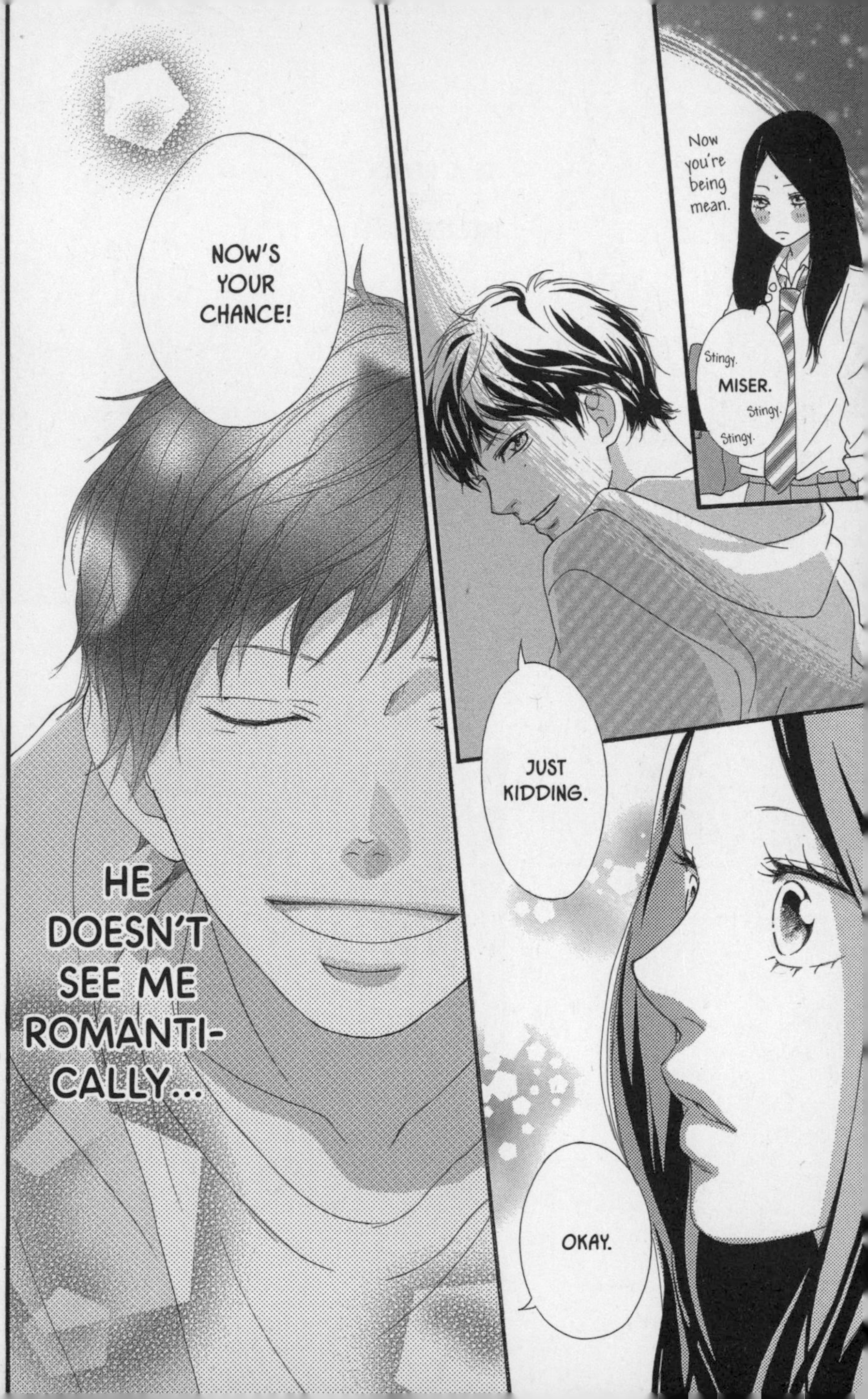
Now you're being mean.
Stingy.
MISER.
Stingy.
Stingy.
JUST KIDDING.
OKAY.
NOW'S YOUR CHANCE!
HE DOESN'T SEE ME ROMANTI-CALLY...

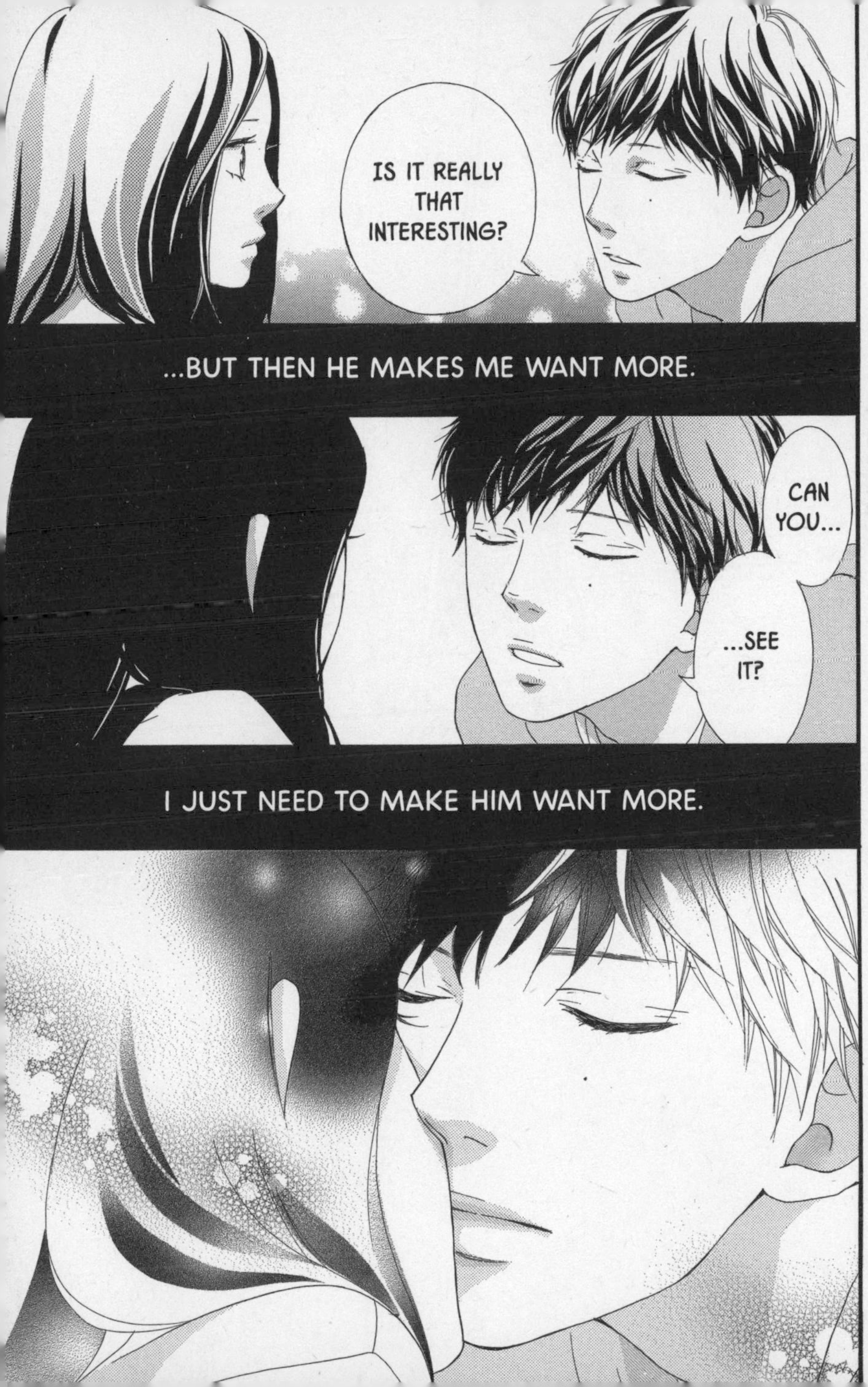
IS IT REALLY THAT INTERESTING?
...BUT THEN HE MAKES ME WANT MORE.
CAN YOU...
...SEE IT?
I JUST NEED TO MAKE HIM WANT MORE.

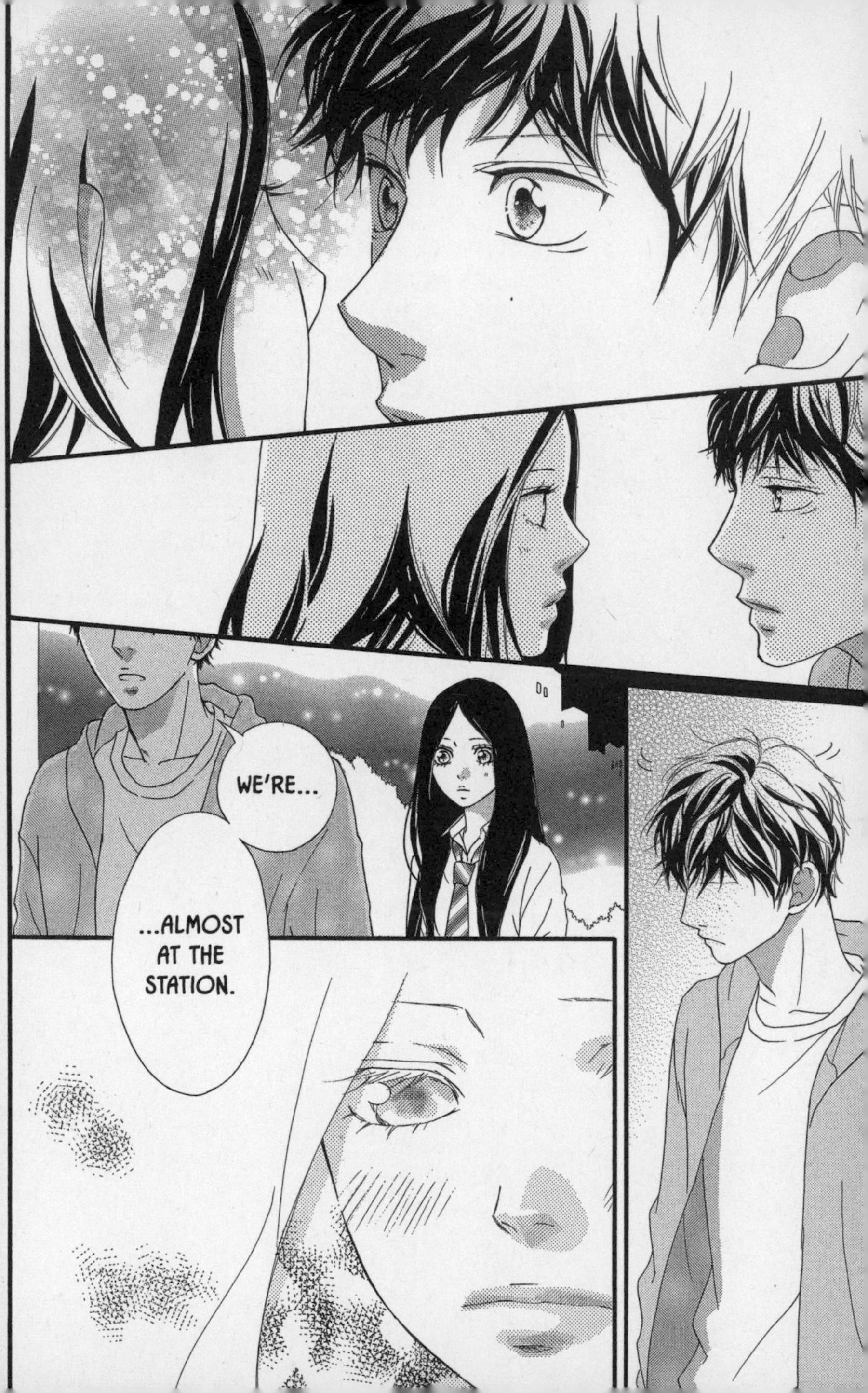
WE'RE...
...ALMOST AT THE STATION.

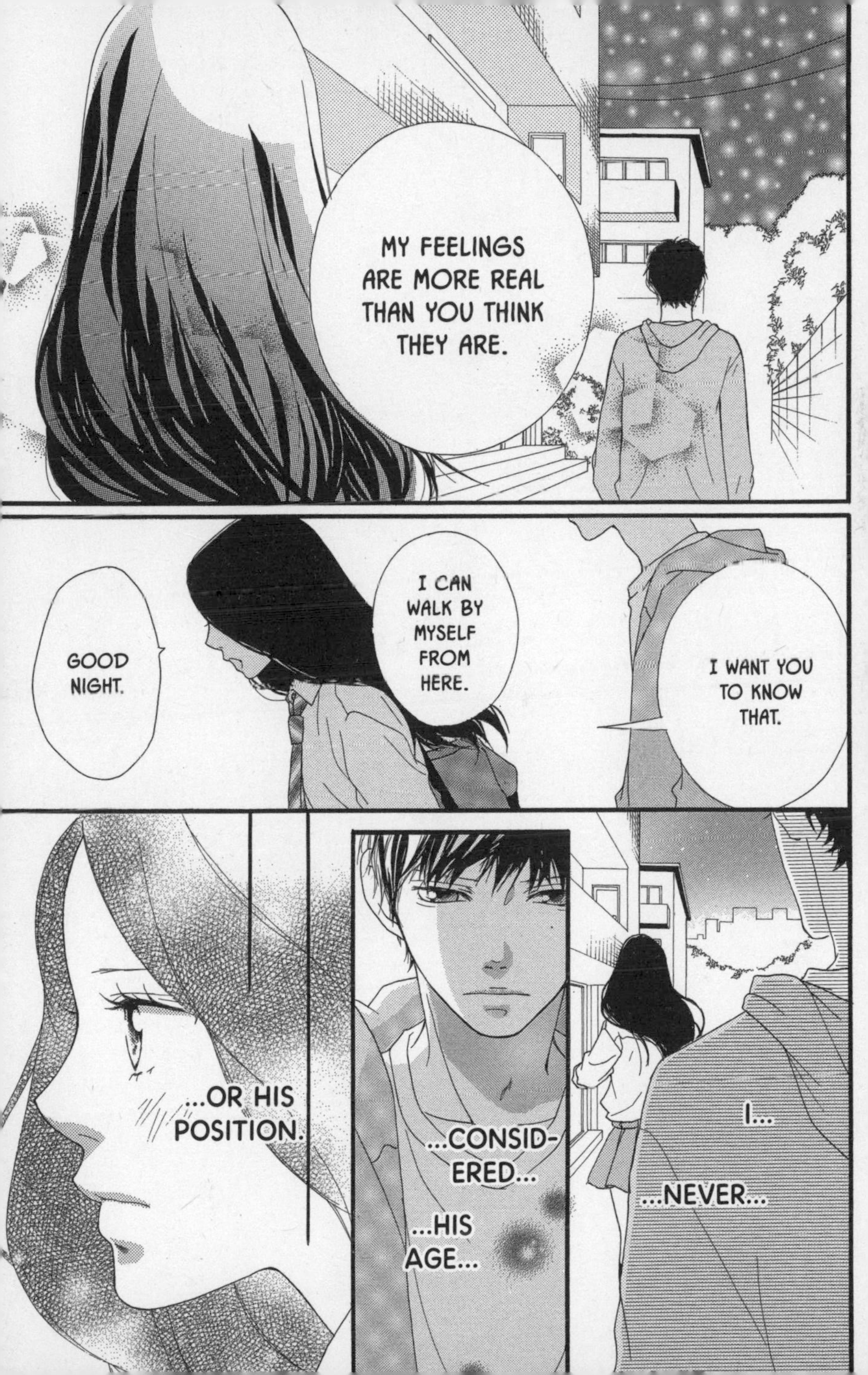
MY FEELINGS ARE MORE REAL THAN YOU THINK THEY ARE.
I WANT YOU TO KNOW THAT.
I CAN WALK BY MYSELF FROM HERE.
GOOD NIGHT.
I...
...NEVER...
...CONSID-ERED...
...HIS AGE...
...OR HIS POSITION.

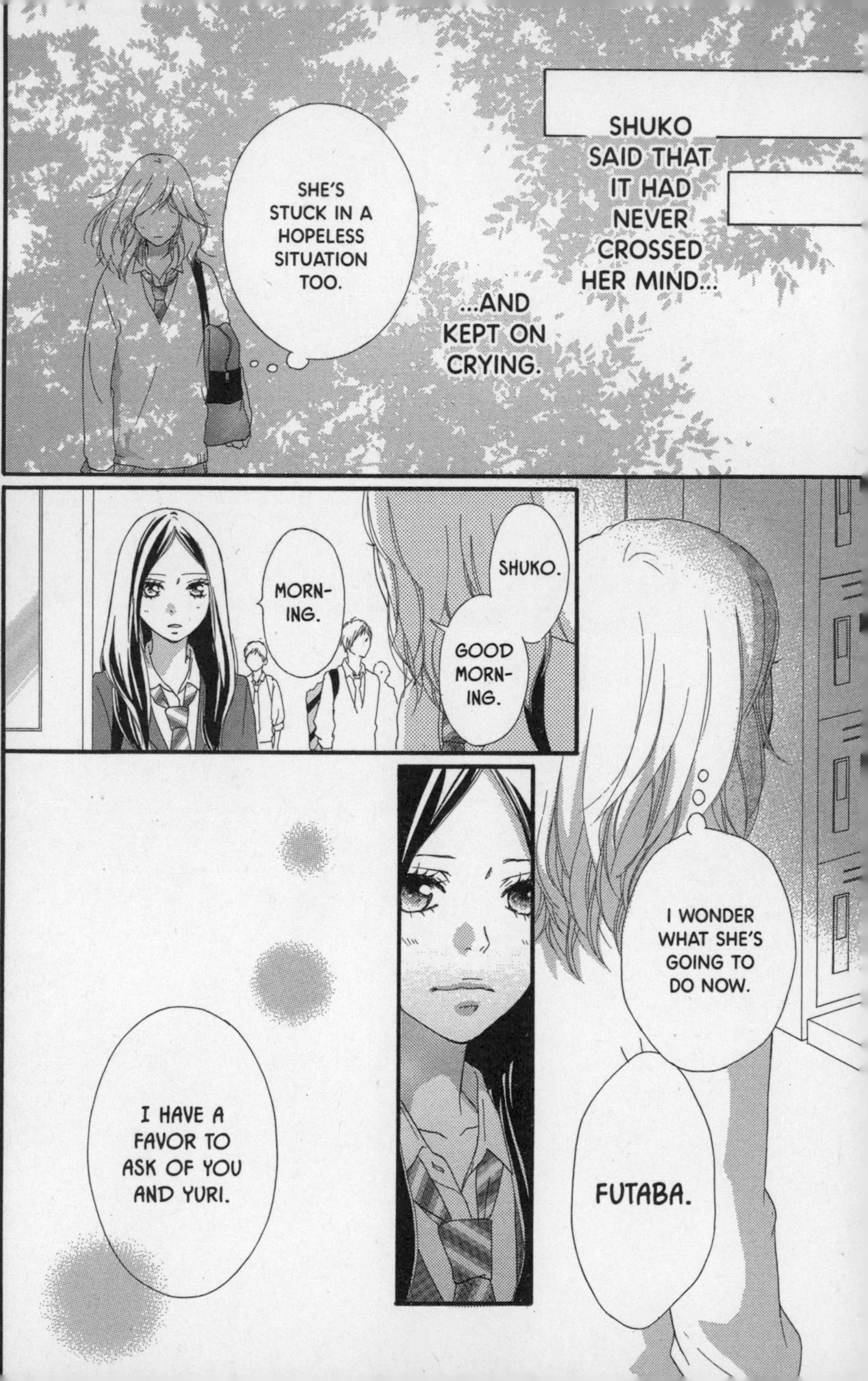
SHUKO SAID THAT IT HAD NEVER CROSSED HER MIND...
...AND KEPT ON CRYING.
SHE'S STUCK IN A HOPELESS SITUATION TOO.
SHUKO.
GOOD MORN-ING.
MORN-ING.
I WONDER WHAT SHE'S GOING TO DO NOW.
FUTABA.
I HAVE A FAVOR TO ASK OF YOU AND YURI.

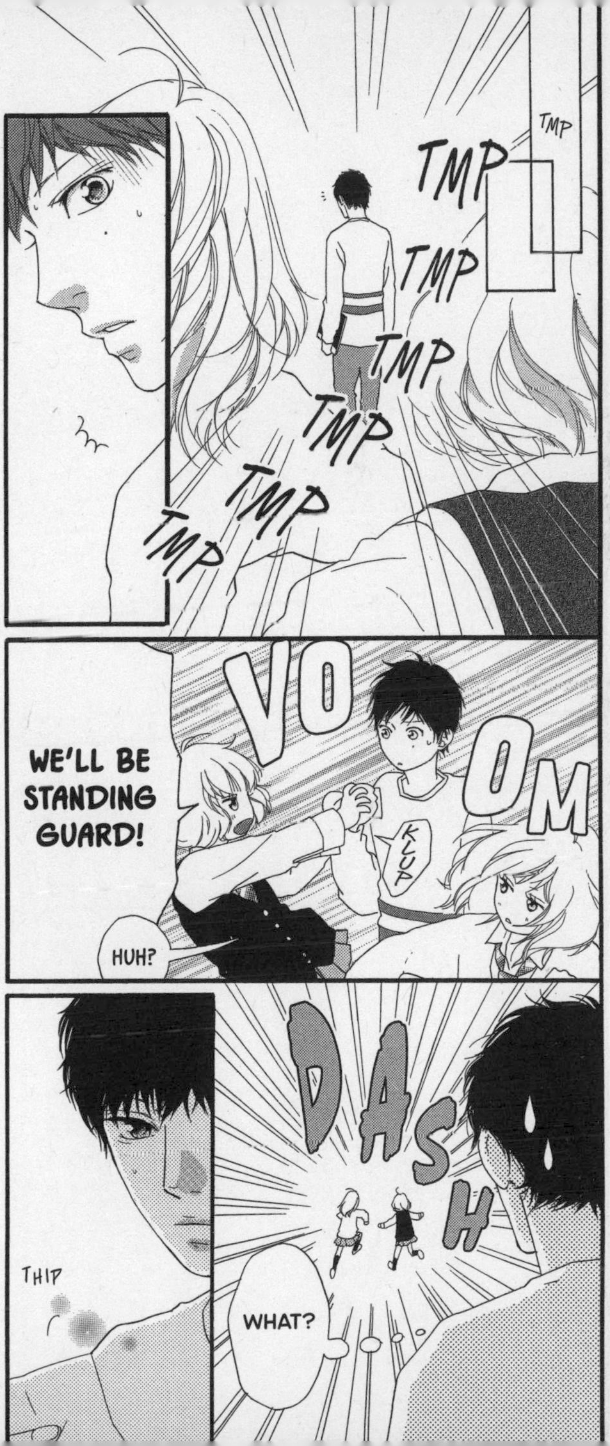
TMP
TMP
TMP
TMP
TMP
TMP
TMP
VOOM
WE'LL BE STANDING GUARD!
KLUP
HUH?
DASH
WHAT?
THIP

In the previous volume I wrote about how I emit sounds whenever I remember embarrassing things from my past. And I am pleased to say that many of you have shared that you do the same! So many, in fact, that I can hold my arms up in victory. Yeahh! From now on, whenever I remember something embarrassing, I'm going to go ahead and snort, hum, and let out whatever comes to me. When my friends and family ask me what's wrong, I'll simply declare it a ritual, laugh, and enjoy myself. Some people wrote that they automatically say things like, "Ugh, I'm such an idiot!" These people are vastly superior and make me feel somewhat inadequate. Why is that?

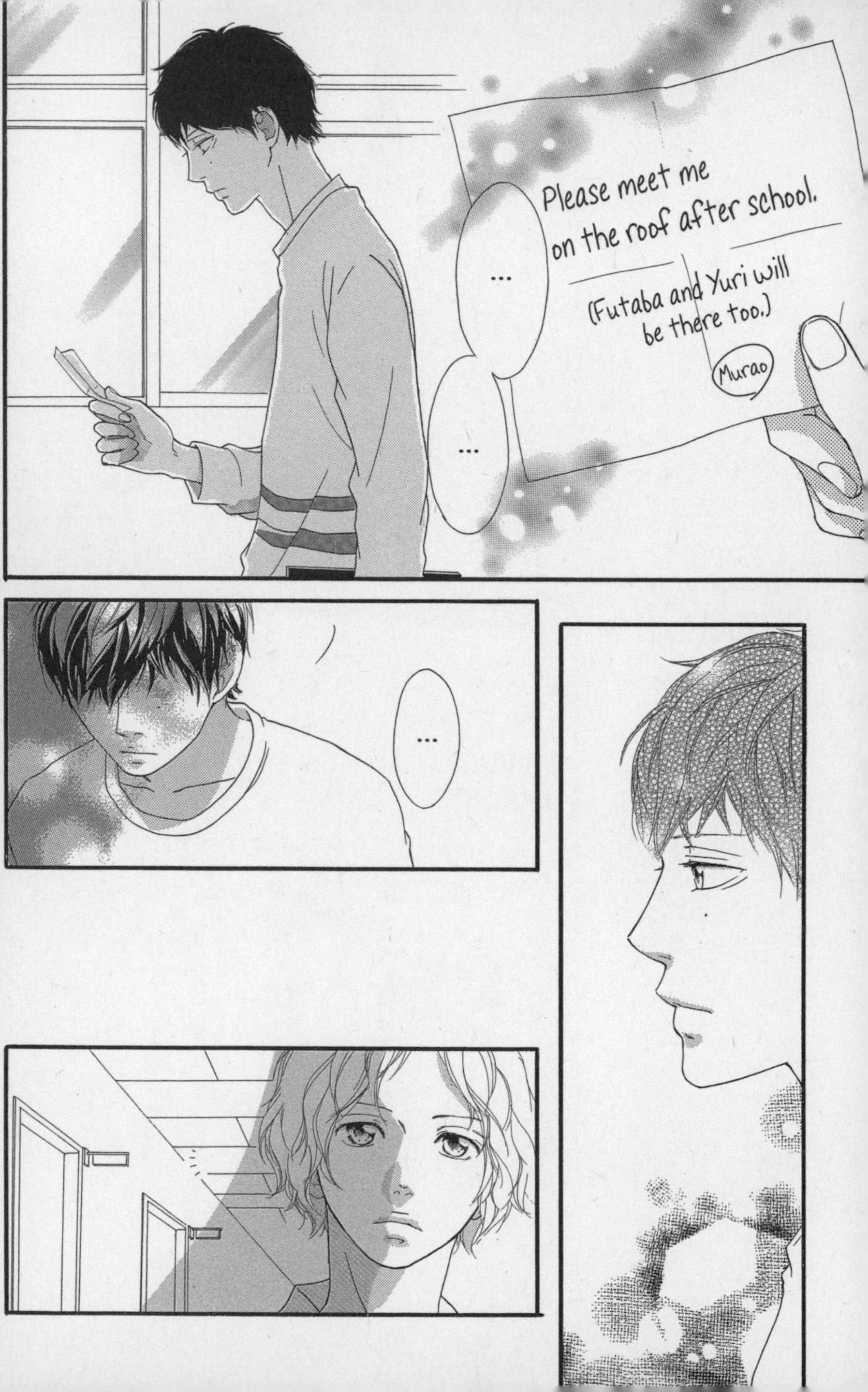
Please meet me on the roof after school.
(Futaba and Yuri will be there too.)
Murao
...
...
...

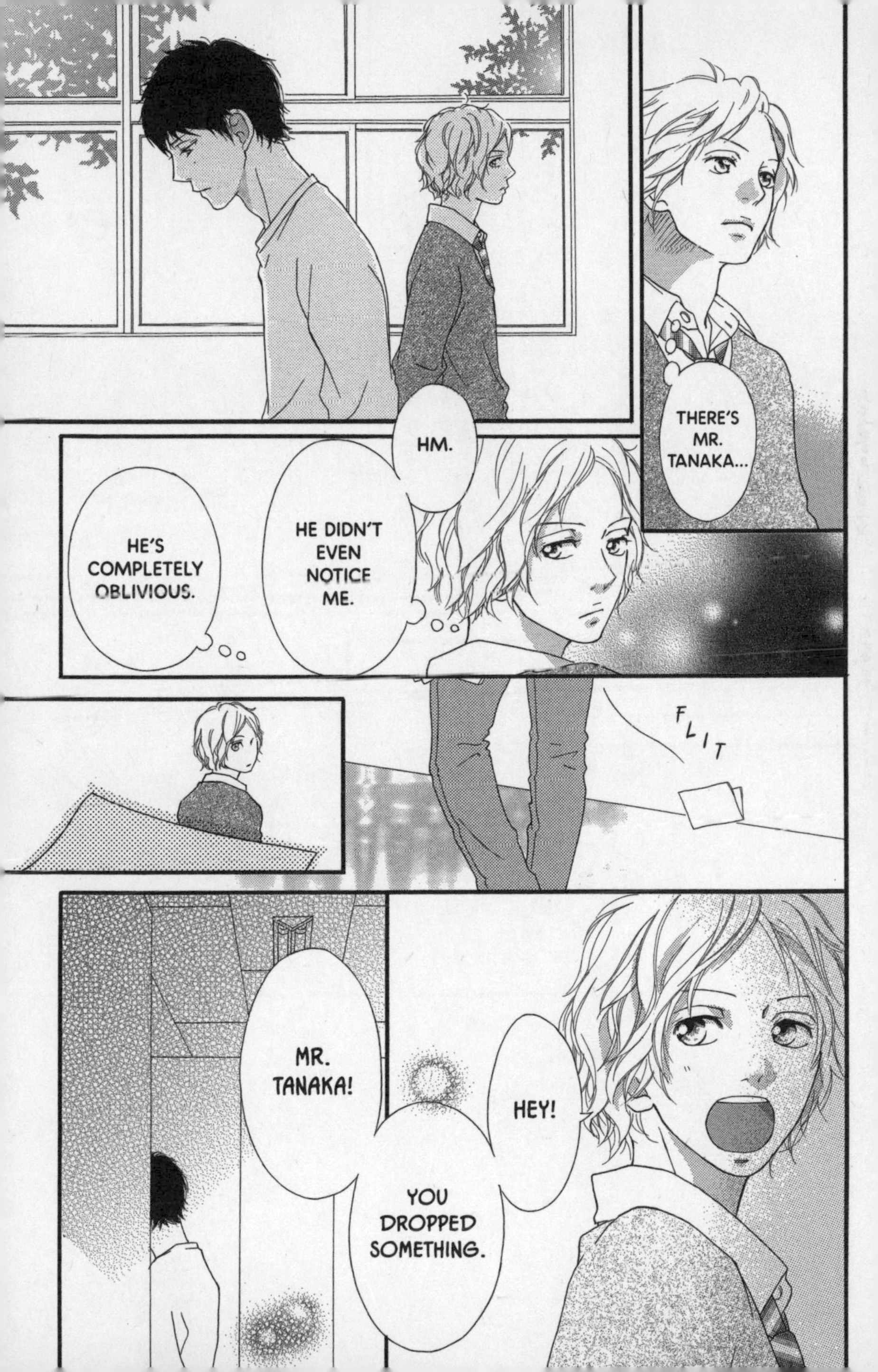
THERE'S MR. TANAKA...
HM.
HE DIDN'T EVEN NOTICE ME.
HE'S COMPLETELY OBLIVIOUS.
FLIT
HEY!
MR. TANAKA!
YOU DROPPED SOMETHING.

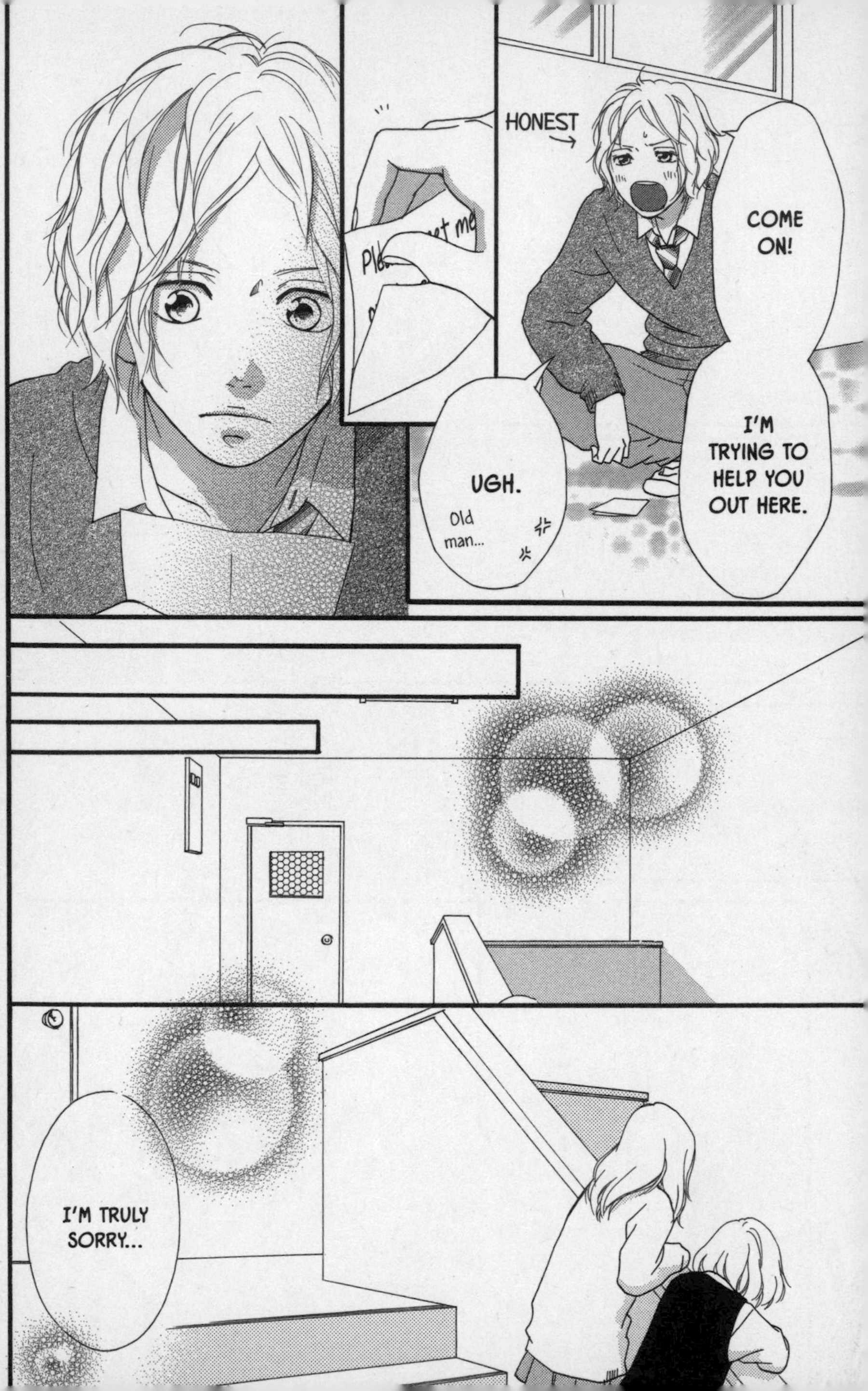
HONEST
COME ON!
I'M TRYING TO HELP YOU OUT HERE.
UGH.
Old man...
I'M TRULY SORRY...

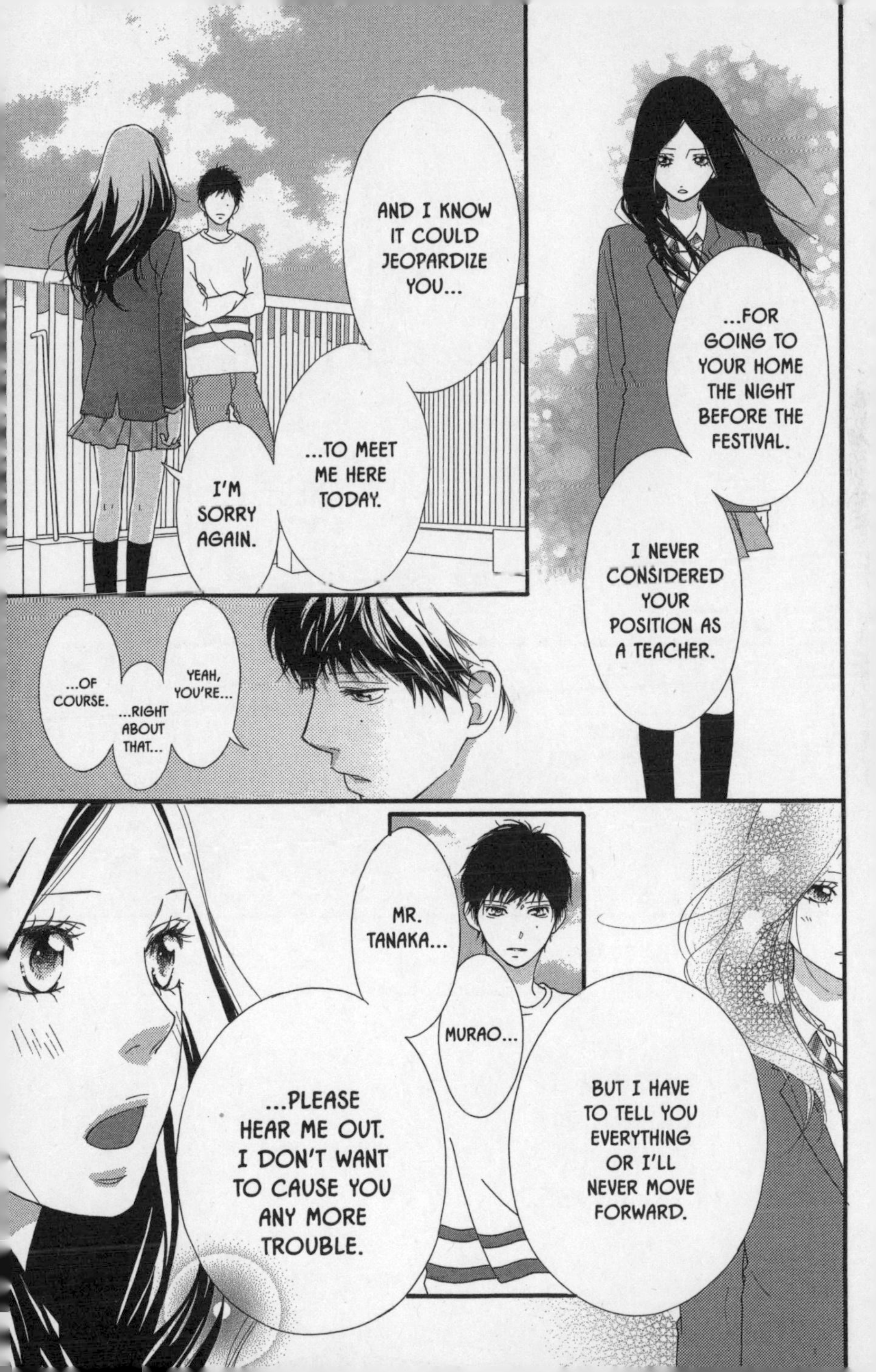
AND I KNOW IT COULD JEOPARDIZE YOU...
...TO MEET ME HERE TODAY.
I'M SORRY AGAIN.
...FOR GOING TO YOUR HOME THE NIGHT BEFORE THE FESTIVAL.
I NEVER CONSIDERED YOUR POSITION AS A TEACHER.
YEAH, YOU'RE...
...RIGHT ABOUT THAT...
...OF COURSE.
MR. TANAKA...
MURAO...
...PLEASE HEAR ME OUT. I DON'T WANT TO CAUSE YOU ANY MORE TROUBLE.
BUT I HAVE TO TELL YOU EVERYTHING OR I'LL NEVER MOVE FORWARD.

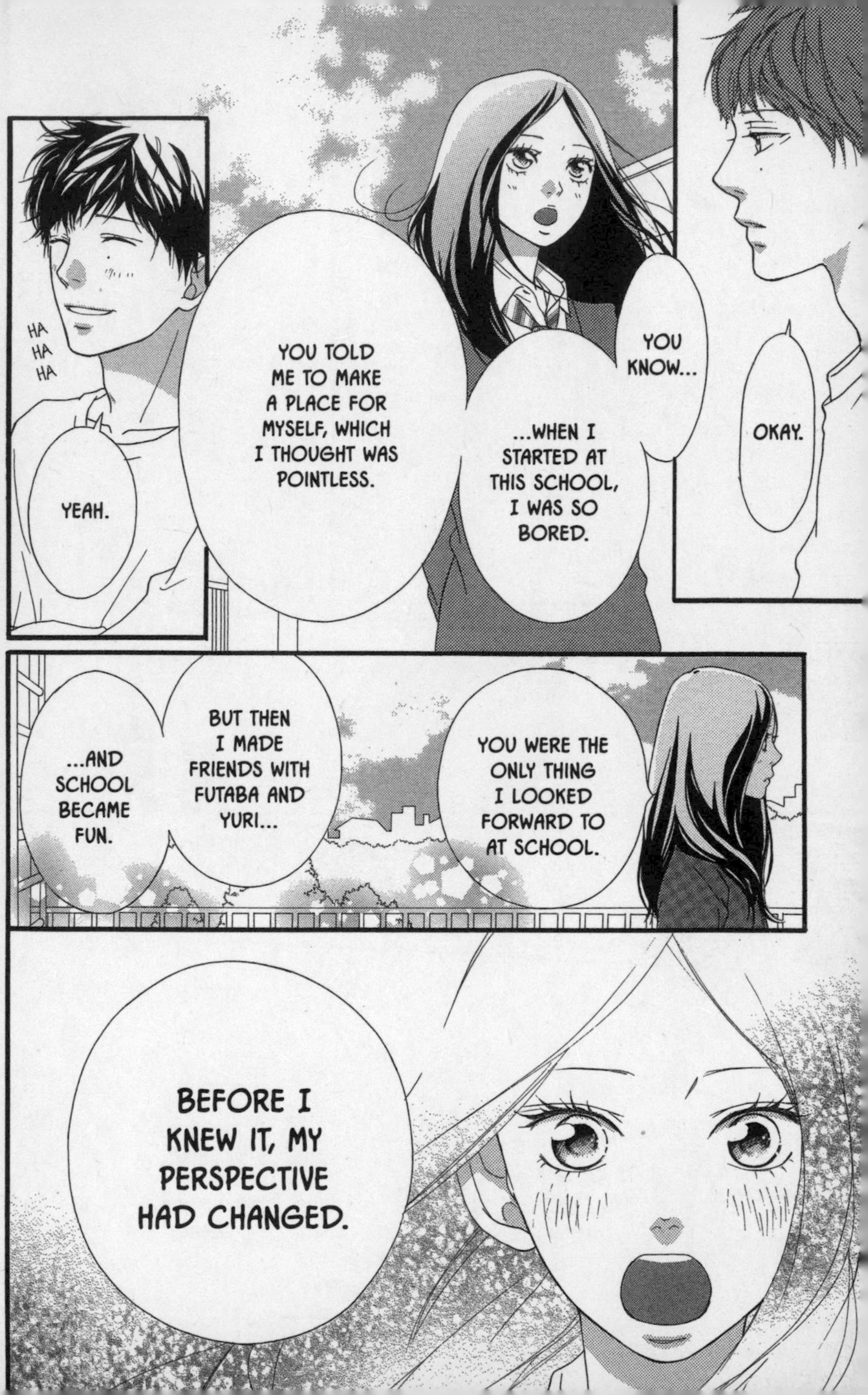
YOU KNOW...
OKAY.
...WHEN I STARTED AT THIS SCHOOL, I WAS SO BORED.
YOU TOLD ME TO MAKE A PLACE FOR MYSELF, WHICH I THOUGHT WAS POINTLESS.
HA HA HA
YEAH.
YOU WERE THE ONLY THING I LOOKED FORWARD TO AT SCHOOL.
BUT THEN I MADE FRIENDS WITH FUTABA AND YURI...
...AND SCHOOL BECAME FUN.
BEFORE I KNEW IT, MY PERSPECTIVE HAD CHANGED.

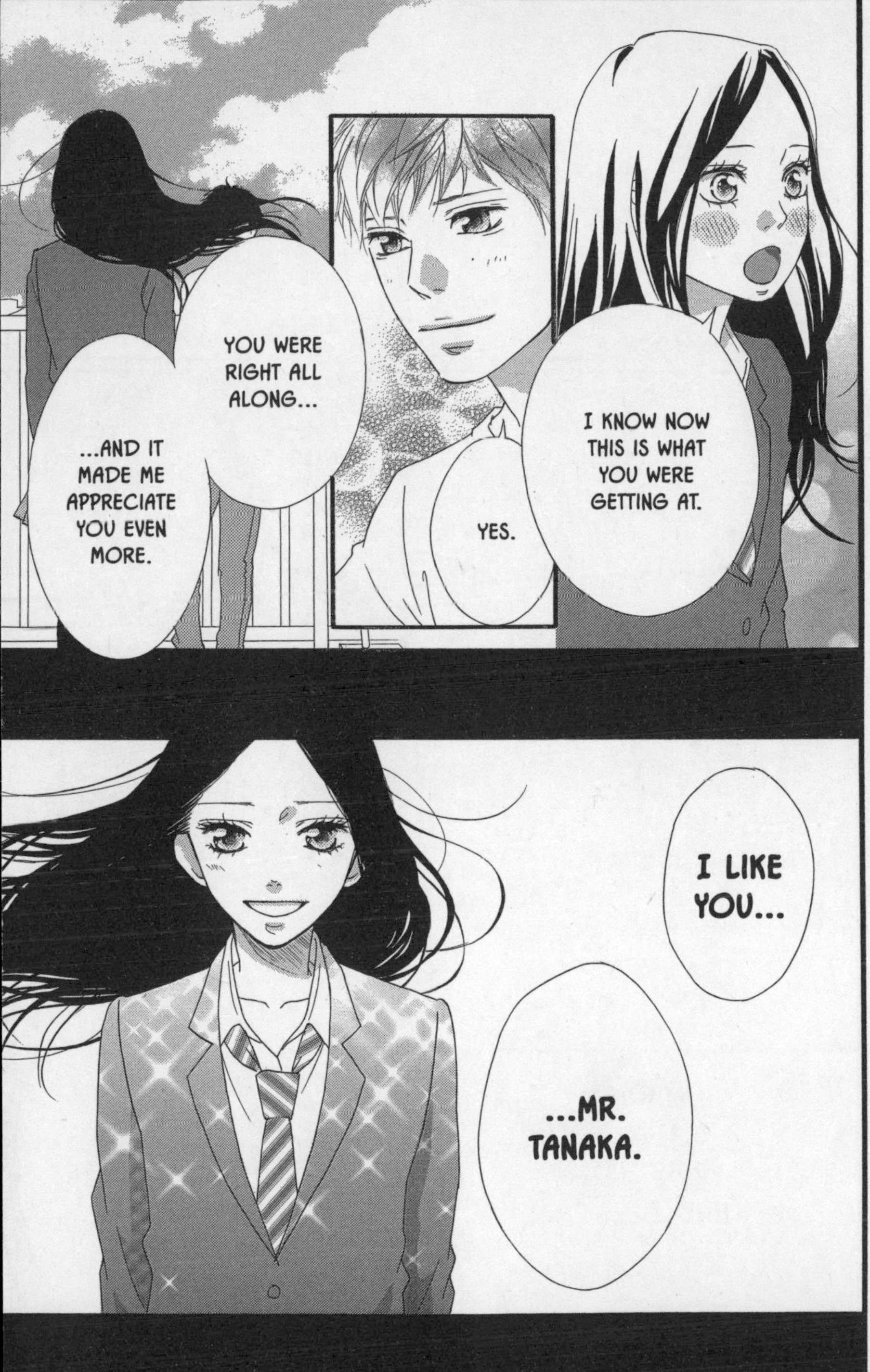
I KNOW NOW THIS IS WHAT YOU WERE GETTING AT.
YES.
YOU WERE RIGHT ALL ALONG...
...AND IT MADE ME APPRECIATE YOU EVEN MORE.
I LIKE YOU...
...MR. TANAKA.

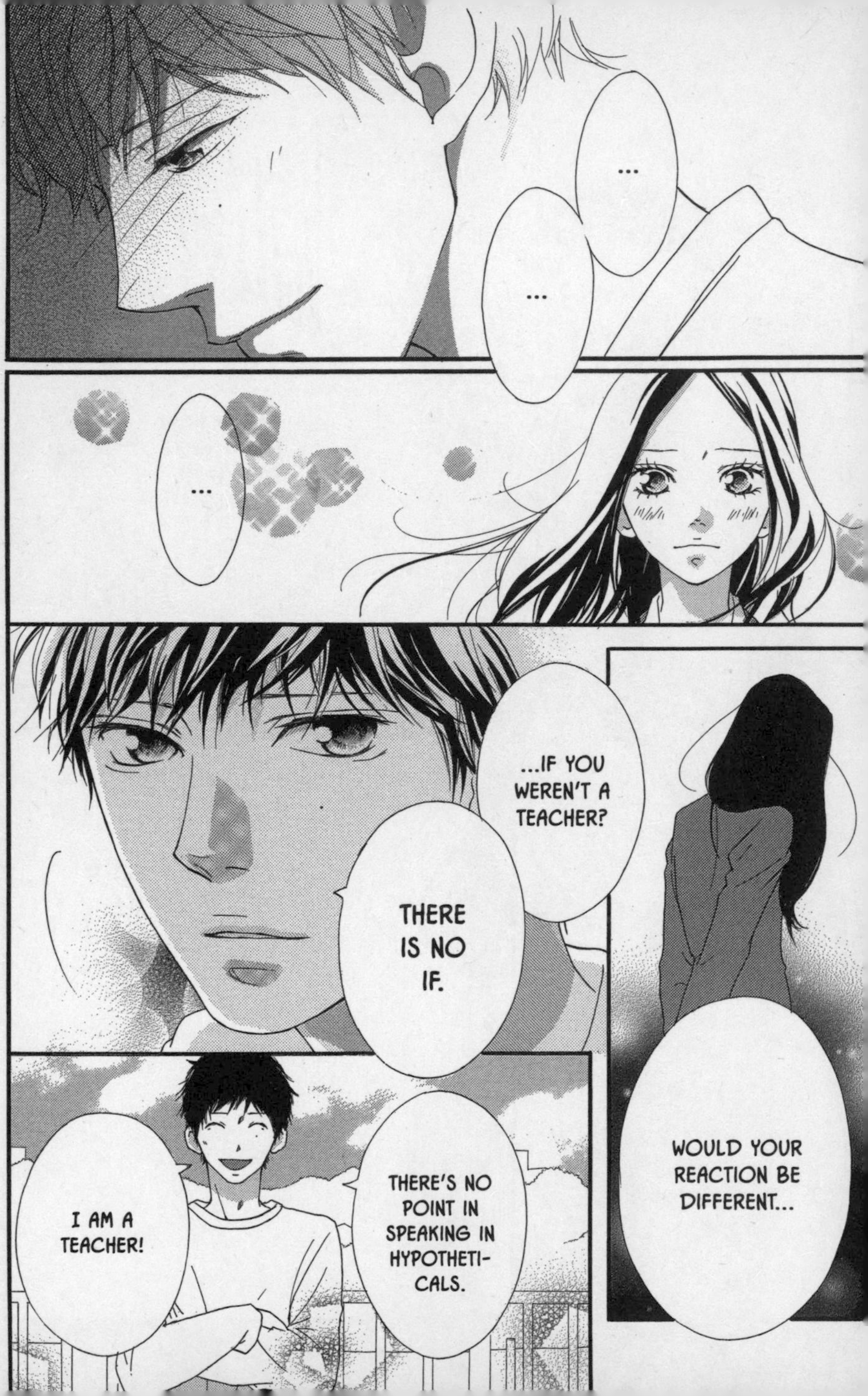
...
...
...
WOULD YOUR REACTION BE DIFFERENT...
...IF YOU WEREN'T A TEACHER?
THERE IS NO IF.
THERE'S NO POINT IN SPEAKING IN HYPOTHETI- CALS.
I AM A TEACHER!

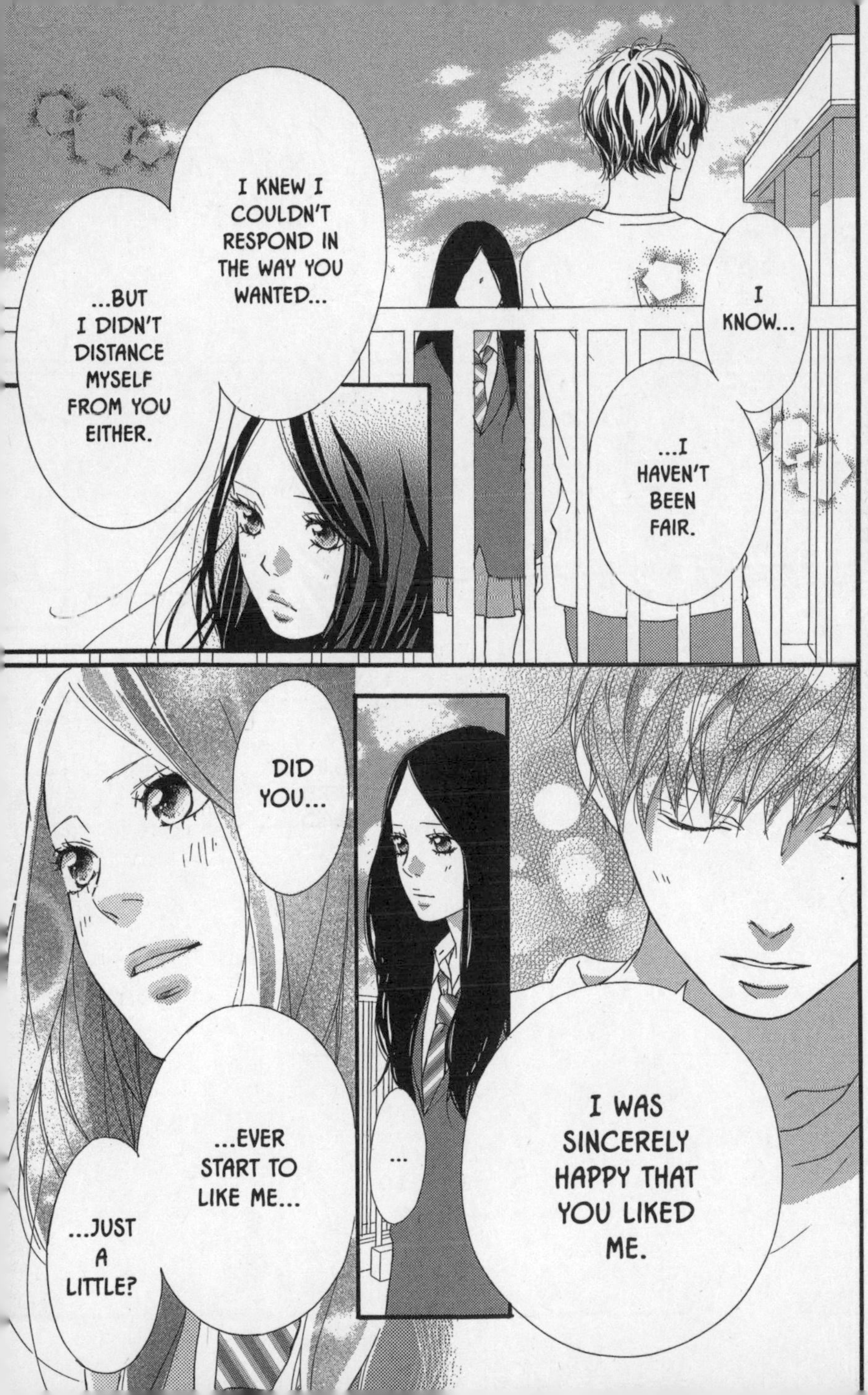
I KNOW...
...I HAVEN'T BEEN FAIR.
I KNEW I COULDN'T RESPOND IN THE WAY YOU WANTED...
...BUT I DIDN'T DISTANCE MYSELF FROM YOU EITHER.
I WAS SINCERELY HAPPY THAT YOU LIKED ME.
...
DID YOU...
...EVER START TO LIKE ME...
...JUST A LITTLE?

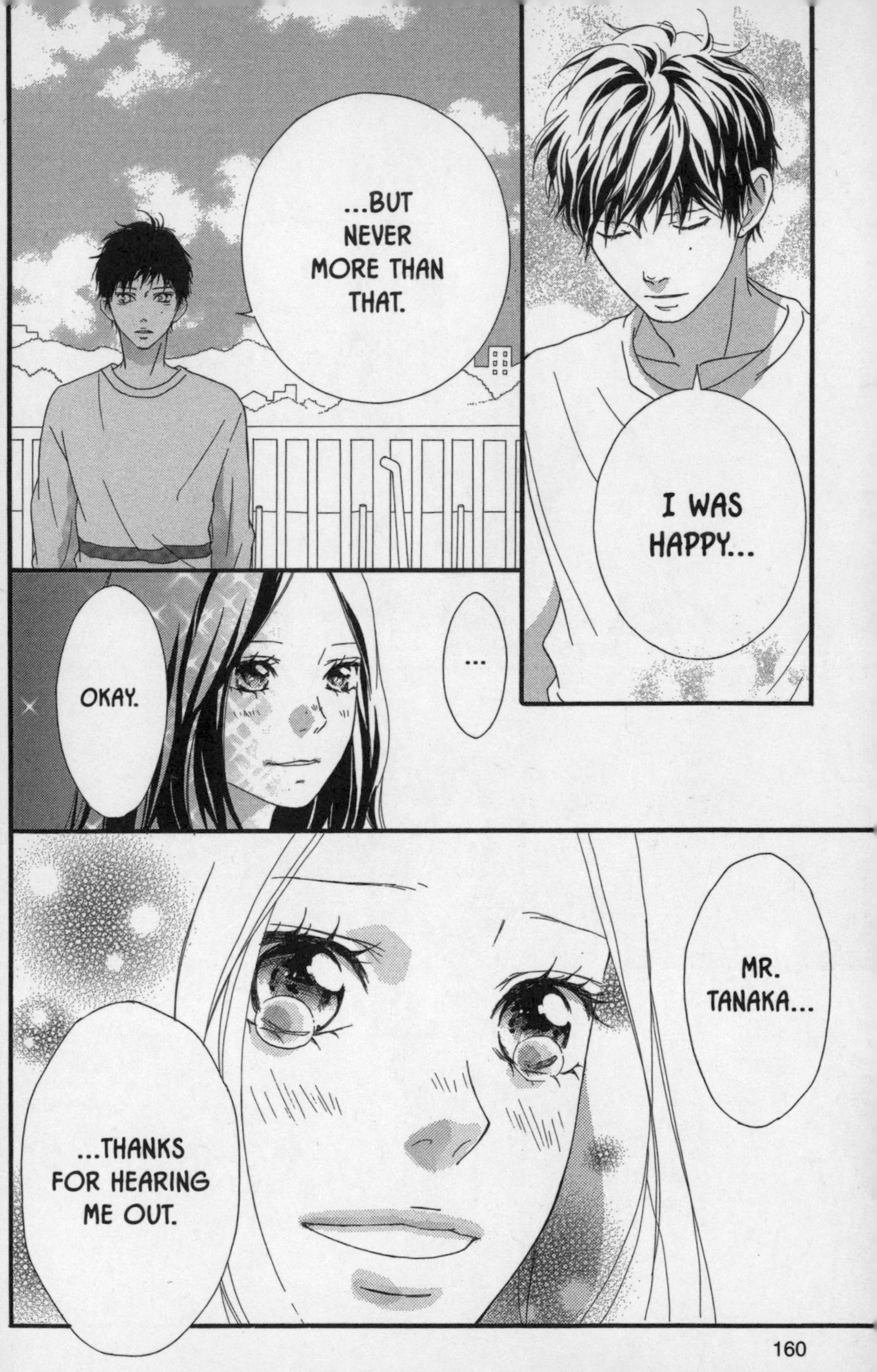
I WAS HAPPY...
...BUT NEVER MORE THAN THAT.
...
OKAY.
MR. TANAKA...
...THANKS FOR HEARING ME OUT.

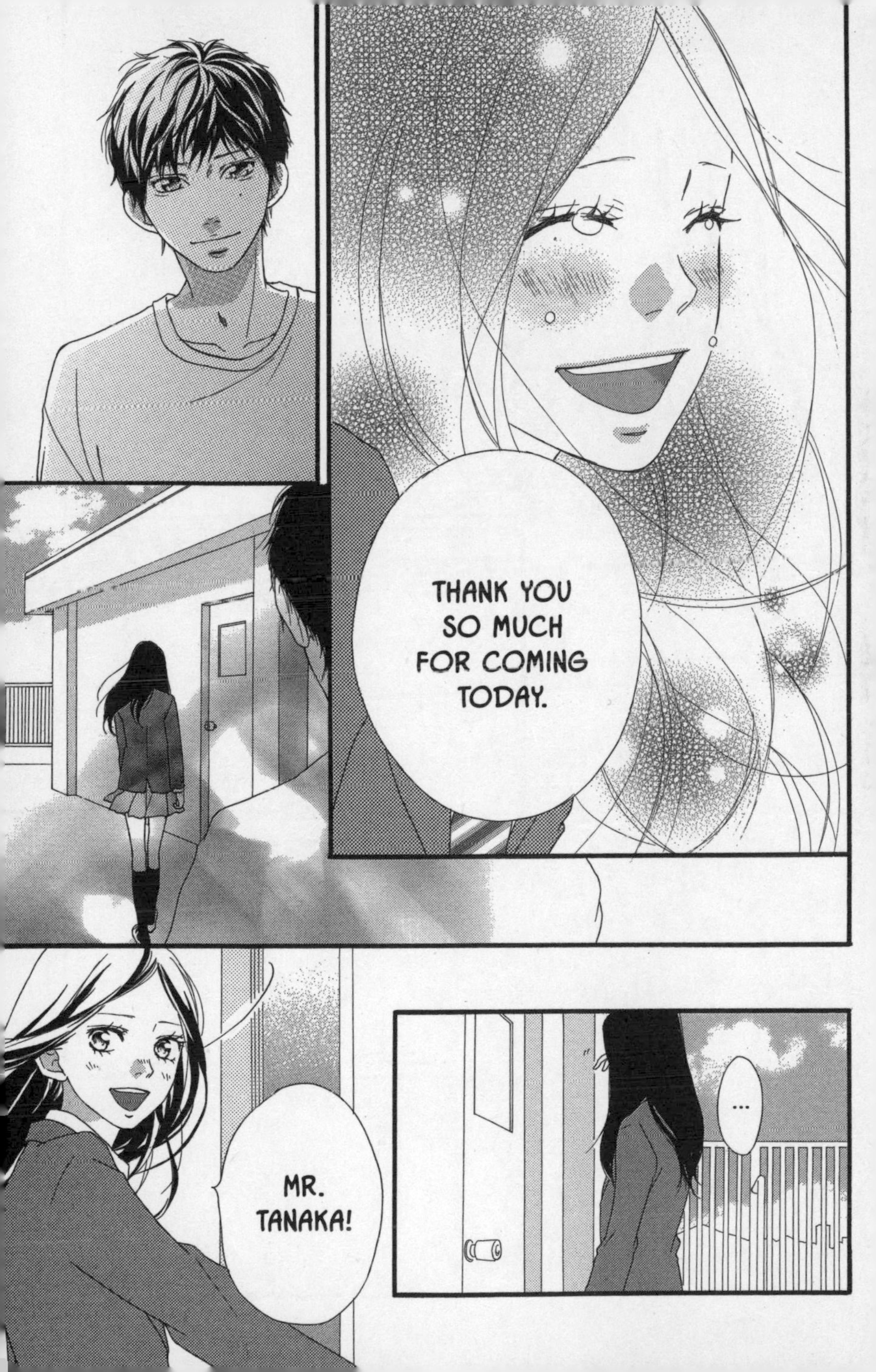
THANK YOU SO MUCH FOR COMING TODAY.
...
MR. TANAKA!

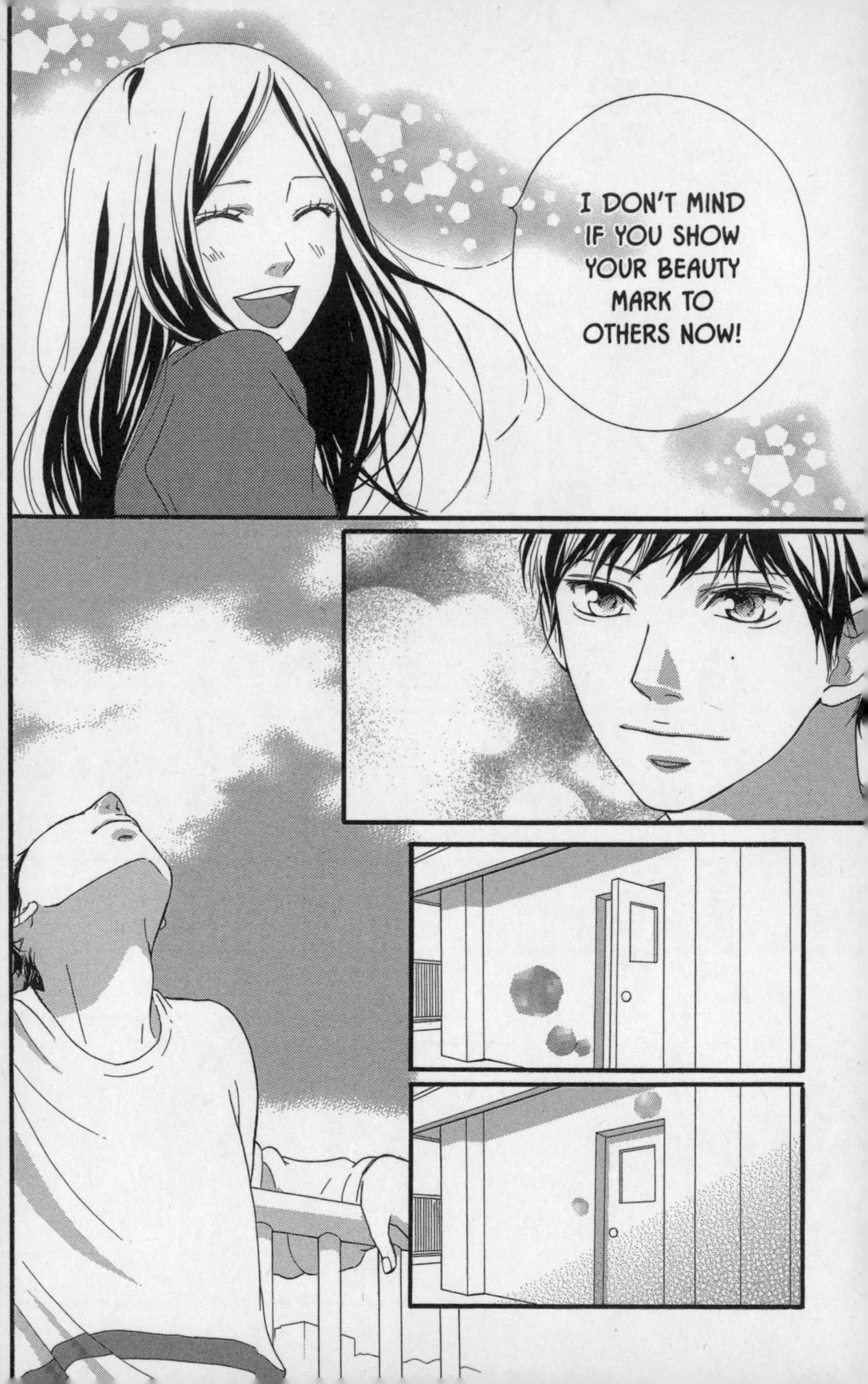
I DON'T MIND IF YOU SHOW YOUR BEAUTY MARK TO OTHERS NOW!

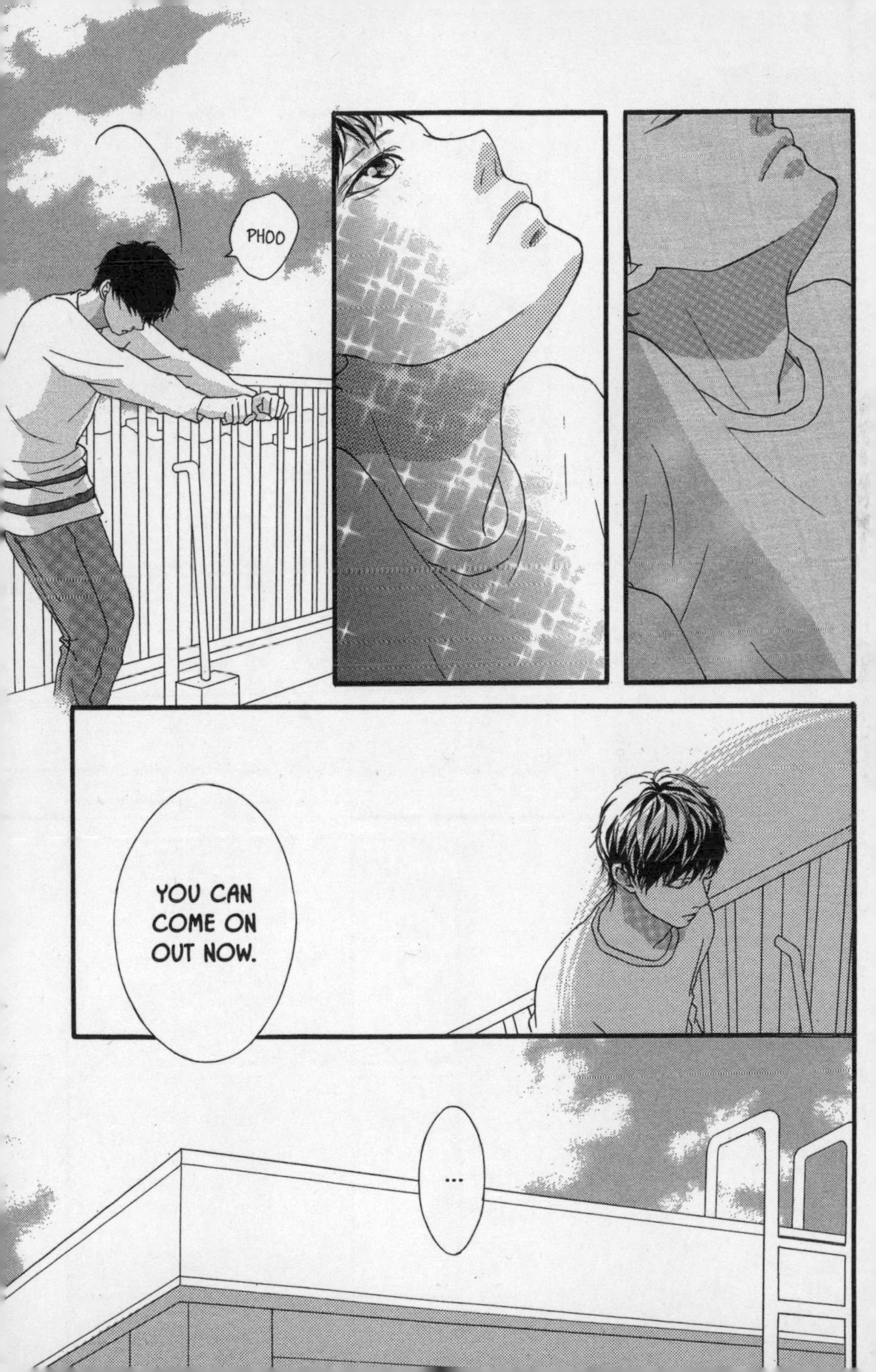
PHOO
YOU CAN COME ON OUT NOW.
...

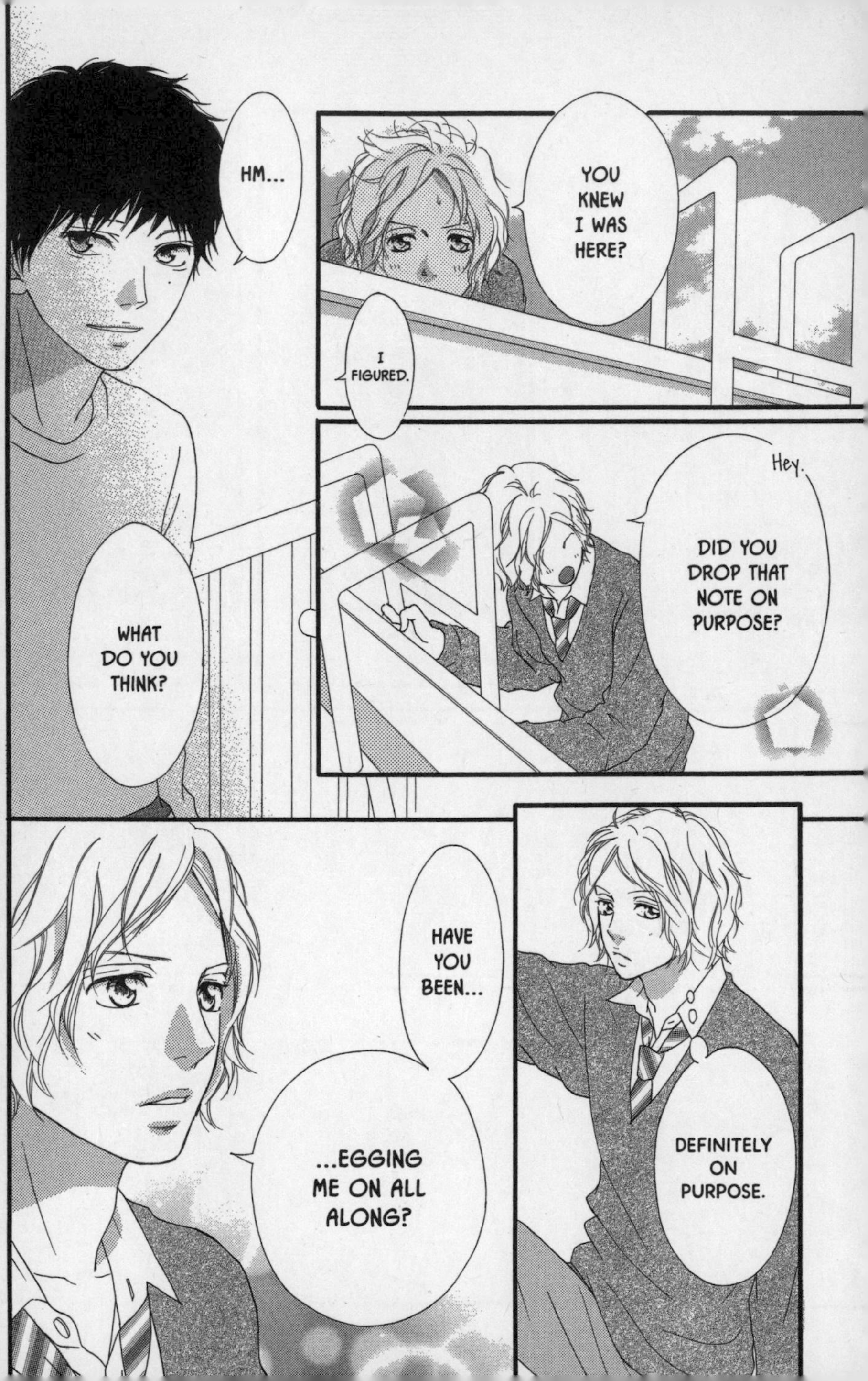
YOU KNEW I WAS HERE?
I FIGURED.
Hey.
DID YOU DROP THAT NOTE ON PURPOSE?
HM...
WHAT DO YOU THINK?
DEFINITELY ON PURPOSE.
HAVE YOU BEEN...
...EGGING ME ON ALL ALONG?

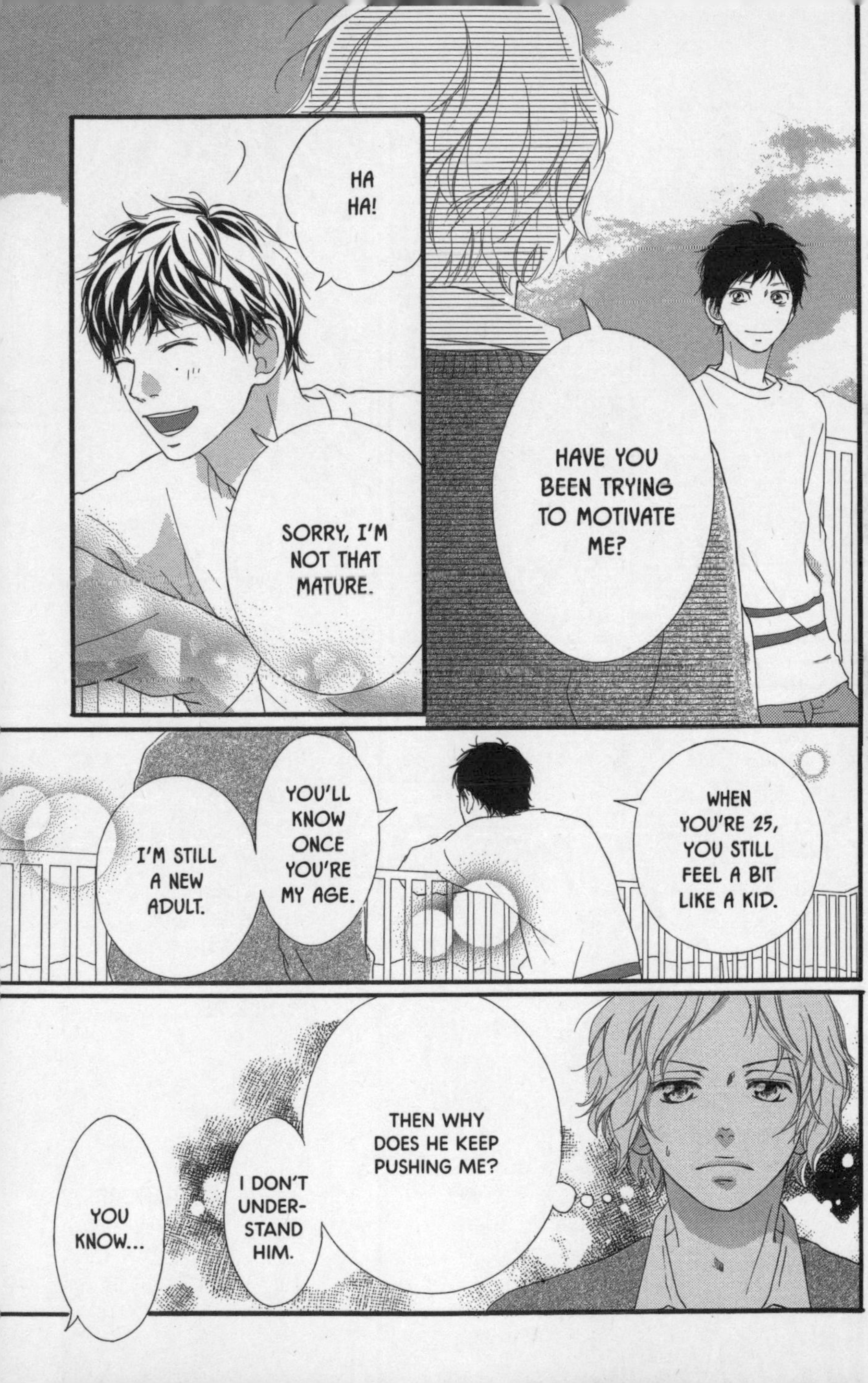
HAVE YOU BEEN TRYING TO MOTIVATE ME?
HA HA!
SORRY, I'M NOT THAT MATURE.
WHEN YOU'RE 25, YOU STILL FEEL A BIT LIKE A KID.
YOU'LL KNOW ONCE YOU'RE MY AGE.
I'M STILL A NEW ADULT.
THEN WHY DOES HE KEEP PUSHING ME?
I DON'T UNDER-STAND HIM.
YOU KNOW...

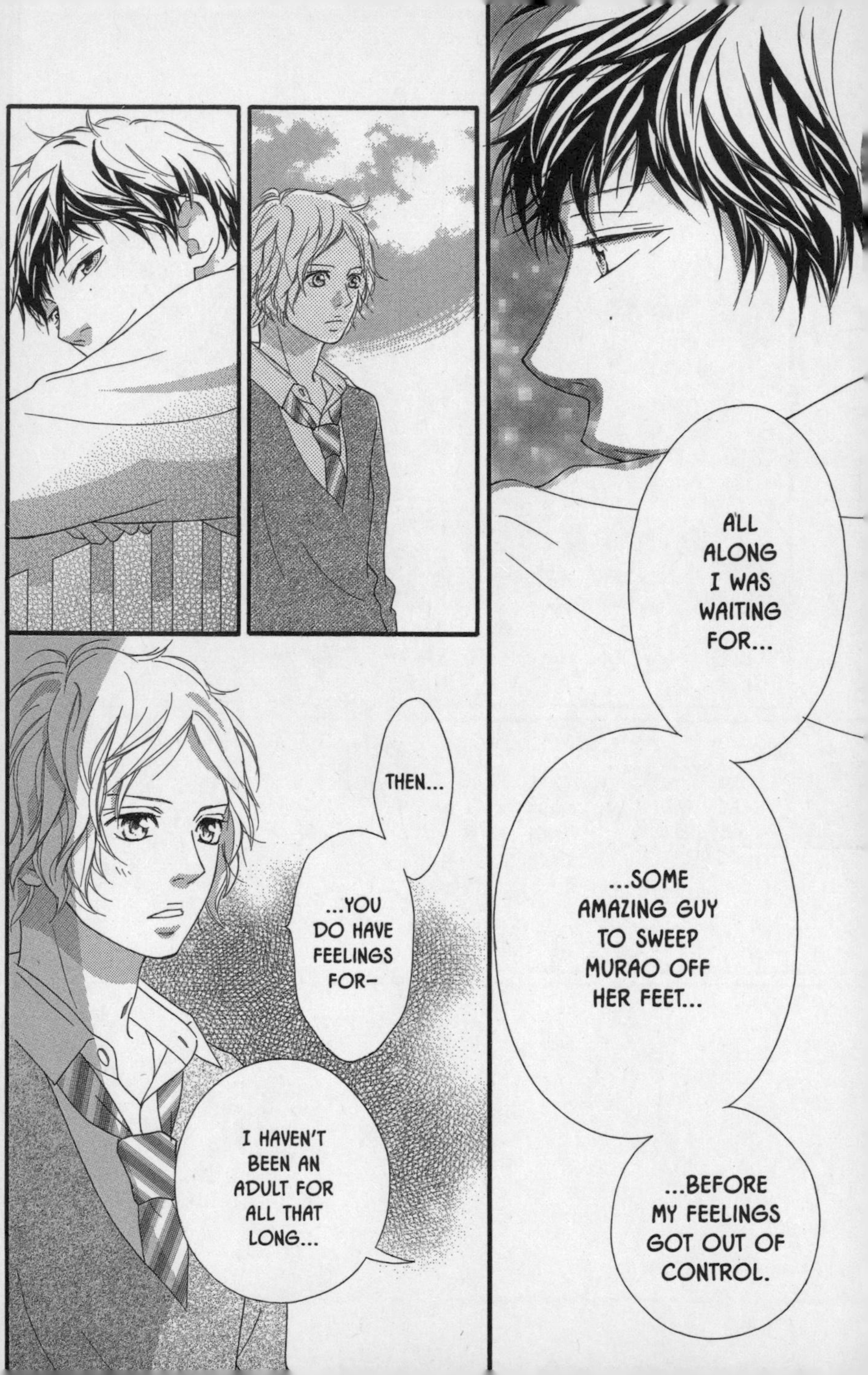
ALL ALONG I WAS WAITING FOR...
...SOME AMAZING GUY TO SWEEP MURAO OFF HER FEET...
...BEFORE MY FEELINGS GOT OUT OF CONTROL.
THEN...
...YOU DO HAVE FEELINGS FOR–
I HAVEN'T BEEN AN ADULT FOR ALL THAT LONG...

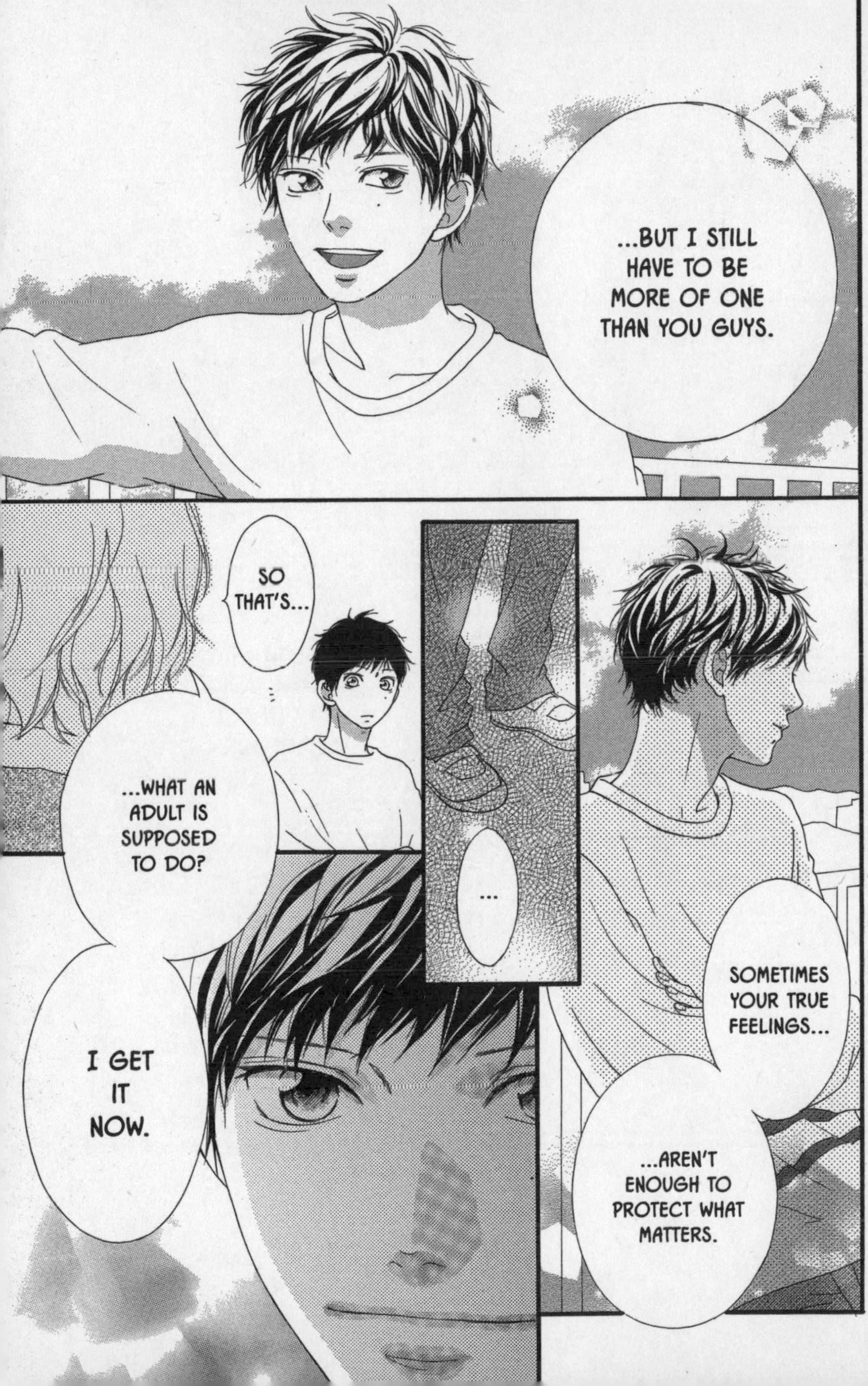
...BUT I STILL HAVE TO BE MORE OF ONE THAN YOU GUYS.
SOMETIMES YOUR TRUE FEELINGS...
...AREN'T ENOUGH TO PROTECT WHAT MATTERS.
...
SO THAT'S...
...WHAT AN ADULT IS SUPPOSED TO DO?
I GET IT NOW.

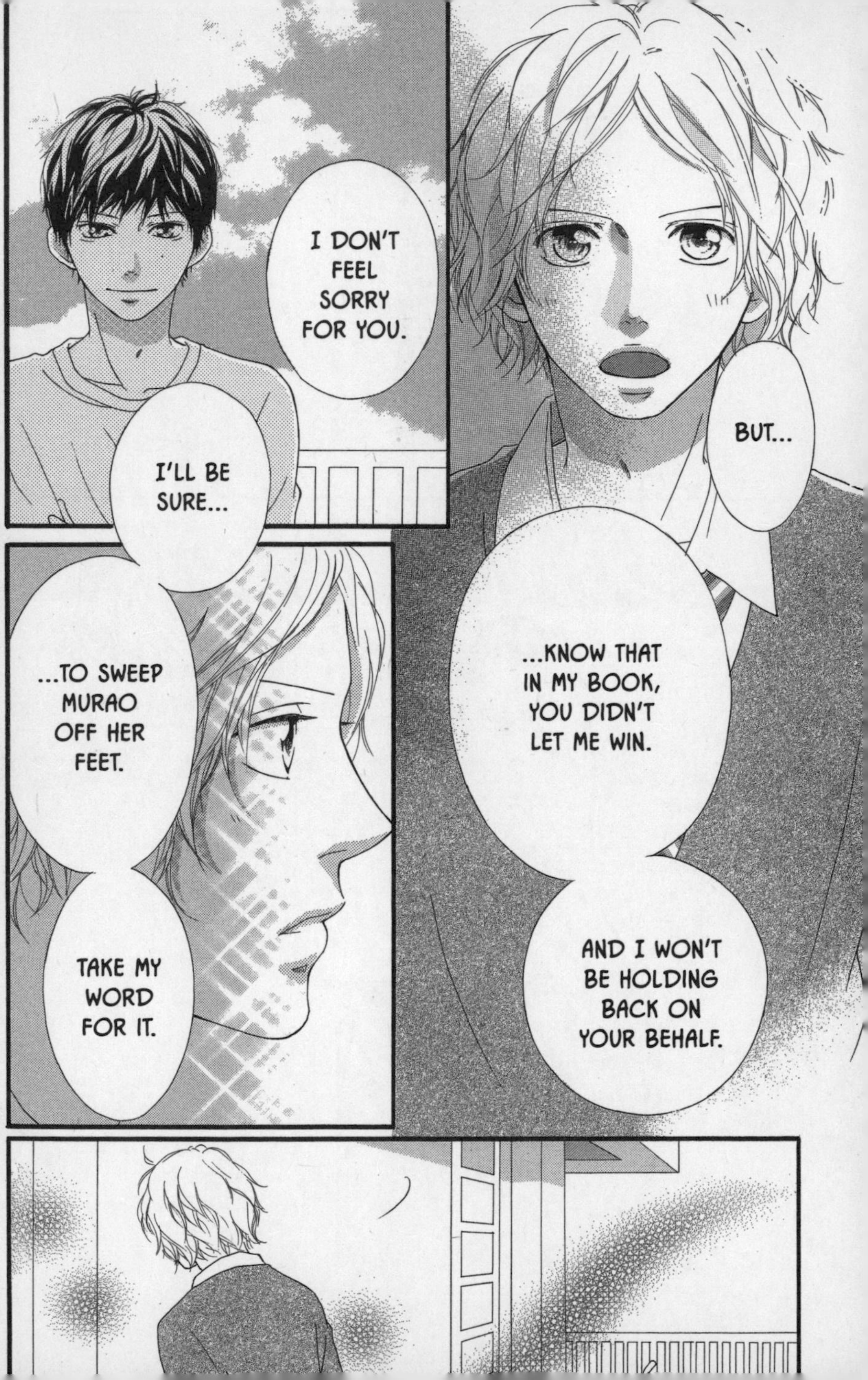
BUT...
...KNOW THAT IN MY BOOK, YOU DIDN'T LET ME WIN.
AND I WON'T BE HOLDING BACK ON YOUR BEHALF.
I DON'T FEEL SORRY FOR YOU.
I'LL BE SURE...
...TO SWEEP MURAO OFF HER FEET.
TAKE MY WORD FOR IT.

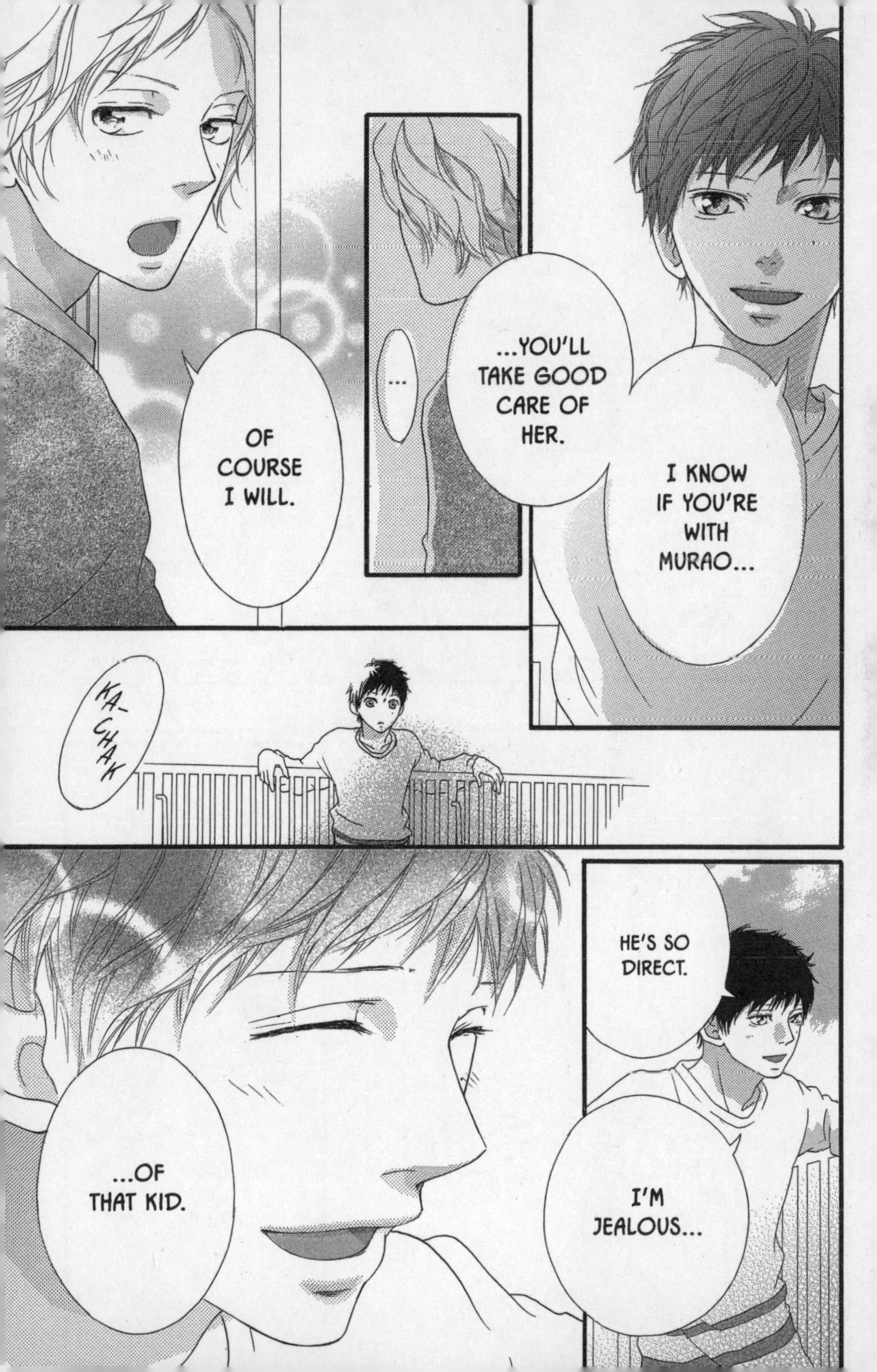
I KNOW IF YOU'RE WITH MURAO...
...YOU'LL TAKE GOOD CARE OF HER.
...
OF COURSE I WILL.
KA-CHAK
HE'S SO DIRECT.
I'M JEALOUS...
...OF THAT KID.

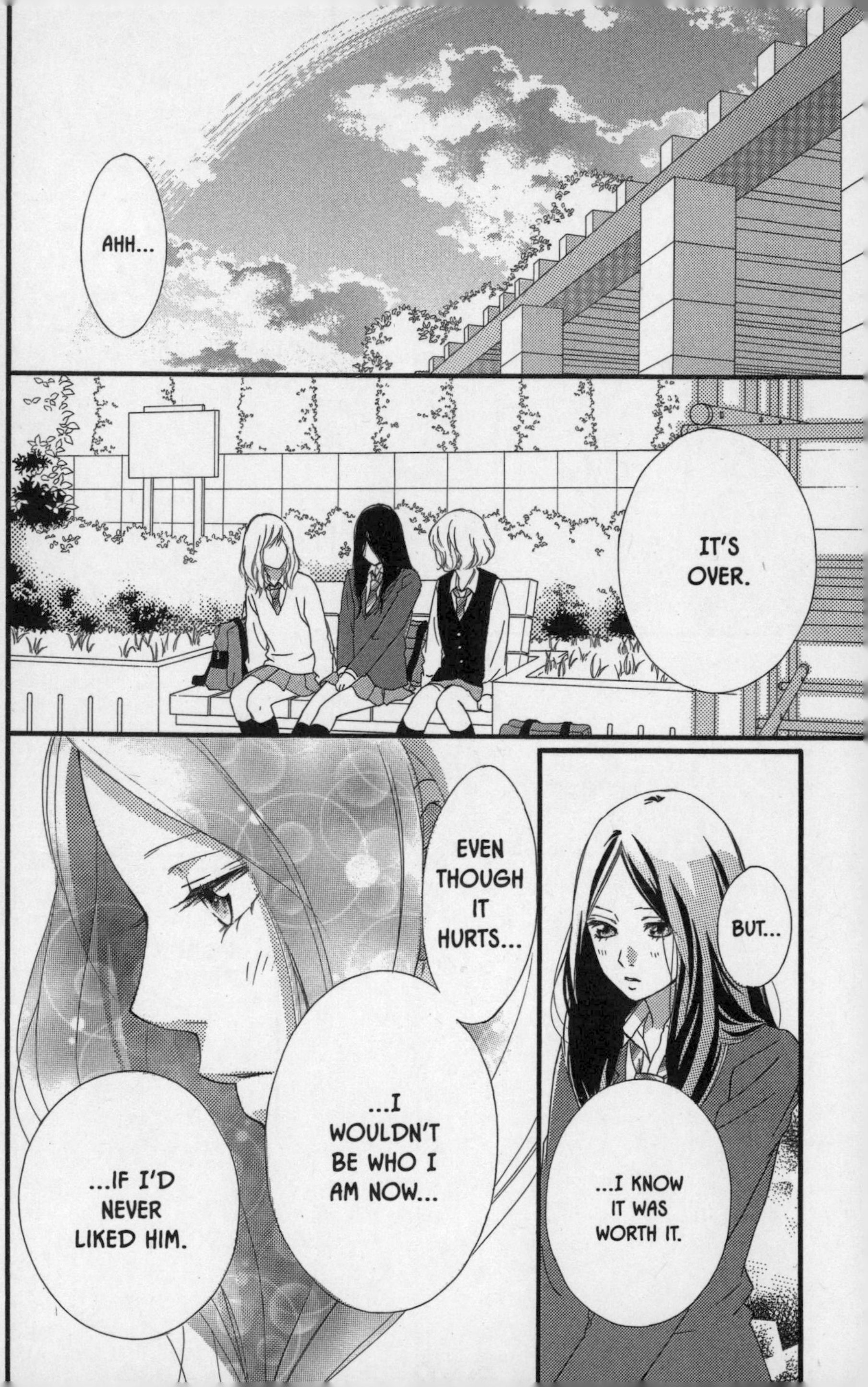
AHH...
IT'S OVER.
BUT...
...I KNOW IT WAS WORTH IT.
EVEN THOUGH IT HURTS...
...I WOULDN'T BE WHO I AM NOW...
...IF I'D NEVER LIKED HIM.

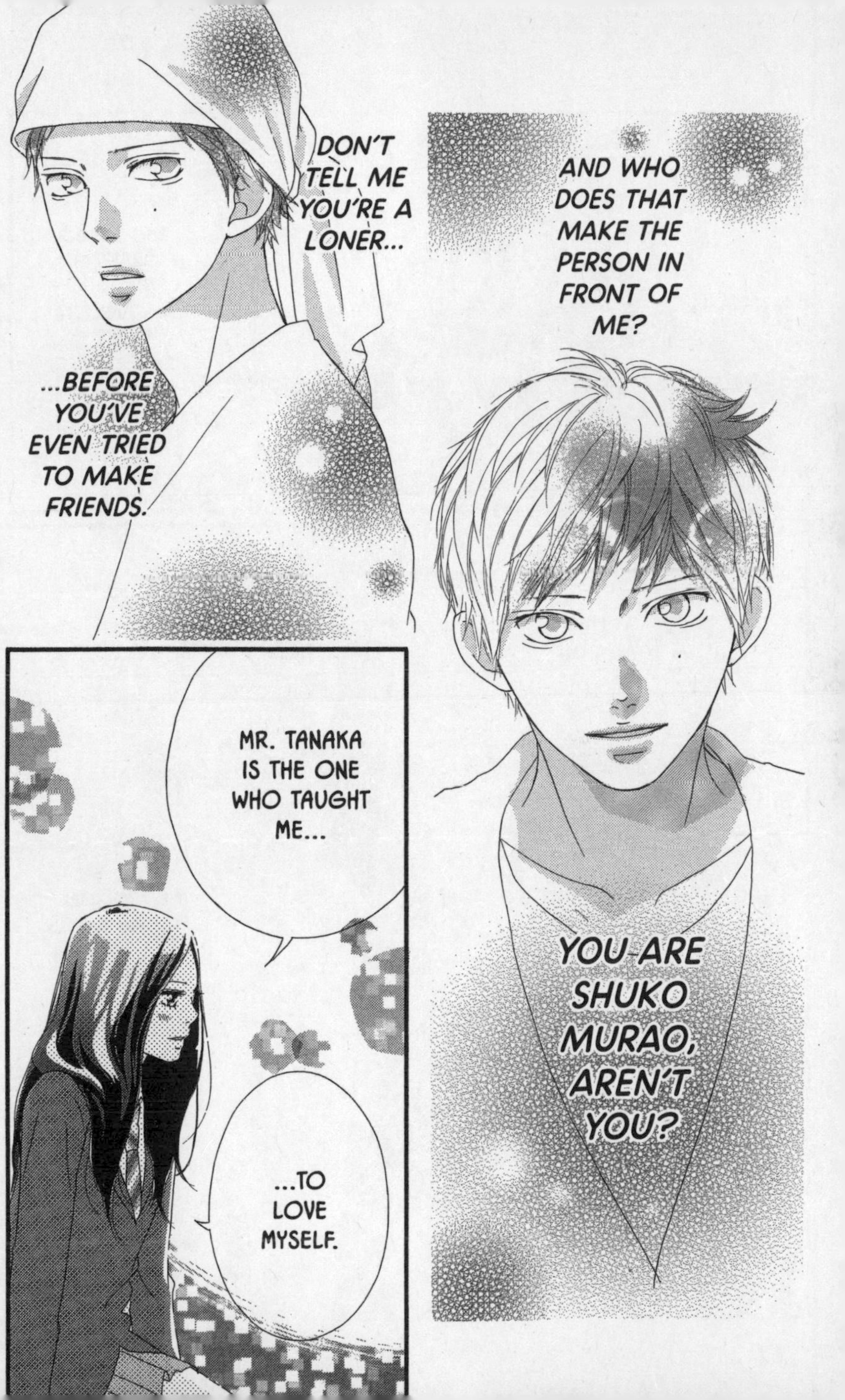
AND WHO DOES THAT MAKE THE PERSON IN FRONT OF ME?
YOU ARE SHUKO MURAO, AREN'T YOU?
DON'T TELL ME YOU'RE A LONER...
...BEFORE YOU'VE EVEN TRIED TO MAKE FRIENDS.
MR. TANAKA IS THE ONE WHO TAUGHT ME...
...TO LOVE MYSELF.

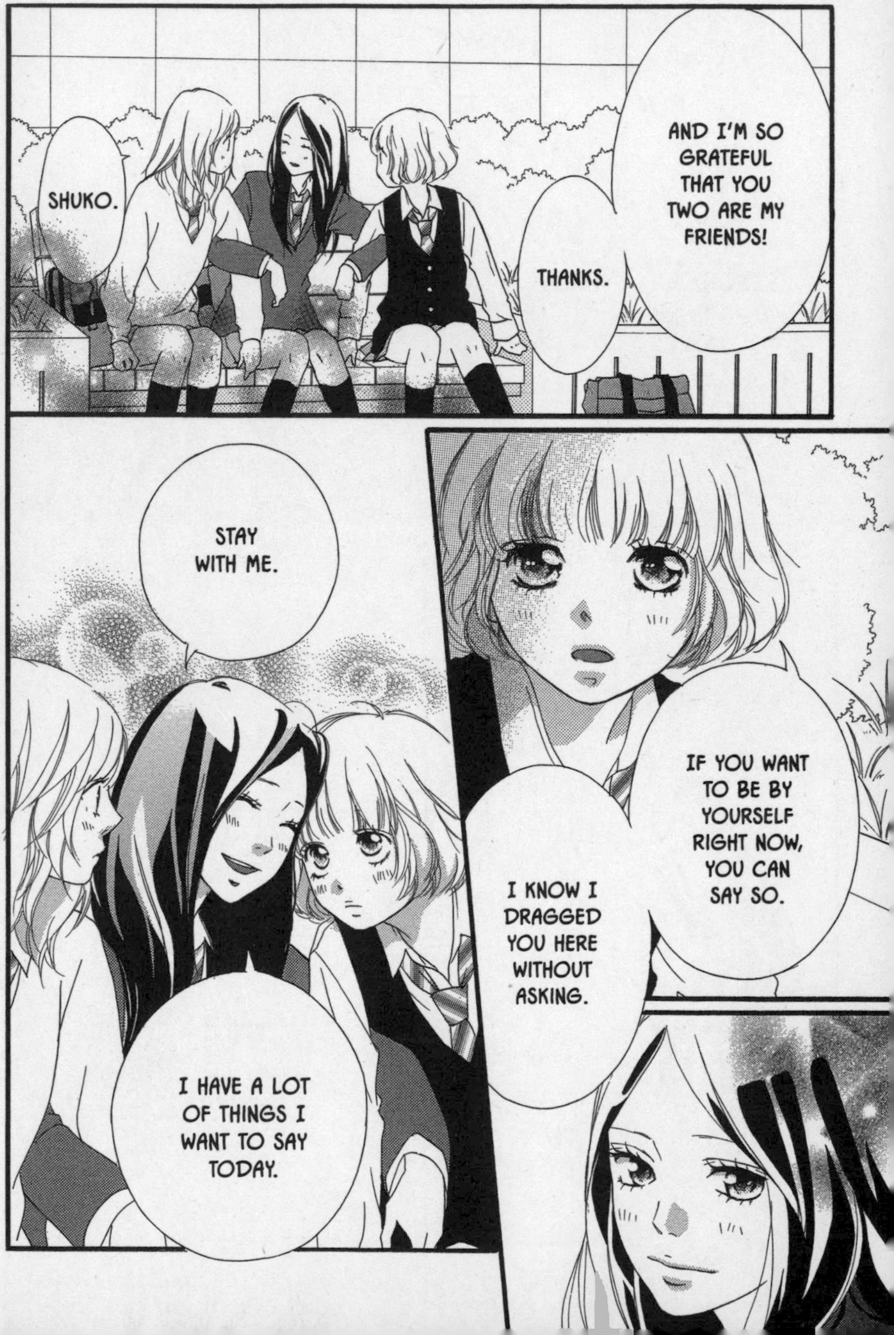
AND I'M SO GRATEFUL THAT YOU TWO ARE MY FRIENDS!
THANKS.
SHUKO.
IF YOU WANT TO BE BY YOURSELF RIGHT NOW, YOU CAN SAY SO.
I KNOW I DRAGGED YOU HERE WITHOUT ASKING.
STAY WITH ME.
I HAVE A LOT OF THINGS I WANT TO SAY TODAY.

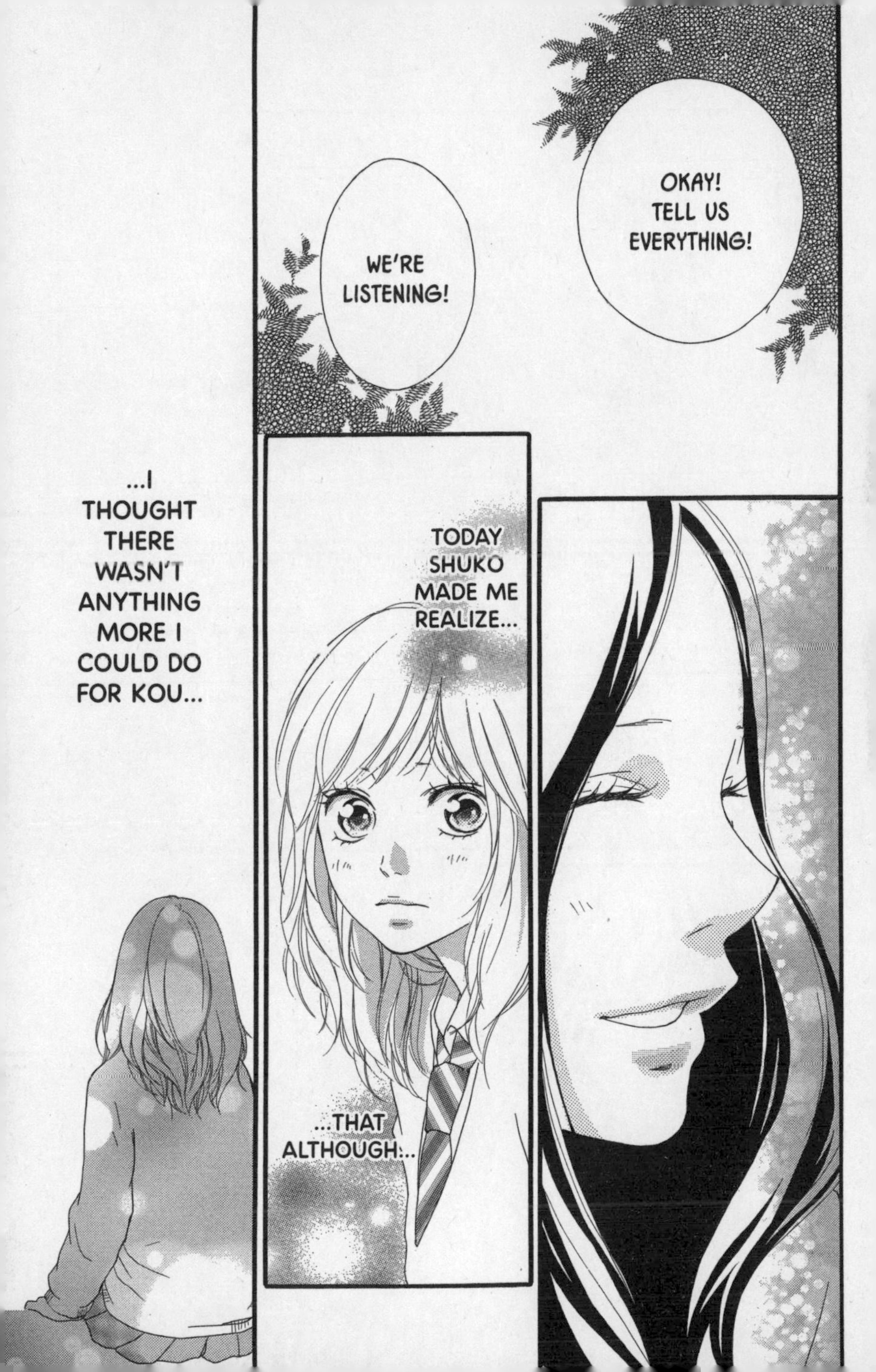
OKAY! TELL US EVERYTHING!
WE'RE LISTENING!
TODAY SHUKO MADE ME REALIZE...
...THAT ALTHOUGH...
...I THOUGHT THERE WASN'T ANYTHING MORE I COULD DO FOR KOU...

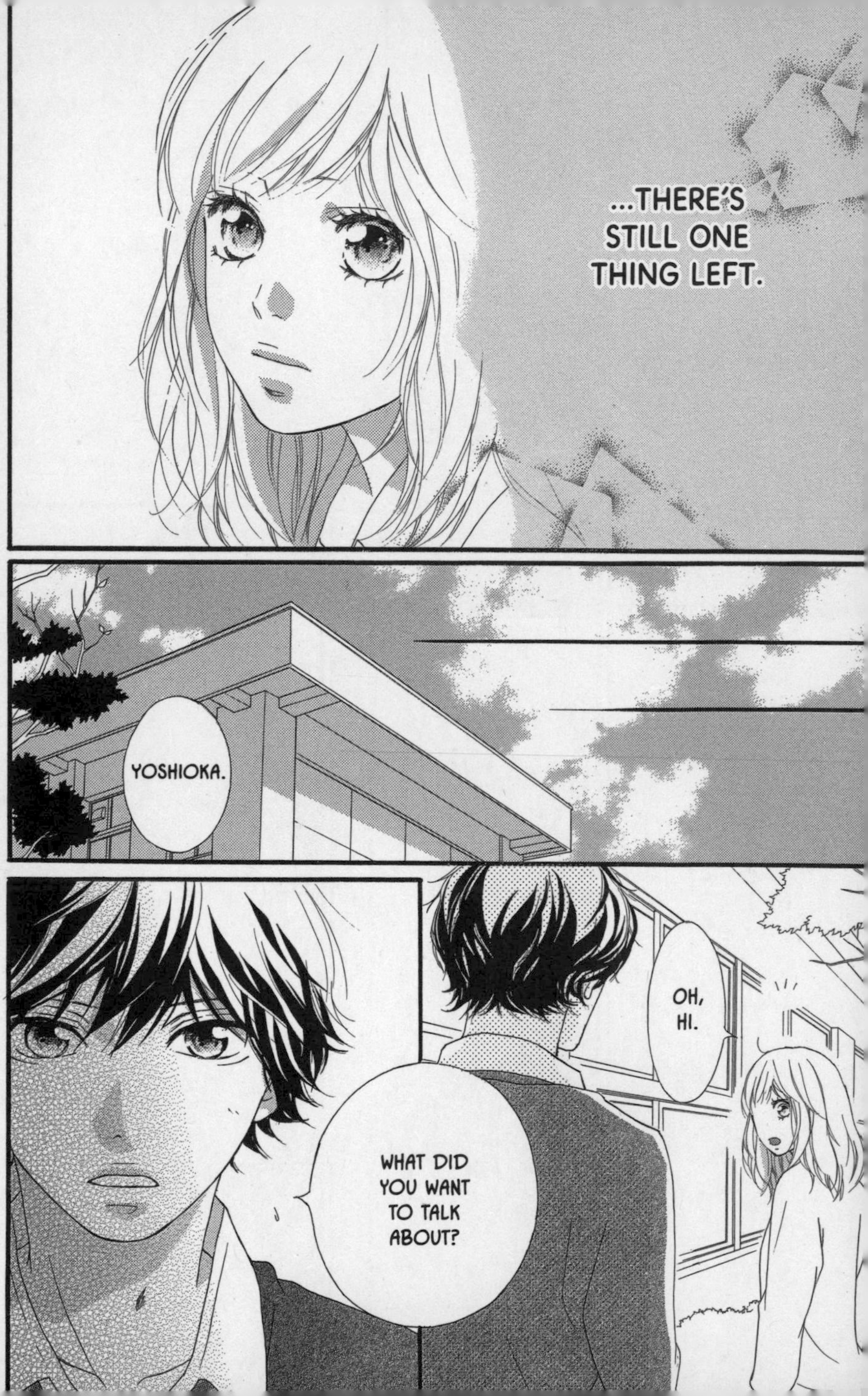
...THERE'S STILL ONE THING LEFT.
YOSHIOKA.
OH, HI.
WHAT DID YOU WANT TO TALK ABOUT?

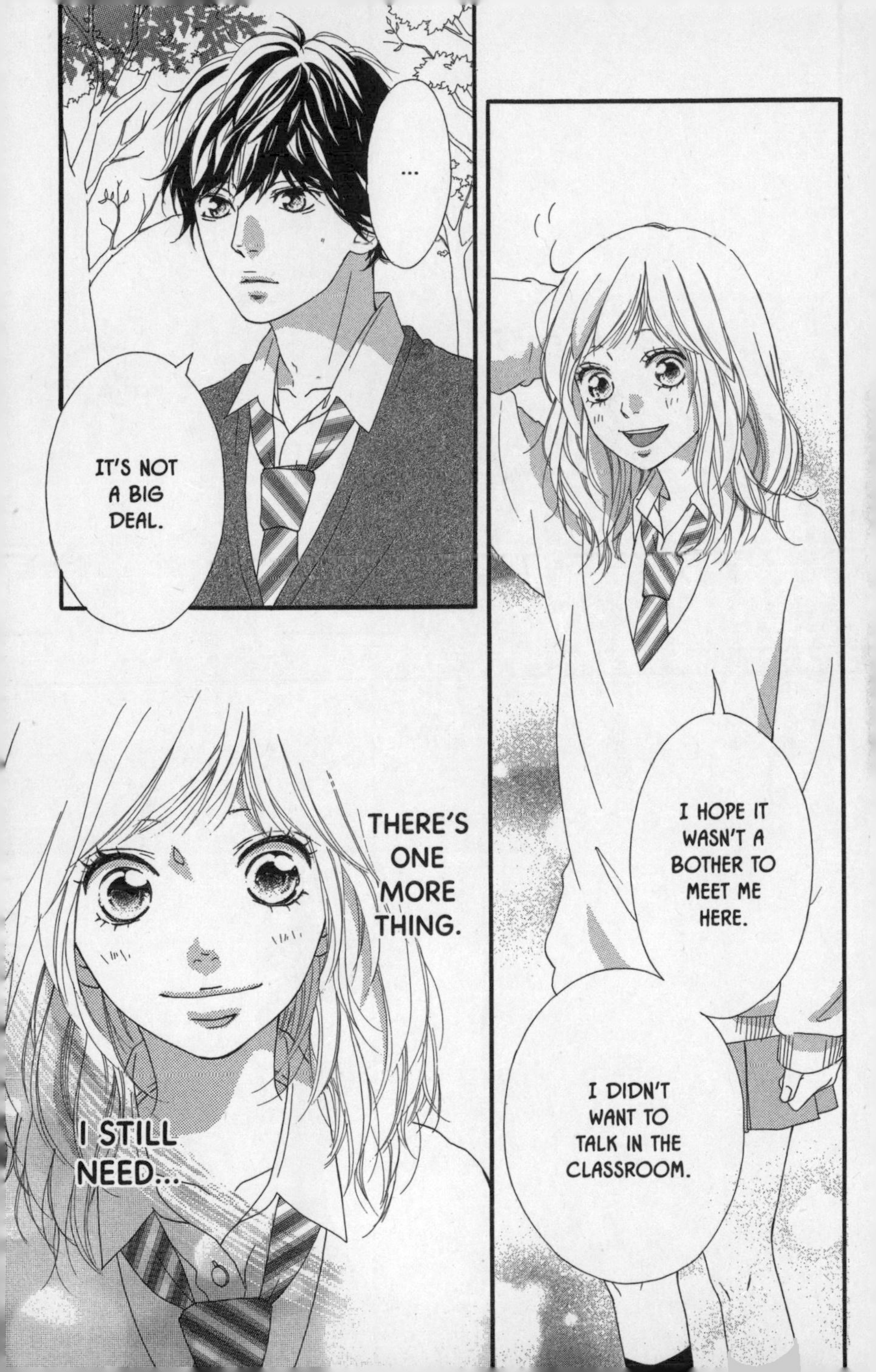
I HOPE IT WASN'T A BOTHER TO MEET ME HERE.
I DIDN'T WANT TO TALK IN THE CLASSROOM.
...
IT'S NOT A BIG DEAL.
THERE'S ONE MORE THING.
I STILL NEED...

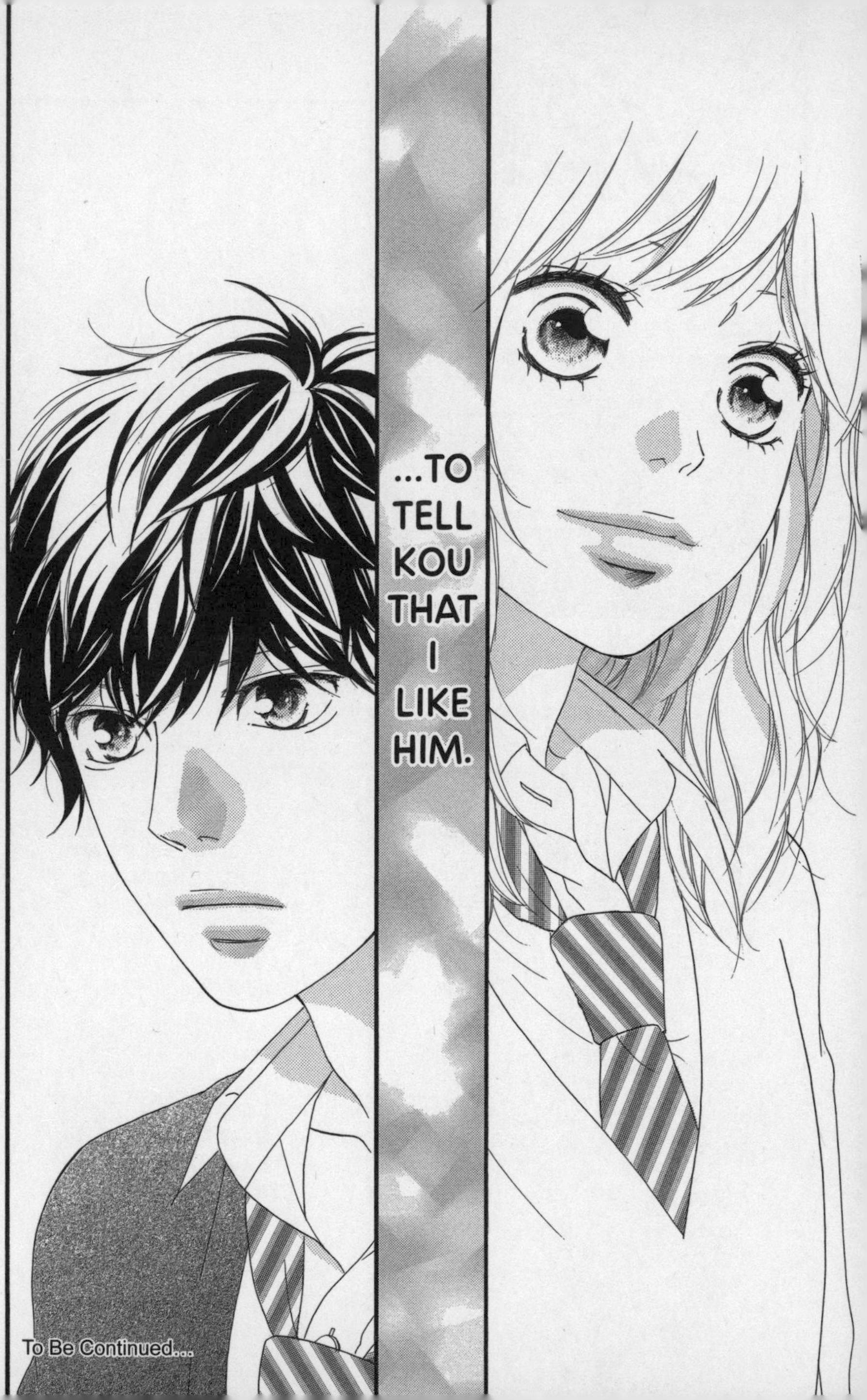
...TO TELL KOU THAT I LIKE HIM.
To Be Continued...

AFTERWORD

Thank you for reading through to the end!

A quiet afternoon, sipping delicious tea while enjoying some literature in a cafe. ← Perhaps this scenario seems lovely to you?

I was constantly talking about how lovely it seemed, so I decided to try it and experience its full loveliness for myself. And when I did, it wasn't fun at all—at least not for me. It was just okay. And that's when I realized that it would be lovely *for someone else*. At that moment, I opened my eyes and thought, "Wow, this is absolutely idiotic!" and went home. When I got back, I changed into my loungewear, rolled over onto the sofa and continued reading my book. And I was sooooo happy. It helped me realize that society's "lovely" and my "lovely" are different.

Sometimes I think about this when drawing Futaba's story.

★ Io Sakisaka ★

Flip to the next page! GO! GO!

HAL I had the privilege of working on the character designs for the anime.

This was of course my first time doing character designs, and initially I was nervous and felt all sorts of pressure and uncertainty. In my manga I get to decide everything, whereas here I would be designing for someone else's story, and I couldn't be sure how it would all fit together. But when I met the director, Makihara, to learn about the story, I immediately saw the dedication of the director and the WIT STUDIO team. It was then that I knew if my character designs weren't right, they would be quick to reject my work and send it back. I remember that being a massive relief.

It was absolutely amazing to collaborate with this passionate team on this anime, and I am so grateful for the opportunity.

To those of you reading this now, I'd love for you to experience all that went into this project.

The release date is June 8, 2013! It's just around the corner!

Also, this is a complete coincidence, but the release date is also my birthday! It's a miracle! (To me.) It's going to be a birthday I'll never forget. I do hope you enjoy it!

My memory has been suffering.
I cannot remember anything anymore.

Until not too long ago, when I forgot
something I would brush it off as not
important. But lately I've been forgetting
things that are important (or so I feel).

I'm pretty disappointed with myself.

My solution was to take notes like crazy,
but then I started misplacing those notes,
and now I don't know what to do...

IO SAKISAKA

Born on June 8, Io Sakisaka made her debut
as a manga creator with *Sakura, Chiru*. Her
works include *Call My Name, Gate of Planet*
and *Blue. Strobe Edge,* her previous work, is
also published by VIZ Media's Shojo Beat
imprint. *Ao Haru Ride* was adapted into an
anime series in 2014. In her spare time,
Sakisaka likes to paint things and sleep.

Ao Haru Ride

VOLUME 7
SHOJO BEAT EDITION

STORY AND ART BY **IO SAKISAKA**

TRANSLATION **Emi Louie-Nishikawa**
TOUCH-UP ART + LETTERING **Inori Fukuda Trant**
DESIGN **Shawn Carrico**
EDITOR **Nancy Thistlethwaite**

AOHA RIDE © 2011 by Io Sakisaka
All rights reserved.
First published in Japan in 2011 by SHUEISHA Inc., Tokyo.
English translation rights arranged by SHUEISHA Inc.

The stories, characters and incidents mentioned
in this publication are entirely fictional.

Printed in the U.S.A.

Published by VIZ Media, LLC
P.O. Box 77010
San Francisco, CA 94107

10 9 8 7 6 5 4 3 2 1
First printing, October 2019

viz.com

shojobeat.com

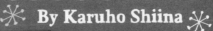

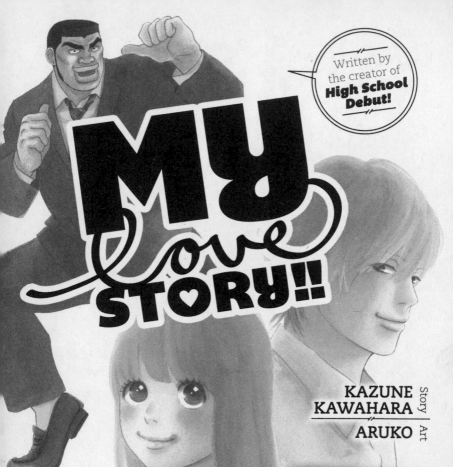

Written by the creator of **High School Debut!**

MY love STORY!!

KAZUNE KAWAHARA — Story

ARUKO — Art

Takeo Goda is a GIANT guy with a GIANT *heart*

Too bad the girls don't want him!
(They want his good-looking best friend, Sunakawa.)

Used to being on the sidelines, Takeo simply stands tall and accepts his fate. But one day when he saves a girl named Yamato from a harasser on the train, his (love!) life suddenly takes an incredible turn!